Anthony Burgess was born in Manchester in 1917 and is a graduate of the university there. After six years in the Army he worked as an instructor for the Central Advisory Council for Forces Education, as a college lecturer in Speech and Drama and as a grammar-school master. From 1954 to 1960 he was an education officer in the Colonial Service, stationed in Malaya and Borneo.

He became a full-time writer in 1960, though he had already by then published three novels and a history of English literature. A late starter in the art of fiction, he had previously spent much creative energy on music and has composed many full-scale works for orchestra and other media. His Third Symphony was performed in the USA in 1975, and *Blooms of Dublin*, his musical version of Joyce's *Ulysses*, was presented in 1982.

Anthony Burgess believes that in the fusion of musical and literary form lies a possible future for the novel. His *Napoleon Symphony* attempts to impose the shape of Beethoven's *Eroica* on the career of the Corsican conqueror. His other books include *The Long Day Wanes: A Malayan Trilogy*; the Enderby novels: *Inside Mr Enderby, Enderby Outside, The Clockwork Testament* and *Enderby's Dark Lady*; *Tremor of Intent*; *The Doctor is Sick*; *A Clockwork Orange*, made into a film classic by Stanley Kubrick and dramatized by the RSC; *The Wanting Seed*; *Honey for the Bears*; *Urgent Copy*, a biography of Shakespeare intended to act as a foil to his Shakespeare novel, *Nothing Like the Sun*; *MF*; *Beard's Roman Women*; *ABBA ABBA*; *Ernest Hemingway and His World*; *1985*; *Man of Nazareth*, the basis of his successful TV script *Jesus of Nazareth*; *Earthly Powers*, which in France was voted the best foreign novel of the year; *The End of the World News*; *Ninety-nine Novels*; *The Kingdom of the Wicked*, winner of the Prix Europa, Geneva; *The Piano Players*; *Flame into Being, The Life and Work of D. H. Lawrence*, winner of the Premio Comisso, Italy; *Homage to QWERTYUIOP*, an anthology of his reviews and journalism; the first volume of his autobiography *Little Wilson and Big God*; the novel *Any Old Iron*; and a collection of stories entitled *The Devil's Mode*.

YOU'VE HAD YOUR TIME

BEING THE SECOND PART OF
THE CONFESSIONS OF
ANTHONY BURGESS

PENGUIN BOOKS

PENGUIN BOOKS

Published by the Penguin Group
Penguin Books Ltd, 27 Wrights Lane, London W8 5TZ, England
Penguin Books USA Inc., 375 Hudson Street, New York, New York 10014, USA
Penguin Books Australia Ltd, Ringwood, Victoria, Australia
Penguin Books Canada Ltd, 10 Alcorn Avenue, Toronto, Ontario, Canada M4V 3B2
Penguin Books (NZ) Ltd, 182–190 Wairau Road, Auckland 10, New Zealand

Penguin Books Ltd, Registered Offices: Harmondsworth, Middlesex, England

First published by William Heinemann Ltd 1990
Published in Penguin Books 1991
1 3 5 7 9 10 8 6 4 2

Printed in England by Clays Ltd, St Ives plc

. . . as I waited I thought that there's nothing like a confession to make one look mad; and that of all confessions a written one is the most detrimental all round. Never confess! Never, never!

Chance, Joseph Conrad

Preface

The first volume of these reminiscences was subtitled *Confessions* in Europe but *Autobiography* in the United States. Indeed my American publisher called the book the first part of *The Autobiography*, as if it were unique. It is, of course, unique in the sense that it is the only autobiography written by myself, but that is not the view that American reviewers took. I do not know why the title *Confessions* was unacceptable to my American publisher. It is hallowed by both St Augustine and Jean-Jacques Rousseau, and I was trying, in my humble way, to emulate the candour of those authors while in no manner laying claim to a comparable literary distinction. I was in the Catholic Church long enough to know that anyone may confess and, indeed, has to. But probably in America *Confessions* does not have a primarily spiritual denotation. There was, and may be still, a magazine called *True Confessions* whose revelations were almost entirely of an amatory nature.

Some of the confessions of my first volume were, it is true, erotic, but these formed a small part of the whole. Nevertheless, many reviewers picked on them for denunciation as though I were a priapic monster or, at best, unforgivably indiscreet. The personality revealed in that volume did not please, but it is never the object of confession, at least in the Catholic tradition, to present oneself as a likeable character. One seeks not admiration but forgiveness. The volume itself did not always please either, but it was unjust to term it, as one lady reviewer did, a 'self-indulgent ragbag'. There is never any self-indulgence in writing, unless it be a pornograph for personal use. Writing remains hard work. If the book was a 'ragbag', so was the life depicted, and so is anybody's life.

It would certainly be self-indulgent to answer the more severe of my critics – a thing rarely possible in the middle of a book (for these two books form one whole) unless that book is by D. H. Lawrence. I am thinking of his admirable *Mr Noon*, which interrupts itself halfway to whip reviewers with rollicking good humour. One cannot regenerate by rebuke the race of reviewers, who are often vindictive by nature. I have practised the craft of reviewing and know how convenient a vehicle it is for the expression of dislike, though I have myself always tried to be objective and assess books as artefacts rather than as emanations of a personality. If I myself wished to be vindictive I would pick on only a handful of reviewers, but all of these are now dead.

There is one man, however, alive at this moment of writing, whose position was far above that of a mere literary hack: he had something to do with the British state's allocation of funds for the promotion of literature. This is Charles Osborne, who, asked to nominate three works which he considered over-rated, chose that 'embarrassingly whimsical novelette *Lady Chatterley's Lover*, that feeble comedy *She Stoops to Conquer*, and whatever has most recently dropped heavily from the pen of Anthony Burgess (no matter what it was or how it may have been critically received)'. This represents a situation suitable for metaphysical enquiry in which a book not yet written has already been judged. It implies also a rather gratifying recognition of a unity in my works, something to do with heaviness.

One of the complaints about the first volume of my memoirs was that it was physically heavy, or too long. In the preface to that volume I threatened that its successor would be as long, or even longer. The threat has gone unfulfilled. I had a more varied life – though not a happier one – up to my forty-third year that I am having now, and this second and final phase has been so filled with work that there is not much to see. In Evelyn Waugh's *Vile Bodies* a film on the life of the reformer Wesley is being made, and there is a five-minute segment which shows him writing a sermon. This volume is like that, only much longer. As for the life itself, it is unlikely to be prolonged much further. Mr Osborne will not see much more dropping heavily from my pen or IBM.

I began the first volume by evoking a period of enforced idleness in a New York hotel in the early autumn of 1985. The idleness, which was a small figure of creative sterility, bred the decision to write of my early life. This may be taken as an instance of the dangers of idleness. I proposed to set forth that life with such candour as was possible to a temperament essentially secretive and mendacious. Out of a phase of similar idleness in a different New York hotel, rather less than one year later, with the typescript of the first volume already in the hands of British and American lawyers, arose the more difficult decision to continue and conclude the story. Why and how difficult the reader will know. As we grow older, the memories of early life brighten, those of maturity and senescence grow dim and confused. We prepare for our second childhood by reliving the first, and we are at last qualified to write about it. A record of more recent life is not merely impaired by the sickness of memory. It can, because of its enforced subject-matter, be a sharp weapon in the fingers of the vindictive. We resurrect the dead when we write of our far past, but they are ghosts, not Lazaruses. They cannot use the laws of the living. I must now write about the living, some of whom may not take kindly to candour. So truth must be occluded or bent and the whole aim of confession vitiated by apprehension. Writers are never as free as they claim, and when they write of themselves, which means also other people, they are least free.

In 1986 I was aware that death was no longer a book to be written but one already in proof and on its way by special messenger. I had flown to New York to deliver to the American Library Association an address similar to the one I had given the previous September to the librarians of Minnesota. The theme was censorship or the manner in which bad law qualified literary candour. I had taken the Crossair flight from Lugano to Zürich, a tiny craft buffeted by Alpine winds, and then the Swissair jet to Kennedy. The food, wine and liqueurs in first class were very refined and they did not settle well. I was bloated with mineral water and yet had a sense of dehydration. This grew worse during the two-hour wait for immigration processing in a shed unconditioned against a very hot New York June. Some travellers fainted. A friendly black wheeled round a tub of tepid water with paper cups. Immigration officers were inexorable in their checking of names against the great criminal ledger that looks like a variorum edition of Ayn Rand. They haggled over proposed length of stay and made shameless enquiries about solvency. I had ordered a limousine through my travel agent and was dehydrated further while waiting for it. It did not turn up, and the Swissair desk gave me a handful of dollars for a taxi. The driver was stoned and his cab reeked of old vomit. It was the New York rush hour and the driver's radio could easily have got through a Mahler symphony and two of Strauss's longer tone poems in the time it took to crawl from Queens to Manhattan. It was on and loud and it played neither Strauss nor Mahler. When we reached the Marriott Marquis Hotel I knew I was going to die. I was revived by delegates of the library conference with quarts of chill Coca-Cola, against which let no man say a word. Then my heart gave over its regular music and, like the percussion section of *Le Sacre du Printemps*, went in either for manic bashing or long stretches of doing nothing. It had to be watched.

In my hotel bedroom I could watch it only by staying awake. It would, I knew, intermit its thumping if I dropped off. After a time it conceded that I was its sort of master, even permitting me to wake with a gasp to confirm that it was still grinding the flour of life, but it behaved now like a rebuked dog that takes its revenge by pissing in corners. It filled my bronchial area with steady phlegm that no hawking could clear. I then knew that the mitral valve must be faulty. The talk I gave to the ten thousand librarians was a wet one, and the microphone picked up very accurately the phlegmy rattle. It did not matter much, since the occasion seemed to call for diversion more than earnestness. I was preceded by a long cabaret show given by black schoolgirls of the city, who waved legs, top hats and sticks in choruses from *A Chorus Line*. After my lecture I was abandoned by the American Library Association and permitted to get on with dying.

I did not, of course, die, but the book of death lay waiting to be opened. I had to spend another ten days alone in New York, waiting to cover the rededication of the cleaned-up Statue of Liberty in an article for the *Corriere della Sera*. After that I was to go to the University of Birmingham (the British one where David Lodge was) to be given an honorary doctorate, and I had promised to write some music for the brass section of the City of Birmingham Symphony Orchestra. I sat in the palmed and fountained concourse of the fortress hotel, set in a very rough area of downtown Manhattan, and scored for four horns, three trumpets, three trombones, tuba and timpani cynically festive music. Its rhythms contradicted those of my heart, and my heart sulked and gushed. Art, however lowly, is the best solvent of a sense of mortality. I smoked foul American cigars which granted me a wide space and distant dismissive gestures, smoking being the new American crime, and I drank whisky sours at the expense of the American Library Association. No kindly fellow-guest came up to say, 'What's that you're doing, fella?' I was alone, except for a young woman from Texas, who was not sure whether or not to write a thesis on my work, and a New York reading man who had bought a novel of mine, *The Doctor is Sick*, in its first British edition at the Gotham Book Mart. He had heard that I was at this hotel and he wanted my signature.

Seeing that first edition brought a lot back. It takes me back now to the continuation of my story. I had not read the book since correcting the proofs, and the dust of the time of writing it lay heavily on its pages. It had been published in late 1960, the year in which a negative medical prognosis was to be fulfilled, though I had never felt less like dying. Now it was time and physical dissolution that were giving fair warning, later perhaps to be confirmed by Dr Liebestraum or Professor Davidsbündler in Zürich. The terminal year allotted by the neurologists was ancient history and therefore very clear to my ageing memory. I can now steer back to it.

Before doing so, I had better make explicit an implied apology. If the reader gains little fun from the image of a man seated at a writing machine, then I am sorry, though I can do nothing about it. I present the life of a professional writer. The term professional, I say again and again, is not intended to imply high skill and large attainment, as with a tennis player. It means commitment to a means of earning a living. In the writer's occupation, action is reserved to fingers that transfer verbal constructs to paper, except for the groaning pacing, the irritable crumpling, the Audenesque analeptic swig, the relighting of a foul cheroot. The writer's life seethes within but not without. Nevertheless, it has to be recorded. This is so that mild wonder may be excited by the fact that the profession can be practised at all. Here then is an account of failures and humiliations but also of qualified triumphs. I apologise for seeming to contradict a native modesty by alluding to these last. But to survive at all as a writer excuses the raising of the bells of three unison trumpets in C.

A.B. Principauté de Monaco. 1990

ONE

I SIGHED and put paper into the typewriter. 'I'd better start,' I said. And I did. Meaning that, unemployable since I had less than a year to live, I had to turn myself into a professional writer.

It was the January of 1960 and, according to the prognosis, I had a winter and spring and summer to live through, and would die with the fall of the leaf. But I could not take the death sentence seriously. I felt too well. After the long enervation of the tropics, Lynne and I were being stimulated by the winter gales of the Channel. Chill Hove sharpened the appetite, and we no longer had to feed ourselves on Singapore Cold Storage carrion and the surrealistic tubers of the Brunei market. The stay-at-home British did not realise how lucky they were. We ate stews of fresh beef, roasts of duck and chicken, sprouts and cauliflowers and Jersey potatoes. There were also daffodils from the Scilly Isles in the flower shops. England was really a demi-paradise. But the serpent of the British state had to flicker its forked tongue.

The departments of the British state knew where I was. I was summoned to the local National Insurance office and asked what I proposed doing about sticking weekly stamps on a card. I replied that it hardly seemed worth while to enter the state scheme, and that the cost of my funeral would far exceed any contributions I could make to it. What was I living on? I was dying on cached Malayan dollars invested in British stock. I was writing vigorously to earn royalties for my prospective widow. When the Inland Revenue got on to me they found nothing, as yet, to tax. My coming death provoked no official sympathy. It was a statistical item yet to be realised. The coldness of the British was something that Lynne and I had become used to seeing as a property of colonial officials. We had forgotten that it was here at home as well.

Also mannerlessness. I worked out a little speech that I proposed delivering to the chinny woman who ran the newsagent-tobacconist's shop round the corner. 'Madam, I have been coming here every morning for the last three (or six or nine) months in order to buy *The Times* for myself, the *Daily Mirror* for my wife, and eighty Player's cigarettes for us both. I have meticulously said good morning on approaching your counter and on leaving it. I have also said please and thank you and made amiable comments on the weather. But not once has there been a reasonable phatic response from your unesteemed chinniness. It is as though bloody Trappists ran the shop.' This was an intended valediction on leaving Hove, but it was never made. At the greengrocer's shop my good morning was met only by a head-jerk of enquiry as to what I wanted. Perhaps the unwillingness to say good morning had something apotropaic about it: say the morning is good and it will turn out not to be. This must be true of American airline ticket agents, who are otherwise friendly enough.

'Good morning.'

'Hi.'

'Good morning.'

'It sure is.'

'Good morning.'

'You'd better believe it.'

We had been living in a region where the uneducated natives had been profuse with *tabek, tuan* and *selamat pagi, mem* and athletic with bows and hands on hearts. It was unnerving to be settling down in double cold, also to be surrounded by so much pinko-grey skin, as E. M. Forster called it. It was like being in a windy ward of the leprous. Like so many repatriates from the East, we found that the tropical past was becoming the only reality. We were in danger of turning into ex-colonial bores and eccentrics. In the winter cold I sometimes put on my suit over my pyjamas: Lynne usually chose these occasions to drag me to a reach-me-down tailor's. We also drank as though we were still sweltering under a ceiling fan. For me, if I was really dying, it did not much matter. For Lynne, ingesting two bottles of white wine and a pint of gin daily, it would matter a great deal.

I got on with the task of turning myself into a brief professional writer. The term professional is not meant to imply a high standard of commitment and attainment: it meant then, as it still does, the pursuit of a trade or calling to the end of paying the rent and buying liquor. I leave the myth of inspiration and agonised creative inaction to the amateurs. The practice of a profession entails discipline, which for me meant the production of two thousand words of fair copy every day, weekends included. I discovered that, if I started early enough, I could complete the day's stint before the pubs opened. Or, if I could not, there was an elated period of the night after closing time, with neighbours banging on the walls to protest at the industrious clacking. Two thousand words a day means a yearly total of 730,000. Step up the rate and, without undue effort, you can reach a million. This ought to mean ten novels of 100,000 words each. This quantitative approach to writing is not, naturally, to be approved. And because of hangovers, marital quarrels, creative deadness induced by the weather, shopping trips, summonses to meet state officials, and sheer torpid gloom, I was not able to achieve more than five and a half novels of very moderate size in that pseudo-terminal year. Still, it was very nearly E. M. Forster's whole long life's output.

Time also had to be expended on finding a house to live or die in. I did not propose meeting my maker in furnished rooms. And so, as spring approached, Lynne and I searched for a cottage in East or West Sussex. We also prepared to furnish it, wherever it was. This meant buying and storing Jacobean and deutero-Caroline commodes and dressers at very reasonable prices. These, to me, were pledges of continued life. They were also the solidities of widowhood. When I died (but the when was being slowly modified to if), Lynne would be able to offer gin or white wine to possible suitors in a polished lonely home of her own. She was only in her late thirties and the beauty eroded by the tropics was returning. Meanwhile, in one of our two rented rooms, I worked at a novel called *The Doctor is Sick*.

I clattered carefully at the dining table. To my right, dingy lace curtains occluded the view of an overgrown garden under a murky marine sky. To my left was a shabby sofa on which, before the shilling-in-the-slot gasfire, Lynne lay reading the *Daily Mirror* or a trashy novel. She had lost whatever literary taste she had ever had, except that she still adored Jane Austen, and one of my duties was to fetch her fictional garbage from the public library. If I brought Henry James or Anthony Trollope, the book would be hurled viciously at my head. It was her fault that I could not take Jane Austen seriously; it was a matter of association. If she could read trash and Jane Austen indifferently, Jane Austen had to be close to trash. But she used my ignorance of that scribbling spinster to trounce my own literary pretensions. In our cups I was catechised:

'How many daughters have Mr and Mrs Bennet?'

'Four, or is it five?'

'Who does Emma marry?'

'A man of decent education, appearance and income. I've forgotten his name.'

'What is the play that is put on in *Mansfield Park*?'

'Something by Kotzebue, I think.'

Lynne never read any of my own books, but she would ask for selected passages from my first, *Time for a Tiger*, to be read to her when she was ill. She was not concerned with savouring literary quality; she merely wanted evocation of her own Malayan past.

I thought at first that her debased taste was a gesture of conformity to our landlady's furnishings. On the walls were pictures of monks fishing and then feasting on fish. All the friars had the same face, as though really brothers, which meant that artistic poverty was matched by real penury: the painter could afford only one model. There were odd knick-knacks (strange that the Hebrew *naknik* should mean sausage) – ceramic buttonboxes, shell ashtrays from Brighton, all my stepmother's paraphernalia. The carpets, blankets and sheets had holes in them. The radio with the sunburst fascia, relic of the thirties, worked sporadically. Winds blew under the doors. Above us dwelt a young couple living in vigorous sin: they slept heavily and let the bath overflow through our bedroom ceiling. They could not be awakened.

I apologise for the irrelevance of that *naknik*. I am evoking a time when I was composing a novel about a man drunk on words, any words, and shoving him against his will into a world of things. Elias Canetti has a novel, *Auto da Fé*, in which an ageing philologist, expert in Chinese, is thrust among criminals. *The Doctor is Sick*, more Britishly and perhaps less ponderously, exploited the same situation. The hero is Edwin Spindrift, a PhD whose speciality is a philology which, in the 1960s, was already out of date, and he is sent home from a college in Burma where he has been teaching phonetics. He has, as I myself had, a suspected tumour on the brain. He also has a dark-haired unfaithful wife named Sheila. In the same neurological clinic as the one where I had been probed, his tests prove positive and an operation is proposed. But he escapes from the hospital and goes looking for his wife, who he suspects is fornicating vigorously all over London. He has had his head shaven in preparation for the scalpel; he wears a woolly cap. He has no money. He gets mixed up with the same lowlife characters I had encountered in a Bloomsbury unknown to Virginia Woolf – the big man who worked in Covent Garden (mornings in the market, evenings sceneshifting in the Opera House) and kept a Tangerine mistress, the vendors of stolen watches known as the Kettle Mob (among them a masochist who paid to be flagellated), the Jewish twins who ran an illegal drinking club.

These Jewish twins, Ralph and Leo, paid a surprise visit to Hove just as I was ready to transfer them to fiction. They wanted to start a small clothing enterprise and needed two hundred pounds to hire sewing machines and pay first week's wages to a young seamstress who was also, they frankly admitted, a shared doxy. We paid the money, though we foreknew the business would fail. All their businesses had failed. Their only stock in trade was their identical twinhood, useful in alibis. As for libelling them in a novel, they, or one of them, said: 'You can't say nuffink worse of us van we done already.' We took them to a pub which a handlebar-moustached ex-squadron leader entered with great laughter. 'Musta sold two cars today,' Ralph or Leo said. When the superior barmaid served our gin, Leo or Ralph said: 'Chip a couple of cubes off yer aris, iceberg.' Aris was short for Aristotle, itself rhyming slang for bottle, meaning bottle and glass, meaning arse. They went back to London with a cheque for two hundred nicker, having ensured that there were at least five Hove pubs we could no longer visit. But they were a pledge that life was going on somewhere, if not in Hove. I went back to the novel with appetite.

Spindrift is forced (by the twins) to enter a competition for handsome bald heads. He wins first prize but disapproves of the vulgarity of the contest. He shouts a filthy monosyllable on television and, anticipating Kenneth Tynan, makes history. In 1960 it was not possible to spell the word out on the page. I had to describe it as an unvoiced labiodental followed by an unrounded back vowel in the region of Cardinal Number 7 followed by an unvoiced velar plosive. Finally Dr Spindrift meets an old Greek acquaintance, a vendor of wine, named Mr Thanatos. Thanatos means death, but we are not sure whether Spindrift dies or recovers from his operation. Nor are we sure whether his picaresque adventures are dreams or reality. He has lived in a world of words but has ignored their referents. The referents get up to bite him, perhaps kill him. Or conceivably they only pretend to.

Spindrift is a very improbable name. I do not think it is to be found in any telephone directory. Spin is a distortion of spoon, and spoondrift is seaspray. It is meant to connote the frivolous insubstantial thrown off by the reality of life's heavy water. Dr Spindrift gained his doctorate by writing a thesis on the Yiddish prefix *shm-* as used derisively in New York Jewish English or Yidglish (Oedipus Shmoedipus, what's it matter what he's got so long as he loves his

mother). I doubt if such a thesis would be possible. I doubt if
Spindrift ever went, as he alleges, to Pasadena to take his doctoral
degree. He is insubstantial to his creator. He is useless to his wife, as
his libido has failed him, and it is in order for her to seek sexual
sustenance in a London of layabouts and failed artists only too ready
to give it. He offers words instead of love. Even the small criminals
he is thrown among are vigorously transacting in a world of realities.
The whisky sold in the illegal drinking club may be watered, and the
kettles sold on building sites by the mobsters may cease to tick after a
day or so, but they are more substantial than words. Spindrift is only
spoondrift, a feeder of philological pobs, and he deserves to die. He
has a neural disease, but this is only a confirmation of a psychical
disease – the morbidity of a useless specialisation. Giving a pair of
improvident Jewish twins a cheque for two hundred nicker was a
recognition, on Spindrift's creator's part, that life was more than
words, that Spindrift could not have been fabricated except by
somebody dangerously like him. To fail at treadling cloth was better
than succeeding with words.

On the other hand, a work of fiction is a solidity that can be
handled, weighed, sold, and its task is to present or distort the real
world through words. Words are real things, but only if they evoke
real things. But things become real only when they are named. And
we can only know reality through our minds, which function
through structural oppositions, typically realised in phonemes and
morphemes. But there is only one knowable mind, and that is mine
or yours. The solipsism suggested in *The Doctor is Sick* – the external
world can be confirmed only by one perceiving mind, even if it is
deranged, but what do we mean by derangement? – is a tenable
metaphysical position, but I was, am, no metaphysician. I was, am,
trying to be a kind of comic novelist playing with a few ideas.
Perhaps it was inevitable that the Germans should make more of this
particular novel than the British. There have been two translations –
Der Doktor ist Übergeschnappt and *Der Doktor ist Defekt* – and a
number of scholarly dissertations from the universities of the
Western Republik. The British have taken it as mere, rather
demented and certainly tasteless, entertainment.

Dr Spindrift is not altogether myself, but some of his experiences
are based on my own, not least the failure of the libido. A Pakistani
doctor at the Hospital for Tropical Diseases had lilted the term with
relish and regret when questioning me about my sexual life. Whether
it was part of a neuropathological syndrome was never made clear.
The fact was that sexual relations between my wife and myself had

practically ceased in 1959, and I did not need a clinical report to tell me why. If, at night, I was too drunk to perform the act and, in the morning, too crapulous, it was probable that I soaked myself in gin in order to evade it. I wanted to evade it because of my wife's vaunted infidelity, intermitted in valetudinarian Hove but, I suspected, ready to erupt again when, if, we settled in a randier ambience. I was prepared to accept the discipline of love but not the abandon of sex – neither in marriage nor, for the moment, elsewhere. Sex, but not too much of it, could be reserved to my novels.

No husband can object to his wife's infidelities if she does not blab too much about them. But to hear about the prowess of a Punjabi on Bukit Chandan or a Eurasian on Batu Road is the best of detumescents. Marital sex develops a routine, but the routines of a stranger are a novelty. Infidelities are a search for novelty, and *dongiovannismo* is more properly a woman's disease than a man's. Don Juan's tragedy is that he finds all women the same in the dark and that they, finding novelty in his routine, are innocent enough to believe that the physical revelation is love. His tragic flaw is to choose the innocent, who pursue him to death. Women thrive on novelty and are easy meat for the commerce of fashion. Men prefer old pipes and torn jackets. Women love gifts (finding novel presents for Lynne on her birthday and at Christmas was strenuous work) and, given the chance, they love amorous variety. The dissatisfaction of wives unable to find it has become, since Flaubert, one of the stock themes of fiction. The flesh of my wife was honeycoloured and sumptuous, but I could not be attracted. She told me how often it had been handled by others, and how well some of them had handled it. I was perhaps better than A and B but not so good as X or Y. I could not subdue my pride, which was a grievous fault, and I preferred to put myself out of the running. This was marital cruelty, though not according to the Catholic Church, which blessed chaste unions. I was always ready to call on my abandoned faith when I lacked the courage to make my own moral decisions.

There was never any argument about the deeper value of our marriage, which could be viewed as a miniature civilisation or micropolis. Or, put it another way, it was complex semiotics. There was a fund of common memories to draw on, a series of codes, a potent shorthand. It was the ultimate intimacy, except that it was no longer physical. I had reacted to infidelity by condoning it; if, as there was, there was to be more of it, that would not affect the intimacy. But the resentment would be all on her side, and it would take forms unrelated to sex. One form would be unwillingness to read my work and to take malicious pleasure in bad reviews of it. Another, not really anomalous, would be to spread the rumour that she herself had produced it, myself not being quite clever enough. 'Anthony Burgess' was, after all, a pseudonym, and it need not be mine. George Eliot and the Bell brothers were women. If she fought for the work, which she did, if insulting agents, publishers and reviewers could be termed fighting, she would be fighting for herself. She cried out for notice while doing nothing to earn it. What she had achieved, which she seemed to me to overvalue, all lay in the past – head girl of her school, hockey and tennis player for her county, swimmer for the principality, pet of Professor Namier, minor star of the Board of Trade and the Ministry of War Transport. She identified with her father, successful headmaster of a minor Welsh grammar school, the more so as she could not quell guilt over the death of her mother. Our marriage was bristling with tensions, but it was still a marriage. It was sustained by love, which I do not have to define.

I WROTE *The Doctor is Sick* in six weeks. As Lynne never read it, it was otiose to wonder whether she would have seen anything of herself in the character of Sheila Spindrift, erring wife. Sheila was dark, anyway, and Lynne was blonde, and, to a woman, the dichotomy is temperamental. All women, with the exception of Ann Gregory, might accept that blondness is a reality that cosmetics cannot efface. Lynne saw herself in the heroine of my Malayan books, what she knew of them, and accepted the blonde, chaste, patrician lady as an adequate portrait. The patrician aspect was important in itself, besides relating her to a writer more important than I. A family tree, engrossed by her primary school teacher sister, was imported, and the name of Lady Charlotte Isherwood of Marple Hall was writ large in gold. The aristocratic heresy is convenient to those too lazy to develop talent, or bitterly aware that they have none. Blue blood is a fine substitute for genius: to Evelyn Waugh his own genius was little more than a calling card for the houses of the great. Class is the great British reality, and the more books I wrote the more Lynne termed me an unregenerable guttersnipe. Many critics agreed with her. As for all my fictional women after Fenella Crabbe, these were to Lynne mere interchangeable mannequins for whom she kindly devised wardrobes. But she was not interested in how these women, dressed by her, looked, nor in what they did. I had, with *The Doctor is Sick*, completed a book that she hoped was saleable. Now stop reading

Richard Ellmann's life of Joyce, just published, and get on with the next.

It had been suggested to me by James Michie of Heinemann that I take a literary agent. He recommended one, Peter Janson-Smith, and I took the train to Charing Cross to see him, the typescript of the new novel under my arm. I would prove small beer to Janson-Smith, who was to handle the work of Ian Fleming, Professor Northcote Parkinson and Gavin Maxwell, but of his goodness he took me on. He began by selling *The Doctor is Sick* to Heinemann, who had already contracted for it, but with a slightly enhanced advance that covered the agent's commission. Janson-Smith was, I suppose, a good agent, but I am not sure what a good agent is. The best agent, it seemed to me at the time, was the one who would try to place a first novel, but I do not think there were many such agents around. When I had published *Time for a Tiger*, received encouraging reviews, and seen the work go into a second impression, I began to receive letters from agents: I had cranked up the car in freezing weather, and now they would drive from the back seat. What I wanted from my agent was publisher's commissions, foreign sales, film options. They were slow to come. I was, it must be remembered, trying to make a living from literature.

I was to do better when I ceased to have an agent. I now gravely doubt the value of a literary middleman. The publisher himself, when you come to think of it, is not much more than that. In the eighteenth century Mr Dilly, a bookseller, could commission a work from Dr Samuel Johnson and not have to be persuaded to display the book in his window. The essential trinity is the author, the printer-binder, and the vendor with a cash register. In America this trinity has become a unity. A young writer, despairing of a publisher's acceptance of his work, will type and copy his book and then sell it on the street. There was, I remember, a young Californian who wrote an interesting but, in publisher's terms, uncommercial trilogy in which the characters of the Popeye cartoons became figures in a theological allegory. He printed his work on an IBM machine and hawked round his copies. He sold only about four hundred of each volume but registered an eighty per cent profit. He managed to live. Later he took to drugs and died, but this does not invalidate his practice. With both agents and publishers hungry for bestsellers, literature will have to end up as a cottage industry.

When bestsellers are boosted, the number of languages into which they are translated is proclaimed with pride. But multiple translation is no index of anything. It is the agent's task to find foreign publishers but not to choose the translator, and many translations are very bad. They cannot be all that bad with what I have termed Class 1 novelists – those in whom language is a discardable quality – but with Class 2 writers, who are given to poetic effects, wordplay and linguistic ambiguity, the translator must be himself a committed writer. I have achieved a reading knowledge of a fair number of the Indo-European languages, and I insist on seeing translations before they are published. This is the kind of time-consuming work which few agents would be willing or qualified to take on, but it is essential if howlers or total misrepresentations are to be avoided. A lot of translations have to be rejected as inept. In a late novel of mine, *Earthly Powers*, the injunction 'Go to Malaya and write about planters going down with DT's' was rendered into Italian to the effect of writing about planters committing fellatio with doctors of theology. A self-respecting author will never boast about the number of foreign countries that know his work: he will consult accuracy and elegance of translation and pride himself, often in old age, on having assembled a limited but reliable stable. Agents will sell to anyone, if the money seems right. They are quantitative people.

They are buffers between authors and publishers, but, to the author, they often seem closer to the publisher than to himself. They will quarrel with an author and even reject him as a nuisance, but they dare not make an enemy of a publisher. They will push saleability more than literary merit, which can sometimes creep into a publisher's list because of a package deal: I will let you have this undoubted bestseller if you will accept this unprofitable pastiche of Henry James. Done. Agents dare not be over-concerned with literary merit, as opposed to adequate literacy, when they have many typescripts to sell. They usually disclaim the higher critical competence. Janson-Smith cautiously made a literary judgement on *The Doctor is Sick* and suggested a change. I snarled, and he withdrew. He knew he was exceeding his brief.

The trip to London to meet him, in an office of which I remember only a large can of lighter fuel, should also have been crowned by a visit to the Neurological Institute for a spinal tap. I did not go. I feared that there would be such an increase in the protein volume of the cerebrospinal fluid that the year to live might be curtailed and discourage a new novel. My failure to turn up seems to have been translated into a negative report from the laboratory, for I received a letter from Sir Alexander Abercrombie informing me that the protein content of my spinal liquor had gone down dramatically and I was now kindly allowed to live. This did not provoke elation but rather new caution: I had to be more careful when crossing the street. If, as I wished, I were to start a very long novel about a minor poet living in a lavatory, the gods might contrive pernicious anaemia or galloping consumption to thwart me. Now that death from a cerebral tumour was crossed off the list, there was still a limitless choice of ailments to draw on, all lethal. Life itself is lethal but, we hope, not yet. I had to beware of what might be called biotic hubris.

THE CHARACTER I was to call Enderby had appeared to me one day in the bathroom of our hovel outside Brunei Town, a wraith conjured by an attack of malaria. He was, for a microsecond or so, seated on the toilet and writing poetry. I proposed a 200,000-word novel about him called very simply *Enderby*. It might be more modest, and placatory of the gods of death, to compose something very much briefer called *Inside Mr Enderby*. Some day *Enderby Outside* might follow, and then he could be seen off in *Enderby's End*. I envisaged an ugly middle-aged man very much on his own, a masturbating bachelor, living in the identical furnished rooms Lynne and I were renting, though mostly confining himself to the lavatory-bathroom, locked in against the world, writing purgative poems in a place of purgation. He has chosen the smallest room, but soon he must be dragged out to engage the biggest one, type of the great historical capitals, synchronically small but diachronically of large size. The Elizabethans pronounced Rome as room, as the Arabs still do: 'Our steel we have brought and our star, to shine on the ruins of Rum' (back to James Elroy Flecker's *Hassan* and my sexual education from the WEA lady). He is married, somewhat against his will, and taken to Rome for his honeymoon, but the marriage is not consummated and he escapes to resume his creative lunette. The Muse however, angry that he should have deserted her for a flesh and blood woman, takes her revenge and deserts him. He attempts suicide but very ineptly. The state health system persuades him that poetry, like masturbation, is an adolescent toy, and that his duty to the new Britain of socialist, or materialist, purpose is to turn himself into an adult. He is helped to do this by a state psychiatrist named Wapenshaw, and he ends the novel looking forward to a job as a bartender in a great hotel.

This is not altogether a bitter conclusion. In *The Doctor is Sick* the philologist Edwin Spindrift purveys nothing valuable, while the Jewish twins who run an illegal club at least try to get people drunk.

Enderby is also a wordman, and his poems are no more than the spume, or spoondrift, of a morbid and antisocial life. It is permissible to despise him and to deplore the way he lives, which is unutterably sordid. On the other hand, he may be taken as the last dogged individualist, the quiet rebel who lives in all of us, affirming the creative impulse, even to no useful end, and, doing little good to the world, at least doing no harm. *Inside Mr Enderby* is moderately ambiguous, and so are its sequels. The poems he writes have their own ambiguities. This one, for instance, coming unbidden to Enderby in the toilet of a train going to Charing Cross and supposed by him to be a song of the Blessed Virgin:

> In this spinning room, reduced to a common noun,
>   Swallowed by the giant stomach of Eve,
> The pentecostal sperm came hissing down.
>
> I was no one, for I was anyone,
>   The grace and music easy to receive,
> The patient engine of a stranger son.
>
> His laughter was fermenting in the cell,
>   The fish, the worm were chuckling to achieve
> The rose of the disguise he wears so well.
>
> And though, by dispensation of the dove,
>   My flesh is pardoned of its flesh, they leave
> The rankling of a wrong and useless love.

That is one of three poems, not previously attributed to Enderby, mildly approved by T. S. Eliot.

Because I had to write Enderby's poems for him, or resurrect old poems of my own to swell his *oeuvre*, I have sometimes been identified with the poet himself. This is not really just. I share with him a nostalgia for a kind of dualism in which the freedom of the spirit is the better confirmed by the filth of the body. Enderby, like myself, is a lapsed Catholic but also a holy anchorite aspiring above the fumes of his filth. His visceral obsession used to be my own. Up to the time of my writing the novel, fiction, with the exception of *Ulysses*, where Mr Bloom spends more than a page in his outdoor jakes, preferred to ignore the bowels. Rabelais did not ignore them, and Rabelais was right. Even sweetest Shakespeare names his melancholy character in *As You Like It* after a water closet and seems to equate depression with constipation. The Reformation had much to do with Luther's costiveness. Also, at the time of writing about Enderby, I suffered from profound dyspepsia. Enderby's stomach is bad, but he brings this on himself with ghastly home cooking. He is ill clad and badly shaven and, since his bathtub is full of poetic drafts, old sandwiches and mice, he is very dirty. I, however, had a tidy Welsh wife who kept me clean and gave me good plain meals. My dyspepsia was probably an aspect of my anxiety about the future, which Sir Alexander Abercrombie's letter now permitted to exist.

My wife, as I have said, read none of my books except the first, but she allowed me to recite in bed certain extracts from *Inside Mr Enderby*. These she found amusing. She contributed to Enderby's cuisine a dish called Spaghetti Formaggio Surprise. She found the character sympathetic and, among women, she has not been alone in this. Many women are perhaps sluts at heart. Many women do not like women.

With Enderby there is a fear of women and a physical distaste for them, unless they can be cleansed into pornographs. I was perhaps here extrapolating a conviction, learned from my marriage, that women are dangerous to the artist. The woman in my novel, Vesta Bainbridge, is the widow of a racing driver who looks forward to being the widow of a poet. Artists are acceptable to women when they are dead – they become an ornament they can pin to their smart black – but they are a nuisance when they are alive, because they are devoted to a rival. Women are not permitted to take art seriously when they themselves practise it, for they recognise that it is a mere surrogate for the creative miracle of bearing children. When Mary McCarthy suggested that the novel was closer to gossip than to art, she was putting the woman's point of view. When women take art seriously they risk self-destruction. They have to try to rise above biology, and nature rebels. They have to be lonely, and this is easier for a man than a woman. Enderby's name implies loneliness. Enderby Land is in the Antarctic. It is in order for him to be cold and removed. When he marries he has to be destroyed. 'The Brides of Enderby', which the church bells jangle in Jean Ingelow's poem about a shipwreck, has shipwreck connotations.

I am ready to be told that the above is nonsense, and not even Enderby would endorse it. His misogyny derives from something very simple and rather comic. He loathes the memory of his stepmother, whose ignorance and sordor have attached themselves to all women. I resurrected my own stepmother to haunt him and made her more distasteful than she really was. Ten years after publishing the book I admitted this provenance in a newspaper interview. Some of her surviving relatives borrowed the novel from the public library and were roused to fury. The symbolic use I made of the detested stepmother was of little interest even to dispassionate readers. Enderby, like myself, has lost his real mother, whom he never knew, and has idealised her into a kind of Virgin Mary. But the Virgin Mary was a mother only to one, and so filiality is denied to Enderby. His flesh and blood stepmother seems to return from the dead in the first chapter, but that is to remind Enderby that she has certain avatars – not only all women but also the sea (*la belle mer* or *la belle-mère*), the state, above all the Catholic Church. Leaving Rome, Enderby tries to write an ode to the 'stepmother of the West'. He wants a woman who is both mother and mistress, but that would mean incest, so he has to have the Muse. Far from permitting Enderby to assume the male role with her, she herself does the impregnating. Sex has to be a merely purgative process, performed, like the writing of poetry, in the lavatory. In marrying a woman who, like all women, is likely to turn into his stepmother, Enderby sins against his art. The Muse is right to leave him. Having lived in purgatory he now has to go to hell. But, because he is a character in a comic novel, he is dragged from the burning and reborn.

The setting of the first part of the novel is the furnished lodgings in Hove, fairly closely described. Some Hove characters got into the book – the habituées of a lesbian pub, a toothless Lancashire cook who said 'Vol au vent's in 't'bloody cupboard', a madman met in an esplanade shelter who believed that the Marxist state would, as though it were Hegel's, ultimately be theophanic. But the locale changed for Enderby as it changed for Lynne and myself. With the book only half-written, we went to live in East Sussex, in a semidetached house in the village of Etchingham.

ETCHINGHAM IS on the railway line between Tunbridge Wells and Hastings. Two miles away is the village of Burwash – pronounced Burrosh: Henry James very nearly got it right – where Rudyard Kipling lived. It is not on the railway line, so, before he bought his Rolls-Royce and hired his chauffeur, Kipling had to catch the same trains as myself. The great Edwardian literary fraternity was in East Sussex – James in Rye, Ford Madox Ford in Winchelsea – but it was not their example that drove me to set up my typewriter in the half-county. Lynne and I had, like all house-hunters, been misled by estate agents' copy to profound depression, and, finding a humble house, totally by chance, newly vacated and not yet processed into agentspeak, we were quick to claim it. I could just about afford to put down a deposit and pay off the mortgage instalments. We were drawing heavily on such capital as we had, and the future in which I was now permitted to live presented grave problems. It was clear that there was little money in my kind of fiction – a hundred pounds advance, as in Ford's and James's day, and a trickle of royalties. If I wrote five novels or so each year we might just about survive, but I doubted my capacity to produce even as many as four. I envied my own Enderby, whose tiny private income and bachelor limitations enabled him to practise an art. I had to produce a saleable commodity and bear the sneers of reviewers who complained of my artlessness. But art insisted on creeping in. That had to be so: my small sales proved it.

The house had 'Applegarth' inscribed on its gate. This was just, because there were gnarled trees which gave sour crabs. There was a shrubby front garden and an extensive one at the back ran down to the stream called the Dodder. This overflowed when the autumn rains were heavy and flooded the sheep pasture beyond as far as the wood which was the beginning of the Kentish Weald. The garden meant a new and time-eating responsibility – mowing, weeding, planting runner beans and roses. Luckily Lynne, as a country girl, knew flowers and had green fingers. We set up croquet hoops.

The house had three storeys. The attic was large, and we turned it into a pub for our own use – bar, dartboard, whisky-advertising mirror, the three Chinese-made high stools which, with our other effects, eventually made their slow way from Brunei. A couple of New Zealand secretaries, admirable girls, had crated our goods, but those crates had stood long on the Brunei docks in monsoon weather. The camphorwood chest had been crowbarred open by customs officials looking for opium, and we found a mummified mouse within. The radiogram, bought in Brunei Town, actually worked. Some books, hollowed out from inside by termites, were not much more than covers and a spine. The Gilbert Wood painting of a pub scene was reframed for the fourth time. The house began to look like a home. We had a cat and kittens.

A month after we settled in we bought a border collie pup which we named Haji. He began as an affectionate baby bear and then grew into a great nuisance. He was intended to be a link with our former English life, the name reminding us of the Eastern intermission. The collie bitch Suky, who had provided puppies for a hundred or so of the pupils of Banbury Grammar School, had been loyal and intelligent. Haji was crafty, disobedient, and ignorant of the sexual life, except in perverted forms peculiar to himself: he tried to rape women visitors. He chased sheep and was shot at by barking farmers. The word *out*, used in whatever context, sent him into a hysterical ecstasy. When it was merely spelt he responded as to the vocable itself. Christine Brooke-Rose produced a novel called *Out*, and I used her name as a synonym for it. He went into a hysterical ecstasy. He wanted to be out, pulling against the lead, choking himself. Off the lead he fought other dogs or attacked their owners. He chased pregnant ewes as far as the Kentish Weald. He had no loyalty, leaving that commodity to us.

We were settled, but we were not at all happy. The villagers were xenophobic and were not impressed at having a writer in their midst. Writers do not fit into any known village hierarchy. Besides, they had had a writer named Rupert Croft-Cooke, a worshipper of Lord Alfred Douglas, arrested for seducing sailors inland, released from jail to write and bugger freely in Tangier. Writers were a bad lot, unlike retired admirals. They were supposed to be drunken sexual perverts who were slow in leaving their morning beds to greet the mailman and ran up long credit in village stores. Alternatively, they were absurd negativities who purveyed goods nobody wanted. This was not merely the attitude of English villages. It had been embarrassing in Hove to have to admit that I was a writer. 'What sort of books do you write? Tecs? Thrillers?' Henry James had laboured in vain: the novel did not exist except in precise genre forms, the most important of which was the dirty book. Say to a French taxi driver '*Je suis homme de lettres*' or to a German barman '*Ich bin Schriftsteller*' and you get a respectful response. Not so with Shakespeare's countrymen.

The wives of authors, when they had them, were considered fair game by lecherous village publicans. The landlord of our one local pub tried to seduce Lynne in the ladies' toilet. She hit out. Thus we had no pub, unless we cared to take the infrequent bus to Burwash, where the villagers, unserved by the railway, were even more xenophobic than our own. When our local butcher, Nelson Jarvis, left Burwash to set up his block and cleavers in Etchingham, he was alleged to have cried: 'Goodbye, Burwash moon.' Kipling had inscribed his son's name on the war memorial by the bus stop, but otherwise he had kept out of the village. The local shopkeepers had sold his cheques at a high profit to American tourists.

A neighbour poisoned our cats and reported us to the RSPCA for

cruelty to Haji. When an inspector arrived he admitted that the
cruelty all went the other way. Lynne slept badly and was prescribed
barbiturates by the Ulsterman doctor who visited from Hurst Green.
She banished me from the bed because I groaned loudly in my sleep,
so I tossed on the second-hand day couch in my study. She installed a
barrel of Kent cider and drank it mixed with gin. I was morose and
insufficiently appreciative of the trouble she had taken to make me a
home. Haji howled at the Etchingham moon and growled when he
was slapped. Drunk, Lynne raved at me and set the neighbours
hammering on the wall. We had had a telephone installed, and
almost our first call was from Lynne's sister, who chided her yet
again for soaking in sun and *stengahs* in Malaya while their mother
was dying and now proposed playing over the line a tape recording
of the voice of the not yet deceased, croaking to her children to live
godly lives and beware of sex. Lynne screamed and slammed down
the receiver. She threw on the floor the salad I was persuading her to
eat and snapped the Malayan tortoiseshell and silver salad fork. She
prepared to hurl my typewriter at the window. I screamed back. She
locked herself in the bathroom and then emerged in calm, saying:
'That ought to do it.' She had swallowed more than thirty
barbiturate tablets.

In suicide it is the gesture that matters. It is meant to promote fear
and regret in loving ones who have not loved enough. The tablets
were quick to start acting, and the fear and regret were now also hers.
She submitted to my pouring salt and water down her throat, but she
collapsed in the first stages of the operation and slashed her forehead
open on the edge of the wash basin. I dragged her, unconscious now
and very bloody, to her bed and then telephoned for an ambulance. It
was slow in coming – the only amenities of village life seemed to be
greenery and frustration – and when it arrived the attendants shook
their heads as her stertorous breathing grew fainter. It was a long trip
to the hospital outside Hastings. There a stomach pump was put to
work. I paced like an expectant father, though more guiltily. Passing
nurses told me to douse my cigarettes. Their cold eyes exacerbated
my guilt. A suicidal wife was the most potent of advertisements for
the brutality of a husband.

Christian theology teaches us that only God knows the nature of
sin, and that humanity demonstrates how fallen it is by its inability to
appraise its transgressions in terms of ultimate reality. Imagine that
God is a field of sentient snow which screams in agony when a man
casually pisses on it. I eat meat on Friday or miss mass on Sunday,
and God is aflame with pain, howling with cosmic toothache. We are

incredulous about this because we are human and fallen. A man can become less incredulous when he innocently (innocently?) harms the woman in his life. There is a huge moral gulf between man and woman, and it would have been better if theology had been in the hands of women, using their own moral system to explicate God's. Don Juan, according to Kierkegaard, was searching for God through woman. I paced the hospital corridors and searched my conscience. I was not sure what wrongs I had committed, but I surmised that they must be vile. The Arabs use the word *nusus* for a man's failure to fulfil the obligations of the marriage bed, sometimes glossed as pleasures. Had *nusus* driven her to attempted suicide? Had I merely (but merely is a man's word) failed in tenderness, appreciation? Was my real sin an anterior one, the dragging of my wife to the tropics and anorexia and the solace of gin? Or was she reacting to the prospect of my death when it was no longer in prospect?

I visited her in hospital twice a day, which meant spending the whole day in Hastings. Enderby, just married, had to wait indefinitely for his Roman honeymoon. A day in Hastings meant the pubs when they were open and the cinemas when they were closed. I did not approve of the pubs. I would order gin and tonic with ice, be served gin and tonic and then be told there was no ice. I would fly into a rage, since tepid gin is no more than an emetic, and be ordered to leave. Clearly I was myself tottering on the edge of breakdown. I saw a film called *Sink the Bismarck*, in which great acts of destruction were effected without hysteria. How much better it would be to be married to that cool darkhaired WRNS officer there with her Roedean accent. Lynne was aggressive. She railed at me with convalescent vigour for pulling her out of the dark. She remembered a story read in childhood about a brown bear that rolled itself into a ball when winter came and unrolled itself in the spring. One spring it failed to unroll itself. She wanted to be that brown bear. She wept for it and for herself. When she was released from the hospital and came home I would have to be better. I thought I had been good enough, but evidently I had not. I was bewildered, leafing through a book of female theology in an unknown alphabet.

The ward sister wore glasses on a sharp nose and was deeply Presbyterian. Lynne resented her imputation of grave sin and, for that matter, civil crime. If you took your own life apparently you merited the death penalty. When Lynne suffered a spasm of *petit mal* on the way back from the sluice and rolled and foamed, the ward sister relented of her just harshness and became, less acceptably, solicitous and also sentimental. I went back to Etchingham to find that the dog Haji had lavishly watered the carpet and chewed a table leg. I cooked myself a free-range chicken in brandy, a more efficacious emetic than tepid gin. Then Lynne appeared at the door in a hired car. Dressed and even lipsticked, she had been led to the hospital psychiatrist and run screaming from his consulting room when he bluntly affirmed that her suicidal anguish sprang from an unsuitable marriage. She had at once discharged herself.

It was a glorious early summer, all blossom and cuckoos. Lynne served herself gin and cider and sternly pronounced that she was not, in future, to be crossed. Neither of us attributed her condition to alcohol. We slept in the same bed and I clasped her for comfort. There was a half-hearted resumption of marital duty or pleasure. I snored. I was banished to my study couch. Soon the spare bedroom was fitted with a bed and a wardrobe and a chest of drawers, and I lay awake long in it, listening for sounds of distress from the master bedroom, working out the plots of three novels.

A NOVEL is primarily an entertainment that should primarily entertain its author. I felt guilty each morning after breakfast when I mounted the stairs to my study, there to be entertained. I was juggling with words in the service of diversion while suffering I could not well understand proceeded with the housework below. The Germans, and especially Thomas Mann, use the term *Künstlerschuld* – artist's guilt – to designate the writer's gloom at his own frivolity in a world that performs dull useful work and is unhappy about it. My *Künstlerschuld* was highly personal: I had to force myself to temper it with the reflection that I was trying to earn a living. Lynne reminded me of this when she occasionally cried upstairs that she could not hear the clatter of the typewriter. She would not accept that writing is nine parts brooding and one part clattering. I finished *Inside Mr Enderby* in late June. Enderby's comic failed suicide was an attempt to exorcise Lynne's uncomic one. I sent the typescript to Janson-Smith, keeping no copy for myself. I had never made copies, even in Malaya and Borneo. I had a naïve trust in the mails. Janson-Smith thought the book was too lavatory-obsessed to be easily publishable. I had better write something else.

The Right to an Answer appeared that summer. On 30 June the anonymous reviewer in the *Times Literary Supplement* wrote: 'The tone of the book is comic, with some initial over-writing, but it takes a turn towards violence at the end. The likeliest scenes are in the local pub, but the Midlands town as seen by one who has become an outsider is sharply described. The reader, though, may well wonder whether the experiences recounted add up to anything of much importance.' The Midlands town, unnamed, was Leicester, where Lynne and I had spent most of our leave from the Far East. That rather smug city I made the backcloth of a drama of marital infidelity and jealous murder, with an overriding theme that seemed to me important enough – the trouble that Britain was going to have with its new Asian immigrants.

John Coleman in the *Spectator* said: 'Not the best of Burgess's books. Mr Burgess might curb his inventiveness: he'd be a first-rate comic novelist if the camouflage of another little joke were down and he looked his subject squarely in the face.' R. G. G. Price in *Punch* wrote: 'I do not quite understand why everybody refers to Mr Burgess as a funny man. He is as accurate and depressing as Gissing, though I agree that he is a Gissing with a sense of fun and an eye for any comedy to be found in his ruined world.' Do reviewers ever consider that novelists are desperate for help, that they are anxious to be told where they go wrong and what they can do to put things right, and that, before they achieve the dignity of *solus* reviews and academic dissertations, they have to rely on those lordly summations in the weekly press? There were not many reviews. The quality Sunday newspapers ignored the book. So did Lynne, though she read the reviews. She coined the judgement 'Mr Burgess disappoints'. Then, after a Saturday noon's drinking session in Robertsbridge, where Hilaire Belloc had drunk port and Malcolm Muggeridge was the present literary celebrity, she attempted suicide again.

This time I brutally forced the barbiturate tablets up and out and threw the bottle in the dustbin. Haji danced and barked and the new ginger kitten leaped wide-eyed to the top of the deutero-Caroline betrothal chest. When the doctor came he brought with him a young man in a flat cap. He was a county official in charge of the committal of the insane to the county asylum. He had a committal form already completed except for the doctor's signature. There seemed to be no place for my own. I threw the young man out. He did not protest: he seemed used to husbandly evictions. Lynne responded truculently to the doctor's firm Ulster tones. Whatever was the cause of her suicidal depression, she must give up the drink. But she did not, and I could not force her: she was, after all, not to be crossed. When the self-destructive impulse returned, as it did several times that year, she could find no easy mode of implementation. There were no barbiturates, only the kitchen knives. The organisation known as the Samaritans spoke calm words to her over the telephone when the fit came on, but she could not hear them because of her sobs. I used the telephone to contact a bookmaker in Tunbridge Wells and open a punter's account for her. That helped. She followed racing form in the *Daily Mirror* and lost only three or four pounds a week.

Meanwhile I had my own troubles, which had nothing to do with the strain of writing for a living. I woke nightly with trigeminal neuralgia, which could be relieved only by tobacco and strong coffee. I went to a dentist in Frant who diagnosed an impacted wisdom tooth. Extracting it he broke it. I had to go to a hospital near Tunbridge Wells to have the root removed under a general anaesthetic. I was thus returning for a night and a day to a locale I had thought to be done with. The real problem was that Lynne could not bear to be left alone at night, even with a dog that flew into an ecstasy of noise at the scuffle of a mouse. She feared the dark, and the fear had its origin in blacked-out wartime London when she had been viciously attacked by four GI deserters. She feared the dark of her sleeping mind: the ultimate dark was a different matter. The married daughter of our grocer was willing to occupy my bed for a night if the sheets were changed. She was willing to do this often, but not for long. A New York publisher, W. W. Norton, had bought *The Right to an Answer* and there was talk of my going to the United States to be launched there. Lynne forbade that: I would be too long away.

The return to a hospital ward was a return to male sodality, the sane subculture of the barrack room. The war had ended fifteen years before, but the nostalgia for nostalgia was alive in a lot of us – away from home we wanted to be home; home, we wanted to be deprived of the right to be there. In the ward I met two men who had read my first novel. It was pleasant to be appreciated and heartening to be temporarily free of the claustrophobia of a tense life with a woman ready at any moment to scream or smash plates. The place of sickness was a place of brief health. I had a monstrous cyst on my back in the site of the jabbings for spinal gin. I requested its cutting in order to prolong my stay. Naturally I felt guilty.

Lynne and I cautiously settled to a country life enlivened mostly with drunkenness and threats of suicide. We had one regular visitor – an official of the Ministry of National Insurance who wished to know why I was not stamping a card. He was a Mr Stanley, a man with a good Lancashire name who, on his first visit, looked at me curiously over his glass of gin. I looked curiously back over mine. He had been Brother John Vianni of the Xaverian College in

Manchester. He had taught me junior Latin. He had, like so many of his confrères, left the order and married. The evocation of a Manchester past was soothing to Lynne. She had been with me to the Xaverian College for a dance, and we had been caught by Brother Nicholas making violent love in the Sixth Form library. An older Manchester returned with a visit from George Dwyer, my cousin by marriage, who was now Bishop of Leeds. Lynne met for the first time very firm Catholic theology with a Lancashire accent. She recalled her studies of mediaeval history at Bedwellty Grammar School. She spoke of St Thomas Aquinas and tried to define mysticism. George Dwyer knew all about my Manchester apostasy and I spoke bluntly of my unwillingness to be rehabilitated. He told Lynne that she had a responsibility to look after her husband's soul. He gave her convincing evidence that hell existed. She did not join the Church but she accorded it more respect than formerly. Even if hell was a myth, two millennia of fire haloed the suicidal act. *Il fallait tenter de vivre.*

I DUG out the yellowing typescript of my old novel *The Worm and the Ring* and began to rewrite it. I tempered its heavy Catholic guilt with an attempt at humour. I finished it in a summer month and sent it to Janson-Smith. Janson-Smith then took it, along with *Inside Mr Enderby*, to James Michie at Heinemann. He showed the lavatorial novel to him first. Michie neither accepted nor rejected it: he thought it might be publishable some day, though under another pseudonym. 'What else do you have?' he asked. It was as if I were a brand name for mass-produced toilet articles. Janson-Smith gave him *The Worm and the Ring*, which was considered immediately publishable, meaning some time in 1961. Roland Gant, the senior editor of Heinemann, who had rejected the work in 1954, now thought highly of it. I was paid another advance suitable for the era of Ford Madox Ford and D. H. Lawrence.

When my half-yearly royalty statement arrived, I groaned at the apparent impossibility of earning a living as a novelist. My first novel, *Time for a Tiger*, had sold five thousand copies, and I had foolishly assumed that its sequels would do at least as well. But *The Enemy in the Blanket* had been suppressed because of a libel suit, and *Beds in the East* seemed, to the superficial reader, to offer nothing that *Time for a Tiger* had not already provided. The first book of the trilogy sold moderately well because it purveyed sad humour in an exotic setting: it was something of a novelty. It also informed, in the manner of heightened journalism, about the conditions of life in a far country rent by an ideological war. When book-buyers buy books, they look for sex, violence and hard information. They get these from Arthur Hailey, whose characters discuss problems of hotel management while committing adultery before being beaten up. Readers interested in a novelist's Malaya got all they wanted from *Time for a Tiger*. The third book seemed supererogatory and it sold fewer than three thousand copies.

But, as the whole world knew, there were some very rich novelists around. There was a category of both author and novel known as the bestseller, and there seemed even to be a formula for selling well, or best. There were even correspondence colleges which taught the formula, although one wondered why their professors, knowing it, were not loftily above having to teach it. I picked up at Heinemann's offices a bound page proof of Nevil Shute's new novel *Trustee from the Toolroom* and saw clearly enough why it had to be a bestseller. There was not much sex or violence in it, but it bulged with information, some of it of a highly technical kind. The characters were unambiguous, meaning that they hardly existed. Style as I knew it hardly existed either, and Nevil Shute, who had been a professional aeronautical engineer, publicly disclaimed style. I could see now that a literary education did not fit one for the popular novelist's trade. Once you started using words like flavicomous or acroamatic, because you liked the sound of them, you were lost. On the other hand, it was in order to write of fallaway sections and finite amplitude waves, since their magic derived from the solid field of technology.

I had to accept that I was what I was, that my books, such as they were, were myself. The only way in which I could pay the mortgage instalments and meet the tradesmen's bills was to offer to the reading public a great deal of what I was. So, with *The Worm and the Ring* and *Inside Mr Enderby* delivered, I turned my verse play *The Eve of Saint Venus* into a novella. Heinemann did not want it. I then tried two novels at the same time – one, called *I Trust and Love You*, based on the fourth book of the *Aeneid*, in which the love affair of Dido and Aeneas was to be set forth in unvergilian amplitude; the other, called *Sealed With a Loving Kiss*, a retelling of John Ford's *'Tis Pity She's a Whore*, a grim story of brother and sister incest. I wasted a month on those. I reread *Salammbô* to get information about ancient Carthage but I needed more than that. I could not, any more than Vergil, bring Aeneas to life. Converted into prose fiction, the John Ford plot seemed improbable. In despair I typed a new title – *A Clockwork Orange* – and wondered what story might match it. I had always liked the Cockney expression and felt there might be a meaning in it deeper than a bizarre metaphor of, not necessarily sexual, queerness. Then a story began to stir.

Lynne and I had come home to a new British phenomenon – the violence of teenage gangs. We had, on our leaves of 1957 and 1958, seen teddy boys in coffee bars. These were youths dressed very smartly in neo-Edwardian suits with heavy-soled boots and distinctive coiffures. They seemed too elegant to be greatly given to violence, but they were widely feared by the faint-hearted. They were a personification of the *Zeitgeist* in that they seemed to express a brutal disappointment with Britain's post-war decline as a world power and evoked the age of Edwardian expansion in their clothes if nothing else. They had originally been called Edwardian Strutters. They had been briefly influential even in Malaya, where national servicemen had worn the attire off duty, and we had seen young Malays and Chinese sweating in heavy serge. Now, in 1960, they were being superseded by hooligans more casually dressed. The Mods and Rockers were so called because the first group wore modern clothes, whatever they were, and the others had motorcycles with rockers or parking prongs. The second edition of the *Oxford English Dictionary* is right in pointing to the leather jackets of the Rockers as a sartorial mark, but it is wrong in supposing that they got their name from a love of rock 'n' roll. Lynne and I saw Mods and Rockers knocking hell out of each other when we made a trip to Hastings.

These young people seemed to love aggression for its own sake. They were expressing the Manichean principle of the universe, opposition as an end in itself, *yin* versus *yang*, X against Y. I foresaw that the Queen's Peace was going to be greatly disrupted by the aimless energy of these new young, well-fed with money in their pockets. They were not, of course, all that new. The apprentices of Queen Elizabeth I's time used to riot, but they were dealt with in a very summary way – sometimes hanged on the spot. I at first thought of making my new novel a historical one, dealing with a particular apprentices' riot in the 1590s, when young thugs beat up the women who sold eggs and butter at prices considered too high, with perhaps William Shakespeare breaking his hip when slithering on a pavement greasy with blood and eggyolk. But I finally decided to be prophetic, positing a near future – 1970, say – in which youthful aggression reached so frightful a pitch that the government would try to burn it out with Pavlovian techniques of negative reinforcement. I saw that the novel would have to have a metaphysical or theological base – youthful free will having the choice of good and evil although generally choosing evil; the artificial extirpation of free will through scientific conditioning; the question as to whether this might not, in theological terms, be a greater evil than the free choice of evil.

My problem in writing the novel was not one that would have worried Nevil Shute: it was wholly stylistic. The story had to be told by a young thug of the future, and it had to be told in his own version of English. This would be partly the slang of his group, partly his personal idiolect. It was pointless to write the book in the slang of the early sixties: it was ephemeral like all slang and might have a lavender smell by the time the manuscript got to the printers. It seemed, at the time, an insoluble problem. A slang for the 1970s would have to be invented, but I shrank from making it arbitrary. I shut the half-completed draft, whose sixties slang clearly would not do, in a drawer and got down to the writing of something else.

HOW FAR did I understand women? I would find out by turning myself into a woman, or rather a girl of the direct, unsubtle, uneducable kind whose womanly qualities would not be obfuscated by books or introspection. I would write a first-person narrative about a girl working in a supermarket, pretty, cheerful, optimistic, married to a rather gloomy young man who suspects that the world is going to pot but is too uneducated to know why. The ambience of these two young people was presented very adequately in the *Daily Mirror*, which was now Lynne's only reading. There was no public library to provide her with trashy novels, but we had television as a substitute, especially the commercial channel beamed from Southampton. There was a weekly quiz programme with accumulative money prizes whose master was a Canadian named Hughie Green. When, in the 1930s, Michael Callaghan brought the *Radio Times* into the Sixth Form library, ready to circle his week's listening ('Dancing Through' with Geraldo and his orchestra, Troise and his Mandoliers), the young Hughie Green was often on the front cover, a youth of our own age in tails and with wide happy mouth, a precocious singing and dancing star, brash and outgoing. We hated him. Now he was sober and greying and had difficulty with some of the harder words in the quiz questions. Him I would put into my book.

The book was a rapid joy to write, a month's work of *bricolage*, for which commercial television and the *Daily Mirror* gave me most of what I needed. As the husband of my heroine works in a used car business, I had to study used car advertisements and drink with a man in a St Leonards pub who knew all the tricks of shady manipulation which make used cars seem less used. There was no difficulty with my shopgirl's idiolect. We heard it all evening long on television. Her husband watches a quiz programme in gloom but thinks highly of the money prizes. He will enter the contest and specialise in questions on English literature. He knows nothing of this, having been, like his wife, to a secondary modern school, but he is oppressed by an image of a past full of great bearded men who transmitted to the future books which warn of evil and coming breakdown, books which my young man knows he will never read. He has a photographic brain and starts to fill it with literary knowledge from an encyclopaedia. He appears on the quiz show week after week, answering the most abstruse questions without difficulty. But when the thousand-pound question comes – who wrote *The Good Soldier*? – he gives, according to the quizmaster's rubric, the wrong answer: Ford Madox Hueffer. The right answer is Ford Madox Ford. Hard breathing, tension, eerie music on the Hammond organ, cries of dismay from the studio audience. But the telephoned literary experts declare that the names are interchangeable. Relief and rejoicing.

The young man, not at all triumphant (it is his photographic brain that has won, not himself), discloses another improbable gift: by fierce concentration he can foresee the racing results in the next day's *Daily Mirror*. He parlays his prize money on the horses and becomes very rich. He has no faith in the world but he feels he has a grim duty to see it. He takes his wife to America and the Caribbean, staying in the most luxurious hotels, and then brings her home to announce that they are both going to die. They have seen the world, and it is corrupt and decaying, and they will both be better off out of it. He produces my wife's barbiturate tablets but his wife fights him off and kills him with a coal hammer. She runs off to France with her husband's money and his body in the camphorwood chest Lynne and I had bought in Malaya. The body is stuck in a French field as a scarecrow and is pecked to the bone by the birds. It is a savage enough ending, but my heroine's optimism is not impaired. The clasped hands of marriage have been reduced to a single hand, but it claps. Hence the Zen title *One Hand Clapping*. I delivered it to Janson-Smith in Christmas week, 1960. It was published the following autumn under the pseudonym Joseph Kell. This meant the launching of a new name, and no money was spent on the launching. The book sank like a stone.

I doubt if it could easily be revived either in Britain or in the United States. The son of John Middleton Murry later wrote his father's life under the same title, and no author can claim titular priority. To give it a new name would be to cheat. The book, anyway, tries to encapsulate a period and an ethos now dead, and I cannot think of it as much more than a *jeu* dashed off to make a hundred pounds or so. But in Eastern Europe it had a late success. It was regarded as a condemnation of money-making, a debased culture, the whole capitalist Western life, than to endure which it would be better to be dead. It was adapted for television in Warsaw and turned into a stage musical in Budapest. It was read in East Germany. It was one of the two books for which I was known in the old Soviet bloc. Needless to say, what money it has earned there remains sequestered.

In the late autumn of 1960 *The Doctor is Sick* was published. As a London novel it received solus coverage in the *Evening Standard*. National reviewers were not enthusiastic. 'Mr Burgess,' said the *Times Literary Supplement*, 'is apparently so anxious to be up to date that he is out of date already.' My kettle mobster admits that he is 'kinky', and this was assumed to be a dead usage. In fact, it was just coming back, soon to be applied to erotic leatherwear. *Punch* found the dialect humour 'as heavy as lead' and the whole brief work fifty pages too long. The poet Geoffrey Grigson, in the *Spectator*, found 'fantastic fantasy, which does not work' and ended: 'The words this novelist employs just don't produce things, or cohere, or make credible, in a sub-smart funniness (quotations from Webster, Eliot, Auden) I found not at all funny.' Maurice Richardson, in the *New Statesman*, said that 'if it were a first novel I should greet it as a promising curiosity. As a fourth it has to be labelled an interesting misfire.' It was in fact a fifth. 'Part of the trouble, I think, is that a cerebral tumour is not a subject a novelist can monkey about with; only a philosophical picaresque vein would have suited.'

I wondered a good deal about what reviewing was for. It was gratifying to be noticed even if to be condemned, wearily half-dismissed, given the impression that the reviewer could have done the job better if only he had been a novelist and had the time. I even sympathised with these hacks, on whom the heavy flux of new fiction imposed a summary approach they must have recognised as essentially insolent. What worried me was the implied lack of an aesthetic in all these highly personal appraisals. I was very ready to learn to write better novels, but the reviewers were unable or unwilling to show me the way. I was later to discover that Geoffrey Grigson disliked the personality ('coarse and unattractive') disclosed in the style and subject-matter of my work, but this seemed to me a false ground for dismissal and contempt. What I, and my fellow-novelists, desperately needed was informed criticism, not hack reviews. To receive such criticism, and even to profit from it, I had to await publication in America. I felt that my own country was letting me down.

Of course, the primary task of the newspaper book reviewer is to inform. I met a man in a pub about this time who loftily said that he did not need to read reviews as a guide to what to read: he could make up his own mind. As the books he read were of the Dennis Wheatley order there was clearly not much mind to make up, but if he had been a devotee of highbrow fiction his boast could not stand. Publishers' advertisements inform, but they are not impartial. We need the lowly craft of the book reviewer, whose partiality at least is not commercial. But we need serious criticism too, and in Britain there is not much of that around, chiefly because criticism is an academic discipline directed towards the literature of the past. In the United States the situation is different.

The *annus mirabilis* of death defeated or indefinitely postponed, of settling back into England and, it was said, writing too much, came to an end with a medium-sized turkey and a red ribbon round Haji's neck. I took stock and saw little future in what was really an imposed trade. I was unknown to the great reading world though the pedagogic one had heard of me. This was because of my history of English literature, written from the angle of a tropical expatriate but found useful in cold climates. A brief course for teachers of English was to be held the following Easter in Oxford, and I was asked to deliver a paper on an approach to literature. Well, if I was still considered to be a teacher I had better return to my primary vocation and earn a steady salary. In the January of 1961 the schools of Kent and Sussex lamented a temporary shortage of teachers. I applied to the Kent authority under my real name to be considered for a supply post. I was told that I was probably rusty and needed a refresher course. There was a course at Oxford at Easter I might attend. I would, presumably, learn a lot from myself.

ONE OF the better reviews of *The Right to an Answer* had appeared in the *Daily Telegraph*. 'It is comedy with the wryest smile since *Measure for Measure*. Its irony is subtle, its wit outrageous and its entertainment value alpha.' That was a high mark, and it had been awarded by Kenneth Young, the *Telegraph*'s literary editor. Young now became editor-in-chief of the *Yorkshire Post*, and he wrote to ask if I would be interested in writing a fortnightly article on current fiction. The fee would be small – six pounds an article – but the prestige considerable. The *Yorkshire Post* was a distinguished news-paper, closely read by Bradford millionaires and Sheffield cutlers and in strongholds of conservative culture on the moors. I accepted, though I felt I was letting my own county down. Lancashire and Yorkshire have despised each other ever since the Wars of the Roses, ritually re-enacted every year in a cricket match. But they become allies to confront the soft and gormless south. I was now to be turned into a journalist.

What Kenneth Young had not mentioned was the money to be made on the side through the selling of review copies. The prospect of this kind of enrichment was not apparent in January 1961, when five or six undistinguished new novels arrived. Reviewing would be an easy sideline conducted by a Kent or Sussex supply teacher. I did not at that time know that January was a slack month for publishing. As the winter advanced to spring the trickle turned to a flood, and the little house had to be bailed out vigorously. Teaching was out anyway, and a good thing too, for I now had the job of selling books at half-price. Every Monday morning I would stagger to Etchingham station with two loaded suitcases ('Leaving 'er again,' the villagers muttered), travel to Charing Cross with them, and then stagger up the Strand to Simmonds's bookshop. Louis Simmonds took everything and paid with new notes. This was real money, to be spent on cigars, cognac, and Gentleman's Relish. I met other reviewers selling review copies, some for some reason furtively. I met Peter Green, who said it was 'big bisney'.

Green liked my work, which, and he was not quite alone in this, he considered as being in the tradition of John Lodwick, a novelist who had been killed when driving a car in Spain, taking four Spanish publishers with him. Lodwick was a good novelist, published like myself by Heinemann, though soon to be dropped out of print and forgotten. He was witty and learned and stylistically distinguished: his following was a coterie one. Authors like to think of their work as *aere perennius*, but it disappears like everything else. It is up to their admirers to resuscitate them, and probably Lodwick will return. Looking back to the early sixties, I reflect on the vanity of the hopes of authors. Heinemann had published a remarkable first novel, *The Rack*, by A. E. Ellis. This, whose setting was a clinic for consumptives and whose theme was pain, was considered by some critics to be better than Thomas Mann's *Der Zauberberg*. One reviewer wrote that he fainted on reading an exquisitely exact description of a lung test. The book has not survived, perhaps because it was both a first and last novel and reviewers could not write: 'Ellis's fifth book cannot be compared with his brilliant first.' But merit is supposed to inhere in a text, however isolated, and a book's vitality, to echo Samuel Johnson, should be a preservative against oblivion. I was learning that an oeuvre, a spate of production, the dinning of a name into the public skull, was the only way to survive, but even that was unsure. Merit is not enough, and it gets buried under the mound of mediocrity. There are far too many books, few of them good.

I was appalled, in my two years of working for the *Yorkshire Post*, at the amount of rubbish delivered by every mail. The Etchingham post office had to take on extra staff. This was just the fiction, unsifted by the literary editor; there must be equal tumuli of biography, travel, cookery, sport, collected journalism. Lynne, expert at rubbish, helped with the sorting. She was now never short of garbage to read, though she preferred television. I naturally had to review the latest Greene or Waugh, but there was the danger of missing, in the very profusion of print, some quiet and unknown talent. Publishers I had never heard of sent their latest offerings, presumably in no hope of reviews. I was so sorry for Alvin Redman, whose logogram was an Indian chief, that I gave a generous brief notice to a moderate bodice-ripper. This was excised by the literary editor, not because the book was unworthy of attention but because the publisher did not advertise in the *Yorkshire Post*. Mills and Boon sent their treacly romances, aware that their market did not depend on either advertising or reviews. But have reviews ever affected sales, except in the great days when Arnold Bennett could make or break a book in the *Evening Standard*? There was a whole underworld of fiction I had not known existed. There was a middle earth too – reputable publishers and dim competent novels, perhaps better than my own. I realised how powerful the competition was, and my heart failed.

For all that, I pushed on. I read the fiction of others in bed and, during the day, tried to write a very difficult novel I was to call *The Wanting Seed*. The title came from a folksong which had, indifferently, wanton or wanting seed in its refrain. The seed was semen and the song was quietly erotic. My book was to be on a theme I had

had long in mind – the population explosion. I had lived in the pullulating East and re-read Thomas Malthus: indeed, I was to write a definitive study of him for a learned American journal. There would, some day, be too many mouths to feed. This was not apparent in the West, except on Oxford Street, and I was probably wrong to make a future England the setting of a novel about demographic disaster: Calcutta or Bombay would have been more appropriate. But this was hypothetical fiction, and it was in order to import starvation from Africa and statutory family planning from China. My England is implausibly overcrowded, and Greater London has expanded to the Channel. There are skyscraper flat-blocks in Brighton and even artificial islands on the sea for population overflow. The task of the three superpowers is to achieve, each in its own way, a balance between food production and population. The superpowers are called ENSPUN, RUSPUN and CHINSPUN (English, Russian and Chinese Speaking Unions), and these implement demographic control according to their own traditions. RUSPUN and CHINSPUN exact the death penalty for exceeding the limit of one child per family, but ENSPUN is liberal and pragmatic. In Britain homosexuality is officially encouraged ('It's Sapiens to be Homo' say the posters) and voluntary castrati (called Castros) earn the higher government appointments. There are mild punishments for philoprogenitiveness, but the democratic tradition of playing the game is upheld. Cricket has become the Sacred Game and is played, for lack of outdoor space, in the old cathedrals. Women play against men.

The cyclical principle of government is well understood: my hero, a schoolmaster, teaches it to his huge classes. There are three phases – the Augustinian, the Pelagian, and an intermediate one like Vico's *ricorso*, abbreviated to Gusphase, Pelphase and Interphase. The Gusphase, based on an acceptance of original sin, does not expect too much from the governed. When the governed behave rather better than could be expected, the notion of original sin is occluded and the Pelagian Phase (which, like socialism, believes people to be fundamentally good) supervenes. Disappointed Pelagianism brings in governmental harshness and draconian laws and the tyrannical Interphase is established. But not for long. Government shrugs at unregenerable man and the Gusphase returns. The cycle resumes and goes on for ever. This playful theory of mine, perhaps not so playful, was meant to be an answer to Orwell.

Most of the narrative of *The Wanting Seed* is set in an Interphase. Food rations are being reduced and the population is growing restive. There are strikes and riots, and these are put down by a newly enlarged police force called, because of their uniforms, Interphase-coloured, the Greyboys. There is also a more sinister body called the Population Police, or Poppol, whose badge shows a broken egg. They check on illegal pregnancies or illeg pregs and haul the miscreants to jail and enforced abortion. But the people rise against this unbritish brutishness and put their faith not in government but in God. God is a dirty word in the positivist state, and Augustus and Pelagius are purely secular myths. Priests, as agents of a superstition based on fecundity (*The Golden Bough* is known in a space-saving logographic form – *Dh Gldn Bau*), are functioning only underground. Now they climb out of their holes and publicly celebrate mass. The cannibalistic overtones of the eucharist encourage genuine cannibalism: a child quite logically says: 'If it's all right to eat God it must be all right to eat Jim Grimshaw.' The police, mostly homosexuals, are the first to be eaten. With the return of public order, generated by private armies, a solution to the threat of world starvation is found in war. Nobody at first knows who the enemy is, but there are ES's or Extermination Sessions conducted in the wilder areas of the world, including Ireland. My hero, who is inducted into the forces against his will, and becomes a sergeant with my own military number, 7388026, discovers that men are fighting women and that the cadavers are being shipped for processing into canned meat. He also discovers two great truths: that man is part of nature, and if he will not breed neither will the animal and vegetable worlds; that everyone has a right to be born, but no one has a right to live. Finishing the novel, I saw that it was very Catholic.

Twenty-eight years ago, when the novel was published, nobody was prepared to take seriously that anthropophagy might be a solution to world starvation, and that overpopulation might thus provide its own solvent. After the disclosure of the cannibalism that kept alive the survivors of the Andes air crash, there was rather less scoffing. Those survivors were well-nourished by the softer portions of their dead companions, though terribly constipated. Buying canned meat in supermarkets, we do not well know what the animal is, the flesh being smothered in additives. One of these days we may well buy *Munch* and discover that it is *Mensch*. There is nothing basically wrong with cannibalism. When, on a trip to New Guinea in my Malayan days, I was given a crisp piece of roasted meat by my primitive hosts, who had just got over the custom of feeding unwanted children to pigs, I only found out what it was after ingestion. I was naturally as sick as a dog, but that was only my culture getting in the way: my stomach was not prepared to object.

The Wanting Seed had little chance of becoming a bestseller. The struggle to earn went on, and it could not wholly be solved by selling review copies at half-price to Simmonds on the Strand. Peter Green began to help. He was a Catholic, a better one than I, married and with a growing family, a classical scholar who had gone the freelance way instead of seeking a safe academic post. He was slaving at journalism, with the odd book on the side, in order to save enough money to emigrate to the Greek islands. He reviewed everywhere, from the *Times Literary Supplement* down to *John O'London's*, was television critic for the *Listener* and film critic for *Time and Tide*. There was for him, as later for me, a grim pleasure in being a Grub Street man: one touched the grubby paw of Samuel Johnson. He introduced me to subliterary modes of earning the odd pound. One was to render reports to publishers on the suitability of foreign works for acceptance and translation. I assessed works on anthropology and sociology and structuralism in a variety of languages, also novels, and was paid a guinea per report. One work I refused to look at was the French translation of a novel by a Danish bestseller whose name I have forgotten. There were far too many Hungarian and Finnish books that got into English through French. I was rebuked over the telephone by a functionary of the firm of Macdonald, who had to deliver a report on the great Dane at a board meeting and had, because of my defection, nothing to say. I realised that I was not, after all, a free writer. One could be rebuked, treated like a servant, threatened with non-payment of one's guinea. I was rebuked by James Baldwin's publisher for being unwilling to dash to London for a party in his honour. I was rebuked by great authors like Bryher for failing to review them in the *Yorkshire Post*.

If I considered a book from France or Italy worthy of translation, I would sometimes be offered a hundred pounds to do the job myself. The contract specified 'good literary English', whatever that was. Lynne and I stayed up for most of the night on three very minor French novels. With the help of the big Cassell's dictionary she would rough out the English and I would then gorblimey it into the good literary form required. But Lynne's tenses were weak, and she would confuse imperfects and conditionals. This would entail cursing retyping and dawn threats of suicide. I sometimes improved the style of the Frenchman, so much so that when *The Olive Trees of Justice* appeared in America (*Les Oliviers de la Justice*, by Jean Pelligri), a critic acclaimed its elegance and searing imagery and asked why Anglo-Saxon novelists could not write like that.

In the early summer of 1961 *The Worm and the Ring* was published. The *Times Literary Supplement* showed unusual kindness. 'The especial distinction of this book is the treatment of the private life of the German master, Christopher Howard, a lapsed Catholic. The terrible dilemma of his small son Peter is described skilfully, tenderly, and slightly light-heartedly. Peter has to reconcile his love of God and the Roman Catholic Church with love for his father. His father praises Luther to him, leaves him access to uncensored books, commits adultery, and finally serves him bacon on a Friday. Mr Burgess has also a gift for caricature which makes the damp grey atmosphere of his Midland town almost bearable.' *Punch* was not so pleased. 'The trouble with Mr Burgess's ebullient disgust is that he will overdo things.' I was also accused of whining, which I perhaps was. I had been angry about Britain's attitude to its teachers when writing the book, and there was a very didactic tirade against bourgeois philistinism. One should never turn resentment into fiction. The book disappeared, for reasons I shall come to, and was slow to reappear. It has never been seen in America and there are no translations.

But *The Right to an Answer*, on its American publication, had done reasonably well for criticism, though atrociously for sales. *Time* said: 'Author Burgess, at 43, is still banging noisily on God's door, insisting on an answer to the riddle of existence.' Despite my shortcomings, which were not clearly specified, 'the author's prose is graceful and precise, his wit is sharp, and he can complicate a comic situation to the point of inspired silliness.' Naomi Bliven, in *The New Yorker*, took the book seriously and examined it at length, finding that it was 'not a joke but a nicely controlled examination of some human predicaments that is cunningly disguised as entertainment'. I had made my American début. The reviewers liked the work, though the great American public was indifferent. It was important, from now on, to appeal to the Americans. They had the money.

Those transatlantic laudations soothed. Soothing syrup was needed in our irritable household. Too much work, not enough sleep, though a healthy diet. Lynne cooked as her mother had cooked – well, but without frills. No *coq au vin* or *boeuf à la bourguignonne*. Wine was reserved for drinking. Lynne's nervous crises had not yet driven her to the tearing of my slowly mounting manuscripts, but she was aware that they might. On my typewriter she left a warning:

> Lynne, in one of her manic rages,
> Tore up ten typewritten pages.
> Wasted work and an opus gone –
> Something for John to ponder on.

Meaning that I still was not making copies. But my attitude to duplicating my work, with carbon or by machine, derived from the condition of writing music, the technique of which is primitive – pen and ink and both sides of the paper, carbon copies impossible, electrical duplicating difficult with orchestral scores. A music manuscript will not easily take second thoughts, and the copy has to be fair. My typescripts too were fair and therefore, in that market where authors' holographs have a cash value, not easily saleable: my work looked like the copy of a professional typist. A man from Israel arrived at our house, a professional manuscript-buyer with a present of Israeli honey-candy. When he saw the perfection of the typescripts that had come back from the printer he shook his sad head and gave me a five-pound note for six of them. Iris Murdoch and Kingsley Amis were, I later heard, doing much better.

Lynne and I now felt that we ought to take a holiday. There were Russian ships sailing from Tilbury to Leningrad, calling at Copenhagen and Stockholm, and then sailing back, calling at Stockholm and Copenhagen with Helsinki added. There was a brief stay in a Leningrad hotel between voyages. The Russians were known to be good drinkers, and Lynne knew she would feel at home among them. When I had finished my day's stint of novelising, reviewing, and assessing the exotic, I started to relearn Russian. I tried to persuade Lynne that she should at least learn the Cyrillic alphabet, so as to know where the ladies' toilets were, and to master a few sweeteners of social intercourse, such as *dobriy dyen* and *spasibo*. But she was above going back to school, unless she could take a time-trip to being once more head girl and outstanding athlete at Bedwellty. She watched *Emergency Ward Ten* on television instead. Her lack of linguistic curiosity worried me, as also the assumption that it was a husband's duty to be a dragoman, as well as an earner, lover and protector. I wrote out TUALET large in Cyrillic but she gave it to Haji to chew up growling. I sighed and slogged away at my word lists and frequentative verbs, and soon it flashed upon me that I had found a solution to the stylistic problem of *A Clockwork Orange*. The vocabulary of my space-age hooligans could be a mixture of Russian and demotic English, seasoned with rhyming slang and the gipsy's bolo. The Russian suffix for -teen was *nadsat*, and that would be the name of the teenage dialect, spoken by *drugi* or droogs or friends in violence.

Russian loanwords fit better into English than those from German, French, or Italian. English, anyway, is already a kind of mélange of French and German. Russian has polysyllables like *zhevotnoye* for beast, and *ostanovka avtobusa* is not so good as bus stop. But it also has brevities like *brat* for brother and *grud* for breast. The English word, in which four consonants strangle one short vowel, is inept for that glorious smooth roundness. *Groodies* would be right. In the manner of Eastern languages, Russian makes no distinction between leg and foot – *noga* for both – or hand and arm, which are alike *ruka*. This limitation would turn my horrible young narrator into a clockwork toy with inarticulated limbs. As there was much violence in the draft smouldering in my drawer, and would be even more in the finished work, the strange new lingo would act as a kind of mist half-hiding the mayhem and protecting the reader from his own baser instincts. And there was a fine irony in the notion of a teenage race untouched by politics, using totalitarian brutality as an end in itself, equipped with a dialect which drew on the two chief political languages of the age.

I ended up with a Russian loanword vocabulary of around two hundred words. As the book was about brainwashing, it was appropriate that the text itself should be a brainwashing device. The reader would be brainwashed into learning minimal Russian. The novel was to be an exercise in linguistic programming, with the exoticisms gradually clarified by context: I would resist to the limit any publisher's demand that a glossary be provided. A glossary would disrupt the programme and nullify the brainwashing. It turned out to be a considerable pleasure to devise new rhythms and resurrect old ones, chiefly from the King James Bible, to accommodate the weird patois. The novel was nearly finished by the time we were ready to travel to Tilbury and board the *Alexander Radishchev*, a well-found ship of the Baltic Line.

In those days the habit of travelling with much luggage had not been modified by a shortage of railway porters. Lynne packed an evening gown and I a dinner jacket. We were thinking of the wrong Russia, or perhaps determined to show capitalistically off in a worker's world of the ill-dressed. That Russians were ill-dressed and that there was a shortage of consumer goods we knew from the British newspapers. A feature writer of the *Daily Mirror* named Marjorie Proops had been to the Soviet Union and wrote home to her readers as 'Marjski', giving the news that 'those Ivans and

Ivanskis appreciate a nice bit of homework,' meaning perhaps herself, but, boy, they sure could do with some decent ragskis off the pegski. For this reason we had filled two suitcases with polyester shift dresses in gorgeous artificial colours, bought at thirty shillings apiece in the Marks and Spencer's of Tunbridge Wells. The *Daily Mirror* always referred to this chain as Marks and Sparks, but I had thought it to be something else or a reference to an unannounced takeover. You could not always rely on the popular press, but this demotic Marjski (whom I was later to stand next to in a pub and find to be a lady with a very patrician accent) was probably telling the truth about ragski. We, or rather I, who spoke Russian, would sell these dresses in public lavatories at a large profit. That would pay for our holiday. It would also pay for board and lodgings for Haji and the two cats. The minder who took Haji away saw what he was getting and put up the price.

We stayed a night in London at the Hotel Russell, and Lynne collapsed during dinner. This was a bad augury for the holiday. It was, I was to discover later, a kind of hepatic exhaustion. It hit her again on the platform of Fenchurch Street station. Then she recovered enough to survey run-down Britain on the journey to Tilbury, all smashed factory windows, merds, rubble, FUCK THE GUVT. Whatever Russians travelled in from Tilbury would see that too and rejoice in our national decay. Their shining ship mocked the run-down docks. A brassy song of Soviet triumph rang from the ship's loudspeakers as we boarded. We had tiered bunks in a cabin with a shower we shared with the neighbouring cabin. Entering the shower-cell by opposed doors, naked I and a naked matron with steel wool pubic hair confronted each other. The shower would not work anyway. The visible ship's company were charming, mostly teachers of English who had been ordered into naval uniform – clean and well-cut – to improve their colloquial grasp of it. The food was disgusting, mostly tired stew with, as at some poor children's treat, an orange for afters. A dark man of unknown provenance in gaudy braces sat next to me, and his wife stood behind him. He did not seem to have met potatoes before. The food was so bad and so scanty that I divined a fiddle must be going on, as in all the mercantile marines of the world. I had seen the chief steward, who wore a London-cut dinner jacket even when supervising breakfast, counting a wad of pound notes – *odannadsat, dvyenadsat, trinadsat* – in a dark companionway before the ship hooted off.

Lynne had learned one word that I had given her out of *A Clockwork Orange*. This was *horrorshow*, a folk-etymologising of *khorosho*, the neuter form of the word meaning good. She mistook its meaning and applied it to the breakfast rice skilly and the fatty salami. The stewardesses, who wore headdresses straight from *Petrushka*, could not reconcile the praise with the frown. If one could not eat one could at least drink, and there were five bars open on a shift system throughout the *sutki* – a useful word meaning night and day seen as a unity. Lynne was taught the Russian way of downing vodka, the shotglassful straight down the hatch, recommended as a specific against seasickness. The sugary Georgian wine induced a sickness of its own. Lynne took to her bunk with a rash caused by wood spirit, exhausted and fed oranges which a sweet-faced young blonde stewardess machicolated or denticulated with a sharp knife in the manner of Swiss restaurants. This took time, of which the Russians seemed to have plenty. Lynne raged at long delays in answering the service bell and quarrelled with a two-ringed steward. I had to take up the quarrel on her behalf, though unwillingly, and met a response of hopeless Russian resignation: it was hard to please people, the human soul exhibited its perverse intransigence even in small particulars. The ship seemed to be an extraterritorial state, not much touched by Soviet optimism. The dinner-jacketed chief steward thought little of Khrushchev and would perform gross imitations of him trying to seduce little girls. He thought highly of Harold Macmillan, Princess Margaret, and stockcar racing. He would down a half-litre bottle of vodka in one, eyes closed against the light like a gardener swigging cold tea.

With Lynne mostly in her bunk, I was free to wander the ship and look for sexual adventure. The deliciously plump stewardess in the third-class bar said that the Norwegian coast was *krasiviy*, and I boldly said: '*Kak tui*.' I should not have used that familiar pronoun: it smacked of imperial contempt for inferiors. I should not have attempted the overtures of seduction. The Russians seemed to have demolished the bourgeoisie only to assume its morals. I gave a copy of the American edition of *The Right to an Answer* to an American girl as an earnest of my competence, energy, refinement, coarseness, other qualities. She read it and invited me to an afternoon on her bunk. It was a narrow bunk and the Baltic was rough. I wanted a Soviet girl but I could not have one. I wished to know how far the sexual act had been modified by Marxism.

Most of the passengers were groups under the control of Intourist. There were British trade union officials who dined in their braces and saw themselves as pilgrims going to Mecca. One, who had no teeth and whose gums were like polished coral, kept saying: 'Stands to reason you can get a good plate of fish and chips on Nevsky Prospect.' He complained that the tea was pure gnat-piss and was rebuked by a serious young woman officer of stern loveliness whose patriotism seemed affronted. 'Lass,' he said, 'I was card-carrying member of t'Communist Party afore you was bloody well wiped.' There were a lot of young people, students in the charge of their lecturers in sociology, who belonged to an organisation known as the Sputnik Club. *Sputnik* meant for them a Soviet space module, but it really signified fellow-traveller. They were a fellowship of travellers who were going to be instructed in the Soviet dream. They were ordered about as on a troopship. 'The Sputnik Club,' the loudspeakers said in good Oxford tones, 'will assemble at once in the cultural salon for the conference on Soviet science fiction.'

Lynne got out of her bunk for this event and fortified herself for it with many shotglasses of vodka. 'You are becoming a real Russian,' admired a stewardess, not the unseduced plump one. Various Soviet science fiction specialists harangued the assembly on the glories of Soviet science fiction, but one complained humorously of the difficulty of screwing the imagination to the right inventive level when Soviet technology was so swift to overtake the fantastically fictional. Lynne cried out: 'Why have you banned *Doctor Zhivago*?' The interpretress, a tall girl with frizzed ginger hair, answered that the question was impertinent but that it would nevertheless be answered. The answer was given truculently by a man of letters who looked like a boilermakers' union official. Pasternak had betrayed the October revolution in wretched prose and worse verse, had evaded the discipline of constructing characters according to the principles of Soviet realism and had opted for decadent Western complexity and ambiguity. Literature was there to affirm the values of the Soviet state and Pasternak affirmed decadent individual pseudo-values in the discredited bourgeois manner. And so on. This was very adequately translated. The Sputnik beatniks cheered. Lynne cried, rightly, 'Bugger the state,' and then fell off her chair. The Sputnik nogoodniks jeered. The holiday was going well.

If the trip so far was proving nothing else, it was making clear to me the excellence of Soviet English teaching. The KGB did remarkable work in their language laboratories, but even at the high school level the techniques seemed to combine scientific rigour and imagination, to judge from the English I heard on the ship. (Some did not speak a word of it, which was better than speaking it badly.) Students moved from Cyrillic to Romic by way of the International Phonetic Alphabet, which eased them into our illogical orthography. The reality was what they read in the IPA, and our messed-up spelling was a kind of humorous nightmare which did not frighten them. They understood why it was messed-up, which is more than most native English speakers do. There was a little too much Shakespeare in their talk – 'The morn, in russet mantle clad, walks o'er the dew of yon high eastern hill,' the two-ringed steward said to me as we approached Copenhagen at dawn – but that was better than the glottal stops and snarls of the Sputnik Club.

In the Tivoli Gardens in Copenhagen Lynne collapsed. She recovered in the bar of the Grand Hotel, where it was difficult to get service. The whole hotel staff was gloating over a letter just received by the management. This was from the secretary of a club of retired SS officials. All these officials had served in occupied Denmark and had thoroughly enjoyed their time there. They wished to organise a reunion at the Grand Hotel and would the manager make de luxe reservations. Lynne collapsed on the docks at Stockholm, and a gull flew down from the head of a statue of Gustavus Adolphus to inspect her. When the ship arrived at Leningrad she could not get out of her bunk. At length she staggered down the gangway to find that all the other passengers had long disembarked and been taken off in buses. There were no officials at the dock gates, and we entered Soviet Russia without showing our passports. For that matter, we had had no trouble with the fatherly customs officer on board who, sparking vigorously from his *papirosa*, dropped ash on the two suitcases full of polyester shift dresses, admiring that a Western lady should require so many clothes. My copy of *Doctor Zhivago*, intended as a decoy, he ignored. Walking the long road to a taxi stop near some decayed ornamental gardens was arduous, what with all those dresses and the rest of the gear. Not much of a holiday so far.

Leningrad seemed at first nothing but carious warehouse façades and a smell of drains and cheap tobacco. There was a Manchester, or perhaps Salford, atmosphere about it. But the Neva shone, as for the ghost of Pushkin, and the architecture of the city centre was impressive, though it was not a Soviet achievement. I told the taxi driver that he lived in a beautiful city. He shrugged. He was entering the depressive phase of a cycle that seemed to me more Celtic than Slav. Lynne ought to get on well here. This driver had a large variety of packs of cigarettes on the seat beside him, all manically torn open. It was as though he was trying to discover whether he really liked smoking. He took us to the Astoria Hotel, where we had booked a room in distant Angliya. I had assumed that it was an affront to offer a Soviet worker a tip, but he cried for *baksheesh*. I gave him fifty kopeks. Everybody wanted *baksheesh*. The bald aged lavatory attendant at the Astoria, busily reading Gogol, wanted it. I had only a fifty rouble note, but he scuffled off to find change.

The spotty girl at the reception desk, who had a bad cold and was reading a novel by Margery Allingham, wanted to know why Yernyest Gemingvye had committed suicide. 'We were all,' she said, 'lovers of Yernyest Gemingvye.' Then we were sent to our room, which first meant confronting the Cerberus of a stern woman in robust middle age on the appropriate floor. The elevator did not work – *nye rabotayet* was blazoned outside the gates of most Leningrad lifts – and I panted from the climb, laden with polyester shift dresses. 'You are sick man,' she pronounced in English. 'Go to your bed.' But it was Lynne who went to it. I had to start selling the dresses.

It was not difficult ridding myself of the first half-dozen. A thin shifty smoking man, not at all a model Soviet citizen, chaffered over them with me, locked in one of the underground toilets of the hotel. He offered one rouble fifty for each, about the price I had paid in Tunbridge Wells. I put on injured scorn. He at slow length increased the price to seven roubles, peeling them with a licked finger from a sizeable and dirty wad. I had made a fair profit, but he warned me of the rigour of the Soviet law. To offer Soviet citizens much-needed consumer goods was to impair the workings of the Soviet economy. I said that I had heard of a death penalty. He shrugged extravagantly at that: we all had to die sometime, and policemen were highly bribable. But prison was always a possibility, and I should do my best to keep out of a Soviet prison. The food was not good and the ambience was filthy. He kissed me and departed, with the polyester dresses crammed into a BOAC overnight bag. If I had more goods to dispose of – Parker pens, Longines watches, even polyester shift dresses – he would be in this underground lavatory tomorrow at about the same time. But he did not reappear. When I came with my new batch, the Gogol-reading attendant looked at me very strangely. I would have to go with care. I took it to the underground lavatory of the Evropa Hotel, where the younger brother, or so it seemed, of my first buyer would not go higher than six roubles fifty. I had to beware of flooding the market.

When, that first evening of our arrival, Lynne felt that she could get out of the lumpy double bed and take nourishment, I suggested our going by taxi to the Metropol Restoran, north of Nevsky Prospekt on the Sadovaya Ulitsa. But taxis were hard to find. The Intourist girl who dealt with them rejoiced when she said we would have to wait not much longer than an hour. Lynne said that in London you could get a taxi just like that, snapping her fingers, and the Intourist girl said: 'You are very uncourteous people and your comparisons are odious. It is not good manners and your manners are bad.' Lynne blazed and slapped her. The girl dissolved into crying and Lynne took her in her arms, not easy since this was a Leningrad giantess. God help them, they needed so much to be loved. Their manic depression was like a parody of dialectical materialism. Thesis of mania, antithesis of depression, but no synthesis. They seemed an undisciplined lot, given to tears and hard liquor; perhaps they needed communism.

The scene at the Metropol was an extravagant display of the Russian gift for drunkenness. Liquor was served only in hundred-gram flasks and accompanied by *shprotti* or sprats which enhanced thirst. Stout women with *Petrushka* headdresses came round with pledgets of cotton wool soaked in ammonia which they thrust up the nostrils of the snoring drunks. When these did not work they thrust them into eyes whose lids they jerked up with thick thumb and fingers. Awakening blinded, the drunks yelled and were kicked out of the restaurant by Neapolitan-looking waiters in tennis shoes. At the table where Lynne and I sat sat a young man and an older woman whom he had been trying to impress with a feast – fried eggs served on long-stemmed ornamental green glass stands, *shprotti*, black bread overtoasted, sturgeon boiled, a multitude of little wrapped sweetmeats, two bottles of Georgian malaga, three or four hundred-gram flasks of vodka. For this feast he could not entirely pay. He began to be dragged and kicked out, while his heartless companion laughed. I offered money, but this was not part of the game. The young man had offered the wrong ploy and accepted his checkmate. No cheating. Fair play.

I had no cigarettes so had to fight my way through the exhilarated to a *papirosa* machine which said *nye rabotayet*. I punched it and it disgorged an endless jackpot. Tough Soviet youngsters fought to get their share. In a gaudy salon off the vestibule people were dancing to a Soviet combo playing 'You Want Lovin' But I Want Love'. It was like wartime – young men in uniform and girls with skimpy flowered frocks and forties hairstyles. Back in the hall of drunkenness a Leningrad giant was thumping something from New Orleans on the piano. He had imparted a Slavic wretchedness to it. 'St Petersburg blues,' Lynne wittily said, fit and animated. She was surrounded by young men, some of whom spoke English. One, Oleg, spoke admirable English, which suggested that he had been trained by the KGB. He admitted later that this was so. Lynne said to him that he looked like her idea of Raskolnikov. A waiter, passing, said: 'As for *Crime and Punishment*, it was a crime to write it and it is a punishment to read it.' I went up to the bandstand to take over the piano, which the giant had abandoned after some fierce and hopeless dissonances ('Temper, temper,' Lynne said). My jazz style struck a senior waiter as unacceptably exotic, and he slammed the piano lid on my fingers. This started a scuffle, but violence was to be expected at this hour of the evening. Somebody had to prime it and it happened to be myself. I sat drinking with Lynne and watched it develop. Where were the police? One thing that had puzzled me from the moment of our arrival had been the absence of uniformed *militsioners* with guns or truncheons. All the police were probably in plain clothes, and they had better, more ideological things to do than put down drunken riots. Then Lynne collapsed.

Her new-found young friends, including the KGB boy, left off their share of the rioting (surely this was *guliganism*, a kind of ideological criminality) and bore her like dead Hamlet to the exit. The doorman was a bearded Bulgarian like the Douanier Rousseau's mailman, and he had bolted the glass-faced doors against a horde of *stilyagi* battering it to get in. They intermitted the battering courteously and let collapsed Lynne out on the shoulders of her bearers, waited for the door to be barred again, then resumed their howls and thunderings. This too was an aspect of the chess mind. Lynne was laid on the pavement. There were, of course, no taxis. But Oleg of the KGB went inside to the telephone to dial 03. A KGB car came and she and I were driven to the Astoria. I had not expected the holiday to be like this.

The next morning I fought with a couple of beefy matrons in a kind of stillroom on our floor to get *zavtrak* or breakfast – blood sausage and cold tea – and then went below to see about getting a doctor or *vrach* and also a morning paper. At the newspaper kiosk the only English journal available was the *Daily Worker*. I had expected this, but I asked for *The Times*. 'If you had been early enough,' I was told, 'you would have got it. They have all been sold out.' I was beginning to understand the Russians now. They were not unlike the Irish – romancers and scrappers. I had expected the steely future, all discipline and automation, but I found dirt and disorder. I found the human condition better displayed in this state founded on cold metaphysics than in any primitive Malay kampong. I feared the *vrach* I asked for: he would bring my stepmother's ikey pikey and paregoric; he would apply leeches.

But no *vrach* came. There came instead three dwarfish paramedics in white, ready to take Lynne away. But she did not wish to be taken away; she merely wanted a diagnosis and a prescription. The most dwarfish of the paramedics sat down with a prescription pad and began to write, in a large unlettered hand, the word **АСПИРИН**. Aspirin would not do, Lynne cried; out with the lot of them. She said she was feeling better now. I was glad to believe her. Alcohol, I was sure, could not be the trouble. I was drinking more than she and I was not collapsing. That basic anatomical truth about the smallness of a female liver refused to dawn. She was suffering from many things – the war, Malaya, my condemnation to death and the presumed relief of my reprieve, my sexual neglect, the precariousness of my livelihood – but not from the drink. God or Bog, look how the Russians drank, and they were all, even the women, brawny colossi in the best of Soviet health. I took Lynne out to lunch at the Evropa Hotel. Lunch began with a couple of hundred-gram flasks of vodka.

The esculent part – beef Stroganoff – was ordered but did not appear for four hours. This was because our waiter went off duty after taking the order and no substitute was appointed. This did not much matter: we were not hungry anyway. But we wished to drink, and nobody would listen. Or rather other waiters would hear our cries for *piva* but rebuke us for impatience: what, after all, were four hours when the Russian people had had to wait four centuries for deliverance from the Czarist yoke? Nay, longer. I wandered into the kitchen area unchallenged and found a refrigerator crammed with litres of excellent Czech lager. I brought in successive waves to our table and opened them with a smart crack on the table edge. We would be all right till evening and the appearance of the beef Stroganoff.

In the vestibule of the Evropa a sort of shop had been opened for the sale of Soviet toys. Roubles were not wanted, only foreign currency. I had pounds and, on my way back from the *tualet*, thought this was as good a time as any for buying souvenirs – a *matrioshka*, which says so much about the Russian soul (grandmother enclosed in grandmother enclosed in grandmother enclosed in grandmother), a bear on a bicycle that clapped cymbals as you eased it off on its disastrous brief journey, badges and brooches depicting the space hero Yuri Gagarin. The *matrioshka* was listed at one pound, thirty-two shillings and fifteen pence. This I could not believe. The delightful frizzed ginger girls in charge said that I had better believe it. They had a typed list of prices in foreign currencies, thick as a PhD thesis. All the prices in pounds, shillings and pence exhibited a total Soviet misunderstanding of the British monetary system.

That old system has gone. Some of my readers may not know that it ever even existed. Before the shameful liquidation of the British penny into a p, there had been an ancient and eminently rational coinage, with twelve pence to the shilling and twenty shillings to the pound. This meant divisibility of the major unit by all the even integers up to twelve. Time and money went together: only in Fritz Lang's *Metropolis* is there a ten-hour clock. Money could be divided according to time, and for the seven-day week it was necessary merely to add a shilling to a pound and create a guinea. A guinea was not only divisible by seven: it could be split ninefold and produce a Straits dollar. By brutal government fiat, at a time when computer engineers were protesting that the decimal system was out of date and that the octal principle was the only valid one for cybernetics, this beautiful and venerable monetary complex was abolished in favour of a demented abstraction that was a remnant of the French revolutionary nightmare. The first unit to go was the half-crown or tosheroon, the loveliest and most rational coin of all. It was a piece of eight, a genuine dollar though termed a half one (the dollar sign was originally an eight with a bar through it). It does not even survive as an American bit or an East Coast Malayan *kupang*. Britain's troubles began with this jettisoning of a traditional solidity, rendering Falstaff's tavern bill and 'Sing a song of sixpence' unintelligible. I have never been able to forgive this.

But the reformists would probably have approved the Soviet fantasy that I met in the lobby of the Evropa Hotel. The system was obviously a British joke; it was reasonable to take the joke further or furthest. My eyes misted for holy Russia as they went over the list:

Gagarin brooch:	£2 21*s* 13*d*
Gagarin tiepin:	£0 29*s* 15*d*
Gagarin banner:	£1 35*s* 17*d*
Khrushchev tea mug:	£2 20*s* 0*d*

I had to tell the delightful girls that this was all wrong. They cried; Russia had been let down. But I gave them a brisk lesson and converted £1 32s 15d into £2 13s 3d. I asked for change in kopeks, but this was not permissible. Nor was change in shillings and pence; their aim was to acquire British money, not to give it away. So I spent an hour converting six shillings and ninepence into a pitiable miniature jack-in-the-box, with threepence left over. I tried to give them the threepence as *baksheesh*, but they were horrified. I bought a threepenny *karandash* or pencil with CCCP on it, and there was joy before these angels at the completion of the transaction. I gave them a bar of Fry's nut milk chocolate, long melting in my pocket, and they kissed me in rapture. I returned to the restaurant to find cold beef Stroganoff and a reproachful waiter: I should, I was told, be on time for my meals.

What could one do with these people except love them? What more lovable people ever existed? They were not to be feared: if they could not get British money right, it seemed unlikely that the arithmetic of their ICBMs would ever add up. When time meant so little, how could one take seriously their manifestos about the urgent need for planning and their threats to overtake the United States in technological achievement? There was nothing in their shops, except for the party élite. Their streets were ill-repaired and their buildings needed a lick of paint. There was no shortage of powerful sparking cigarettes with cardboard mouthpieces; vodka and kvass flowed. They lived in a dream of drunkenness or ideology, sometimes both. They did not see the external world: the broken windows and filthy façades did not register on their retinas. They were, in the metaphysical sense, idealists: matter was no primal reality. And yet what could they have except this outworn philosophy of nineteenth-century materialism, in which the brain secreted thought as the liver secreted bile? Democracy? Drunken fights in the Duma. Monarchy? They had had that.

And these delightful girls were so damnably dressed. I had better resume my selling of polyester shift frocks. No, damn it, I had better start giving them away, an *Angliskiy podarok*. Lynne collapsed after picking at beef Stroganoff and her downed flask of Georgian cognac, and I dialled 03, mentioning the name of Oleg Petrovich Potapov. A KGB car with a dour driver appeared with speed and tried to take us to KGB headquarters. After a brief fist fight we were permitted to be dropped at the Astoria Hotel. There Lynne lay down.

My giving away of a whole suitcase load of polyester shift dresses in the vestibule of the Astoria naturally aroused suspicion. I tried to explain that this was an expression of British love and generosity. Some of the older women, off whom a peasant belief in miracles had not yet rubbed, accepted the gifts with joy, tears, muscular embraces. One, examining the horse's teeth, said that her daughter was to be married on *Sabbota* and needed white, not vermilion, cerulean, electric blue. I dashed upstairs and brought down white. She looked at it critically, accepted it without grace. Well, it took all sorts, even in holy Russia. I gave a crimson dress to a scarlet woman, though officially she no longer existed in the Soviet Union. She at once accepted this advance payment and said we were to go to my room. Regretfully I had to tell her there was a woman already there.

I did not give all the dresses away: that would have been carrying love too far and losing much money. In the lavatory of one of the Metro stations I disposed of what were left, at six roubles the piece. I also sold my cheap wristwatch at a high price: here what did time matter anyway? I was relieved to be unburdened; I had had the impression that two men in raincoats were following me. Leningrad was a big city, but Lynne and I were beginning to stand out. We were not items in one of the bodies led forcibly by Intourist guides to pig farms and refrigerator factories where junctions were achieved with a sly hammer and nail. We were on our own. We were known, through Oleg, to the KGB. Lynne collapsed spectacularly and I gave away polyester shift frocks. But at least the illegality was all over, unless my buyers were arrested and blabbed about an *Angliskiy turist* staying at the Astoria.

But the time was coming for us to leave the Astoria, Lynne to go into a Soviet hospital and myself to stay with a young man named Sasha in his wretched flat in a block by the Kirov works. For the hospital stay was to last ten days, and the hotel rates were high for foreigners. The processing of Lynne into the intricate hospital system was not sought by either of us. I had taken her to a low loud tavern and, emerging, she said she felt ill. Wait, I said, breathe deeply of the good Baltic air, and I will look for a taxi. I marched with a high-ranking army officer the mile or so to one of the taxi stands. I called him *tovarishch* and he, correctly, called me *gospodin*. He too wanted a taxi, but there would be none available, we were told at the stand, for an hour or so. I dashed back to where I had left Lynne to find a crowd round her: she was lying on the pavement. The foolish woman had refused to learn a single word of Russian except *khorosho*, and, conscious but supine, she was having no luck with Malay. She kept pointing at her wedding ring, meaning that she was waiting for her husband, but the crowd thought she wanted to sell it. Somebody had evidently telephoned for an ambulance, for one shortly appeared. Dwarf paramedics hoisted her aboard. It was not quite an ambulance as the West knows ambulances, more of a Zis or Volga saloon car with the back cut out of it, so that Lynne had to be injected into an open boot, with her feet waving at the traffic. She and I were driven fast to a *bolnitsa*.

The Soviet hospital system seemed to me highly sensible. Like Dante's Inferno, it was organised as a series of concentric circles, with first-aid posts on the outer circumference and clinics of progressively greater professionalism on the inner ones. Lynne was taken like Dante from circle to circle, and this meant a repetition of the same inductive procedure. *Familiya?* was first barked, meaning family name. Lynne muzzily thought that the family way was being diagnosed. A female doctor, very irascible, snarled: '*Ya nye skazala familivay – ya skazala familiya.*' I was pleased to hear this. There are some grammatical rules in foreign languages that one cannot take seriously and one, for me, was the existence of feminine endings in Russian preterites. Well, here it was – *skazal* (I said) for a man, *skazala* for a woman. I wrote down our *familiya* – Uilson – and I added Lynne's baptismal name Llewela. I was interested to see how these Leningraders would deal with it. I represented the unvoiced L with an X (as in *loch* and *Bach*) followed by an ordinary Russian lambda. Nobody believed that such a name was possible. Hospital business was held up while I gave a lesson on the Cymric hissed lateral. I was, perhaps still am, too much of a Dr Spindrift in that novel I mentioned, too linguistically frivolous. After all, my wife was sick.

Lynne's clothes were wrenched off and her underwear admired. She was put into a Soviet cotton nightgown and into a bed. She tore the sheets. This annoyed no one. She was a *krasiva Anglichanka*, and her antics were to be cherished. She was wheeled away, loudly protesting to their broad Leningrad smiles (you did not get a treat like this every day), and I was told that I could come back some time. I was a free man, with roubles in my pocket, but not enough roubles to stay much longer at the Astoria. Sasha Ivanovich Kornilov was one of the solicitous young men who had helped to carry Lynne out of the Metropol. He worked, I knew, at the Ermitage, this being the Winter Palace converted into a sumptuous art gallery of Western loot, all for the workers and their wives. Sasha, or Alexei, had to dole out tickets at the entrance. I found him there and told him what I needed – cheap lodgings for a week or so and a hermitage or sanctuary from possible prying officials. I could, he said, have the bare floor and a blanket for three roubles a day – a good deal cheaper than the Astoria. He gave me his key. So I took the Metro to the Kirov Works station and walked to the Ninth of January Park, finding a hideous flatblock with a rain-striated bas-relief image of a worker in heroic overalls. Comrade Kornilov's flat, I was told by an ancient *babushka*, was on the ninth floor, number eleven. I lugged my bags up there, lay on the floor to recover breath, then made tea in the samovar, drinking it from an old jar in which there was still a spoonful of blackcurrent jam. Quite the little Russian.

I stayed for over a week, eating what I found when I joined the shopping queues at the state stores elementally labelled with their products, meaning sometimes their lack of them – *riba, myahso, kleb, moloko*. The flat was a single room and filthy, with tacked American pin-ups, ikons of Khrushchev and Yuri Gagarin not in evidence. It was enlivened by almost nightly vodka parties, with our old young friends from the Metropol, including watchful bespectacled Oleg. There were discussions about the warlike intentions of John F. Kennedy, the evident lies of the Soviet press, the shortage of consumer goods. These young men were not taken in by anything or anybody. They read foreign newspapers. You could not stifle free traffic, either of goods or ideas, in a great port. They loved jazz and bought records from tourists. I was clearly not the only Westerner to engage in the illegal marketing of commodities. At last I made love to a girl of the Baltic. She was Finnish, not Russian, and her name was Helvi. She had been in some kind of trouble in Helsinki and was now, off and on, the mistress of Sasha. She was growing tired, she admitted, of Sasha's embraces. She needed someone maturer, gentler, more experienced. Her Russian was much on my level. She was blonde and underfed. For the moment she had no work. She had tried to be a projectionist in the cinema of the Kirov District Soviet but she had snarled up a thousand versts of some epic of the steppes. She had also worked as a cleaner in the children's workshops of the Kirov Works Club but had not been considered clean enough. She was thinking of emigrating to Moscow. Big opportunities in a great city like that. Helsinki was a load of *kal*.

I visited the Pavlovskaya Bolnitsa every day. Lynne was better because she was not drinking; thinner because she was not eating either. The doctor in charge of her case, Anya Petrovna Lazurkina, was a tall and pretty woman who wore discreet earrings. She spoke German and made it more or less clear to me in that language that my wife had wept *bitterlich* about not being loved and seeing no end in her existence. She had been drinking too much, said Dr Lazurkina, because of her lack of occupation. She needed work as well as love. Her liver had been out of order but had much improved since the administration of salts of Soviet manufacture. She must not drink vodka, to which she seemed to have an *allergiya*. I could do something now about taking her home. I had open return sea tickets? *Khorosho*. Take the next sailing of the SS *Baltika* and secure the suite that was occupied by Nikita Khrushchev when he sailed to the United States. That will grant your poor wife space and ease and better service. I thanked her. There were, of course, no hospital fees. This was a socialist country.

So we sailed back to Tilbury on the *Baltika* in the private suite of solid Edwardian furnishing, with a bathroom a positive Laocoön of sturdy pipes. Oleg came on board to see us off. He said: 'I will now show you how easy it is to escape from Soviet Russia, if one so wishes. I will hide in your bathroom there. When they come round to ensure that all are ashore who must be ashore I shall stay in that bathroom and only leap off the ship when they are removing the gangway. It is easy to get out if you want to. I do not want to. I love Leningrad.' I could see that it was very easy to learn to love Leningrad. I had been growing into something of a Leningrader myself. Not that young people called the city Leningrad: they preferred to think of it as Peter. Lenin was not yet a sufficiently venerable myth to have his name attached to the true centre of Russia, Moscow being only a village. As the sirens opened their throats and the ship prepared to leave Peter, Oleg athletically disembarked and waved at us from the quay. I waved back, not without tears. The novelising machine in my brain had already begun to process the materials of our Russian visit into a plot. We had entered the Soviet Union without showing passports; we could quite easily have left with a refugee crouching under the growling water pipes. No novel-reader would believe how easy it all was: the stereotypical USSR of polished police efficiency and fundamental ill-will – Frederick Forsyth stuff – was what popular fiction needed. But, of course, I could not produce popular fiction.

Lying in Nikita Khrushchev's bed, not bunk, Lynne granted that the stay in a Soviet hospital had done her some good. She had been embraced and kissed by motherly nurses who scolded her for demanding cigarettes and gin. She had been fed wholesome soup bloody with boiled beet, black bread and butter, glasses of tepid tea with gooseberry jam as a sweetener. She was convinced that Dr Lazurkina had lesbian tendencies. Nonsense, I said. Homosexuality is not permitted in the Soviet Union. And then a blond steward minced in without knocking to ask if we would like some *lyod* or ice. He twittered long lashes and spoke with the languid suggestive vowels of Rudolf Nureyev. He had a powerful belief in the virtues of ice, though in what sphere those virtues operated was unclear. 'The iceman cometh,' Lynne was to say whenever that coy knock, she insisted on a knock, in future sounded. We built up a large supply of ice, slow to melt as we met unseasonable Baltic cold and storms. Lying in the bed, not bunk, of Nikita Khrushchev's cabin companion, I composed for the ship's orchestra a jazzy little piece called *Chaika*, full of seagull riffs on the alto *saksofon*. I did not rise to hear it performed. The bandleader came in without knocking to say that we were the only passengers not up and dancing. The Russians were damned liars. Sasha had sworn that he had a Siberian cat, five feet long and red-spotted, as a household pet. But he had only Helvi.

Lynne got up briefly to down vodka, this time the pepper variety, and promptly collapsed. The ship's doctor, who spoke no word of English but was knowledgeable about London's ecclesiastical architecture, delivered the best advice: *'Nye kurit i nye pit'* – don't smoke and don't drink. He examined Lynne with an explosive *papirosa* in his mouth and a strong aroma of Bombay gin. So she got back into Khrushchev's bed and watched the ice accumulate. When we arrived at Tilbury the immigration authorities took her ice-blue eyes and nordic blondness, combined with her Welsh accent and exhausted stagger, to signify that she was an illegally entering Russian with a forged passport. The name Llewela was not any British name that they knew of. Our bags were severely examined and our cartons of *papirosi* and *sigareti* found heavily dutiable. There were too many grim policemen around. It was like entering a fictional dream of Soviet Russia.

The LONG article entitled 'Novel, The' in the latest *Encyclopaedia Britannica* was written by me in 1971. It contains the following:

> In some countries, particularly Great Britain, the law of libel presents insuperable problems to novelists who, innocent of libellous intent, are nevertheless sometimes charged with defamation by persons who claim to be the models for characters in works of fiction. Disclaimers . . . have no validity in law, which upholds the right of the plaintiff to base his charge on the corroboration of 'reasonable people'. Many such libel cases are settled before they come to trial, and publishers will, for the sake of peace and in the interests of economy, make a cash payment to the plaintiff without considering the author's side. They will also, and herein lies the serious blow to the author, withdraw copies of a whole edition. Novelists are seriously hampered in their endeavours to show, in a traditional spirit of artistic honesty, corruption in public life; they have to tread carefully even in depicting purely imaginary characters

and situations, since the chance collocation of a name, a profession, and a locality may produce a libellous situation.

I had a particular libel case in mind, and this was waiting for me on our return from Leningrad.

Miss Gwen Bustin, secretary of Banbury Grammar School and once Mayor of Banbury, had been reading *The Worm and the Ring* and had been eager to identify herself with the fictitious school secretary of the book. The strength of her case rested mainly on an onomastic coincidence: her own doctor had the same name as the doctor of the secretary in the novel. A letter from her lawyer made the standard accusation of malice, and my publisher promptly withdrew the unsold part of the edition. Now I was to await the delivery of a writ. It was possible to avoid the serving of it only by refusing to answer the doorbell. But I still had to shop. Loaded with groceries, I was accosted by a young man on a motor cycle on Etchingham's only street. His smile was bland, as in Gilbert's First Lord's Song, and I had to admit that I was who he presumed I was. He shoved the writ into my top pocket, both hands being full, and sped off. Gwen Bustin, described as *sole feme*, was taking me to court.

In the chambers of Heinemann's legal advisers I met a bulky florid Queen's Counsel who looked forward with relish to a long and, he hoped, somehow historically significant trial, since he proposed thrashing out in very general terms, though with a wealth of cited precedents, the nature of a putative tort that seemed to him to harm no one except its putative perpetrator. It would cost much, what with juniors and refreshers, and I could conceivably lose the case, but at least things might be clarified. I was gloomy, especially when I saw a photograph of Gwen Bustin in civic robes in the *Evening Standard* with the headline EX-MAYOR GWEN FIGHTS LIBEL. According to the terms of my contract with William Heinemann Ltd, I was liable to pay damages and probably the plaintiff's costs, as well as my own. In a sense, the Queen's Counsel was right to wish to attack in open court a legal situation of desperate vagueness, in which British jurors were notoriously against professional writers, who wrote dirty books and were rich. Constantine FitzGibbon had recently published a novel called *When the Kissing Had to Stop*, about a Soviet takeover of Britain in the unforeseeable future. He had presented a fictitious night club in his novel, but he had adventitiously given it the name of one that actually existed, and this night club had sued. The author could not exculpate himself by appealing to an invented time in which this night club could not possibly exist.

When, two years later, I began to write about William Shakespeare and put into my fictional study a Mistress Bustin of Banbury, I was warned by Heinemann's law men, though my reference was neutral enough. Mistress Bustin was merely a cheese-chewing Banbury Puritan.

I did a thing I should not have done. The opposed camps had settled to their long sleep, awaiting the convenience of the legal calendar. I made contact with the enemy. I wrote a letter to Gwen Bustin, full of groans about illness and poverty, denying any malicious intent and apologising abjectly for any harm unintentionally done. She replied, perhaps on her solicitor's advice. Perhaps her solicitors feared the case and could not put in to bat a QC of fame and power comparable to my own. Gwen Bustin regretted what I had done and regretted the whole situation. Heinemann sent her a hundred pounds. The case never came to court. But *The Worm and the Ring* joined the immeasurable mound of pulped books. This was no way to earn a living.

In the autumn of 1961 *Devil of a State* appeared, nearly five years after its composition. This was a novel that had been feared to be libellous, and I had been locked in Heinemann's cellars for two days, there to remove the story from its Borneo setting and to relocate it in East Africa, a territory I did not know. The state of Naraka (Arabic for hell) was now a caliphate somewhere around Zanzibar, rich in uranium, not Brunei oil. Malay and Iban had to go and invented languages took over. I regretted the fantasisation: what virtue the original novel had resided, as with the Malayan books, in its fairly truthful representation of a British colonial reality. The British Adviser had to become a functionary of the United Nations, a very implausible fiction, and I had to take a paint brush to the browns and make them black. The satirical bite was blunted in the fairy tale ambience. But the book was a sort of success in that it was made a choice of the Book Society.

I divined here the hand of Peter Green, aided by William Golding: both were big names on the selection committee. Their kindness did not noticeably bring in much money. It did bring, however, copies of the book to be autographed. There seemed to be a special class of novel-readers around, mostly well-heeled ladies who read only such fiction as the Book Society provided. They assumed a right to signed copies. It would have been reasonable to expect a letter accompanying the book (often with an EX LIBRIS Lady Tulkinghorne or the Hon. Edna Sprout-Fairfledge already affixed), saying: 'I realise that this must be a great nuisance, having to unpack and then repack the thing and take it to the post office and pay for the stamps, but I *would* really be quite overjoyed if you would be good enough to autograph this book, which I did *so much* enjoy.' But there was usually an upper-class bark: 'Quite likeable really. Put your name in.' There is too much of this sort of thing. I still receive books for autographing from Fiji and the Cayman Islands. Or I receive requests for autographs without books, often confusing me with another author. I even get peremptory demands for signed photographs. Signed copies, I have discovered, are saleable, and there are even shady agencies that will buy autographs. I have hardened my heart. If, as there sometimes are, there are international postal certificates accompanying the request, I keep these for my own use. The books I throw away or, if they are first editions, sell. This is undeniably criminal, but I was inured early to seeing authorship as an irregular pursuit.

The reviews of *Devil of a State* were, for the most part, no worse than the book deserved. But Julian Mitchell, a young novelist who saw in my work more than his elders and professed himself to be even influenced by me, which may explain why he gave up fiction for the theatre, said in the *Spectator*: 'Mr Burgess makes these people not only horrifyingly credible and brilliantly appalling, but also symptomatic of the collapse of the tradition they are hopelessly trying to prop up. His venom is sprayed with the accuracy of machine-gun bullets on exploiter and exploited alike.' John Gross, in the *New Statesman*, said that the book needed 'pruning and tidying up', operations I thought I had already performed in the cellars of Heinemann. The *Times Literary Supplement* wanted 'more fact and less laboured fantasy . . . Characters waver uneasily between satire and fantasy. The book does not even work up to a climax: a *dea ex machina* just holds up a policewomanly hand and stops it dead.' It was generally felt to be inferior to Evelyn Waugh's *Scoop*.

By the end of 1961 I had published seven novels and a history of English literature. I had no sense of achievement: that could only arrive when my bank statements affirmed that I was making a living out of a writer's trade. What money was coming in was mostly small dividends from Lynne's investments and such fees as I earned from reviewing and translating. But there always seemed to be enough money to buy drink. I had discovered a distinguished wine merchant in Hastings who supplied some of the Oxford colleges. His announcements of special acquisitions were too tempting to ignore – a dozen of rare Malmsey going cheap, Russian *champanskoe* (sugary with nostalgia for Leningrad), a cognac so old it could not be dated,

Highland malts with a tang of the ling. I could not pay for these out of royalties.

Bill Holden, the Canadian public relations officer of Heinemann, granted Lynne and myself a chance to see how other professional writers were getting on by inviting us to publication parties. The first of these we attended was to celebrate the autobiography of the musical comedy singer and dancer June, who, like a by-blow, had no surname. Her husband was an American businessman who, on my being introduced to him, was at once sick on the carpet. There were not many genuine writers around; it was all raddled theatrical glamour ('Darling – ' kiss kiss – 'your book is *wonderful*. So *true*, my angel. It brings *so much* back.' And, presumably, up). I asked Bill Holden how many copies this wonderful book was likely to sell. About four thousand, he said, adding something that chilled me: 'It's the four thousand copies of people like you that keep Heinemann going.' This meant that Heinemann would be satisfied till the day of my death, or my discovery of creative inanition, with moderate sales on which no author could be expected to live. Few books sold, or sell, on their own merits. They have to be pushed, and pushing is costly. The firm, no longer in existence, that had pushed Mailer's *The Naked and the Dead*, had ruined itself with pushing. It was clear that I was not to be pushed. Reasonable reviews in quality periodicals enhanced the publisher's prestige; moderate sales did not impoverish. So, at June's party, I saw my future.

At other, more literary, launching parties Lynne behaved much as she had done at the Duke of Edinburgh's garden fête in Brunei. She was truculent on both our behalfs: the publishing world was much like the Brunei administration, dedicated to reducing us to frustration and squalor, to which now add indigence. She took in free drink and canapés what we could not get in earned royalties. She attacked Kingsley Amis and L. P. Hartley and Gore Vidal for doing better than I, or we. Although she did not read my books she had a powerful proprietorial attitude to them; indeed, sometimes she claimed to have written them. The name Anthony Burgess had already become, with the prospective aim of easing the tax position, the sobriquet of a duo. I had no better claim to it than she; ergo, she had written the books. Unassailable Welsh logic.

During the winter of 1961–62 I began to suffer from profound dyspepsia which whole snow showers of bicarbonate of soda failed to ease. It was probably psychosomatic but I feared an ulcer. I tried to bring the condition to a head by feeding myself a midnight supper of cold pork and mixed pickles with potato salad, following that with a hunk of cheddar and beetroot, with pickled walnuts for good measure, washing all down with a pint of overcold claret of poor quality. I slept like a baby and woke eager for breakfast. No ulcer, then. My mind was trying to attach its perturbations to my body. Its bluff had been called. From now on dyspepsia became the normal due of a civilised man, the fruit of gorging or too much gin. Lynne and I faced the spring of 1962 in moderate health. She did not collapse, reserving that to holiday trips. I began to write *Honey for the Bears*, sometimes alternating that working title with *St Peter's Summer*. This was, of course, based on our trip to Leningrad.

I FOUND this novel rather slow going. Slowness, anyway, was to be accounted a virtue, something enjoined by reviewers who assumed that, writing too much, I was writing too fast. But the new slowness, and occasional disturbing blocks, had something to do with a theme that went deeper than a mere tarted up travel book. The book was to be about something that I could not fully understand till it was written, if then. Only the surface – Lynne in a Leningrad hospital, the illegal sale of polyester shift dresses – was common to the truth and the fiction. The fiction was to have at its centre characters who were pure invention – Paul Hussey (transformed in Russia to Pavel Gussey) and his American wife Belinda (named by her Amherst College professor father for the heroine of *The Rape of the Lock*). They propose selling Western consumer goods in the Soviet Union in order to provide money for the widow of a friend of Paul, his homosexual attachment to whom has never been clearly articulated. In Russia Paul is brought to realise his sexual nature; so is Belinda. Belinda accepts, through falling for her woman doctor in the Pavlovskaya Bolnitsa, that she is lesbian. She elects to stay on in Russia, thus, in the symbolism of the plot, declaring that America and Russia are the same place, and that the alignment of the future has nothing to do with the opposition of the superpowers, rather with their identification, leaving it to the small countries to conserve the past while Russamerica creates a timeless plasticity. Paul runs a small antique shop and stands for a Britain living in the past, confirming its new impotence through a kind of sexual dubiety. Paul says to one of his Soviet interrogators: 'You've no idea how comforting it is to have no future. It's like having a thoroughly reliable contraceptive.' The Russian says: 'Or like being sterile.'

There is another character whose name is unknown and sex

ambiguous. Paul calls him/her Dr Tiresias. He/she looks to a future beyond any conceivable political one dreamed up by Russamerica – one in which the almighty state has withered away and only the appetites of the individual have any validity. He/she is looking east, to a theology in which opposites merge, to a peace unintelligible to statesmen. His/her epicenity is a symbol of appetites which transcend sex as they transcend politics. All this was difficult to work out in the framework of a novel that should seem to be a mere diversion. My former lighthearted approach to the craft of fiction was being severely modified by new pressures.

In May 1962 *A Clockwork Orange* appeared. One anonymous summation in a trade paper was not untypical: 'An off-beat and violent tale about teenage gangs in Britain, written in out-of-this-world gibberish.' The *Times Literary Supplement* was more specific: 'A viscous verbiage . . . which is the swag-bellied offspring of decay . . . English is being slowly killed by her practitioners.' I was considered an accomplished writer who had set out deliberately to murder the language. It was comforting to remember that the same thing had been said about Joyce. My taste was questionable. 'The author seems content to use a serious social challenge for frivolous purposes, but himself to stay neutral.' Robert Taubman, in the *New Statesman*, said: 'The book, written in a combination of Jacobean English and nadsat, is a great strain to read,' adding: 'There's not much fantasy here.' No British reviewer liked it, but the producers of the BBC television programme *Tonight* were interested enough to invite me to be interviewed by Derek Hart. They did more. They dramatised much of the first chapter of the book very effectively and made more of the language than the theme. I showed myself to be an adequate television performer. The BBC even paid a small fee, more than French or American television does, the view of both being that one should be delighted to publicise one's work for nothing.

In 1962 there was only one BBC television channel. Though most viewers preferred the offerings of the independent network, it was said that a good nine million people watched *Tonight*. I took the train from Charing Cross back to Etchingham in cautious elation. Surely at least one per cent of those who had had this superficial exposure to *A Clockwork Orange* would buy the book. I would become moderately rich; I had had the accolade of a television appearance and would now be a sort of public personality. But the book sold badly, rather worse if anything than previous novels of mine. I learned the great lesson of the dangers of over-exposure. Viewers had been told enough about the book to be able to discuss it at cocktail parties: the reading of it would be wearisome, as the press had already announced, as well as supererogatory. The British were, I considered, stuffy and desperately conservative. They did not want experimental fiction and they hated ideas. I began more and more to look to America.

A Clockwork Orange was published in New York by W. W. Norton Inc. later in the year. Eric Swenson, Norton's vice-president, insisted that the book lose its final chapter. I had to accede to this lopping because I needed the advance, but I was not happy about it. I had structured the work with some care. It was divided into three sections of seven chapters each, the total figure being, in traditional arithmology, the symbol of human maturity. My young narrator, the music-loving thug Alex, ends the story by growing up and renouncing violence as a childish toy. This was the subject of the final chapter, and it was the capacity of this character to accept change which, in my view, made the work into a genuine if brief novel. But Swenson wanted only the reversible artificial change imposed by state conditioning. He wished Alex to be a figure in a fable, not a novel. Alex ends Chapter 20 saying: 'I was cured all right,' and he resumes joy in evil. The American and European editions of the novel are thus essentially different. The tough tradition of American popular fiction ousted what was termed British blandness.

Though they were reading a somewhat different book, American reviewers understood what I was trying to do rather better than their British counterparts. *Time* said: 'It may look like a nasty little shocker, but Burgess has written that rare thing in English letters – a philosophical novel. The point may be overlooked because the hero tells all in nadsat which serves to put him where he belongs – half in and half out of the human race. The pilgrim's progress of a beatnik Stavogrin is a serious and successful moral essay. Burgess argues quite simply that Alex is more of a man as an evil man than as a good zombie. The clockwork of a mechanical society can never counterfeit the organic vitality of moral choice. Goodness is nothing if evil is not accepted as a possibility.' Robert Gorham Davis in the *Hudson Review* said that the novel clearly turned Alex into an inarticulate apostle of existential or even Christian freedom and 'by a perverse logic, images of violence are put at the service of a dreadful, dead-end concept of freedom.' David Talbot in the *New York Herald Tribune* wrote: 'Love cannot exist without the possibility of hate, and by forcing men to abdicate their right to choose one over the other, society turns men into automata. Thus Burgess points his stunning moral: in a clockwork society, human redemption will have to arise out of evil.'

It was gratifying to be understood in America, humiliating to be misread in my own country. American critics forced me to take my own work seriously and to ponder whether the implied moral of the novel was sound. Brought up as a Catholic (and the book is more Catholic or Judaic than Protestant), I naturally considered that humanity is defined by its capacity for St Augustine's *liberum arbitrium*, and that moral choice cannot exist without a moral polarity. I saw that the book might be dangerous because it presented good, or at least harmlessness, as remote and abstract, something for the adult future of my hero, while depicting violence in joyful dithyrambs. But violence had to be shown. If I had begun my story with Alex in the dock, condemned for crimes generalised into judicial rhetoric, even the gentlest spinster reader would rightly have complained about evasion. Fiction deals with the concrete and the particular, even in Henry James, and the sin of showing juvenile brutality was, for me, behovely. But I was sickened by my own excitement at setting it down, and I saw that Auden was right in saying that the novelist must be filthy with the filthy.

I discussed this matter of the novelist's moral responsibility with George Dwyer in his Leeds bishopric. I was invited to a *Yorkshire Post* literary luncheon at which he said grace. George had written his master's thesis on Baudelaire and knew all about flowers of evil. Literature, even the kind celebrated at a literary luncheon, was an aspect of the fallen world and one of its tasks was to clarify the nature of the fall. Thoughtful readers of novels with criminal, or merely sinful, protagonists achieved catharsis through horror, setting themselves at a distance from their own sinful inheritance. As for thoughtless readers, there was no doing anything with them. With the demented, literature could prime acts of evil, but that was not the fault of literature. The Bible had inspired a New York killer to sacrifice children to a satanic Jehovah; the murderer Haigh, who drank the blood of the women he slaughtered, was obsessed with the eucharist. The guest of honour at this literary luncheon was C. P. Snow, whose wife Pamela Hansford Johnson was to write a book about the Moors Murders. The child-killer Brady confessed to having possibly been moved by his reading of the Marquis de Sade's *Justine*. Lady Snow said that if the life of one innocent child could be saved through the obliteration of the world's literature, then we should not hesitate to set fire to it. That was very much a non-Catholic view. George Dwyer knew we had to live with the devil.

This visit to Leeds was, in a way, encouraging. Charles Snow was a novelist of high reputation, and this was enhanced by his inhabiting the corridors of power. He was friendly with Maurice Edelman, member of parliament for one of the wards of Coventry, also a reputable novelist, whose help with the details of parliamentary procedure Snow acknowledged in writing his *Strangers and Brothers* sequence. Maurice Edelman became my friend, and I dedicated *Honey for the Bears* to him: he knew Russia and spoke the language and saw what the book was about. I was to be glad of the support of these two men in 1963 in a totally Leeds connection. I was glad, at the Leeds luncheon, to hear Snow commend my reviewing in the *Yorkshire Post*. Nobody else had commended it. Nobody else seemed to know of it. To generate a response in *Yorkshire Post* readers, I had made some ridiculous statements in my articles – pointing to the influence of Italo Svevo on Bernard Malamud and ascribing *Tobacco Road* to William Faulkner. I received only one letter from unliterary Yorkshire, and that was when I alleged, in an aside, that English orchids had no smell. This was severely contested by a lady from Bradford. Contemporary fiction meant to Yorkshire chiefly John Braine. Braine was there at the luncheon, with his silver-grey Mercedes, reward of authorship, parked outside. He was known to me as the man who, in the company of Alan Sillitoe and Keith Waterhouse, had said: 'It's a solemn thought, but if a bomb was to come through the roof at this moment the whole future of English literature would be in jeopardy.' Braine thought highly of his own work. *Room at the Top* demonstrated that there was no incompatibility between high fictional achievement and the acquisition of brass. At least not in Yorkshire. Look at Jack Priestley, whom Braine called, as Beaumont might have called Shakespeare, 'the old man'. If I represented Lancashire, then Lancashire was on a sticky wicket.

I was at least trying to match Jack Priestley in prolificity – a virtue in him but a sign of failure in me. 'You're writing too much, lad,' said John Braine, getting into his silver-grey Merc. 'But I suppose you have to.' True, I had to. In the autumn of 1962 yet another novel appeared – *The Wanting Seed*. The anonymous reviewer in the *Times Literary Supplement* saw that, having published nine novels, I could be appraised like Picasso or even Beethoven, at least in the sense of having periods (the term was not inappropriate: I had been asked unkindly at a party whether I had published my monthly novel yet). The first period was exotic, the second repatriate, the third fantastic, meaning *A Clockwork Orange* and the new book, which was considered 'a remarkable and brilliantly imaginative novel, vital and inventive. Inevitably it will be compared with *Nineteen Eighty-Four* and *Brave New World* . . . but the comparison is not really helpful.

Nor is the comparison, so often made, with Evelyn Waugh, for here only Mr Waugh's *Love Among the Ruins* is really relevant, and that is a minor work, almost a squib. *The Wanting Seed* is most certainly neither.' This was the sugar taken before the pill of Miss Brigid Brophy's review, which appeared in *Washington Post Book Week* with the American publication of the work. British reviewers in American periodicals seemed encouraged, by distance and permitted length, to exhibit a leisurely viciousness to their compatriots which might have been bad form in Britain. Miss Brophy is worth quoting very nearly in full:

> 'Half-baked' might have been invented to characterise the new Anthony Burgess novel. Not that Mr Burgess himself would invent any such term. He would prefer 'hemicaust'. His prose glitters with shards of Greek – embedded, however, in mud, for, apart from his Greekisms and a couple of words in Chinese script, Mr Burgess writes in pure, old-fashioned English clichés. He has borrowed a medical turn of description from Aldous Huxley. A flimsy copy of Orwell's vivid atmosphere of shoddiness, shortages and the synthetic hangs over the work. He also makes sly but fatuous allusions to English literature as it appears in the academic syllabus. Literary digs (Jackie Priestley, Joan Wain) are brought in on the cabaret entertainer's assumption that the topical must be witty. His war of extermination between the sexes gives him his few good scenes. Although he seems to be stating the dangers of over-population, he sides emotionally – indeed mystically – with fertility. The best dystopian novels express loathing for the present through a nauseous future. Reading Burgess's book is reminiscent of those queasy days when you feel like vomiting but can't actually bring anything up. Finally, he has stolen his last and moving sea-washed paragraph from the French.

I present the prosecution but offer no defence. I agree with the accusation of half-bakedness. The novel needed a longer gestation, but I needed money. A painter, as Evelyn Waugh pointed out, can work again and again at a subject until his execution comes out right. It is unseemly to rework a novel already published, and it was unseemly of Waugh to make his readers pay twice for the same book. The second *Brideshead Revisited* represents not so much artistic second thoughts as moral ones at variance with the original concept. The turning of the three books of the *Sword of Honour* sequence into a single-volumed novel entailed merely minor changes – elimination of certain secondary characters chiefly – but made the reader feel guilty about preferring the original to the revised version. Reworking does no good, though I have spent the last twenty-five years thinking that it might, and that *The Wanting Seed* could, in my leisurely old age, be expanded to a length worthy of the subject. The idea was more original than many critics wished to believe. Samuel Johnson said of *Gulliver's Travels* that it was only a matter of thinking of big men and little men, but neither he nor anyone else had thought of them. So with the cyclical pattern of *The Wanting Seed* and the cannibalistic final solution, my own modest proposal. I have wanted to remake the work by turning it into a film or a cartoon book, but Harry Harrison, on his own confession during the downing of a bottle of Scotch in my New York flat, stole the ending for the film of his *No Room! No Room!*, called *Soylent Green*. The young French artist who has half-made a visual version, on *Astérix* lines, of *La Folle Semence* (originally *Le Prix de la Viande*, a better title) can find no publisher. Miss Brophy's 'half-baked', anyway, was right. The book needed to be longer in the oven.

But I cite her review not merely to agree with her on this. I reproduce it as an example of the kind of criticism fired more by antipathy than by a desire for honest appraisal. 'Although he seems to be stating the dangers of over-population, he sides emotionally – even mystically – with fertility.' There seems here to be a deliberate unwillingness to understand what the book is about. Is there perhaps also a concealed attack on my vestigial Catholicism? The accusation of 'stealing' from Paul Valéry's *Le Cimitière Marin* rings strangely in the age of T. S. Eliot. The whole thing adds up to: I dislike with my guts, and now I will justify the dislike with my head. You can put a writer down by comparing him adversely with writers he has not even tried to emulate, and you can humiliate him with references to cliché and fatuous allusions which you do not have to specify.

I learned a lot from this review. Following the reviewing craft myself for a living, I learned that it was ignoble to take pride in what Geoffrey Grigson called 'swingeing', confirming the colloquial usage of 'criticise'. I was doing a fair amount of criticism now – regularly for the *Yorkshire Post*, sporadically for the *Listener*, the *Observer* and the *New York Times*. If literary editors found me useful, it was not because I could swinge: it was because I delivered clean copy on time. Reviewing a new novel, I was aware of the pain that had gone into the writing of it and tended to compassion even when the book demanded a summary dismissal. Flaubert was right when he talked of his novels as machines damnably difficult to construct: you do not sneer even at an engine that does not go and then, pleased with yourself, mix the reward of a gin and tonic. It seemed to me that Brigid Brophy – whose own books I rather admired – was pleased with herself for having so swiftly and ably demolished my novel. If this was so, it had to be condemned on the moral grounds of the critic's responsibility. For judging a book is very much like judging a life, and who among us is so pure of heart as to want to assume the judge's office? Leave lives to God and books to posterity.

I finished writing *Honey for the Bears* while staying at small Yorkshire hotels on a lecture tour of the dales. Lynne permitted me to go: in fact, she needed me to give up my bed to one of her friends, the divorced wife of a Canadian ophthalmic surgeon in Banbury. So long as she was not left alone in the night full of owls and barking foxes it did not matter much who shared the house. The lecture tour, arranged by the *Yorkshire Post*, was a flimsy affair compared with its American counterparts. There were small literary clubs which met to discuss the achievement of Daphne du Maurier or Nicholas Monsarrat ('master of the sea yarn') or to compare Poirot with Lord Peter Wimsey. I did not feel that it was yet proper to discuss my own work, which nobody knew anyway, so I spoke on T. S. Eliot and Dylan Thomas. I also spent a night in Manchester with my step-relatives, all of whom, applying the Northern Catholic work ethic to their trades of tobacconist, newsagent, travel agent, were prospering. My own failure to prosper had something to do with my old apostasy. Fiction was a dangerous enterprise because it seemed to throw doubt on conventional morality, and my stepsister Madge considered even Catholic John Braine's *Room at the Top* to be a shocking book. I had converted what I termed paternity lust into art, while the rest of my adoptive family was fulfilling God's ordinance and breeding fast. I seemed to have more grandnephews and nieces than I could count. And so across the Pennines to Yorkshire, where I clattered at my novel during the day and, in the autumn evenings, took buses to villages and amiably chatted about literature in village halls. When I got home I had to sleep on my study couch: the Banbury divorcee refused to leave.

She left at length, taking her cats with her in two wicker cat-baskets, and I imported a second-hand upright piano. I soothed myself with Chopin and Debussy. I did more: I attended an audition organised by Southern Television in Hastings, which proposed putting out a series of amateur talent programmes. I played one of my own works, a Rachmaninoffian rhapsody whose title varied according to the place where I played it: if it was in Leeds, it was 'Song of a Northern City'; if, as now, on the Channel coast, it became 'Song of the Autumn Tide'. The talent spotters were not impressed: they wanted electric guitarists; above all they needed the *young*. I was not young. Nor was I all that well.

The new trouble was pains like toothache in the left calf. I had to walk with a stick or, preferably, not walk at all. I had a book called *Synopsis of Medicine* (I did not, despite Miss Brophy, have to get my 'medical turn of description' from Aldous Huxley) and from that I learned that I probably had thromboangiitis obliterans, or Buerger's disease, to be found mostly among middle-aged Jews who smoked too many cigarettes. Middle-aged Catholics probably qualified too, though not middle-aged Protestants. I gave up my eighty or so cigarettes a day and took to an excessive number of panatellas, but the pain persisted. The arteries, apparently, were closing up. The condition ended in gangrene and amputation. Television showed, in the series *Emergency Ward Ten*, a man, a Cockney Jew, ready to have his leg lopped off so he could carry on smoking. I was frightened. I went to see an arterial specialist in Tunbridge Wells, a charming woman of much my age. She played a stethoscope over the leg and heard thrombotic thumps. Sooner or later, she said, the arteries would have to be exposed, scraped clean of cholesterol, and then sewn up again till next time. Smoking was deadly, she said, smoking, but alcohol dilated the arteries and did good. As an earnest of this, she went off duty and drank gin with me in a Tunbridge Wells pub. I had to try a change of diet, cutting out animal fat and turning to sunflower oil. Come back again and we will see how you are getting on. She, strangely, knew my work: at least she had read unfavourable reviews of it in the *New Statesman*. It was a pity that a probably promising author should have a leg to worry about as well as bad reviews.

I went back, having cut out eggs and eaten nothing fried at all, but the stethoscope still registered the wrong thumps. I was amiable, submissive, as I always am with keepers of the great somatic mysteries. I was perhaps too amiable. This doctor, a married woman and the mother of two children, fell in love with me. This was not supposition on my part: she wrote a letter declaring passion and proposing that we make love in her surgery after hours. I came down for breakfast in the spring of 1963 and found that Lynne, opening all the mail, had read the declaration. Since the Gwen Bustin libel suit I had become timid about tearing open envelopes and I left that to Lynne. For once a literary review served me well. *Honey for the Bears* appeared in the same week as the letter, and Christopher Ricks in the *New Statesman* devoted a whole article to it. His title was 'The Epicene', and he seemed to argue that my novel was an attempt at making a case for homosexuality. It was becoming possible, in the newly permissive sixties, to state that people were homosexuals without incurring legal rigour, and Ricks appeared to have no doubt that I was given both ways, perhaps more the deviant one than the other. I was delighted to learn this, and I was able to write an eloquent letter to my doctor referring her to her current *New Statesman*, which contained an admirable summation of my sexual position, though Professor Ricks, I said, had not taken it far enough. I had fought hard, for my poor wife's sake, to become wholeheartedly heterosexual, but I did not know how to do it. Forgive me for my failure to respond to your flattering and indeed heartening avowal, but you see, thanks to Professor Ricks, how things are. The sclerotic calf-ache has eased somewhat. Things are being cooked in oil. They were, in fact, not. To follow my doctor's dietetic advice would, for Lynne, have been submission to a kind of rival. There was some sex going on now, though not much. She fried in lard, a daughter of the cold north.

She also slowly simmered a suspicion that, *Honey for the Bears* apart, there might be something in Ricks's hint about my sexual proclivities. Other authors, Oscar Wilde and Somerset Maugham for instance, had discovered their homosexuality in middle age. That I might prefer men or boys to women, meaning herself, would explain a great deal. She worked out a scenario, not yet to be articulated, in which our Malay houseboy Yusof was a character, as well as a blond German to whom I had seemed to be attracted at a village dance in Leicestershire. It occupied a good deal of her inner time.

1963 WAS a strange year. It was a year in which it seemed possible that I might start earning money, though not from the writing of fiction. I had become used to a small but steady sale of my history of English literatue, and Longman, its publisher, sent a regular spring cheque for about £200. This year their cheque was for £3,000, which seemed excessive: there had to be a mistake; the money was really meant for one of their textbook princes (*English for Foreign Commis Waiters*). Nevertheless, I paid the cheque into the bank and, when Longman's accountant apologised for the error and sent a cheque for rather less than £200, I drew a cheque for the mistaken amount and mailed it. The trouble then was that the Inland Revenue Department, uninterested in my disbursements, tried to tax that sum as income.

But then I was paid a genuine unreturnable £3,000 for writing the history of a great metropolitan real property corporation, which was celebrating its first centenary. There was an organisation which looked after the subliterary concerns of great commercial bodies, and it made these pay far more than the small commercial firms which were publishing houses. It was almost like the film world. The patrician gentleman who was arranging, of his goodness, a subvention of genuine literature, asked me to meet him, after lunch, on the steps of the Travellers' Club – not, I noticed, inside: I had not reached that level. He took me to the offices of the corporation, where we met an ageing executive who loved it like a father. I gathered what material was available and found it insufficient for a book. I contrived a Dickensian fantasia full of mean streets, chophouses, smoky taverns, cantankerous eccentric clerks on high stools in dusty chambers. Over all brooded a London particular. There were one or two revelations in the available documents which seemed to me to be shady – such as the driving out of smallholders by droop-lipped bullies in order that the headquarters of a great insurance company might be erected. Still, the failure to renew leases was part of the heartening history of London: there would have been no Globe Theatre for the Lord Chamberlain's Men if John Brayne (no connection with the man of the silver-grey Merc) had not dangled the promise of lease renewal before the Burbages, owners of the Shoreditch Theatre, and then failed to fulfil. Anyway, the book was never published. Too literary, or something. But I was paid the money. The upstairs bar bulged with bottles.

More money was to come in with the death of Lynne's father, who had promised not to leave it all to his second wife, the Guinness-loving lady of good yeoman stock. Lynne and I travelled to Leicester to visit him in hospital, where he was alternately sucking on oxygen and Capstan full strength. Travelling back on the Sunday train I observed some young people who were covertly deriding me. They had a copy of the *Sunday Times*, which I had not yet seen, and they seemed to be comparing a dim photograph in the book review pages with the dour smoker of panatellas who was waiting for his wife to collapse. Get Lynne on a journey and collapsing was always imminent. The trouble was that she sometimes collapsed in the train toilet and was in danger of taking us on to Penzance. The young people had apparently been reading a review of *Honey for the Bears* by

Julian Jebb. This was one of a breed of fringe littérateurs who were, in what were now called the media, gadflies to their elders and betters. They made statements like 'What a clever old thing jolly Jack Priestley is' and 'Renegade Catholics are becoming a bit of a bore'. Julian Jebb slashed my novel but was not entirely unkind. If, he seemed to say, he did not exactly demand that I give up writing fiction through manifest lack of talent this was because he recognised that even bad writers had, alas, to earn a living of sorts. I read this review when we reached home. Perhaps unreasonably I blamed Julian Jebb for exposing my mediocrity on a crowded Sunday train. I took Lynne, who was clearly depressed by her father's condition and probably felt a renewal of filial guilt, on a swift holiday to Gibraltar and Tangier. From Tangier I sent Julian Jebb a postcard with a picture of shitting camels on it and the message 'Thinking of you here'.

Gibraltar was Major Meldrum OBE territory, the scene of military failure. Why did one insist on going back to the past? We had gone back, the previous summer, to Ambleteuse in the Pas de Calais, where, ten years before, Lynne had made love in the sea with a M. André Pécriaux. There he was still, somewhat fatter, but ready to make love again, though preferably not in the sea because of his rheumatic twinges. On returning home Lynne received from Pécriaux's wife a long letter in purple ink which was an almost exact reproduction of the jealous effusion of a decade back: '*Ah, vous, madame, avec votre incapacité typiquement anglaise de pouvoir comprendre la nature de l'amour conjugale . . .*' This did Lynne good. She could not return to the triumphant head girlhood of Bedwellty Grammar School, when her father was smoking but vigorous and her mother as yet unaware of her sexual sins, but it was a kind of rejuvenation.

The return to Gibraltar rejuvenated me in the wrong way. It tapped the vein of outmoded revolt and made me spill drink on harmless retired army officers. I was now permitted to stay at the Rock Hotel, whence other ranks had been barred. I was served for my first breakfast broken haddock in tepid water and broken fried eggs in cooling grease. I dumped these back in the kitchen and played hell in broken Andalusian. So this was the broken glass dump we, with enforced myopia, had imagined to be a fairy palace. Lynne was in bed. Lynne was nearly always in bed on holiday. The hepatic exhaustion was stimulated by a change of scene. She would rise to go out to lunch with me and, having ordered grilled swordfish, see it arrive on the table only to wish to go back to bed. Over in Tangier in the Miramar Hotel she lay in bed while I incessantly rolled cigarettes of adulterated *kif* for her. William Burroughs, author of *The Naked Lunch*, admirer of *A Clockwork Orange*, would read funereally Jane Austen to her as she lay. His cured junkie heart homed to Regency stability.

Tangier was all junkies ('land of the great grass,' they called it) and pederasts. It was also German tourists who were ready at table for the first sitting of dinner a good hour in advance, eating dry rolls and calling for more. I was interested to watch one German *paterfamilias* after lunch collect the sugar lumps from the deserted tables and dump them in a napkin. He needed them for a picnic, he said. The manager said: '*Sie brauchen auch Milch*' and poured on the lumps a whole jugful. Why did the Germans, in this admittedly rather feeble manner, continue to want to be hated? It was best to eat out, away from them, with the expatriate literary pederasts, Robin Maugham, Rupert Croft-Cooke, and their smart-suited Tangerine companions. After a drinking session with one of them Lynne turned her sharp blue eyes on me (*sa-rupa pisau*, Alladad Khan had used to say: like a dagger) and put the straight question: was I perhaps really a closet homosexual? To my surprise she cited verbatim Christopher Ricks's review: 'Homosexuality is not wicked, not ethereally spiritual, not necessarily the source of anxiety or agony, not incompatible with other things, but rather a pleasant virtuosity . . .' I denied the charge, though admitting that I should like to be omnifutuant just as I would like to have been born a Jew. She had stolen a glance at the pages of the new novel I was writing, in which I seemed to be presenting William Shakespeare as a homosexual and a syphilitic one at that. My true sexual nature was beginning to come out in middle age. This, I said, was all nonsense. What I would have liked in Tangier was to seize one of these kohl-eyed houris in a yashmak and kiss her from her neat brown ankles up. One evening when Lynne lay in bed, making me read *Persuasion* to her (William Burroughs's lugubrious American tones were not right somehow), I said to hell, I was going to visit the kasbah. Ah, she said, to find little boys. She called the hotel doctor, told him I was unstable and violent when drunk, and, against all my protests, had him feed me a sleeping draught. Then I passed out and woke late with a parched mouth. This was no way to spend a holiday.

There was no time for holidays anyway. There was much to do. The following year was the quatercentenary of Shakespeare's birth and I had to bring out a novel on his love life. This piece of fiction was the hardest I had ever undertaken. I had had to read hard and learn to think like an Elizabethan, even talk like one. How to use 'withal', when to change from the polite to the intimate pronoun system, what meanings to give to 'honest' and 'politician'. I had already read out on the BBC Third Programme part of the first draft of the opening chapter, and I was far from satisfied. This was no time for a holiday, and yet a holiday had been needful to stop me going mad. I had had to disinfest myself with *kif*, absinthe, and Mediterranean wind of doubts about my ability to write not only that novel but any novel ('Anthony Burgess is a literary smart aleck whose novel *A Clockwork Orange* last year achieved a *succès d'estime* with critics like William Burroughs, who mistook his muddle of sadism, teddy-boyism, jive talk and Berlitz Russian for social philosophy. Now he tries again with a novel about a black market expedition to Leningrad by an ill-mated couple . . . The work offers no clue to Mr Burgess's fixation on things Russian. Nor to some critics' conviction that he is a first-rate satirist.' I had read that on the flight to Gibraltar.) Sitting in the North Shore airport, awaiting the flight to London, I read a review of *Inside Mr Enderby* by Joseph Kell, in the *Observer*. This was so favourable that I have forgotten its content.

Back in Etchingham post office a mountain of other people's fiction awaited me. But then there arrived from the offices of the *Yorkshire Post* a lone volume, meticulously wrapped, unsullied by contact with Alvin Redman tripe and Mills and Boon sub-erotica. It was *Inside Mr Enderby* by Joseph Kell. That previous autumn, during my tour of the bookish villages of the Ridings, I had had lunch at his club with the editor of the *Yorkshire Post*, Kenneth Young, and had, as I well remembered, forewarned him about the publication of a new novel by me under a new, or fairly new, pseudonym. Let that book not be sent to me but let it be reviewed by someone else, preferably Peter Green. Kenneth Young had said nothing, but he seemed now to be disclosing a sense of fun hitherto concealed. He apparently wanted me to review my own book, so I reviewed it. I wrote, under the heading 'Blasts from the Smallest Room' (changed by the literary editor to 'Poetry in a Tiny Room'): 'This is, in many ways, a dirty book. It is full of bowel-blasts and flatulent borborygms, emetic meals ("thin but over-savoury stews," Enderby calls them) and halitosis. It may well make some people sick, and those of my readers with tender stomachs are advised to let it alone. It turns sex, religion, the State into a series of laughing-stocks. The book itself is a laughing-stock.' Then I turned to cleaner fiction. No one, discovering the double identity, not the editor himself, could complain that I was boosting my own work. I was going out of my way to put people off.

I was surprised at the response of the literary world to this harmless piece of foolery. A week after the publication of the review the *Daily Mail* disclosed that Joseph Kell was really Anthony Burgess, who had chosen a disguise in order to be paid for advertising his own work. Kenneth Young appeared on Granada Television to denounce my treachery and summarily, in public, to fire me. There was no response of either regret or satisfaction from *Yorkshire Post* readers, who first as last ignored me when I was not writing about inodorous orchids. I had just sent a review article to the *Observer*, in which I discussed books by V. S. Naipaul, Penelope Gilliatt and John Wain. This article now became deeply suspect (I presumably might be all those writers in disguise) and was neither published nor paid for. I gained temporary fame as a literary villain. I was even invited to sit at the high table of a Foyle's literary luncheon and wondered if this would be a kind of pillory and I a target for bread rolls. Ah well, Daniel Defoe had been in the pillory too. Maurice Edelman MP and Sir Charles Snow, establishment pillars, had the guts to defend me in the national press. Are we losing our sense of humour? After all, Walter Scott had reviewed the first of the Waverley novels, and at great length too. A novelist who reviewed his own work might be presumed at least to have read it, which was more than could be said for some well-regarded hacks who would read only its blurb. Edelman said that I was a good comic novelist who had carried over comedy into real life to a response of a pretence of moral shock. I was comforted by this support, but my wife was not. She wept slow tears. I had dishonoured myself and, since she was also Anthony Burgess, at least to the Inland Revenue, her too. My literary future was in jeopardy. Good prose would be seen to be bad. William Shakespeare would not die in 1616.

My literary future was not, in fact, especially harmed by this nugatory crime. Crime never harmed a man much, unless it involved the dirtier varieties of sex. No revelation of Burgessian turpitude could make my prospects more dismal than they already were. I had written much fiction and reviewed widely and un-brophianly, and I was sneered at for over-production and reviled for compassionate blandness. Burgess could not be trusted as a novelist, since he might really be someone else, perhaps a paralytic Irish soak named Joseph Kell, or it could be the other way round. He clearly could not be trusted as a reviewer, since he might really be V. S. Naipaul, though, to the thoughtful, this must seem unlikely. Still, the untrustworthy novels might still be published, sauced piquantly by their creator's vileness, and the newspapers of former colonies, which had been founded on a rejection of the hypocrisy of the motherland, ought to fill in the vacuum left by the defection of the *Yorkshire Post*. True, there would never again be such a mound of saleable review copies, but my left leg would not have permitted me any more to lug them to London (Leavin 'er again, he do be).

There were, in the field of humble sèrvice to literature, many roles still to fill. Thus, the British Council asked me to write a pamphlet on the state of the contemporary British novel, which, as a reviewing hack, I knew something about. I could not put myself in the pamphlet but I toyed with the notion of including Joseph Kell. But who was Joseph Kell compared with Iris Murdoch and William Golding and Anthony Powell? I was also asked to write a monograph on Iris Murdoch, but this was calling my bluff. I did not really know what she, and so many of the other British illustrious, were getting at. The BBC asked me to prepare an exhaustive apparatus for students of Golding's *Lord of the Flies* – author's biography, notes, dramatisation for recording – and this I did. But I had my doubts about Golding: he dealt in original sin without theological backing; he was gaining fame and money out of supposititious evil. I had my doubts about a large number of British novelists.

A reviewer who is not himself a novelist is permitted to slash, for he is not able to be accused of envy. I had, I remembered, written a prescient epigram about critics when I was seventeen:

> Behold a prodigy – ballless born:
> Shielded so by a natural fence
> From the feared charge of impotence,
> He laughs your little prick to scorn.

But it is always dangerous for a novelist to attack his fellows, for nobody will impute to him a passion for aesthetic excellence that he has learned through his practice though not attained. He is jealous, no more. I have never been able to understand the fuss that is made about John le Carré, who not only earns large royalties but is praised for his literary qualities. Philip Roth said that *A Perfect Spy* was the best British novel since the war. When I underpraised this book in a long review, there was an immediate charge of envy of his genius and earning capacity. This was not so. I have always envied the rich, but I do not necessarily envy the way they become rich. John le Carré writes competent novels of espionage in a traditional style. They are considered better than those of Ian Fleming and Len Deighton because they are more authentic and, perhaps, because they are less entertaining. The inability to entertain is supposed by some to be an aspect of high seriousness. The trouble with most of my contemporaries, in my view, is that they do not seem to have heard of James Joyce.

I was prepared, during this period of shame, to serve James Joyce, whom, even when discussing Alan Sillitoe or John Braine, I was always dragging irrelevantly into my reviews. A BBC television programme was to be made on sex in literature, and I was asked to tell the camera about sex in James Joyce. A television van came to Etchingham, and the villagers assumed it was there to honour the village itself or show up the horror of its lack of drainage. Or, at least, it might be there for Lady Percy or the Rector, whom Mrs Catt called His Holiness. But it was for me. The film has probably been long destroyed, but it showed Lynne apparently illustrating sex by beating a Yorkshire pudding batter. The dog Haji damaged a camera in fun and, not in fun, tried to rape the producer's secretary. But the producer, Christopher Burstall, proposed that we together go further than a mere Joyce snippet and make a sixty-minute film on the author in Dublin. This meant long preliminary discussions over sumptuous luncheons in the West End. I could see the point of television.

I had been watching much television with Lynne, chiefly because she had quarrelled with the new landlady of the local pub, perhaps with less cause than when she had quarrelled with the precedent landlord. There was no late night bus from Burwash, where she had as yet quarrelled with no landlord, and there was not much else to do in the evenings. Thus when I became one of the television reviewers for the *Listener* there was no true imposition of extra work. I watched no more than before, stayed up all Friday night to write my weekly review, dispatched this by the London train, then spent Saturday morning in bed. I have always, despite jibes to the contrary, been a slow worker. My predecessor as reviewer of documentary programmes put out by the BBC for the BBC's own hebdomadal had been Peter Green, who wrote at enviable speed. He had now packed his bags for Mytilene and there proposed translating Juvenal at retsina-lubricated leisure. He had recommended me as his successor and I was accepted, on condition that I did not review any programmes in which I myself appeared.

I find it informative to re-read some of the articles I wrote a quarter of a century ago, since they are a kind of record of the ethos of the early sixties. In retrospect that seems a golden era, but Britain was suffering as always a decay of energy and enterprise. On 6 June 1963 I was inveighing against the British housing shortage and the British brain drain, as revealed in two separate programmes: 'Four million slums and three million substandard houses, our apparent inability either to build houses or afford them; industry's unwillingness to apply new techniques; the frustration of self-exiling scientists; our feeling that efficiency is ungentlemanly and only right for damned foreigners – everything added up to a malaise which calls for a more general documentary analysis.' On the same evening Professor A. J. P. Taylor was improvising a history talk on the screen. Back in 1938 he had written on one of my history papers: 'Bright ideas insuffi cient to conceal lack of knowledge.' I was now able to pay him, word for word, back. It is always just a matter of waiting.

The Profumo affair was the big shocking theme of that summer. It is only in this year in which I write that we are able to see the enormity of its conclusion. In July 1963 a man named Stephen Ward committed suicide. This was during his trial at the Old Bailey for an alleged crime of living off the earnings of prostitutes. The evidence had been heard but the verdict not yet delivered. Yet this verdict was a foregone conclusion. The judge, Sir Archie Pellow Marshall, and the counsel for the prosecution, Mervyn Griffith-Jones, had con-verted a criminal trial into a display of hypocritical moral outrage and, by tone and implication, virtually impelled the jury to find the defendant guilty. Ward did not wait for his condemnation. He, in his own words, disappointed the vultures by taking an overdose of Nembutal tablets. That he was not guilty was evident then and has, in the quarter-century since the trial, been thoroughly confirmed by witnesses who admitted perjury. Ward was a sacrificial victim for the British establishment or, as Lord Goodman puts it, 'was the historic victim of an historic injustice'. His defence counsel put it more bluntly: 'It was a political trial because of Profumo. Judge Marshall murdered Stephen Ward. It's as simple as that.'

Stephen Ward was the alumnus of a minor public school, which was a stroke against him to begin with. He was educated neither at Oxford nor at Cambridge but at a college of physiotherapy in the United States. He became well known among the figures of the British establishment as a skilled and often salvatory osteopath and as a highly talented black and white portraitist. He had a flaw which may be considered tragic: he loved women. He loved them not in the manner of highly venerated satyrs like John F. Kennedy, for his sexuality was feeble and best satisfied by voyeurism and shoe-fetishism. He liked to be surrounded by beauties of all social classes to draw them and, if they were poor, to help them. He took satisfaction in the educative labour of converting provincial floozies like Christine Keeler and Mandy Rice-Davies into courtesans worthy of statesmen like John Profumo, the Secretary of State for War, and fascinating exotics like Yevgeny Ivanov, naval attaché of the Soviet Embassy. An essential adjunct of the entourage of Lord Astor, who needed osteopathic soothing after equestrian exercise, Ward was given a cottage on the Cliveden estate. There were great parties at Cliveden, and Profumo and Ivanov were drawn together in a common interest in the female flesh that Ward innocently made available. He was not a procurer in the grosser sense of the term: he was aesthetically satisfied at seeing his Pygmalion statues come to life in a worthy ambience. He was not directly responsible for the security danger that arose from the contiguity, in a sexual context, of Profumo and Ivanov. Indeed, MI5 was glad to see Ivanov buzzing round the honeytrap and made Ward a trusted if unpaid agent of a possible Soviet defection. But Ward's intelligence connection was not mentioned either at the trial or in the ultimate report of Lord Denning.

Lord Denning said of Ward 'the most evil man I have ever met', meaning that Ward liked women and liked other men to like women. His promotion of high-class fornication was perhaps morally reprehensible, but morality, then as now and heretofore, is only invoked by the establishment when it suits its book. This has given the British as a whole a reputation for hypocrisy, which is perhaps unjust. Ward had another flaw than the love of women. As artist and physician he was democratic in a way the establishment could not well understand: neither beauty nor the possession of aching bones was a monopoly of high society. Ward went to low dives and met pot-smoking black men. He was the nexus which made it possible to speak of Profumo and the West Indian thug 'Lucky' Gordon in the same breath.

George Wigg, who as an Army Educational Corps lieutenant had found fault with my scheme of enlightenment in 1942, was a Labour MP at this time. He was later ennobled and ended his days sadly looking for whores. He raised the question of Profumo's conduct in the House of Commons. Morality seemed more important than British security, which became a rabid concern of the FBI at the time of blustering Khrushchev and the Bay of Pigs, manifested in a belief in a universal call-girl conspiracy which might have trapped Kennedy. Profumo lied to parliament but later retracted his lie and resigned his seat. He virtually brought the Macmillan government down, but he was granted the opportunity to repent and be purged by doing social work. His wife, the actress Valerie Hobson, stuck by him, and he was eventually made a Commander of the British Empire. He remains wealthy and has recovered respect. But a victim had to be found to cleanse the establishment, and this was poor Ward. The police allegedly suborned witnesses, his friends deserted him, the women he had raised to courtesanship lied like troopers. Lord Denning produced his report, and the world was safe again. Or at least the Wilson administration persuaded us that it might be, once the legacy of Tory misrule was eliminated.

Both Cliveden and Ward's cottage were literally exorcised, and the exorciser said he had never before met such a reek of evil as exuded from the latter. As always, the British establishment deliberately confused crime and immorality and made a scapegoat of a man of eccentric ways but undoubted talent. We have had to wait to see the whole unclean affair in perspective. While I was reviewing it as news all I had to report was Lord Hailsham's 'fulminant credo, a lay sermon on the general moral decline of which the Profumo affair may be regarded as a symptom' or Peregrine Worsthorne's statement that 'the call-girl cult could be seen as an unworthy flower of a suspect and lopsided affluence'. There was a blurring of the whole sad business in a discussion programme on the sexual morality of politicians in general, which, I said, reminded us 'that Curzon and Lloyd George did, like Falstaff, in some sort handle women, but they never perpetrated any barefaced denial. A minister's sexual morality was his own affair, a minister's lie was his country's.'

Of politicians in general, as television showed them, I said that 'they were a kind of Jonsonian humours, predictable, identifiable with what they stood for, hardly worth interrogating'. I did not think much of young artists either. A programme on art students provoked the comment: 'They were as guilty of as wretched a gallimaufry of phoney aesthetics and scruffy underdog whinings as ever steamed up from the dog-end-littered floor of a Soho wine-club. Anyway, said these students, in the last analysis we only paint to please ourselves. Gurt topfloor ararakis wertle dickdock. This is written to please me, and to hell with communication.' I noted that navvies take twelve pints of beer 'in the confidence that they will be quickly sweated out on the job. There are worse things, God knows: coffee bars, the Beatles, the cult of the disc-jockey, watching *This is Your Life* for pleasure, giving some harmless ancient the boot for a giggle.' I was harsh, in November, on the Miss World 1963 contest: 'I thought the standard of beauty was not so high as in other years –

too much standardisation of the coiffure, the inevitable false
eyelashes twittering away. Let's have these girls judged, for a
change, coming straight out of bed or emerging from a by-election
tussle.' I was harshest of all on a Christmas Eve programme called
Elizabeth Taylor in London – 'a waste of public money, an impertinence and an insult, an invitation to a feast of nothing . . . The
eponymous goddess was a jaw-dropping vision of totally meaning-
less allure – Yves Saint Laurent icing, delectability of fairy gold, the
poor little box of tricks of Zuleika Dobson.' Given a black and white
television and a midnight typewriter I could be quite a devil. I see
myself now in the summer dawn, having written an article entitled
'A Stink in the Profumeria', yawning down at the back lawn, where I
had installed a device that saved me from the labour of mowing – a
wide bottomless cage full of guinea pigs, to be kicked from grazed to
ungrazed segment. Some of the guinea pigs have burrowed under to
freedom. I limp down to them and, scared of a scolding, they burrow
back in again. Then I limp with my stamped addressed article to the
early London train. I had no time for mowing the lawn, anyway.

1963 WAS the year in which, according to Philip Larkin, sexual
intercourse began – 'between the end of the *Chatterley* ban and the
Beatles' first LP'. Mervyn Griffith-Jones had been counsel for the
continued banning of Lawrence's book. He lost, but he succeeded
with the prosecution of Stephen Ward. The sixties got off to a good
start with a licence to print the word 'fuck', a new translation of the
New Testament which made the gospels plainer but killed the
magic, and the cult of youth. The miniskirt was not for mature
women, and there was a new kind of popular music intended for
teenagers. I disliked the Beatles, who survived the scorn of the *Daily
Mirror* to become a world myth, but, in the spate of trash that has
succeeded them, I am inclined now to find there a sort of twilight
merit – shaped melodic lines and a modicum of literacy before
analphabetic recitative took over. I did not go so far as one American
magazine editor, who offered me good money to celebrate them as
the new four evangelists. Charles Manson, of course, went further,
seeing them as breastplated archangels in the Book of Revelation
(the breastplates were electronic guitars). I was, in fact, uneasy about
the youth cult – though, later, unintentionally, I was to contribute to
it. I detested their servitors the disc jockeys, especially a Yorkshireman who was eventually awarded the Order of the British Empire.

There was a weekly television showcase of new pop discs in which, I remember, a song called 'Who's Afraid of Virginia Woolf?' was played. One of the grinning appraisers said that this Virginia Woolf must sure be some swinging chick: I rushed to the toilet to vomit. Ministers of religion bowed to the tastes of the young and accommodated pop-singing guitarists in their services. There were rock masses. Independent television celebrated Easter with a crucifixion ballet to a rock beat. I had now been back in Britain for three years, and I was ready to get out again. But there seemed nowhere to go.

I suppose I was dour about the new sexuality because no ageing man likes to see the young doing better than he did. Swinging was for the young, bingo for the old, and the middle-aged had to be satisfied with dull jobs, plain wives, and aseptic suburbs. At forty-six I did not wish to be old, but I could not deny that middle age was now supposed to start at about twenty-five. I hungered for these girls in miniskirts, but they were not for me. Long-haired louts in pubs called me 'dad'. At least I was not going bald. But Lynne was visibly ageing, her once delectable legs thinning, her fair hair losing its lustre. I sublimated lust into a novel about lust, which I called love. The secondary title of the fiction I was writing about Shakespeare, *Nothing Like the Sun*, was 'A Story of Shakespeare's Love Life'. The primary title, taken from the sonnet beginning 'My mistress' eyes are nothing like the,' referred not only to the Dark Lady he lusted for but to the poet himself, effulgent in his work but perhaps very ordinary in his life. I had taken one theme from Joyce's *Ulysses* – Anne Shakespeare's adultery with Richard (though not Gilbert) Shakespeare – and another from Thomas Mann's *Dr Faustus* – the possibility that great tragic art related to syphilis. I was fairly sure that Shakespeare had contracted syphilis – his description of its symptoms in *Timon of Athens* is, in the context, gratuitous, but there is an urgency in the manifest of disgust, wholly accurate, that suggests a sufferer seeing himself in a mirror. He could have got syphilis from the Earl of Southampton or the Dark Lady, perhaps both. That he had an affair with the Earl seemed to me at least possible, but that might be the way of advancement rather than of temperamental conviction. Passion for a dark woman is well authenticated in the sonnets, and it was so powerful that it led to disgust – 'The expense of spirit in a waste of shame/ Is lust in action . . .' Who was the Dark Lady? Dr A. L. Rowse is dogmatic about her being a Sicilian, but Professor G. B. Harrison, aware of black brothels in Clerkenwell, thought she might be negroid. I present her as a Malay brought back from Sir Francis Drake's circumnavigation, and I give her the name Fatimah. The name is presented acrostically, with the first two vowels suppressed in the Arabic manner, in the lines

>   . . . My love is as a fever
> Feeding on that which does preserve the ill,
> The uncertain sickly appetite to please.
> My reason, the physician to my love,
> Angry that his prescriptions are not kept,
> Hath left me . . .

The name is more fully spelt out, first forward then backward, in a juvenile sonnet I fathered on the boy Shakespeare:

> Fair is as fair as fair itself allows,
> And hiding in the dark is not less fair.
> The married blackness of my mistress' brows
> Is thus fair's home, for fair abideth there.
> My love being black, her beauty may not shine
> And light so foiled to heat alone may turn.
> Heat is my heart, my hearth, all earth is mine;
> Heaven do I scorn when in such hell I burn.
> All other beauty's light I lightly rate:
> My love is as my love is, for the dark.
> In night enthroned, I ask no better state
> Than thus to range, nor seek a guiding spark.
> And childish I am put to school of night
> For to seek light beyond the reach of light.

Needless to say, not one reviewer spotted this improbable acrostic.

Nor did any reviewer remark on the structure of the novel – two parts and an epilogue, with ten chapters in each of the two parts, the chapters of the second part exactly double the length of their counterparts in the first. Some scholarly readers noticed that, in the first chapter, the river Avon is made to 'spurgeon', this being a reference to Caroline Spurgeon's study of Shakespeare's imagery, in which she cites 'back to the strait that sent him on so fast' as descriptive of the back eddy under the Clopton Bridge. Noticing it, they gleefully cried out an anachronism, failing to see that the narrative is prefaced by some remarks by Mr Burgess, a character who is telling the story of Shakespeare's love life to a group of

Malayan students (whose names are given and reappear in the text), who is growing drunker and drunker on Chinese rice-spirit, and who finally identifies his alcoholic collapse with Shakespeare's death.

Despite that irresistible 'spurgeon' (and 'spurge' means to emit foam, which is what the river does), the text is pretty well free of anachronisms – no Freud or Jung and no word that Shakespeare himself would not have known. It was in contriving exact Elizabethan pastiche that the agony lay, as well as a great deal of laborious research. The composing of the novel was a thing tempting to put off – who would read, who would praise, who would buy? – but if it were not published on 23 April 1964 when could it possibly ever be? I slogged at the book and delivered it on time, then I briefly collapsed and lay with the guinea pigs. Then I had to start writing a more or less popular study of linguistics more or less commissioned by the English Universities Press.

'A HYPOTHESIS may have a mental existence and the ginger-and-white cat that sits by me at this moment of writing may have a physical one: to the user of words they inhabit the same area of reference' – that sentence brings back the writing of *Language Made Plain* in the autumn small hours of 1963. The cat was Sandy, and he rested his sleeping head against the typewriter carriage, resisting its unsteady travel to the left. On the table, besides the materials of writing, were a number of tins of Brazilian cigars, sent by a cigar club to which I subscribed. The book was made as much out of smoke as of strong tea firmly enwhiskied, brewed by the pint mug – a Bavarian *Stein*, in fact, that had lost its metal hat. It was also made out of reading and independent speculation. Its intended reader was Sir Charles Snow, to whom, and his wife Pamela, I had dedicated *Nothing Like the Sun*, though, plain writers both, it was not really their pint mug. Charles distrusted wordplay, being a scientist, and was not really impressed at a telegraph I had once had to send. Invited to a New Year party at his house, I was unable to travel because of high drifts on the roads so telegraphed: WAS SNOWBOUND BUT AM SNOWBOUND. Charles, in his 1959 'Two Cultures' lecture, had contended that literary men feared the big wind of modern science. I responded: 'There are other forms of science than the study of matter. I can tell Sir Charles nothing of nuclear biology; can he define a phoneme for me?' No, he could not, so here was I doing it for him.

I felt that not only literary men but plain lovers of literature should know something of the basic material of the art – the structure of speech, the nature of meaning, the volatility of both. But I felt also that the British, some day to enter the European Community, had to overcome their insular resistance to foreign languages and learn the basic phonetic and morphological principles that underlay language in general. I had brooded over my wife's lack of curiosity in the Arabic and Cyrillic alphabets, and I tried to show how fascinating, even miraculous, was the Semitic emergence from pictograms to syllabaries, then to the unique wonder of the alphabet in all its cognate forms. My wife was bored when I read out, over iced gin, the day's writing. Free forms and bound forms, autosemantemes, synsemantemes, dull, dull, dull. Dull, or rather not highly signifi-cant, to Charles Snow. There was a nearly total lack of interest among literary people in language and, for that matter, the sister discipline of music. Shakespeare scholars responded dully when I told them of the two solmised themes which were the poet's singing to us out of the past – the CDGAEF intoned by Holofernes in *Love's Labour's Lost*, the CDE low B insolently chanted by Edmund in *King Lear* (from this Richard Addinsell had made his main theme in the *Warsaw Concerto* pastiche). Literary people just did not care about sound.

There was one exception, and this was Kingsley Amis. Obtuse critics like Miss Brophy had missed the peculiar music of Amis's prose, imputing unwilled dysphony or cliché to very cunning clumsiness matching the clumsiness of life. Evelyn Waugh had never quite understood that Augustan elegance cannot work in the novel. Henry Fielding, who lived in the Augustan era, knew that the rhythms of life oppose those of the intellect. You can only write the fiction of Gibbonian periods if you are homosexual or belong to the Church Triumphant. If you are sweatily involved in the setting down of life as it comes, thick and hot, you must seem to some to write clumsily. Anyway Amis, more than any other contemporary writer, knew what sound was all about. Reading *Language Made Plain*, he was the one man willing to join me in confuting Bloomfield's dogma that a bound morpheme could not make sense as a single utterance. 'I'll just go upstairs and say good night to your son.' The proud parents respond with '/z/', the plural morpheme, meaning that they have more than one son now. The professional linguist might be scared of contradicting Bloomfield; the sound-conscious novelist, exploiting language as it is colloquially used, need not be so timid. In Amis's *Girl 20*, we hear the lazy assimilations of the young and the middle-aged imitators of the young, who say 'vogka' and 'tim peaches' and 'corm beef'. The linguists have not recorded such locutions for posterity; they have had to leave it to a novelist. Charles Snow, the scientist, was content to say of one of his characters that she left the 'g' out of her 'ing' in 'singing', instead of 'she turned the voiced velar nasal continuant into a postdental one'. How seriously could one take his bludgeonings of literary men for being ignorant of science when he neglected the science closest to his art? Amis, in the first pages of *I Like It Here*, has his hero turn off the radio and stop Frank Sinatra in mid-phoneme. That is not quite accurate – it should be mid-allophone – but it is better than J. B. Priestley's having someone put an aspirate after his esses in words like 'scissors'.

The men of letters who were also men of sound – how many were there? I was drawn to the few I find and still am. *Language Made Plain* was intended to make more of them, but it probably failed. The devoting of the year 1963 to a novel on Shakespeare and a book mainly on phonology did not represent a splitting of interests. We know what Elizabethan speech was like (there is, for the non-specialist in phonology, an accurate phonemic analysis in John Florio's English–Italian dictionary *A World of Words*, 1598 and 1611), and it was necessary for me, writing *Nothing Like the Sun*, to hear in my head the authentic tones of Shakespeare's London. The work emerged from the press as printed graphemes, but to me the dialogue was resuscitated dead sound. When, in 1964, I tried to celebrate the quatercentenary by publicly reciting Shakespeare in Elizabethan phonemes, the public was mostly disgusted. It wanted to believe that Shakespeare spoke like John Gielgud, not like an Irish Bostonian. He was diminished in its ears by sounding hayseed and provincial.

In the summer of 1963 Lynne's father died. He was buried in Leicester, but she would not travel to the funeral. She pleaded exhaustion, but there was probably a mixture of psychological motives – fear of her sister's sentimental grief, a kind of symmetry of absence (she had been in Malaya when her mother died but, with a bank loan, she could have flown to the burial. Let it be that she could not because ill; let her present posture of illness rub on to that), doubt that she could sustain the ceremony of mourning without breaking down in referred guilt. I went alone. I gave to Hazel, Lynne's sister, a paperback copy of *One Hand Clapping*, which I had dedicated to her. She said it ought to sell well because it was kitchen sink fiction. She picked up such indices of modishness from the popular newspapers. She was sentimental about her father's death but also talked of legacies.

The proving of the will did not take long. Lynne received a few thousand pounds, and she proposed spending them on a house in London. There was a professional need for my going to the capital: on Shakespeare's four hundredth birthday the BBC was to open a second television channel unbeamed, for some time to come, to East Sussex. My articles for the *Listener* would require that I saw its programmes. But Lynne dreamed rather of London pubs: the country life was beginning to pall. We would spend high summer and the Christmas season in Etchingham; for the rest of the year we would be Londoners. I studied the estate agents' advertisements and found a terraced house in Chiswick that would meet our, her, purse. There was a long lease and the property would cost less than £3,000.

The past to me is the period before the Second World War; everything after is the present. To a later generation the past is the period before the new currency was imposed and inflation began, when a £20 fee for a magazine article was good money and it was possible to buy a leasehold house for a couple of thousand, with a ground rent of £10 per annum. I remember the author Arthur Calder-Marshall saying to me, as late as 1967, that if a writer could earn a steady £40 each week he was doing well enough; whatever he earned over that was champagne and a little caviar. It was true. In 1964 I woke cautiously to find myself well off, with a solidity of bobs and tosheroons and oncers in my pockets. It did not seem right that an ill-selling novelist like myself should have money in the bank. But the money came from journalism and the great new dangerous boon of television appearances. The novels were the topping up, the spume or spindrift. They had been meant to be the means of basic subsistence. I had become the least fatigable of hacks. Like Dr Johnson, I would write on anything. I even became an abortive lexicographer. But that was not yet.

We had had a vacation in the spring. Now we proposed another in the fall. Lynne was to have the opportunity of collapsing into a variety of hotel beds, for we were to take a Mediterranean air tour, a free world equivalent of the Intourist excursions we had successfully avoided in the Soviet Union. It turned out to be a bad idea in itself, though useful fictionally. A hired car from Burwash took us to Gatwick airport, where we were told to leave most of our luggage behind, since chartered aircraft imposed a limit on it. The other passengers were a decent middle-class herd of meagre drinkers and unadventurous eaters, glad to be bossed by a Mr Lodge, a dragoman who put on a little woolly cap like Dr Spindrift's, so that he might be identifiable to his flock when he led them through mobs of redolent pickpockets and bottom-pinchers. We stopped briefly in Jersey, where he ordered us to disembark and take a glass of Jersey milk laced with cognac. Then we were flown to Seville, where Lynne vomited blood copiously in a hotel toilet. It was an omen which we were too stupid to read. She was slow in boarding the airport bus, and Mr Lodge publicly rebuked her. The atmosphere was that of a school trip. Lynne felt very ill and was plainly exhausted when we reached Marrakesh. The French proprietress of the Hôtel Maroc blamed her sickness on the *cuisine espagnole*. I drank heavily and alone in the hotel bar. In our bedroom I found a young Berber in a striped waistcoat preparing to get into bed with Lynne and arguing about how much she was willing to pay for his services. An American lady, he alleged, had given him five hundred dirhams. He had to be punched and thrown out by a weary husband. There was no repose on any of our holidays.

At Tangier the time had come to pay Mr Lodge back for his insolence. In a seaside bar-restaurant run by a young English viscount who had a passion for dirty Berber boys, I met a fat man in a tarboosh and striped galabiya who ran a dirty Berber boy agency for visiting white pederasts. I gave him a hundred dirhams and fifty small white cards with the name Mr Lodge written on them in Arabic script. Mr Lodge was staying at the Rif Hotel and some of the dirty Berber boys were to visit his room in sequence, armed with his name – *min sin tok roh* space *lam waw jin* (it went beautifully into Arabic) – and offers of their services. Meanwhile, despite her sickness, Lynne's sharp blue eyes (*sa-rupa pisau*) searched for signs of pederastic inclinations in myself. Puzzled, she found none. William Burroughs appeared at the Hotel Velasquez to read Jane Austen to her. Then Mr Lodge emerged tired and cross ready for the flight to Tenerife. In Tenerife, at a remarkable jerry-built hotel where, if you slid open your bedroom window you slid open also the windows of your neighbours, Lynne came out in violent red spots. I bought penicillin and hired a *practicante* for a few pesetas. It was a shot in the dim light but it seemed to work. She got up ready for drink and psychic visions. The hotel bar, she said, was the scene of some past disaster: she saw dim wraiths raising arms of appeal. The bartender and waiters crossed themselves: the site of the hotel had been that of the village, now razed, where many of the inhabitants had died from cooking in infected oil.

Tenerife seemed to be a place for psychic visions. I lay awake on our last night, 21 November 1963, reading *El Cid*: it was, belatedly, to help my Spanish. I read the moving scene in which the young leader leaves his wife Jimenez: they part tearfully and it is like the parting of the nail from the flesh – *la uña de la carne*. I went to sleep and dreamed of a crowded street in an American city. There was an automobile procession, and a young leader stood up in his car to receive acclaim. 'The Kid, the Kid!' the crowd cried. The name of his wife began with a jota. The American Cid was brutally murdered; his wife J— was in anguish and the parting was violent enough to tear the nail from the flesh. I woke at dawn sweating. We flew to Gatwick, picked up our deposited luggage, and took a car back to Etchingham. Lynne retired to bed and I switched on the television set. Both channels were empty. I saw why when at length a news programme reported the assassination of President Kennedy. I had to believe in the capacity of dreams to tear the veil of the future.

I belong to the generation that had, in the thirties, been fascinated by J. W. Dunne's *An Experiment with Time*. The reversibility of time had proved a useful theme for J. B. Priestley's stage plays *Dangerous Corner*, *Time and the Conways* and *I Have Been Here Before*, but they did not convince of the viability of Dunne's thesis. Dunne went too far in supposing that one could, in waking life, soar above the temporal landscape and fly freely from past to future and back to past. He seemed to be right, however, in positing a parachronic state for the dreaming mind and demonstrating that the materials of dreams were drawn as much from the future as from the past. I find few of my own dreams to be Freudian. Indeed, I sometimes dream of a Freud who is puzzling out the meaning of the dream in which he is embedded. When a dream haunts me but refuses to give up its meaning I often find that it is enough to wait, perhaps months, to find the source of its images in future time.

Some little while ago I dreamed vividly of lecturing in an American college. I saw clearly a group of students, one of whom was Greek and was taking notes in the ancestral language. The dreaming mind had gone to great trouble in setting up the décor, including a very large reproduction of Millais's portrait of John Ruskin. I was lecturing on Ruskin, a subject I would not willingly choose, and most of my facts seemed on waking to be accurate, including the dates of his birth and death. But I ended the lecture by affirming: 'John Ruskin's greatest tragedy was that he turned into an elephant.' The class to my dreaming horror howled with derision, the Greek student (bespectacled and in a Fair Isle sweater) more than any. 'No, no,' I cried to him, 'I don't meant that as *metaphora* but as the literal truth.' The roars were so loud that they brought students peering in from the corridor. Then the dream ended.

I found it necessary to write the dream down, to make an article of it in fact and sent it to the *Saturday Review* in New York, to which I was contributing a monthly free-wheeling page. The response of the readers was mostly one of disgust that a reputable periodical should waste space on such rubbish, though one or two sent me their tentative interpretations. 'Elephant' went back to the childish 'effelunt' and referred to Ruskin's wife Effie, with whom, shocked at the revelation that women had pubic hair, he refused to sleep. I, as a minor writer, was jealous of Ruskin's achievement and was denouncing his prose as elephantine. But why had the oneiric machine gone to such trouble? Ruskin had not been in my head for years. I have still not uncovered the deeper meaning, but I was to find out the origin of the images several months later. I was in the Milan apartment of my Italian translator, Francesca Dragone, and she had on the table a new book on Ruskin by an Oxford friend of hers. On the walls were, recently acquired, engravings of the worship of Siamese elephant gods. Images from the future had coalesced, but dramatically and even farcically. A dream seems to want to unify disparate elements in the manner of a metaphysical poem, and it will try to make the unity plausible through the elaborate realism of the décor. The emotional element may have something to do with the effort entailed in piercing the future.

A dream I had in December 1963 was of Lynne and myself celebrating the arrival of the following spring by drinking gin only a little diluted with human blood. She at once threw this up. I interpreted the dream in terms of the new American presidency and the sacrificial downing of Kennedy's blood. I found a few years later that its meaning came closer to home. Tough-minded readers who either do not dream or see dreams as discardable waste matter, exhaust fumes of the brain, are not entitled to feel superior to persons who, like myself, feed on dreams and are sometimes violently shaken by them. For literary creation is much like the dreaming process, and dreams fuel all the arts, not just the landscapes of Salvador Dali. Igor Stravinsky saw his puppet Petrushka in a dream and in a dream saw and heard the triple-stopping which solved a problem in the composition of his violin concerto. Tread softly for you tread on my. The Golden Age is *alcheringa*, which means dream time. The word 'dream' itself is as mysterious as the phenomenon. *Dream* is a song in Anglo-Saxon and it is cognate with the Greek *thrulos*, meaning a noise. Has humanity graduated from an aboriginal sound to wide screen and Technicolor? Films are dreams and dreams feed hungrily on films. I know so little about them and yet, though I often dread having them, I am lost without dreams. Lynne was lost too: she could dream a whole saga in nightly instalments. Her dreams, she said, were better than life, except when an animal with sharp teeth tore at her vitals. That certainly was prophetic.

I should, at the beginning of that December, have been more concerned with Lynne's health than with Kennedy's death, which already had a mythic resonance. But she seemed to be well enough at home: only our disastrous vacations provoked fatigue, collapse and vomiting. 'C'est la faute de la cuisine espagnole' and also of Spanish gin, manzanilla, and the impurities in Tangerine *kif*. In Etchingham our doctor paid daily visits, more social than medical, and she showed no symptoms that perturbed him. My intermittent claudication concerned him more. When, as I always did, I drew, coloured and rhymed a Christmas card for Lynne, I wrote on it: 'A house in Chiswick will be the best physic.' It turned out to be the worst.

In December I went up to London for two purposes – the conveyancing of the house and a luncheon appointment with a young Italian woman who provided the publisher Bompiani with an annual report on the state of the British novel. She had written to express interest in my work, an interest not otherwise shown much by Italians. My only Italian literary connection so far had been with a certain Donatella Manganotti in Bologna, a lady erudite in the cut-up and fold-in experiments of William Burroughs who wrote essays about him in learned Italian journals. She had tried to draw me into the reticule of Burroughs scholarship, assuming a worship of the master on my part very like hers. There was too much of that sort of thing going on – my own creative work ignored, my over-generous laudations of other writers augmented into a supposed scholarly passion. I was sick of being left out of the compendia which exalted Alan Sillitoe and David Storey.

The young woman to whom I now gave lunch in a Greek restaurant on Chiswick High Road – roast sucking pig and too much Pommard – had read all my fiction and thought highly of it. She had learned English by reading Henry James defiantly during the last days of the German occupation of northern Italy – heavy going for an Italian schoolgirl – and had studied American literature at Mount Holyoke in the United States. She was married to a black Bostonian named blasphemously Ben Johnson, son of a lawyer and translator of Italo Svevo, but was now separated from him. She was living in the East End of London and translating Thomas Pynchon's *V*. She was dark-haired, beautiful, lively, and hated equally the Italian state and the Roman Church. I was powerfully attracted to her, she at least to my work. I had taken possession of the Chiswick house on payment of the deposit and had, with miraculous prescience, stuffed it with gaudy cushions. On these, after our sucking pig, we made love. Then she disappeared from my life, but not for ever.

TWO

In the early spring of 1964 Lynne and I travelled to 24 Glebe Street in Chiswick to assume residence. We travelled on a half-heartedly cleaned up coal truck with two cats in a basket and the dog Haji. I lay in coal dust with Haji on a lead, and he slavered at the great world he had not seen before, while Lynne quietened the cats in the driver's cabin. These cats were the Sandy of *Language Made Plain* and a half-grown kitten named Dorian, whose colour it would be otiose to specify. We had furnished the house with little taste out of a great store in Hammersmith. The previous owner had installed a bar with ingenious concealed lighting, and I blew the coal dust off our three Chinese bar stools and placed them in position. It was early evening, opening time, and there was an off-licence at the end of Glebe Street. I staggered to our new home with a crate of Gordon's gin and a bottle of the bitters manufactured at Ciudad Bolivar on the Orinoco. That would do to start with. Then we went out, greedily rather than thirstily, to sample all the Chiswick pubs, with Haji choking himself on his lead. All along Glebe Street tough tomcats assembled at their garden gates at nightfall, and some of them dealt Haji token paw-thumps as we passed. I was reminded of some of the schools I had visited on teaching practice in Lancashire, where children were thumped by their teachers as they entered: that was for doing nothing; wait till they started doing something.

We had been starved of pub life. Lynne began as she meant to go on, standing no bloody nonsense from publicans, berating them for lack of ice and, in one Irish-run pub, hitting out at a crone who sang 'Ireland was an island when England was a pup, and Ireland will be Ireland when England's buggered up' but conceded later that Lynne had the blue eyes of old Erin. I was reminded that Irish independence was, for many of the Irish, an undelectable fruit. James Joyce's father had grumbled about it, regretting that that scoundrel Lloyd George had given the Irish what they wanted. An expression of Irish wrongs had to continue, preferably on English soil. Many of the Chiswick pubs had Irish landlords and jukeboxes which discoursed loud IRA songs. Irish labourers contended, when not wasting their English tax-free earnings on one-armed bandits, that there was only one bloody writer and that was dead Brendan Behan. They had not, of course, read him or seen his plays. If I contested this view I was liable to be thumped. Lynne became very Welsh in face of the Irish. Our life in London, an abstract civic space imposed upon the fields, as Auden called it, was likely to be more physical than in the country of real things like sheep and turnips. But I demurred at having to take up her quarrels and transfer them to a region of fists.

We had hired a television set, and I was ready for the inauguration of the new BBC channel. But there was a problem here. For the first time in my literary life there was to be a publisher's party to celebrate my new novel, and it was to be held on the evening of BBC-2's first transmissions. The problem was solved, probably by Shakespeare's ghost, with a failure at the Battersea power station and the postponement till the following evening of *Kiss Me Kate*, an inspired choice for the occasion. My own homage to Shakespeare, *Nothing Like the Sun*, did not go down so well. Robert Robinson, well known as a radio and television quizmaster, complained that pedantry dripped from every sentence like sweat from a nose. D. J. Enright related the book to my other work and said that I flayed my characters so savagely that the reader turned against the creator. 'Whom Mr Burgess loves is in for a sticky time.' The *Times Literary Supplement* found the language 'deft' but the syntax too modern, and alleged that the sexual content needed more subtle handling. Elizabeth Jennings said that the novel was vastly inferior to Brigid Brophy's father's *Gentleman of Stratford*, that it made claims that could not be substantiated and was written in a bogus archaic style. It was pretentious because it was not possible to combine novelistic farce with learned research. 'It seems a pity that *Nothing Like the Sun* should be so disappointing.' That statement is, surely, a mistress-piece of pleonasm.

Ah well, I had done my best. It seemed that I was always biting off more than I, or anybody else for that matter, could possibly chew. The opposed summations of the British reviews were that I had chewed too hard and not chewed hard enough. When the American edition came out, *Time* was unkind – 'He loads in the sex scenes but makes his Shakespeare a timid, ineffectual Stratford bumpkin, afraid of impotence and baldness, who could hardly tell an iamb from his two left feet' – but the *New York Times* said: 'Bawdy, extravagant, word-drunk, *Nothing Like the Sun* is a piece of staggering cheek that comes triumphantly off.' A magazine called *Choice* said that the epilogue, 'Shakespeare's dying delirium, is writing of the highest order'. Not quite so, really. I had taught myself the trick of contriving a satisfactory coda by what, in music, is termed aleatory means: I flicked through a dictionary and took whatever words leaped from the page. I did this again at the end of my Napoleon novel: the effect is surrealist, oceanic, and easily achieved. What hurt me most, I think, about the reception of the Shakespeare novel was that nobody seemed to spot the musical references. For example, a barber tells Shakespeare of the massing of troops in Picardy, and the barbershop lutenist accompanies his statement with a final tierce. I was referring to the tierce da Picardie, a major triad at the end of a piece in a minor key.

But musicians, who of course did not review the book, saw that there was something musical going on in it, and I was able to write a long article on Shakespeare and music for the *Musical Times* and to give a talk on the same subject, with musical illustrations, in the BBC's *Music Magazine*. The deafness of a great number of literary critics was being attested again not only by their ignorance of music but by their failure to read my book with their ears. And, when *Language Made Plain* came out, it was left to the linguistic experts to find fault rather than to the literary reviewers to find revelation. I sensed that I had a friend in the great slang lexicographer Eric Partridge, who saw what *Language Made Plain* was trying to do and, assessing the novel in the same article, praised *Nothing Like the Sun* as 'a narrative and an interpretation at once profound and engrossing, torrential in its surging narrative, molten in its emotional impact, magisterial in its employment a style rich, vigorous, and deeply moving: a book that, leaving us stunned and exhausted, also and more importantly leaves us wealthy.' That was more than generous, and I quote blushing. I was learning where my friends were not – not among women reviewers, not among those of the literary who disdained the craft of sound, but not among refugee Austrian musicians either. My audience remained narrow, and it would never make me much money. It was the audience of James Joyce, though not necessarily of Joyce scholars. But *Nothing Like the Sun*, and this pleased me, found favour with actors too: they knew Shakespeare in a way that Shakespeare academics did not, and my portrait of a player with a mad irrelevant talent fixed to his back like Richard's hump, bisexual and unsure of himself, rang some kind of bell backstage. We must all be thankful for what we can get.

The Shakespeare quatercentenary got along nicely without me, except for a couple of lectures I gave to American matrons visiting Stratford. I was concerned with what Shakespeare's plays could tell us about the man's life. Being a writer myself, I knew that the autobiographical is hard to hide, and I guessed that Hamlet's speech over the skulls in the Elsinore graveyard was mostly the poet's own reminiscences – the early days in a Stratford law office, acquaintance with London lords, Dick Tarleton, head of the Queen's Men, as Yorick. The gravediggers' discussion about crowner's quest law clearly, in my view, went back to the suicide by drowning of Kate Hamnett at Stratford in Shakespeare's youth and the wrangle, transferred to Ophelia, about her right of Christian burial. This is not the scholarly way, which is concerned with a text, but I was never a scholar. Drunk, I even thought I saw Shakespeare, a stooping bald commercial traveller, on Stratford station. There were also three Punjabis, one of whom said '*Om peshab munkta*' (I want to piss). I was able to say: '*Ap khuch karab bolta*' (You've said a bad thing). The man's discomfiture appealed to Shakespeare. As for my other discourse, on Shakespeare's spoken English, this, as I have already indicated, did not go down well either in Stratford or in London. The dropped 'g's (as Priestley would have it), the aitchlessness, the Dublin 'ea' in 'sea' and the Lancashire 'o' in 'nothing' were too much in the spirit of *Time*'s 'ineffectual Stratford bumpkin'. To demonstrate that Queen Elizabeth I spoke in that way was *lèse-majesté*. I gave up.

I had my London life to live now, and Lynne had hers: the two conjoined in London pubs, of which there were, and are, a great many. The dog Haji liked pubs, where he could pretend to strangers that he was starved of love at home, and insisted on being taken to them. Left alone in the house he barked loud and long and had the neighbours complaining. In pubs with low tables he knocked over full pints with his tail; everywhere he attempted the rape of ladies, pawed the chests of male strangers, snarled at me when I thumped him. He was a dog not meant for towns, nor for the country either, for there he chased pregnant ewes. At Turnham Green underground station, where the trains ran overground, he was quick to note that the District Line had a stop but the Piccadilly Line none. This meant that District Line trains had a slow take-off, while the Piccadilly Line trains hurtled through. These latter he wished to race, himself at ground level, they on high. He escaped from the back garden by climbing the wall and ran to Turnham Green to do this: it became a manic obsession. The Piccadilly Line trains were the pregnant ewes of the capital. The local police got to know him, and hence me, too well. I was always buying tickets for police concerts.

The literary confrères I was beginning to meet I met alone, or with Lynne, in pubs. I needed to meet writers to whom, as for me, writing was an agony mitigated by drink. These writers were very rarely fellow-novelists, who were mostly depressed by small royalties and had no interest in discussions of literary technique. They were mostly poets who worked in schools or advertising or the BBC and did not relate their art to the earning of a living. There was chiefly Martin Bell, a slave of the Inner London Education Authority by day, a drinker and poet in the evenings. He lived in Chiswick and knew the Chiswick pubs. There was something goliardic about him – shabby, bad-toothed, always with a volume of Empson or Wallace Stevens in his pocket, a genuine alcoholic who had to be dried out at intervals, doomed to die of drink and be posthumously neglected. His collected poems, to which I contributed passages of musical notation for a reason I cannot now remember, are out of print. I cannot find him in the anthologies. Haji would regularly knock him over. To Lynne he should have been a horrid example but she took him as a competitor in the knocking back of double gins. With him it was a great joy to spout words as the alcohol warmed. The digging out from memory of lines from *Volpone* or *The Vanity of Human Wishes* with the twelfth glass is the true literary experience. I mean that. Verse is for learning by heart, and that is what a literary education should mostly consist of. I know the whole of Hopkins by heart, a good deal of Marvell, many of Pound's Cantos and most of Eliot. Also the lyrics of Lorenz Hart and Cole Porter. What is wrong with prose is that it is not learnable by heart and faults of memory in trying to recite it (the opening of *A Tale of Two Cities*, Overton and Dr Skinner in *The Way of All Flesh*, the Moses oratory in *Ulysses*) do not seriously impair its rhythms or even its lexis. I longed to write a new *Don Juan*. Mrs Browning's *Aurora Leigh* was a fine idea, but it should have rhymed. Verse has not necessarily anything to do with poetry. A return to heroic couplets might save British civilisation.

The kind of London life Lynne wanted was one of heavy drinking in company, seasoned by contention. The pubs closed too early for her but, on payment of an annual subscription of five pounds, one could obtain membership of most of London's night clubs. In 1964 I was asked to submit details of my life and achievements to the publishers of *Who's Who*, and under Clubs I wrote: the Neptune, Toby's Gym, the Half-and-Half, Dick's Corner etc. But Clubs meant the Athenaeum and the Reform. Under Hobbies I meant to put wine and life, but these coalesced into wife. It was true enough, except that Lynne was really a full-time occupation.

She had to be dragged back to Etchingham in the summer of 1964 so that I could write a book on James Joyce. Concentration on heavy writing in London was virtually impossible: it was a place for drink, journalism and literary politics. Peter du Sautoy of Faber & Faber had seen and heard my television talk on sex and Joyce and thought I might produce a useful popular introduction to the man and his work. I was dubious about the commission he offered, since I saw that its fulfilment might make it too easy for critics of my own work to see me as a satellite of Joyce, which was not true. No post-Joycean novelist can learn anything from him except a certain eccentric scrupulosity in the handling of language, usually interpreted as clumsiness. His literary experiments were meant for himself alone: he drained all the possibilities of formal ingenuity in two massive novels which are not quite novels. After Joyce the novel in England had to start all over again. The pedagogue in me opposed the novelist soon to be confirmed by my entry as novelist in *Who's Who*.

I planned a book to be entitled *Here Comes Everybody*, one of the fillings out of the initials HCE in *Finnegans Wake*. I wanted to stress Joyce's universality and a potential popularity obscured by the academics of the blossoming Joyce industry. It was not an easy book to write. I should have gone first to Dublin to drink in, all too literally, the Joyce atmosphere. But, despite the family's Dublin connections, I had never been there and I was scared of going. Ireland might drag me back to my Irish origins and particularly the Irish chapter of the Church of Rome. I might weep out my sins and demand to be let back in. A visit to Dublin would impair a hard-won independence. So, in the introduction to the book, I stated that an understanding of Joyce did not entail first the buying of an Aer Lingus ticket in order to vomit in the Liffey. He was universal, not narrowly Irish, and he had affirmed his independence of Ireland by seeking European exile. This was disingenuous.

I became newly Joyce-soaked under the apple trees, escaping briefly to London to see something on BBC-2 which could not be ignored in my *Listener* articles. It was always possible to pretend to have seen something which one had not and write that Mr X's programme on Y showed much ingenuity but not all that much originality. The danger was always that the programme might be cancelled. I knew that in the shady world of cultural journalism there was a lot of trickery going on. One indigent poet I knew sold his review copies as soon as he had received them, making do with the blurb on the dust cover. Film critics sent friends as deputies. Robert Robinson, reviewing television programmes on television, had denounced Perry Mason as a glove-puppet private eye. There were plenty of horrid examples about to force one to keep one's integrity.

I pored over the Joyce texts again while Lynne fretted: she was no Joycean. It was easy enough to explain what was happening in *Ulysses*, both in the separable narrative which had recently been dramatised, even on television, as *Bloomsday*, and in the language and symbolism. *Finnegans Wake*, in which text and raw narrative material are inseparable, drove me frantic. I had known the work ever since the Faber pamphlets *Anna Livia Plurabelle* and *Haveth Childers Everywhere* in the thirties, and I had had the first edition of the completed book in 1939. As the book recounts a dream, and none of us properly understands his dreams, I had been content to find much of *Finnegans Wake* unintelligible, but now I had the task of creating an easy paraphrase for newcomers to Joyce. The root of the book seemed to be the metathetising of 'incest' to 'insect'. Humphrey Chimpden Earwicker, the keeper of a pub in Chapelizod, is ageing, and so is his wife Ann. Though, towards the end of the book, they attempt the sexual act, it is a mere marital duty and a failed one. Earwicker lusts after his daughter, but not even his dreams will admit this: hence the metathesis and the twittering of insect life. Joyce, whose dream encloses that of Earwicker, enables his ignorant publican to extrapolate his sense of guilt on to the whole of history. Izzy, the desired daughter, who is also all temptresses from Eve to Kitty O'Shea, is a split personality whose symbol is an X – lips pouting to kiss a mirror image – and she emerges frighteningly as Joyce's own schizophrenic daughter Lucia. There was a story in the book, and a very disturbing one. It was a fantastic autobiography in disguise and it upset me deeply. What upset me even more was the personal revelation it primed: that my sexual estrangement from Lynne had something at least to do with thwarted paternity. Attacked in the London black-out by four GIs, she had aborted and been forbidden pregnancy thereafter. I wanted a child, preferably a daughter. I did not then know that I had a son, not by her.

I was destined to go to Dublin and work for Joyce on his own territory. Christopher Burstall, to whom I was to dedicate *Here Comes Everybody*, had fought with Huw Wheldon, head of BBC television arts programmes, about the making of a sixty-minute study of Joyce – the first visual one ever – and had won. In February 1965 I flew with him to Dublin, along with a technical team (the generator truck went by sea). Lynne was left behind in Chiswick.

Interested in determining the nature of my sexuality, she had made friends with a pair of bonded homosexuals and introduced them into my company to see what my reaction might be. They seemed lively enough boys, given to fantasy, who preferred to bicker before an audience. They were only too ready to stay with her, usurping her double bed, severally seeking her support in their nightly quarrels. So I was granted a fortnight's leave of absence.

Burstall and I and his production assistant put up in the Dolphin, where Yeats had held his celebratory dinner after receiving the Nobel Prize. It was already decaying fast, with morning ice appearing in cracks in the bedroom ceiling. It was a cold February but an unnaturally dry one. The technicians scorned the dying Dolphin and chose a bijou novelty on the outskirts, complete with vestibular muzak. And so, scriptless, we began to improvise a film to be entitled *Silence, Exile and Cunning*.

I had two themes, both of which might yield to visualisation. One was that Stephen Dedalus, who called on his artificer father, inventor of flight, had to be Icarus, the flyer who flew too near the sun and fell into the sea when the wax of his wings melted. The image of the falling boy merged with that of the falling Lucifer who, like Stephen, had cried '*Non serviam*'. In other words, Joyce's art entailed a kind of self-damnation. The other theme was simpler and perhaps facetious, though facetiousness in Joyce is raised, or lowered, to a level of profundity. Stephen Dedalus, or Joyce, rejects Mother Church to embrace the ideal of fatherhood as represented by a half-Jew of Hungarian extraction, Leopold Bloom. Bloom lives in Eccles Street, pronounced Eck-lez, and this takes over from *ecclesia*. A priest in the church on Gardiner Street was very willing to vest himself fully and recite the Latin credo at the altar while the camera rolled: '. . . *et in unam sanctam et apostolicam ecclesiam.*' Cut to ECCLES ST. Number 7, Bloom's Ithaca, was being demolished to make way for office blocks, but the destroyers were persuaded to hold off for a day while we filmed in what would have been the Blooms' bedroom. Much speech was slurred by the need to down much whisky in freezing pubs. Some of my monologues were unacceptable in London. They had to be redone as voice over.

What I had feared might happen happened. The heavy whisky intake induced sentimentality and remorse. I sat late in the Dolphin lobby with a porter who kept saying 'Dhere dhere, fella' to my helpless howlings, 'we've all been trough it in our toime,' and then: 'Is dhere anytin I kin get ya at all?' I asked for milk, very cold. 'It's a funny ting ya should ax for dhat, for dhere's divil a dhrop in the whole place. If ya'd axed yesterday or the day before, sure dhere'd have been gallons of dhe bloody stuff, and dhe same if ya was to ax tomorra.' I was in a very bad way. The hound of heaven was not just snuffling: he was baring his fangs. Stephen in the first section of *Ulysses* is prepared to take his morning tea without milk, thus rejecting all his mothers. The night porter at the Dolphin was an agent of my continuing apostasy. On the other hand, milk might have sobered me up. We must never take symbolism too far.

Anyway, Dublin disturbed me. It was ancestral ground and also holy. There was no whiff of sexual sin in it under the smell of roasting hops and peat. The sins were venial and were mostly drunkenness and calumny. As Joyce had demonstrated in his story 'The Dead', in Ireland there were no true divisions between dead and living, mythical and real. An old Dublin woman swore that the Blooms lived on Capel Street. In Glasnevin cemetery I met Dominic Behan, glassy-eyed and looking for his dead brother Brendan so he could piss on the fucker. The categories of logic did not apply, despite Catholicised Aristotle. The servant in the Cork hotel who brought a telegram to a man's room and was asked to shove it under the door replied that he couldn't because it was on a tray. That makes sense: he saw the tray and the telegram on it as a single entity. Freudians say that the Irish are the only race impervious to psychoanalysis. Dreams is it you're wanting now? Sure, I can tell you some lovely ones.

There is also lying, as in holy Russia. I appeared on a television programme called *The Late Late Show*, held at eight in the evening and conducted with one busy camera. The theme was obscenity in literature and the main target of abuse Edna O'Brien – 'Sure if she was my daughter I'd have her over me knee' – but a government official praised Ireland as a land of free speech in which state censorship had no place. In the following morning's newspapers he was violent about the need to keep Ireland pure by banning Edna O'Brien and her like. As for James Joyce – when the programme was over a participant said earnestly to me: 'Have you read the bloody man at all? It's all fucking filth and obscenity.' This tied up with the old lady who said to Lady Gregory after the *Playboy of the Western World* riot: 'Sure, and isn't Mr Synge a bloody old snot for using a word like "shift"?'

Dear Dublin. She was not to be despised. Her literary men, living, dead, or dying, like Brian O'Nolan or Flann O'Brien or Miles of the Little Horse, drunk but upright in the Bailey, attested the virtues of the continuing Catholic tradition. St Thomas Aquinas had been diminished into matter for pub citation, but at least he had been read. Literature was speech and a bard was a drunken reciter. I imagined myself moving over to a damp house in Sandymount or Ringsend and trying to write a novel. I would start the grey day hung over and trembling and staggering to the just open pub for a ball of malt ('and I'll trouble you for a glass of fresh water') to cut the phlegm. 'What are ye writin dhen?' And then I would, with babbling nerves, give out the whole jimbang lot and find it unnecessary to write it down.

Dublin, turning literature into sound, turned it also to stone and water. I delivered lines to the camera outside the Martello tower in Sandycove and followed Stephen Dedalus's protean ramble over the sand. Joyce had been right to wish to get away from it all and turn the solidity into a text. Textuality equalled reality. Chapelizod was all too real a place, and Earwicker's pub – called the Dead Man because drinkers tumbled out at closing time to be run over by the trams – was still standing. This was not at all right. Transubstantiation was needed. You turned flesh and blood into a printed wafer. The Eucharist was a sane sacrament rejected by the insane. Sane as a doctrine of art as well as the invention of a religious genius. The sooner I got out of Dublin the better.

When I returned to Chiswick, I found that the hound of heaven had pursued me over the airways. I gave Lynne a toy Wicklow donkey and then confided that I was going back to the Church but was also scared of going back to the Church. Going back to the Church I would have to return to accepting the doctrine of everlasting punishment, which I did not want to do. I wanted to be like ordinary people who did not give a damn about the next world. Then I wept, Haji growled, the two cats stared at me from the outside windowsill. Lynne was very brutal about my confusion and threatened me with Bishop George Dwyer or, easier, with whatever Maynooth priest presided at the local church with its Italianate campanile. Her blue eyes were more *sa-rupa pisau* than ever. She telephoned the presbytery to find out the times of confession. But I would not go to confession. 'Make up your bloody mind,' she cried, but I could not. All I could do was to put Haji on his lead and have him tug me and her on a round of the Chiswick pubs. That helped.

What also helped was the transmission of the film that had been drunkenly made in Dublin. The craft of cutting, the addition of sound effects, the conversion of my talking self (often in back view to accommodate the sober dubbing) into a mere image on the small screen transubstantiated the reality into a kind of art. What could have been the most frightening scene of all was of myself ashen in a church pew while T. P. McKenna's voice spoke, in artful echo, of the pains of hell. But it had become television drama, no more, and I was only an actor in it, nursing a BBC cheque in my pocket. Still, the film evidently had the power to move others to tears and breast-thumping. I received letters from strangers who, long out of the Church, had been impelled by the gravity of my face and diction, to say nothing of the sermon on hell, to consider going scampering back. But the intention of the film had been otherwise: it had been merely to relate the art of a Dubliner to the city that begot him.

The film still exists. I resaw it midway through this account of the making of it. Those of us who are mere writers, not film actors, have the ghastly opportunity, thanks to the videocassette, of seeing how we once were. Photographs are not the same: we are defined by our shrugs and nose-scratchings and stutters. In the Joyce film I seem to combine the cattle broker and the bishop. The speech is certainly episcopal and has the deliberateness of the drunken farmer on market day. I am bulky and dark-haired and very serious, solemn indeed like a bloody owl. The black and white seem to antedate the film to the era of the Russian Revolution: BC for before colour is an acceptable designation. Myself apart, it is a good film and reflects that it was possible for the BBC to expend time, money and skill on its productions before the politicians grew scared of raising the licence fee. It is even, in its small way, a classic. The voice over of the Dublin actress as Molly Bloom in the ravaged icy bedroom is very moving, as is Sean Mac Reamoinn's Bloomian monologue about the decay of the cityscape. The film has been the rounds of the American colleges. It has led young people to Joyce. It was worth spending that drunken remorseful fortnight in Dublin.

A SITUATION had arisen in the literary world that could only be called Shakespearean. Shakespeare was an actor who could, presumably, be seen most afternoons on stage on the Bankside; he was also a writer. We writers of the deutero-Elizabethan age were now becoming actors of a kind: at least we were appearing on television and being greeted in the street as known faces. This did not noticeably enhance the sale of our books. Literature and its prac-titioners were feeding the great demotic medium, or at least that cultural annexe of it which paid a sort of lip-service to the old Reithian dream of broadcasting as public enlightenment. The BBC's first television channel enlightened, but it had to compete with the commercial channel, which enlightened as little as it could. The new channel, BBC-2, tried to enlighten most of the time, and the Joyce film of early 1965 was a kind of attempt at enlightenment. BBC-2, defining superior entertainment as enlightenment, had already presented two superior novels – Ford Madox Ford's *Parade's End* and Evelyn Waugh's *Sword of Honour* – as television serials, and these proleptically opposed the televisualisation of John Galsworthy's *Forsyte Saga* on BBC-1. Galsworthy was not superior entertainment, and he attracted a large audience: on the Sunday evenings when he was presented, ministers of the various churches had to change the times of their services. Paperback reissues of *The Forsyte Saga* placed it in an ancillary situation – a verbal adjunct to a visual experience regarded as primary. Ford Madox Ford, on the other hand, did not become a pocket bestseller. The audience for BBC-2 was small, though television was teaching us all to reorientate our notions of quantity. A million was small compared to nine million, but those writers who, like myself, sold a few thousand copies of our books, saw it as astronomical.

If one kind of enlightenment was the adaptation of a difficult book to the black and white screen, another was the reduction of literature to a gàme. It was assumed, perhaps rightly, that those who wrote books also read them, and writers were drawn, for a fee of a hundred pounds, into a Sunday performance called *Take It or Leave It*. Four writers were made to look respectable by the make-up department (Lynne would touch up my grey with a very temporary dye) and placed on a platform with Robert Robinson as quizmaster. Two actors would read out in turn from works of literature and the writers were asked to identify them. The game was not competitive. The right answer was flashed on the viewer's screen, though not the participants' monitor, and the viewer had the superior pleasure of knowing who wrote what while his literary betters stumbled. John Betjeman regularly said: 'Surely that's Thackeray' while the viewer's screen said Edgar Wallace or John Dryden. What might be called the cream of the British littérateurs of the sixties paraded in changeable fours, all eager for a hundred pounds (Cyril Connolly said that the title of the programme ought to be *Money for Jam*) – Lord David Cecil, Angus Wilson, Kingsley Amis, Philip Toynbee, V. S. Pritchett, Elizabeth Jane Howard, Bernard Levin, John Gross. It was considered only decent to allow an occasional publisher in, but Anthony Blond, identifying a passage as from *Scouting for Boys* by Lord Baden-Powell, added gratuitously that there was a statue erected to that hero of Mafeking in West Germany, with the inscription *Der Grosse Britische Homosexuell*. This had to be cut.

It was mere play, suitable for the pleasure-loving sixties, but it had its useful resonances. Unable to identify a passage from *Diary of a Nobody*, I said, 'Oh, it's probably from *Augustus Carp Esquire*.' The session was held up while both Amis and Robinson exclaimed that now three people knew the book. This got the comic masterpiece back into print after forty years of neglect. Unneglected writers were, on an ear test, found to be negligible. Mary McCarthy, the sole American, failed with John Gross to recognise a passage from Saul Bellow's *Herzog*, though they had been together on a jury that gave the novel an international award. Christopher Fry was thought paltry, except by the Poet Laureate. Once there were two stutterers on the same panel. There were no drunks. Despite the regular fee, I was uneasy. We were debasing literature into a parlour game available to millions. We were yielding to the temptation of public display. Was it proper for us to show our ignorance so nakedly?

But there was one television game which was based on the complacent acceptance of ignorance by the ignorant, so long as it was the higher ignorance. A team of actors, all charm and fine timing, confronted a stutter of writers. A word it was presumed nobody would know, usually technical or archaic, was flashed, and a choice had to be made from two false definitions and one genuine. When I was on the programme I was given the word 'trank'. I got it right – the piece of leather from which gloves are cut – but admitted foolishly that I knew the word already: it had come out of my research for *Nothing Like the Sun*. This caused embarrassment: I was not supposed to know. In the hospitality room afterwards I was avoided, except by the producer, who said that it was a bad show, meaning my contribution. I was never asked again.

Living as I did, for most of the year, in Chiswick, I was near enough to the Wood Lane Television Centre to be called on in emergencies – to improvise an obituary on Somerset Maugham or Evelyn Waugh, to fill in a gap on the open-ended show called *Late Night Line-Up*. It was this programme which went out in the first live colour transmission. Angus Wilson was on it with me, and his companion called: 'Angus, your silvery hair looks *lovely* on the monitor.' Angus beamed, saying: 'Yes, I washed it last night.' These odd jobs were a means of learning about the gap between unsyndicalised freelancers like myself and the heavily unionised technicians. Obituarising on Waugh, I was put off by an assistant lights man yawning while reading the *Daily Mirror*. He could not be rebuked without danger. In another BBC-2 programme I was delivering my lines from near a table which the studio manager wished to be moved. Helpfully I moved it myself, only to hear the whistle blow. I had to apologise to avoid a strike.

The temptations of television appearances, which were easier than writing, were among the factors that were to drive me from Britain. In 1959–60 I had written a lot of books; now I was writing none. I was also too willingly putting myself into a position of literary inferiority by interviewing other writers on radio – Paul Scott, Arthur Koestler – or joining in symposia which made much of Ian Fleming. The lure of the easy cheque for the casual job was putting a trickle of cash in the bank but blurring my sense of vocation. I was a complaisant hack, ready to review anything for anybody. I would appraise a book on stable management for *Country Life*, adding snobbish fictions like 'When my father sold the old place . . .' and talking of my rural estate (the semi-detached in Etchingham) and my town house (the Chiswick hovel). I maintained critical integrity, however, although it was not likely to impress *Country Life* readers. Kenneth Young, my former editor at the *Yorkshire Post*, produced a book on the Balfour Declaration which I found superb and said so. He wrote a letter expressing surprise at my 'magnanimity'. I was not being magnanimous: the ability to write a good book does not necessarily have anything to do with its author's morality.

In 1965 I found myself in black tie and dinner jacket almost every evening, for I was now drama critic for the *Spectator* and concert and opera critic for *Queen*. It was hard to reconcile these two posts one with the other and both with the writing of television reviews for the *Listener*. I felt the eyes of more conscientious critics on me when I went to the theatre bar during the first interval. Would I come back? Often I did not. When the possibility of my becoming food and wine critic for another magazine was being dangled I took fright. Enough was enough already. Goethe said that we must beware of wishing for anything in youth because we would get it in middle age. I had wished for journalistic work as a subvention of serious fiction. But now there was no time for serious fiction. One day a parcel arrived from Messrs Heinemann, and I said: 'Ah, the proofs of my new novel.' But I had written no new novel.

I was determined to write one in the summer of 1965 and also consider the compilation of a dictionary of current slang for Penguin Books. Eric Partridge had invited me, over lunch at the Savile Club, to cannibalise his own great dictionary to the limit, but I feared that I was not really a lexicographer. The lexicographer's work is never done. He has more correspondence than the novelist, for people will go mad about words while ignoring literature. New words are born every day. New ingenuities of etymology from country vicarages and old people's homes have to be rejected with courtesy. Still, I was tempted. The lexical bulk of any dictionary is to be found under 'S', but the true linguist thinks of 'S' as accommodating two different phonemes – the 's' of 'sit' and the 'sh' of 'shot' – while the 'B' entries – initialising unequivocally with the 'b' phoneme – present the true superlative of weight. If I could get through 'B' without too much groaning I would take on the whole task. But I warned my agent not to take an advance.

This agent was not the one James Michie had recommended all of five years back. Peter Janson-Smith, busy with Gavin Maxwell's otters, Parkinson's Law, and James Bond, handed me over silently to his new associate Deborah Rogers. She had trained with the highly professional agency of Lynn Nesbit in New York. It was not long before I suggested that she start up in business for herself, and I became her first client. Deborah Rogers was a young woman of good family and considerable blonde beauty with wide literary connections. Beauty is no disadvantage in any profession, but in business it can, especially to susceptible artists, be a disturbing impertinence. Deborah, being beautiful, could do no wrong. Despite my doubts, she took the Penguin advance. Having slaved over the dictionary for a month in summer Etchingham, I found the pushing on with the task impossible. I expressed regret, made Penguin Books a gift of 'B' (completed except for 'bovver boots', which had just come into the slang of the violent young) and returned the advance, but I still had to pay the agential ten per cent.

There is more waste and frustration in the professional writer's life than the mere reading public can know about. Commissions are sometimes accepted and then found impossible of fulfilment. I have known writers who have worked hard on the documentation of a life of Lloyd George or Marie Antoinette and even completed several hundred pages of a first draft, only to find that the machine will no longer go – a lack of temperamental fuel, an inability to steer, a sudden shocking boredom with the whole journey. One is not paid for work wasted, though one's literary agent may be. It is right to return an advance to the commissioning publisher, but it is dangerous to accept the advance in the first place. It feels like money earned because time and energy have been expended. But work is not necessarily a work. Appalled at waste, a writer will sometimes push on hopelessly to complete a book that he needs no reviewer to tell him is abysmally bad. The need to earn generates guilt, and guilt is partially dissolved in alcohol: that is where a good deal of the unearned advance tends to go.

I needed to write a new novel, and I had ideas for it, but, as Mallarmé said of poetry, fiction is not made out of ideas. If poems are made out of words, novels are made out of people, and freshly invented people refused to walk in my head. Instead of writing I painted. Painting, like musical composition or playing patience, is mindless: it asks for an ocular skill, not a cerebral one. With eye and hand busy, the brain, unpressed, might beget characters and give the characters something to do. I had started drawing again, studying anatomy and perspective, and I proposed to Peter Dawnay of Sidgwick and Jackson that it might be a good plan to revive the illustrated novel. Sidgwick and Jackson, at that time, had a very poor contemporary list, relying for income mostly on Rupert Brooke and Lyall's *Languages of Europe*. It was agreed that they should publish my first two pieces of fiction, long gathering dust – *A Vision of Battlements* and *The Eve of Saint Venus*, both with drawings by myself. But my drawings were not good enough, and the task of illustration was left to the young Edward Pegram. *The Eve of Saint Venus* was reviewed kindly enough, and Sidgwick and Jackson gave a celebratory party at the Café Royal. Here I met Peter Dawnay's father, equerry to the Queen Mother. He told me that he had asked Her Majesty, when with her in the Royal Enclosure at Ascot, if he might borrow her binoculars. She graciously acceded and then, leaning towards him confidentially, added: 'They bring things closer, you know.' The party, a very lavish one, signalled Sidgwick and Jackson's renaissance as publishers of distinguished fiction. It also fired Peter Dawnay's conviction that he was skilled at spotting talent and led to his founding his own publishing house. I joined him as a director. In a year we were finished.

I was painting, then. There was a certain infantile pleasure in oozing oil paints on to the palette and then on to the stretched canvas, but I wanted to paint like Giorgione, not like Picasso. You could not, I believed, plunge straight into modernity: you had to have the agonies of mastering traditional techniques first. In the same way I believed that you had to be able to write strict classical fugues before being Schoenbergian, and Schoenberg would have agreed with me. Film composers in Hollywood flocked to the exiled Schoenberg, hoping to pick up startling devices of *appliqué* modernism, but Schoenberg had them working at four-part harmony. I painted imaginary portraits, highly academic, fagging on, like Fra Lippo

Lippi, at flesh. One morning, hung over, my brush-hand trembled as it approached the canvas. 'That,' Lynne said, 'is tremor of intent.'

Well, there at least was a title. The clinical term for the shaking hand of the alcoholic as it reaches out to pick up a bottle or glass is properly intentional tremor, but *Tremor of Intent* would do well enough. The title at once begot images – the shaking of the assassin's finger on the trigger, a shiver of doubt before a sexual encounter. The male face I had painted was of no one I knew, but the inexpert colour of it suggested stage make-up, disguise. There was what Ian Fleming called a comma of dark hair on the brow. James Bond and not James Bond, a spy story but something more. The title soon began to seem irrelevant. Foreign publishers have never been happy with it. Though Germany was to call the finished book *Tremor*, the Danes preferred *Martyrenes Blod* and the French *Un Agent Qui Vous Veut du Bien*. Books are merely christened, and baptismal names mean nothing.

The novel had various roots. Lynne had suggested to me the theme of a man brainwashed into a belief in Marxism through the sexual allure of a Russian woman. What came out of that was a man married to a German girl who uses sex to inflame him with a sense of national guilt, a conviction that England is the twentieth-century enemy of the utopian ideal embodied in totalitarianism. The name of the man, a scientist who defects to the Russians, is Roper, taken from St Thomas More's son-in-law. He is Catholic, which makes him an imperfect English patriot, and he is led to believe that he has an Elizabethan Catholic martyr in his family. He is, apart from his scientific attainments, unintelligent, and he is easily filled with a total resentment of England, historico-religious as well as political. He has to be dragged out of Soviet Russia by an intelligence agent named Hillier, or so Hillier's instructions say. Actually both are to be murdered on Crimean soil by a different kind of agent – a neutral assassin employed by an organisation called Panleth, that is ready, for money, to send anybody to Lethe. Hillier is to be killed on the instructions of MI6, which has received notification of his impending retirement and is disturbed at the prospect of his selling secret information. Roper is to be murdered because he knows too much about the private life of a British statesman. I called the novel an eschatological spy story, meaning that it tried to present the Cold War between Russia and the West as a figure of an ultimate conflict – between X and Y or *yin* and *yang* – which paradoxically sustained a universe which was really a duoverse. In other words, hostile symbiosis.

On one level, it was meant to be a parody of the popular espionage novel. This seemed to be as much the fictional genre of the age as the tragedy of blood had been the dramatic genre of the Elizabethans. Fleming's fantasies could be taken with minimal seriousness as modern fairy stories – ogres were killed with courage and ingenuity – but John le Carré had come along with his rather heavy-footed studies of the true espionage situation, books written without humour or fantasy though said to be reliable in matters of intelligence procedure. I tried to suggest in *Tremor of Intent* that the whole spy business was ludic, that it unconsciously dramatised an ultimate cosmic war which could never be resolved, but that it ineptly parodied that war by failing to define good and evil in theological terms. The West was good and the Soviet system evil, but, as John le Carré had the insight to intimate, the moral division was not so simple. It disturbed me, and still does, that Britain's major contribution to the sub-literature of the time should be in a genre that reflected nothing of the reality of Britain's position in the world of the Cold War. James Bond, a more sophisticated Richard Hannay, belonged to the time of imperial power. The contemporaries who spoke mythically for British intelligence were all defectors – men like Philby, Maclean and my namesake.

In my novel I blew up James Bond's wenching and eating into two chapters of gastronomic and erotic extravagance. Dwye Evans, the chairman of Heinemann, said that if these two chapters were excised I might have a rattling good yarn. But I did not want a rattling good yarn: I was trying to be both serious and comic at the same time, exploding the pretensions of the popular genre while making it serve a metaphysical end. My retired spy Hillier ends up as a priest living in neutral Dublin (where the swastika is the trademark of a laundry), ready to engage the real or eschatological enemy. This conclusion was not greatly liked: like knowing the meaning of 'trank' in that television word show, it was not quite playing the game. Regular reviewers of spy fiction were confused by the book; such theologically-minded critics as got hold of it found its implied morality distasteful. I was saying in effect that there was as much nobility in a commitment to evil as to the other shop, and that only the neutrals had to be destroyed. This seemed to some to tie up with *A Clockwork Orange*.

Lynne, having created a wardrobe for my chief female character, vomited blood again, far more than in that Seville toilet. She vomited so much blood that she had to be removed to hospital for a transfusion. With totally culpable unwillingness to face the truth, I diagnosed an ulcer while the doctors said nothing. I should have read my medical dictionary and discovered that this was a portal haemorrhage and a signal that she did not have long to live. She must, in the late spring of 1965, have divined some kind of doom, for she insisted on our paying a visit to South Wales 'for' she said, 'the last time'. We were not to go to Bedwellty, scene of her schoolgirl triumphs, but to Abergavenny. Near Abergavenny was the village of Gilwern, where her uncle and aunt, William and Gwenllian Powell, both now dead, had kept a pub. She was devoted to the memory of the Powells and, when in Malaya I had been looking for a pseudonym under which to publish *Time for a Tiger*, she had suggested Anthony Powell. I had to tell her that there was already a distinguished novelist of that name, so she compromised with Anthony Gilwern. Roland Gant at Heinemann made the simpler decision of using my two middle names, and Anthony Burgess was his creation. As for Gilwern, we did not go to it. We drank heavily in Abergavenny, since there was nothing else to do except make love in a Trust House bed. We made love, though not successfully. I could take no pleasure in a body that had once been as sweet as cinnamon but was now being wrecked through drink. There is an all too palpable male signal of lack of desire which cannot be dissembled. Surrounded in Abergavenny by Welsh voices like her own, she wept for what she had been. She was only forty-five but she recognised her physical decay. She blamed it on going to Malaya, though not on learning to drink deep in Malaya. And then she drank deep in Abergavenny and became fierce-eyed and lively, ready for argument, anecdote, fist-fights. She was, God help her, never dull.

I was at that time writing an occasional 'London Letter' for the *Hudson Review*. The one I wrote from Etchingham in the late summer of 1965 described myself alone with Haji and the two cats, heavily drinking iced gin and eating hard-boiled eggs peeled over the kitchen sink. I was pressing on with my novel in order to earn a small advance and royalties that reflected the publisher's regret that it was not a rattling good yarn. The shorn sheep announced their condition – baaaare – while Haji howled to be allowed to round them or savage them, he was not sure which. The young cat Dorian was savaged by a water rat and limped home with a torn mask the vet had to repair. He lay, sorry for himself, on my lap while I typed *Tremor of Intent*. The elder cat Sandy slept by the typewriter, resisting the movement of the carriage. Out on the lawn the guinea pigs in their bottomless cage chewed busily at the grass. I was falling in love with my young heroine Clara and vicariously trying to savage her. This damnable

sex, as my old headmaster, transplanted into the book, had used to
say. I was forty-eight, and the youth of England were claiming sex
for themselves. In a King's Road pub I had seen a teenager in a topless
dress. Such erotic displays, designed perhaps to make the ageing
groan, had no effect on young males, who were now narcissistic and
dressing in Crimean army uniforms with medals for valour. I saw on
the lawn a full-grown cuckoo bullying its robin fosterparent to be
quicker with the worms.

Lynne came out of hospital with thinner limbs and a dramatically
swollen belly. She was subdued: I divined that someone had spoken
to her sternly. Conversation on both our sides was evasive: there
were two taboo topics – the way she looked, the way she drank.
There was defiance in the manner of her pouring the first gin of the
day. She asked for a lot of ice, perhaps an unconscious desire for a
haemostat. From then on one of my duties was to keep the ice bowl
filled. She began the day with iced water, to which she developed the
routine of adding gin as a mere seasoning. It was like adding milk to
tea. One then drinks tea, not milk. She drank iced water, not gin. It
was a kind of semantic trickery. Our local doctor either refused to
divulge that the dropsical swelling was ascites or else did not know.
He gave her diuretic tablets. For my claudication, while his hand
was in, he prescribed what proved to be a totally irrelevant medicine,
though it cost the National Health Service dear. Lynne collapsed
again, but this time there was no haemorrhage. A hepatic specialist
was brought from Hastings. He spoke brutally to me: 'Tell her if she
takes another drink she will die.' When she recovered I said: 'If you
take another drink you will die.' She asked for iced water and sauced
it with gin. *Liberum arbitrium*. We are all free. She would die of
theology.

We went back to London in a hired car, the cats in their basket,
Haji surrounded by many copies of *The Times*, collected against this
journey, for he was regularly and lavishly car-sick. Lynne settled to a
dull routine she was to maintain to the end of her life, which was still
more than two years away. She came down dressed in slacks and a
ponyskin jerkin to iced water, the *Daily Mirror*, and a rocking chair. I
did the shopping in limping agony (old men would cry across the
street: 'You all right, mate?') and had to queue in a Viennese
Feinbäckerei for cream cakes. Lynne, who had never had a sweet
tooth, was now avid for these: some obscure change was proceeding
in her metabolism. I did the kitchen work and she cooked. I changed
the bed linen and made out the laundry lists. I paid the bills. In the
evening we played Scrabble in Malay or did the *Times* crossword

together, and I watched the television programmes I had to review. Taking another drink and dying meant going to the Chiswick pubs. With her gin-sauced iced water she felt virtuous. It was I who got drunk now, though to a creative end.

Peter du Sautoy at Faber & Faber commissioned me to edit Joyce's *Finnegans Wake* into a beginner's version. This meant scissoring the whole big work down to about two hundred pages of print and adding a linking commentary as well as a long explanatory preface. I could tackle the mad work of cutting only when reeling under Irish whiskey. It was not a task for the sober. The professional Joyce scholars had apparently balked at it, so it was left to a foolish amateur Joycean to attempt the impossible and give those scholars a chance to gloat over his ineptitude. There was not much money in the assignment – a fraction of a fraction of the royalties that went to the Joyce estate – but undertaking it was a homage to an author to whom posthumously, or so I was beginning to suspect, too much homage was being paid. He must, as the homage grows absurd, be grinning in purgatory. The Joyce industry was becoming dangerous, dangerous because techniques of textual nit-picking were being applied to him which, if attached to neglected authors like H. G. Wells or popular authors like John le Carré, might open up similar vistas of symbolism and make literature collapse altogether. Finding new subtleties in *Ulysses* was proving, in America at least, a path to academic promotion. Both *Ulysses* and *Finnegans Wake* were ceasing to be fiction and turning into mystical codices. My *A Shorter Finnegans Wake* attempted to cut to the narrative bone and show that there was a story there about an ageing father's sexual fixation on his daughter. The academics were not pleased.

One of the problems in fashioning this version was crudely physical. The 1939 first edition had been printed with great pain, and in subsequent editions errors had been corrected with approximate exactitude. The text could not well be disturbed: it slept on the bed of the page and was not permitted to move even a finger. The pages had to be renumbered for my truncation, but the position of any passage had to stay where it was in the complete version, and the blanks had to be filled with just enough commentary to accommodate the space. Expansion and contraction of my own text followed physical exigencies, not hermeneutic need. Once disturb the original text and Joyce's words might dissolve to more of a pudding than they already were. The printers were apprehensive, but they were sharp-eyed. Joyce has a verbal invention exactly one hundred letters long to symbolise thunder – a thundred-letter word, I called it. The structure appears ten times, though each time with a different lexical content. The counting printers discovered that there were one hundred and one letters in the tenth grumbling peal and wondered if there had been an initial printing error in 1939. But of course Joyce was up to his old symbolic tricks: the total number of thunder letters is one thousand and one, which relates Earwicker's dream to the *Arabian Nights*.

A DEAD Irishman was dominating my attention, and not for the last time. A living one wrote to me about my work. This was George Dwyer, Bishop of Leeds, who had read *Nothing Like the Sun* closely enough to descry chunks of disguised verse in its prose.

> Out of the urgent coupling,
> The stave, the chordee of summer morning,
> The melting of the island of winter heat,
> He came, crowned with more than was asked for.
> Only from them, the makers, was hidden the
> Enormous pulse of the engines, whose
> Switch they touched by an alien curse
> Concealed in the fever of rose or apple or mirror.
> One would ask only a candle, whose doomed flicker
> Is grateful enough; but that other gift embarrassed –
> Fire that could not be handled or tamed to
> Humble sufficient processes. With that passage
> From intolerable heat to water is remembered
> The ocean in runnels, the ocean in the corn,
> In the fruit-skin's pressure, and death becomes
> The desirable crown of the foul river.
> But instead it was fire that was found,
> Ironically bestowed, lurking in the comfort of light.
> The fuse of water sooner or later leads
> To the ghastly miracle implosion which
> Would not blast its frailest tabernacle.
> When the warning bell announced to the crouched hearers
> The water suffused by fire, there could be no escape,
> Nor could the burden be purged in news
> Casting no shiver over dawn sleep. Oneself
> Was the storm's centre, the heart of the giant flower.
> The smallest room he could rent, though with only

A single friendly door fronting the
Light and music of traffic or carnival,
Would at length – when the picture was burned,
The mirror with its dream panorama destroyed –
Still in an atomy of dust open
The desert and the howl of the time wind . . .

There is a good deal more of this, and it is very Catholic. It was originally a pseudo-poetic meditation fathered on the hero of *The Worm and the Ring*, that now banned novel, in which he muses on the wrong he has done his son by begetting him. For procreation means the bringing of a soul into the world, and that soul must face the possibility of damnation. I transferred the meditation to William Shakespeare, for whom it becomes an interior monologue when he is riding from London to Stratford, having heard that his son Hamnet is sick and probably dying. Dying, even at the age of eleven, the possibility of eternal damnation has to be with him, God being what he is. If it is better not to have been born, it is also better not to beget, especially when the process of begetting is an irrelevant ecstasy: the switch of huge malevolent engines is touched in the pleasure of coupling.

George Dwyer saw what the meditation was about. He saw a lot of things. He was a television hero in Robertsbridge, where Lynne and I had so often gone for our noontime boozing. For the medial lord of Robertsbridge was Malcolm Muggeridge, who had been an atheist before being subjected to George's apologetics on the small screen. George had, with genial Manchester Irish bluffness, shown Muggeridge a light he had at first winked at. But now he was flooded with it and slowly proceeding towards Catholic conversion. It was probably not this that led George to his translation as Archbishop of Birmingham, but that kind of exposure did no harm. Anyway, in a postscript to his letter about the Shakespeare novel, he announced that he was to be so elevated and I was cordially invited, along with Lynne, to the ceremony and the sacred booze-up afterwards.

Lynne would not or could not go, but she insisted that I attend and that I take with me one of her two homosexual friends, those who, singly or jointly, had failed to excite me but had protected her from night terrors on my Dublin trip. This friend worked in a bookshop and could get time off. He was jumping at the prospect of seeing an archbishop fully vested, for he was one of those homosexuals who loved the pomp of even the Anglican Church and was himself saving up to buy the accoutrements of an autocephalic archbishop, which apparently anyone could become. It was the high camp aspect of his deviation. I stayed the night with him and his companion, so that we could take an early train together, and Lynne brought in as night protectress the wife of the local greengrocer. The companion, who was lower on the social scale than his lover and hissed irritably a good deal, served a very elaborate dinner while we listened to records popular with homosexuals. These were mostly of patriotic airs sung without satire by, photographed floridly on the sleeve, a man got up as Dame Clara Butt; the encomium at the back of the sleeve referred to him as 'sir', using the honorific as a pronoun. Then my two hosts went to bed with a teddy bear and I dossed or tossed on the sofa.

In Birmingham I perceived that I was announcing a putative homosexuality to the Catholic world: this may have been Lynne's subtle intention. It was no longer a crime to be homosexual, but it was certainly a sin. My, or Lynne's, friend, fair and willowy and, incidentally, dressed in a kilt of a clan not his, was practically provoked to orgasm by the blaze of vestments in the Pugin church that pretended to be a cathedral. All my surviving Manchester step-relatives were there, shocked. While we sang 'Soul of my Saviour', the Maynooth man next to me said: 'Fella, dat boyfriend of yours dere is singing de wrong words.' At the massive reception after the ceremony, Archbishop Dwyer, now very fat (it was well known that he had kept a good table in his Leeds palace), announced that he would leave his bones in Birmingham, if anybody could find them. Then the drink flowed, the nuns genteelly tippled, and the younger priests attempted doubtful songs and grew glassy-eyed. My, or Lynne's, friend would have proposed his instant conversion to the camp and boozy faith if only he had not committed himself previously to becoming an autocephalic archbishop. I prevented him from throwing his arms round George Dwyer as a potential brother in elevation and got him on to the train. I left behind a riotous party with plenty to talk about.

I proposed some day to write a novel from the viewpoint of a homosexual and achieved this in 1980. Apparently the impersonation worked, for the book found its way to the shelves of Gay Lit in American bookstores. Lynne could believe what she wished, but I have always been afflicted with a powerful but banal heterosexual drive, unmodified by the sight of Greek or African boys lying naked in the sun. Yet the conviction that I served or was served in the other shop would now be well established in the parts of Catholic England that knew me, and the literary, or specifically theatre-going, world would have its suspicions too. The son of the Chiswick greengrocer was mad about literature, and a room had been set aside for him above the cauliflowers which was a very respectable library, lovingly dusted by his mother. There were even copies of the *Paris Review* on a polished table. This boy, who was about eighteen, was desperate to see James Baldwin's play *Blues for Mister Charley* at the Aldwych Theatre, but, though his mother queued for him daily at the box office, he could not get a ticket. I, as drama critic of the *Spectator*, was forced to see it, and I invited the lad along. I picked him up in a taxi and found him dressed in worn jeans and a leather jacket, which was not proper for a first night in the orchestra stalls. I was black-tied, like Bernard Levin and the other critics, who all had a good look and a nod or two of confirmation. I was into rough trade. I left after the first act, alone. It was not a good play anyway.

IN EARLY 1966 Lynne permitted me to go to America. The greengrocer's wife or the two homosexuals would protect her London nights, but I had better not be in America too long. One of the few books not by Jane Austen that she re-read was John Malcolm Brinnin's account of Dylan Thomas's wenching and boozing in New York and elsewhere in the United States and, of course, his dying in Manhattan after the insult to the brain of a load of double whiskies. I, it was implied, would be seduced, though perhaps not lethally, by a free and generous society which, at that time, was suffused by a brief Anglomania – something to do with the miniskirt, the asthenic model Twiggy, and the film *Tom Jones*. Make it brief, then. There was no cause to do otherwise, for I was being invited to take part in a swift literary conference at the University of Long Island and to stay in the apartment of a sober Jewish academic on Brooklyn Heights. The conference was to last three days and was to concern itself with problems of literary translation.

It was important for me at the time to go to New York: I wanted to find out how my literary reputation stood there, to pick up any journalistic commissions that were going, and to take what sexual comfort I could find in that, so I understood, very open society. In England I had been, as it were, nocturnally faithful. I was super-stitious enough to have visions of Lynne lying bleeding on the mornings of my return from an illicit night out. The Dublin television trip had presented no sexual temptations; New York, I foresaw, might be different, and the Atlantic would be a barrier to guilt. So I flew tourist class by Pan Am, which, as Ian Fleming pointed out, serves the most experienced chicken in the world, and sat next to an American girl who had been on a pilgrimage to Liverpool, the new world centre of popular culture. I travelled with a swordstick, not for defence but as an aid to walking, for I was in the active phase of intermittent claudication. Those were the innocent days before weapon checks were introduced to airports.

The opening session of the conference was held in the former Paramount Cinema overlooking the East River: it had now become the great hall of Long Island University. The Provost of the University was, to me, all that an American academic administrator ought to be, for the huge desk in his office was a disguised refrigerator crammed with ice and canned beer, and he had a bookcase of false leather spines hiding scotch, bourbon, and gin. He introduced George Steiner as chief speaker by telling him that he, George, had better give a good performance, for Eddie Cantor had rolled his eyes and Fanny Brice her can on that august platform. So George affirmed that, after Auschwitz, language and literature were dead, and that a certain Monsieur Béquette was, which was right, reducing literature to silence. George was articulate on behalf of inarticulacy, eloquent in his denunciation of eloquence. His point was that the Nazi enormities had rendered language powerless to express them, and that even the tirades of *Timon of Athens* and *King Lear* were inadequate to find objective correlatives for the states of mind they had induced among the civilised. It did not seem to be an auspicious beginning to a conference dedicated to the universality of literature, and I was later reported to have denounced George as a bloody fool, which was not strictly true. He was not and is not a bloody fool. His problem is that he knows too much.

Some years later than this first meeting with George, I reviewed a volume of the Supplement to the *Oxford English Dictionary* in the *Times Literary Supplement* and picked on, for gentle derision, a citation from Steiner used for the illustration of a meaning. In the music of *Tristan and Isolde*, according to him, one could hear the noise of the breakdown of nineteenth-century industrial civilisation. George wrote me an angry letter in which he accused me of letting the intellectual side down and of being, on various literary occasions, memorably drunk. He forgot this later and was, on our next meeting, amiable enough. We have both, in print, been kind to each other's work. The trouble I have with literary people is rarely literary: it is mostly to do with music. George once said that it was impossible to hear music in one's brain. In the German language, he said on that Long Island occasion, there was the music of barbarism, a snarl deep in the Teutonic forest. The German language would never recover from its Nazi degradation, and even a neutral word like *spritzen* must always carry the memory of Jewish blood spurting under the Nazi knife. I do not think this is true. The word was used to me by a Berlin waiter when I had ordered chicken *à la Kiev*: he warned me that butter would *spritzen* if I did not cut carefully. And it is not true that the Teutonic languages are cursed: those of Scandinavia carry connotations of bland health and winter sports. And George praised the Teutonic forest of Shakespeare's language. But he is a great man if a non-existent musician.

I do not remember much of that Long Island conference, except for the chill from the East River. I was less concerned with literature than with gefilte fish and sex. The young academic with whom I lodged on Brooklyn Heights gave me a duplicate key to his flat, but I could not make it work. A dumpy blonde Brooklyn lady in a bathrobe came out of the next-door flat to help, but she could not make it work either. All I could do was to take her afternoon hospitality and her bathrobe off. She was not a refined lady – she said 'you was' and 'ain't that sumpn' – but she was attracted to what she called my British accent. Lying with me was like lying with somebody in the movies, George Sanders or sumpn. This was a mirror situation of the wartime seduction of English girls by GIs, who spoke like Robert Taylor. And there was George Steiner talking of the death of language.

Human sexuality, as we are always discovering to our innocent surprise, has few international variations. It is the true universal speech. I was glad to have this confirmed in Brooklyn, but I did not want continued confirmation from the same confirmer, who was divorced and lonely. That damned key had better be made to work. But I met a lady, far more literary than my Brooklyn neighbour, at a party given by Panna Grady in Manhattan. Panna Grady, a literary hostess of strange but compelling beauty, had her apartment filled with the great cultural names of the period – Andy Warhol, who dithered at me, Norman Mailer, who said: 'Burgess, your last book was shit,' and Alan Ginsberg who said: 'Tell Bill Burroughs we'll be back there and up his ass.' Also others. But there was a delightful dynamic girl, fizzing with the champagne of the February Manhattan air, who took a fancy to the author of *A Clockwork Orange*, the only work of mine that had made any impression on the fractional percentage of Americans who read books. She, like many others, and not only in the United States, had expected its author to be acneous, brutal, coarse, in strange garb, burbling nadsat or slavering over Ludwig van, swinging a bicycle chain. She was delighted to find a soft-spoken man growing grey and old. The term gerontophily is vague, and the age limits it covers have never been defined, but greying seems a prime qualification, even a fetish, to some gerontophiliacs. Silk-ash kept from cooling, says Hopkins, and ripest under rind. So I went back with her to her cold-water flat in Greenwich Village and did not further, during the day or so left, have to fiddle with the key on Brooklyn Heights. I extended my stay beyond the end of the conference. I toyed with extending it indefinitely. I thought I had fallen in love. Really, I supposed, I was suffering from an ageing man's infatuation with youth. And perhaps with New York, city of, as Leon Trotsky called it, prose and fantasy.

Perhaps the violence of the city is a necessary aspect of its dynamism. The intellectual dynamic seemed reserved to the Jews, of whom I met many at the Young Men's Hebrew Association on Lexington Avenue. The New York sandwich, a mere piece of etymology, a disregardable slice of bread under a square meal hidden, is an example of the way in which American things grow beyond their origins, and so is the YMHA, reduced to the Y and notable for its Poetry Center. For there were delectable Jewish princesses there, and old men who spoke of Kafka and Kierkegaard. I gave a talk there, introduced perhaps inaccurately as the ultimate pessimist, and established a useful reputation for articulacy and clarity without the prosthesis of a microphone. Useful, for I saw that American money for my kind of author lay less in royalties than on the lecture circuit. The writing of novels makes one a novelist, but a novelist to Americans is someone who exposes himself as a person preferably bohemian, drunk, fornicating, smashing his host's furniture, giving a hungover talk. They prefer, as Alroy Kear says, the living dog to the dead lion. Americans will listen, but they do not care to read. *War and Peace* must wait for the leisure of retirement, which never really comes: meanwhile it helps to furnish the living room. Blockbusting fiction is bought as furniture. Unread, it maintains its value. Read, it looks like money wasted. Cunningly, Americans know that books contain a person, and they want the person, not the book.

Lynne, with woman's insight, divined that I had left something in New York, seed or heart or both. She seemed well, even comely, when the cosmesis of a wig, to cover hair that had lost lustre, and a caftan, to hide what I did not yet know as ascites, were applied for literary parties. Well through going easy on drink, she went harder on drink but was not noticeably less well. Well enough to walk to pubs near Turnham Green, she grumbled at my limping and my groans from sclerotic calf-ache. She sent me to a Harley Street specialist who confirmed what had been delivered in Tunbridge Wells: that the arteries were seizing up with an excess of cholesterol and would have to be opened and scraped. But, quite recently, this had happened to a man in Etchingham, and he had died. Spirits, this specialist said, especially cognac, would keep the passages clear until a time for scraping could be arranged. I left his surgery in a state of full intermission and walked two miles, drinking a large brandy in every pub I met on the way. A fellow-sufferer, also on brandy, said that vegetable oil and garlic would work wonders. I had heard this before, and so had Lynne. But she, daughter of the north, abhorred garlic and kept to lard. I ate what I was given and got on with my work.

The main task that year was writing a book for Faber & Faber called *The Novel Now*. I was qualified, thanks chiefly to the *Yorkshire Post*, for such a commission: I had read, or at least received, the novels of all the nations for two and a half years. This, and the later bizarrer commission it engendered, the article 'Novel, The' in the *Encyclopaedia Britannica*, had the effect of making me seem somehow outside fictional practice though well inside the trade of non-academic appraisal. Rex Warner, in his novel *The Wild Goose Chase*, had imagined a world in which fiction was only the raw material for reviewers, who were invited to parties where their reviews were praised, while the subjects of them languished in cold attics. It seemed reasonable to Faber & Faber that I should intermit the writing of novels and produce a book which was really a mammoth review article. I had brought this on myself. Young aspirants to journalism wrote me letters asking how one became a reviewer. Ladies at parties said: 'Oh, you write books as well as reviewing them, do you?' Everybody's tame reviewer, I bridled at the neglect of what I thought of as my primary trade. But it was a trade I did not practise much in 1966 and for much of 1967, and it was because the stress of the creative labour involved was matched neither by critical appreciation nor by money. I had only myself to blame. The emphasis of the times was on the glamour of the television appearance and the quickly thrown off, preferably sensational, chunk of journalism. Novel-writing was truly an occupation for a cold garret, a prolonged courting of the muse of the debased epic. In that sybaritic quick-buck era true novelists were true heroes. I was not proving heroic enough.

ANOTHER LITERARY sideline began to offer itself, one that I was pretty well qualified to practise. This was the translation of foreign opera and oratorio libretti into singable English. I could read music and I could write words: twin skills became Siamese. BBC-2 wished to present Berlioz's *L'Enfance du Christ* as a Christmas treat for the cultivated. Colin Davis the conductor and Berlioz specialist wished it to be done in the original French, Berlioz's own, but this seemed inappropriate for a feast that the British could claim to have invented. So, though he grumbled at every line I wrote, he allowed me to turn the work into *The Childhood of Christ*. Not even a novel could be harder work. Berlioz devised words of no great poetic resonance and found melodic lines to fit them. I had to wander the streets, gloom in the pubs, toss in my single bed coaxing English rhythms out of a French conception. There is no consonance between French prosody, which, since French is stressless, is totally syllabic or quantitative, and the rhythmical system of music. The ghost of a stress comes, when it comes at all, in perverse contradiction of the genius of English. '*Comment s'appelle-t-il?*' Joseph is asked of his foster-son. He replied: '*Jésus.*' The question can be rendered, keeping the original rhythm, as 'What is his name then?' But the answer can only be 'Jesus', and Berlioz's notes contradict the English by gently stressing, with a down-beat, the second syllable. There was no way out of changing the down-beat to an up-beat – horror of Davisian horrors, tampering with the sacred notes of Berlioz. The chorus sings '*La terre*' and flicks the final *e*, mute in speech, on a quaver at the beginning of a bar. What can one do in English? Extend that quaver to a minim, if the harmonies allow, and attach 'earth' to it. W. H. Auden had been asked to make the translation, but it had to be a rapid, or journalistic, job demeaning to a major poet. Anyway, Auden found it too difficult. I, the universal mug, was all too persuasible.

It was a killing task, but time could not be taken off from it. For Christmas was a feast unmoveable even by the BBC, and parts had to be copied, singers rehearsed. Lynne fretted at being housebound while I sharpened fresh pencils and blew eraser crumbs from the score, but I could not work at a bar counter while IRA songs blasted from the jukebox. Nor was I tempted to go to quieter pubs where there was a piano for trying Berlioz and Burgess out. Trying out is no help, I snarled; I can hear the damned thing quite clearly in my head, thank you. She wept. She could not understand the agonies of the assignment. The comic potentialities of English were an aspect of the pain. When English becomes self-conscious, in oratorio and also in historical films, it seems automatically to become risible. If Oliver Cromwell says 'Pass the salt, please', the audience roars. If Jesus Christ says 'Yes, my friends', sanctity and seriousness are exorcised. Joseph (or Joséph with a second syllable stress) gives the name of the holy child, and the response is '*Quel joli nom*'. Try putting that into English in a slow melodic line. Even 'A noble name' will bring the house down.

I was recently asked to make a new translation of the libretto of *Carmen*. The Toreador's Song, which the score calls *Couplets*, has '*Toréador, prends garde de toi, toréador, toréador,*' a foolish line excused by Bizet's direction that it be sung '*avec fatuité*'. There used to be an English version which went 'Toreador, now gua-a-a-ard thee', not really acceptable. My rendering of the whole refrain was

> Toreador, the flag of battle flies.
> Gird up your youth,
> Fame is the prize.
> Though fear besmear the dagger-point of truth,
> Take that chance in your stride.
> Remember, two dark eyes
> Look on in pride,
> And love is by your side.

When this number went into rehearsal I received perturbed telephone calls from the director to say that the entire cast was rolling over the stage with hysterical laughter. Perhaps the 'fear' and 'besmear' had something to do with it: I never could resist an internal rhyme. Even parts of *The Childhood of Christ* were sounding like Lorenz Hart, though not Richard Rodgers. One is always drawn to Broadway to find the triumphant exploitation of the genius of spoken English – which, say what they will, is a language more comic than tragic – by marrying the cunning rhyme to the musical phrase. But the atmosphere of Broadway is bitter-sweet Jewish-ironical. Opera and oratorio try to be serious, and English shows up their pretensions.

When *The Childhood of Christ* was produced, very expertly, on BBC-2, the critics praised the words of Berlioz as well as the music, attributing more English to him than he could have learned from Harriet Smithson. When, fairly recently, *L'Enfance du Christ* was produced, beautifully but blandly, by commercial television, it was done in French, with a new translation by myself flashed in subtitles. This translation, like the one for BBC-2, followed the rhythms of the music. The critics mostly scoffed at my words, saying that they would have preferred a literal rendering of the original. But my, and the producer's aim, had been to show what the singers might have been singing had they not, because of the need to sell the programme abroad, been committed to French. An intelligent kind of synaesthesia might have persuaded the critics that they were actually hearing the words they were only scornfully reading. But the obtuseness of critics is a great sorrow to the creative.

Politics is described as the art of the possible, but art is never termed the aesthetic exploitation of the possible. What critics often ask for is the impossible, though this may be a salutary means of extending the borders of art. A horn-player in the Hallé Orchestra when Hans von Richter was rehearsing it in *Siegfried's Journey to the Rhine*, complained that his solo was impossible to play. The complaint was translated for Richter, who then put out his hand for the horn, took a mouthpiece from his pocket, and played the passage by heart with great panache. He gave back the horn, and there has never since been a complaint about the unplayability of Wagner. But a cornist may be instructed more easily than a critic. Critics should not say 'Mr A could surely, if he had tried harder, have found a rhyme for "fugue" ' or 'Signor Z's very respectable tenor voice is marred by his inability to reach a high E flat'. It is conceivable that some critic or other has blamed a bassoon for not going lower than the B flat below the bass stave. There are limits to what an artist can do, and it is important that the critic distinguish between crass unintelligence or unadventurousness and what is imposed by the obduracy of the medium the artist is using. Occasionally the medium can be forced to yield. No rhyming dictionary gives a rhyme for 'fugue', but Lorenz Hart might have written

> They're playing a fugue? Oh,
> You go,
> Hugo.
> I can't abide polyphony.
> I'd rather have a diamond from Tiffany.

This is still not a rhyme for 'fugue'. It will be a long time before tenors can reach high E flat or bassoons go down to A. But language, and I am thinking of the critics of literature pure or applied, has its own intransigent laws, and these cannot be bent, not even for the most exigent critic. A better English version of *L'Enfance du Christ* or *Carmen* or Weber's *Oberon* (which the Scottish

Opera Company and I rescued from a hundred and sixty years of oblivion) will some day supervene on what I did, but that will depend on the free working of talent, not the critic's demands. The critic, like the artist, must bow to the possible.

I raise this matter of the possible not only in connection with the torment of producing a singable English translation of *L'Enfance du Christ*, but because of a literary event of 1967 which had everything to do with the linguistically possible. This was the publication of Robert Graves's translation of the *Rubaiyat* of Omar Khayyam, which I reviewed at some length in the magazine *Encounter*. Graves did not know Persian and followed a literal crib provided by Omar Ali-Shah. I, having overcome the obstacle of Arabic script when learning Malay, had at least stumbled through the *Rubaiyyat* in the original and seen how right Fitzgerald had been in following Omar's rhyme-scheme. Graves, deriding what he termed 'Fitz-Omar', claimed to have produced something very close to the meaning of the Persian, though this was not strictly true. But, he said, in striving for verbal accuracy he had had to forgo rhyme. I said in my review: 'It's useless for Graves to protest the difficulty of matching the Persian form in English while at the same time retaining the poet's meaning: the poet's job is to overcome such a difficulty.' Was I being one of those critics who demand more than the possible? It seemed to me that we were on that borderline where more honest or thoughtful criticism would have confessed doubt as to the real problem – a problem of the limited resources of language or of the limited talent of the poet? Graves, had, for one of his stanzas,

> Ah me, the book of early glory closes,
> The green of Spring makes way for wintry snows;
> The cheerful bird of Youth flutters away –
> I hardly noticed how it came or went,

which I suggested could be deblanked into something like

> I see the book of early glory close,
> The green of Spring make way for winter snows.
> The cheerful bird of Youth flutters away –
> I hardly notice how it comes or goes.

I was generally attacked for presuming to dictate to a major poet. If I had been a poet myself, even minor, my suggested emendation might have been acceptable, but I was only a novelist, or a reviewer of novels, and I must keep my dirty paws off the higher art.

Yet novelists deal in words as much as poets and are usually more aware of the rhythms of speech, which carry so much of the burden of their meaning (what was wrong with Graves as a poet was that he had an ill-developed ear for speech-rhythms). If prose-writers become increasingly unsure what poetry is, they remain powerfully conscious of the nature and importance of verse, the formal antithesis to their own medium. They are fascinated by it and want to practise in it. The poet Martin Bell, who often sat sadly getting drunk in the Chiswick house while I wrestled with *L'Enfance du Christ*, could not help. Poetry was his medium, not verse. He adored opera but he had no knowledge of the relation of words and music. If, as is needed, the operatic repertoire ever gets wholly into English, that will not be the work of poets. It will be done by versifiers who earn their primary living from prose. It will not, of course, be done by critics.

Ah, critics. *Tremor of Intent* appeared in 1966, with a nude girl and gun-toting spy on the cover, than which, said *The Month*, 'Mr Burgess's umpteenth novel is, though not for the squeamish or the prurient, much subtler.' The *Times Literary Supplement* said that it was 'a marvellously entertaining book, but when the fireworks die away there is not much left in the cold darkness to warm or to sustain.' *Time* kindly said that it was one of the best novels since *The Spy Who Came in from the Cold*, which one or two American reviewers suggested I had plagiarised, though I had not in fact read it. John Gardner in the *Southern Review* was to say that I was a good writer, but not a great one. 'His characters do not fight towards the impossible with the same demonic intensity as those of Lagerkvist, and they are not cruelly broken when they fall.' I am still looking for this Lagerkvist to learn how to break my characters with greater cruelty. The *Saturday Review* said that I failed to discover adequate metaphors for radical evil; hence, 'devoid of seriousness, the work degenerates into a kind of theological farce'. For God's sake, reviewers, lead us to the light, tell us what we ought to do, instruct us in the craft of the possible. *America* said: 'This eschatological spy novel may strike some as also scatological: it had a definite preoccupation with sex.' When reviewers do not know the meaning of the words they use, then authors must doubt their capacity to teach.

I took *Tremor of Intent* with me to the United States in early 1967 with the intention of reading part of it aloud to three thousand students at Vanderbilt University in Nashville, Tennessee. Nashville was to be a great centre of popular music of a mock-rural kind: I had a different music to retail. There is a chapter in the novel consecrated to an immense sexual bout between the spy Hillier and an Indian lady named Miss Devi, who has been instructed in love by the *Kamasutra* and a Tamil manual called *Pokam*. Some woman reviewer had assumed that *Pokam* was a crude invention on my part, but though the Tamil word *pokam* is unrelated to poking it has certainly to do with sex. There may be a book of that name, but I am still to discover it. What all reviewers had missed in that chapter was that it makes sense only to the ear, being compounded of the rhythms and cries of rutting. It even ends, as I was to find in Nashville, with the sweat and exhaustion of the reciter. What looked to some critics like senseless surrealism is as close to phonographic realism as I am ever likely to want to get. The customs official who processed me at what had been Idlewild but was now Kennedy saw only photographic pornography on the dust-cover, but after saying, 'You wanna read something better than that, fella,' he let the book through. I flew to Boston and gave a talk at Amherst College, then I proposed travelling back to New York for the weekend, with the end of contacting the girl in the cold-water flat in Greenwich Village. But Eric P. Swenson, my editor at Norton, insisted on my staying at his country mansion outside Hartford, Connecticut, and travelling towards it on a decrepit train from Springfield, Massachusetts. It was probably just as well: that fizzing girl might have fizzed off after some other author. I had had enough humiliation from American reviewers without having to receive it also at the door of a cold-water flat.

What I learned chiefly in Eric Swenson's ménage was the complex family constellations that spring out of divorce. There is not all that much divorce in Britain, where casual adultery feeds the need for sexual change, but the aura of the theocratic death penalty for adultery still clings to America, even outside New England, and multiple divorce, which looks to the European like serial polygamy, is the moral solution to the problem of the itch. Love comes into it too, of course, but in Europe we tend to see marital love as an eternity which encompasses hate and also indifference: when we promise to love we really mean that we promise to honour a contract. Americans, seeming to take marriage with not enough seriousness, are really taking love and sex with too much. They are romantic in a way that the French are not. They cannot abide cynicism. There was not much point in envying the rich writers of America, Saul Bellow and Norman Mailer for instance, since all their money went into alimony. Talk among the literary successful was mostly about where to find a good divorce lawyer. Writers were great ones for multiple divorce, being romantic, idealistic, and sexually imaginative, or so my superficial investigations were teaching me. Publishers naturally divorced less. Eric Swenson had divorced once, and so had his wife. He and she had met Lynne in the Café Royal on a visit to London, and they could not understand how she could talk so brazenly of my infidelities and hers. Why no divorce? Americans assume an ingrained masochism in the British (I once saw on American television a comedian ineptly impersonating a Cockney garbage collector, having him say: 'Oh yes, I'm very 'umble, sir, Cor stroike a loight, and I'm already trynin' me daughter to grow up into a doormat, sir'), probably with justice. My novels were said to be working models of referred masochism, and my married life glowed dully with self-torture.

Anyway, Eric Swenson's wife Brook, a charming name for a charming woman, was pregnant on my visit with my coming goddaughter, or earth child as Eric put it, but had a son by her first marriage to match a daughter from his. These two children were much of an age, ten or eleven, and the boy was precocious enough to say to the girl: 'I am your lord and master and order you to take off all your clothes,' to which she replied: 'I wouldn't do that for a thousand bucks.' An interesting situation, in which the half-sib relationship is technically incestuous but cannot really feel like it. My friend Erica Jong is the only writer, so far as I know, to take divorce as applied to children casually enough to make a cartoon book out of it. Her little heroine, Megan, grows up in two households with two sets of parents and even two dogs. I have heard earnest American sociologists say that American children have a *right* to the divorce experience as an enriching element of an advanced civilisation. I was learning all the time from this great country of everybody's future.

I flew to Kansas City and was driven though the middle of the night to the town of Manhattan, of which Dorothy Parker wrote:

> Manhattan is an island.
> Manhattan is a drink.
> Manhattan is a city,
> Or so the Kansans think.

The state university was there, but there were no bars. Prohibition was still around in regions little touched by European morality, though it was modified sufficiently in most states to accommodate liquor stores. Even Utah, the dryest state in the Union, where even the taking of tea or coffee is a sin of stimulation, has a liquor store in its international airport. Salt Lake City is the only place in my late sober years where I have had to be carried, full of gin, on to an aircraft. Having bought a bottle of gin you had better drink it. Next door to the Holiday Inn of Manhattan I found a store with bottles of Old Crow and Roma Rocket, but no, as they are termed, fixings. I sipped neat all day in a bedroom that reeked of old cigars and broken air conditioners and gave a scarcely sober lecture in the evening. Students asked questions like: 'Mr Burgess, what is your precise threshold of credibility?' A delightful country.

An ingenious country, too. I had to fly to Kansas City in order to fly to Nashville, but dawn fog had grounded all the commercial aircraft. I was agitated, since I was due to recite at noon, so the kind and resourceful staff of the little Manhattan airport wheeled out what looked like an ancient Focke-Wulf, together with a pilot who was not only ancient but deaf. We flew low, and it was my task, as a coopted co-pilot, to identify landmarks. 'Do you see a kinda big lake down there, fella?' I nodded. 'Okay, that means we're on the right route.' Airport controllers bawled over the radio: 'For Christ's sake identify yourself,' and my pilot said: 'What's that he says, fella?' 'FOR CHRIST'S SAKE IDENTIFY YOURSELF.' 'That's okay, we're nearly there.' So we landed bumpily on the Kansas City airfield and, dragging my heavy suitcase, I ran to the Nashville plane, which was over-ready for take-off. I sat panting with my suitcase on my knees, despised by all as one who had got up late and nearly missed his flight.

I was borne from a chill Kansas spring to a southern summer full of magnolias. At Vanderbilt there was a kind of literary festival at which Richard Ellmann compared, remarkably, the techniques of Auden and Yeats, and Louis Simpson read his poems and enquired of a fellow-writer about good alimony lawyers. I dripped sweat and lost pounds over my recitations and, next day, received a reward for putting all my available beef into the erotic chapter from *Tremor of Intent*. A massive blond football-playing student shyly brought his small dark girlfriend to me and said: 'You put things right between us, sir. We'd been, you know, kinda not hitting it off, but that thing you read out made us both kinda horny and, you know, things were okay last night and things are okay today, so gee, thanks.' Did this mean that the chapter was pornographic? Or could pornography, or perhaps pornophony, reside in the way it was read aloud? I was glad, anyway, to have done something for American youth.

This was brown-bag territory, meaning liquor in brown bags had to be imported into restaurants, which served only fixings and ice. Nothing could better promote drunkenness, which, on the part of these Southerners, in its turn promoted virulent hatred of the North. Looking for the lavatory in the house of Professor Sullivan, I opened the wrong door and found myself gazing at a well-kept Confederate museum, with swords unsheathed and brightly polished and uniforms brushed and stuffed, it seemed, with the ectoplasm of defeated heroes. Hatred of the Union spat out from an old lady who would liefer have had the rule of the Hanoverians back than the rule of the Yankees. That bastard Lincoln, that super-bastard Sherman. The bastard Lincoln, who was excoriated by the old lady as though still up there, terribly constipated, in the White House, had fought, true, not for the manumission of black slaves but for the preservation of the Union. But how important was the Union? That there were two distinct American nations I was seeing for myself. The South had been, still was, a different country, lashed to Northern conformity by carpetbaggers. I recited the lines:

> In the long sunset where impatient sound
> Strips niggers to a multiple of backs,
> Flies yield their heat, magnolias drench the ground
> With Appomattox! The shadows lie in stacks.

And here was their author, Allen Tate, sixty-eight though looking much younger, a link, the last link except for the young Robert Lowell, with the greatest British novelist of the century, Ford Madox Ford, who had prophesied that America's great literature would be a Southern product; and so it was, except for the North-Eastern Jews.

Tate's niggers were no longer to be called that, though the term here did not have the pejorative harmonics that the progressive had forced upon it. It was a classical term, the straight Latin *niger*, for some reason often employed in the feminine form *nigra*. In New York, Deborah Rogers's favourite author Ralph Ellison, whose *Invisible Man* was a masterpiece, was to tell me that, reading William Faulkner, he had met 'nigger' on every page, but he was confirmed in his American Southernness by Faulker's unique insight into an ethos regional, not racial. In Nashville, the blacks with a racial conscience kept to their own schools and colleges; the lowlier blacks, porters and waiters and butlers, were Uncle Toms mainly in their bossiness. A drunken black butler at a faculty cocktail party held in the Palladian mansion of Vanderbilt's young President bossed the show and sustained a friendly insolence, unrebuked. The South was his as much as the whites'. The adoptive avuncularity of Uncle Ben's rice or Aunt Jemima's pancake mix was not contemptuous or facetious.

I played 'Back Home in Tennessee' and 'Sleepy Time Down South' on the Bechstein, and these Americans marvelled, in their isolationist innocence, that an Englishman should know those tunes. For a faculty member whose speciality was John Dryden, I recited parts of *Absalom and Achitophel* in Restoration pronunciation, really a refined Dublinese. The English department looked back to a period of Augustan order and courtliness, an agrarian society maintained through gross inequality. The Yankee-haters, who still chafed at their defeat, were ready to justify the past of slaves and Southern gentlemen in the manner of Augustine St Clare. Miss Ophelia, an Abolitionist, contends that British factories, terrible as they are, are not plantations. He replies that the English labourer 'is as much at the will of his employers as if he were sold to him. The slave-owner can whip his refractory slave to death – the capitalist can starve him to death. As to family security, it is hard to say which is the worst – to have one's children sold, or see them starve to death at home.' Not that anybody read *Uncle Tom's Cabin* any more. That was a wicked Northern book. This was also, I remembered, the view of the Catholic Church of my boyhood. We were all warned off seeing a silent film version of the book at the Manchester cinemas. The old economic tie between my native city and the Southland was a matter of forgettable history, but not the treachery of Cottonopolis in assisting the Yankees in the Civil War. Meanwhile the cotton still grew and was picked by blacks with white overseers.

I flew to New York, brooding on the South and Harriet Beecher Stowe, whose Miss Ophelia is called by the slaves 'Miss Feely'. She is an Abolitionist who cannot bear the touch of a black skin: the sobriquet is ironic; she has to learn to feel. There seemed, despite everything, to be a symbiosis in the South; in the North-East there was an agreed apartheid. None of this was my affair, but American history was, since it began as British colonial history. History was something that the students I had met wanted to see as a nightmare from which they had awakened. They were ready now for a prolonged present, the gift of rock music and drugs. At La Guardia airport I telephoned the girl in the cold-water flat. She was in and agreed to have lunch with me at the Algonquin. She had changed, as young people do. I watched her forking in her chef's green salad ('Go easy on the garlic, okay?') and noted the budding herpes on her lip. She was no longer bemused by *A Clockwork Orange*: she had moved

on to writers like Brautigan. I was kinda old. That was true: I was
fifty, matched with an ageing wife four years younger. It was time
for me to stop lusting after brash girls. As for my cold-water one, she
was not above living on the old, meaning an allowance from a father
who ran a small plastics works near Albany, ostensibly to study
Creative Writing at Columbia, actually to sleep with visiting
authors, and even indigenous ones, in order to see whether their true
sexuality matched their fictitious. It was perhaps not a bad idea and
might make an interesting book unpublishable because of libel. I
heard my British voice, vaguely episcopal, and hers, bright and
classless, speaking of sodomy as presented by Norman Mailer in *An
American Dream*. Buggery was kinda a man's thing, there was not
much erogenous about her particular ass. Hatted lady lunchers heard
this, appalled. I was glad to pay the bill and take my taxi to Kennedy.
There was no farewell kiss.

GIVE UP womanising and concentrate on work. But I was not quite
sure what work was. It ought to be the novel, but it was increasingly
journalism. There were three thousand dollars to be earned from
Playboy for an article about precognition. What, apart from my
dreams, did I know about precognition? The assumption of
authority that went into a long think-piece and was an emanation of
the high fee paid could be regarded as an aspect of fiction, but it was
dishonest in a way that fiction – lying and posturing in the service of
truth and dignity – was not. There was much less than three
thousand dollars to be gained from the *Sunday Telegraph* colour
supplement for a trip to Berlin, West and East, and an account of the
life, or lives, there. This meant philosophising superficially and
coming to the brash unequivocal conclusions appropriate to popular
journalism. I went as soon as the two homosexuals were able to
move in safely with Lynne, and I settled for a weekend at the
Kempinski Hotel on the Kurfürstendamm. In those days there was a
severe limit placed on the money one could export from Britain, and
there was no danger of my responding to the whores who called, as
though living in a book by Christopher Isherwood, '*Komm', Süsser.*'
I went with a taxi-driver to a transvestite night club ('*Es ist nicht
billig,*' he warned, nor was it) where a bass-voiced *lustige Witwe*
introduced young male naked dancers with silicone in their chests.
West Berlin was playing at being the Weimar Republic. Over in East
Berlin the entertainment was more wholesome, being mostly drink

served by miniskirted girls who insisted on checking one's coat. I had a French photographer with me to illustrate the article, but the authorities at Checkpoint Charlie confiscated his camera. He would have loved to snap the saplings growing from city roofs, grown, I presumed, out of seeds defecated by birds, somehow emblematic of a sad half-town in which wild life was not much disturbed, either by the noise of traffic or public gaiety. I had expected the Berlin Wall to be a monstrous monument of totalitarian efficiency, high, blind and forbidding, but it was only a bricolage of decayed buildings.

After that first visit, East Berlin became for me one of the metaphysical cities. If ever I wavered in my acceptance of Western capitalism, I had only to return to that grimness unenlivened by the gaudy posters of commercialism to wish to scuttle back to nudes and Mammon. Between the preceding paragraph and this, I crossed over on a summer Saturday. I was with a girl from Hamburg who had not previously visited the Democratic Republic; she was not permitted to enter at Checkpoint Charlie, so I took the S-Bahn with her to Friedrichstrasse where foreigners had to wait long and unsmoking, prodded by beardless boys in uniform. What terrified me was the weekend emptiness: no one about, for there was nothing to be about for; meagrely supplied stores all shut; a three-kilometre walk to the one sad café open; callow youths with guns patrolling the streets. Leningrad had been different: the communism there tempered a natural ebullience, and not too much. The East Berliners were in their wretched element, having passed immediately from one totalitarian régime to another. The damnable hypocrisy of the half-town, pretending that the West was the true prison and the gunmen were protecting the freedom of the citizen, stood for a metaphysic based on lies, the biggest lie of all being the perversion of the term *demokratisch*. Under the roof of the Friedrichstrasse S-Bahn platform two boys with sub-machine-guns paced, their eyes on potential refugees from communist prosperity. It was a relief to get to the Zoo station and all the howling injunctions to consume.

On that first visit to both Berlins, I returned footsore from inspecting the free side of the Wall, peeping over and being jocularly threatened by armed official thugs, and went thirsty to a *Bierstube* called *Der Moby Dick*, with an inappropriate blue plastic whale in the window. I took a seat outside in the sun, but none of the young men who ran the place came to serve me. After half an hour I walked in and asked why. 'Because,' I was told, 'you are of the generation that started the war.' I went for a beer elsewhere.

Of course, at fifty I was old, and, to those young idealists of *Der*

Moby Dick, I must have been of Hitler's generation. There were no gradations of eld any more: fifty was as bad as ninety. Youth and age had become spatial concepts with a Berlin Wall between them. It seemed wrong somehow to have to be taught that lesson in the old capital of the bad children of Europe. Berlin had tried to mess up both my father's life and mine. West Berlin, grousing rightly at the bizarre split of the Wall, could convert guilt into self-righteousness, a live capitalist island in a totalitarian sea, flashing the skysigns of the Springer empire across at the sundered brethren. I found no guilt in Berlin. There were Himmlers and Goerings in the telephone directory, and the waiter in the Kempinski dining-room, serving me with the white asparagus that are the summer speciality, said: '*Mein Herr*, good can out of bad come. These from fine bone-manure in the east are grown.' And, of course, George Steiner was wrong about *spritzen*: it was only butter that gushed from the chicken Kiev.

What could I write about West Berlin except that, to my ingenuous mind, it ought to be, like the walls of a kitchen, filmed with the scum of blood? I was pleased at the Tempelhof airport when I tried the wrong door and an official boomed '*Verboten!*' That provided an easy summary: the German mentality ran to the forbidding of things, including remorse. When the article was published, a number of letters arrived from Berliners, most, I noted, in exile, who complained of my moralistic tone and affirmed that the town had always been gay, antinomian, mocking of authority, and had fizzed with the finest anti-Hitler jokes in all Europe.

I had made myself into a novelist, and novelists are perhaps the last people in the world to be entrusted with opinions. The nature of a novel is that it has no opinions, only the dialectic of contrary views, some of which, all of which, may be untenable and even silly. A novelist should not be too intelligent either, although, like Aldous Huxley, he may be permitted to be an intellectual. It is in order for him to make aesthetic judgements, though these will tend to partiality and the reflection of his own practice. But it is dangerous to turn him into a little seer or twopenny philosopher, though this is probably bound to happen when professional philosophers and churchmen have so little useful to say about moral or social problems. London in the sixties was offering too many opportunities to novelists, poets less, to spout half-baked views on television or in the press.

Or in the magistrates' court. The American author Hubert Selby Jr had published a book called *Last Exit to Brooklyn*, a series of interlinked fictions about perverse and violent sex in the squalider purlieus of New York, and this work came up for trial as a piece of outrageous pornography. I was persuaded to offer myself as a witness for the defence in Marlborough Street court, there to assert that the aim of the pornography was to promote lust (though what was wrong with lust? Were we not all – well, some of us – the product of it?) and that the book on trial was there to engender compassion for those whom genes or history had led into inverted sexual practices. The magistrate believed that *Vanity Fair* had fixed the techniques of expression of sexual relations for good and all, and that upstarts like Emile Zola were going too far. The trouble with my deposition was that I had to pretend that a very mediocre book was good art whose literary qualities were its best defence. The work was eventually, in that decade that had begun with the end of the *Chatterley* ban, cleared of the pornographic charge and permitted to stand, along with Lawrence's eroticon, as a signal of our new permissiveness. Frank sex was from now on to excuse feeble art. Foolishly perhaps, I wrote a preface for the reissue which, by its very presence at the head of the book, looks like a commendation. My view was that not even bad books ought to be banned.

I had also let myself become involved in a public argument about Arts Council awards to indigent or idle writers. I was asked by Arthur Crooke, editor of the *Times Literary Supplement*, to write a letter to his journal protesting about the intrusion of state subvention into what could be considered a field of pure commerce. Crooke wanted controversy and he got it. I held that it was in order for symphony orchestras and ballet companies and opera houses to be publicly subsidised, since their huge apparatuses of expression had been developed in an era of cheap art and no trade unions. It was not possible to economise on the production of *Der Ring* or *Le Lac des Cygnes*. But the creative writer ought to be in Shakespeare's position, purveying what looked like popular fodder but was really more. By trickery, the novelist should seem to be providing a plain story but actually be working in other dimensions, those of symbolism, poetry, philosophy. Moreover, creative writers should work hard enough to be able to subsist without state hand-outs. There ought to be a sort of stubborn pride in scribbling independence, of the kind that Dr Johnson had represented before accepting a pension. One lady novelist had told the press that she could not write during the summer months because she had to go to Lord's to watch cricket, hence she needed state money. H. E. Bates, who had written hard to little critical applause, agreed with me and lambasted the lazy, adding that state subsidies to authors went straight into the coffers of the distilleries. He had to apologise for this.

The point I made in my letter, and had to make again on television as a member of a panel that included Cecil Day Lewis, now Poet Laureate, was perhaps little more than a desire to make other writers suffer and slave as I had been doing: it was grim Lancashire unwillingness to be beholden to anonymous favour-doers, hatred of the sense of being under an obligation to the state (though this was not the Soviet state and, save for its paltry cultural annexe, not greatly interested in the arts anyway), a comic turn of the ah-paid-mah-way order. The television programme made me appear grudging and certainly eccentric. I was eccentric again when I was passionate on television about the sin of the impending decimalisation of the coinage. I might not have seemed so eccentric if I had not been harnessed with a spokesman for duodecimalisation (the figure 10 to stand for a dozen, 100 for a gross). Yet this spokesman spoke good sense about the unviability of packing whisky and eggs in tens (five by two made for cartoning either over-flimsy or over-expensive). But my rage about the loss of the half-crown or tosheroon sounded hollow under the studio lights. I had better get out of England once more and become the faceless creator of what I called literature. I was betraying myself into the postures of a personality. Personalities were what the age demanded.

I WAS having some difficulty with the writing of fiction, and this was because I had fulfilled my ambition of becoming a busy hack, at home with the easy article and the even easier shoddiness of tea-room chat on the small screen. I had started a novel called *It Is the Miller's Daughter* and made the mistake of publishing its first chapter in the *Transatlantic Monthly*. Seeing this in print, I saw how impossible its continuation was. The novel was to be about flour and water, especially water. It was set in a French village near the Belgian border, and its hero, a lowly farm-worker, lived with his grand-mother, who fed him soup ladled from a pot simmering on a fire which never went out. The soup had been bubbling ever since the days of Louis XIV, so that it stood for the continuation of history: the boy spooned in history twice a day. The life of the village centred round an ancient well, but men arrived from Paris to condemn its water as poisonous: it contained an element called *bebasan* (this, improbable in the context, is the Malay word for freedom). Water

was to be laid on from a remote reservoir, and my unlettered hero
guessed with peasant wisdom that the state would infect the water
with its own poison – that of submission to a central authority. The
village poet spoke enigmatic lines:

> Love water, love it with all your being,
> But only from the tap, never the spring –
> Tasteless but grateful in summer, embracing the hollow
> Of any vessel, but never never follow
> Water to the source, never never call
> On Master or Mistress Water in the fall
> Of rivers or the sea churned by the rough
> Winds' enmity. Water from the tap is enough.

The hero, in love with the miller's daughter, was to run away with
her to a Belgian village beyond the reach of the dangerous state, only
to betray this rich-fleshed girl into poverty. They would be unable to
pay the rent of a hovel leased from the landlord of the inn, a gross
man who believed himself to be God, but the landlord's son would
steal wine from the inn cellar and sell it cheap to the owner of a
bistrot, thus securing rent-money for the couple. Caught in the dark
by his father, the son would be clubbed almost to death, but the
appalled father would recognise him in the light and take him for
nursing to a new house on the hill. Unaffected by all this, a Monsieur
Geist, living in an upper room of the inn, would be typing nonsense
all day, occasionally letting a sheet fall through the window for the
mystification of the drinkers. Encouraged by the son's sacrifice, the
hero and his bride would return to their village, smash the state's
water supply and unseal the well. It was an impossible story, and
every writer of fiction has such impossible stories incinerated or
gathering dirt in a cockloft. The trouble always is the guilt the author
feels at having given birth to characters who are left inanimate,
suspended, unfulfilled. They gibber at him during his bouts of
insomnia, saying: 'If you cannot use us, destroy us,' but they refuse
to be destroyed.

I started another novel which I was able to bring to completion. In
1960 I had written half the story of the poet Enderby, neglecting the
other half for reasons I have given earlier. Now, under
the title *Enderby Outside*, I pursued the poet's life. He has been cured
of writing poetry, an antisocial activity, and is a barman in a big
London hotel. His mother's name was Hogg, and the remaking of
his personality entailed adopting this name and forgetting the one

attached to his poetry. Thus, as he is called Piggy Hogg, his bar is
named Piggy's Sty: Circe has worked on him and made him one of
the herd. A great luncheon party is held at this hotel to honour a
singing group based loosely on the Beatles. One of the group, based
loosely on the late John Lennon, has published a volume of verse,
received the Heinemann award, and been made a Fellow of the Royal
Society of Literature. Reciting one of his poems after the luncheon,
he horrifies Enderby because the poem is Enderby's own. Enderby's
former wife, Vesta Bainbridge, has become the manager of the pop
group, found some of Enderby's poetic drafts in her apartment, and
ruthlessly fathered them on to a representative of debased art. A
failed and jealous former colleague of a pop-poet shoots him and
hands the gun to Enderby. Enderby escapes, aware that a just
assassination has been performed on his behalf, and takes the
air-cruise that Lynne and I had taken in 1963, ending up in Tangier.

The shot-at pop singer is named Yod Crewsey, and his group is
called the Fixers. He is a blasphemer against art but also against
religion, because first his death is given out and later his resurrection.
Meanwhile poetry has returned to Enderby, though first, like
Endymion, he has to be loved by the moon, embodied in a
selenographer named Miranda Boland (*merenda*, an Arabic alternative for *qamar*, meaning moon, and *bulan*, the Malay for it). Enderby
takes over a beach restaurant in Tangier from the failed poet
Rawcliffe, who dies in agony from cancer, recognising a just
punishment for his own debasement of art as a scenarist for bad
Italian films. The sun-goddess visits Enderby in the bar of *La Belle
Mer* (which, sounding the same as *la belle-mère*, reminds its proprietor that his stepmother will never be far away); she opposes the
white goddess of the moon; she seems also to be the Muse in person.
Enderby rejects her invitation to sleep with her for what he considers
to be the right motives – his age, his ugliness – but she makes his
unwillingness to plunge into the fire a proof of his minor status as a
poet. He does not dare enough, he is a mere poetaster. But wait – has
not the Muse perhaps mistaken him for Rawcliffe, who was
undoubtedly minor? In an appendix, as well as in the body of the
book itself, some of Enderby's poems (especially those that T. S.
Eliot once marked with a tick of approval) are presented to the
reader, who must make up his own mind about them. Few of the
reviewers seemed willing to dare a judgement. In *Punch* it was to be
written: 'It would be helpful if Mr Burgess would indicate whether
these poems are meant to be good or bad.' Critical impotence cannot
go much further.

I was to see later that I had prophesied the murder of John Lennon. I have less against him now, in the period of pop garbage, than I had at the time of writing. The madness of the adulation he and his colleagues met in the sixties appalled me. Even serious musicians were bemused by pop music, which tied up with youth, the miniskirt, easy sex and was coloured by middle-aged regret that they had been born too early. The musicologist Hans Keller was to be seen on television deferring to four haired louts (not the Beatles) who clashed guitars and howled illiteracies. 'First, gentlemen, though, I must deplore the noise level. You see, I was brought up on chamber music,' to which the answer was, 'Well, we was bloody well not.' Keller bowed humbly and led into a musical dissection of some inanity which had seventeen bars because its perpetrators could not count, not because they had tried to loosen the four-square stricture of traditional melodic form.

I wanted to escape from the sixties, and thought I could do so by yet another exile from England. It was possible to do one's escaping only in the sterling area: the buying of property outside it imposed the payment of a large dollar premium to the government; the exportation of one's earnings was difficult to arrange. The early swinging sixties had been presided over by Harold Macmillan, the Conservative premier who rightly told the country that it had never had it so good; they ended with the socialist administration of Harold Wilson, on to whose Liverpool constituency had rubbed some of the glamour of the Beatles. He spoke of a legacy of Tory misrule and a forthcoming technological revolution. I had met him at a cocktail party given by Charles Snow and knew he was dangerous because he was small. When I told him I came from Moss Side, he expunged the district as lost and Tory. He was to speak of literature as a minority sub-culture. He was arranging for workers in solid commodities to be subsidised by workers in invisibilities like literature, the printer and binder representing labour, the writer not. As for the right to wander the world freely, this was being denied by the currency export regulations. A week on the Costa del Sol was in order, a flight round the world possible only for the salesmen of British goods, who despised the world by despising its languages. There seemed to me to be something rather unhealthy about this progressive Britain of the sixties, choked as it was by bureaucracy. A local bureaucrat named Mr Eliot had told me that, as a great favour, I would be permitted to pay my national insurance contributions by cheque, whereas the less lucky had to line up in the post office to buy stamps to stick them on a card. I was sufficiently stung to write that he and I surely were not little children to find magic in a wearisome ritual; it was my money his department wanted, and I was earning that by writing, not by wasting time in a post office queue. I wanted to get out, and the only place to get out to seemed to be Malta. Lynne and I would fly off in early 1968 to take a look at it.

I had never had strong political beliefs. If I was a kind of Jacobite Tory, like John Dryden and Samuel Johnson, this was because socialism was positivist and denied original sin. Harold Wilson had even sneered at the 'theology' of certain Tory thinkers. The socialists were either optimistic or cynical, and I was neither. I had never, not even as a university student, written anything that could be construed as politically progressive. I had never been tempted by Marxism, and what I had seen of Marxism in East Berlin made me want to retch. If I had voted Labour in 1945, that was because, with millions of others, I believed that a Tory administration under Winston Churchill would hold weary men in the forces to keep an eye on the Iron Curtain. I had been unwavering in my lack of faith in statesmen, and it had worried me that certain writers I admired had expressed strong socialist views, which argued an unseemly naïveté in dedicated followers of truth, since a political party can represent only a fraction of the human reality which government is meant to serve. Kingsley Amis and John Braine had been very much men of the left, but now they were swinging towards a reactionary stance that denied artistic progressivism as well as political.

A fortnightly luncheon club of these holistic Tories met at Bertorelli's in Soho. I was persuaded to join them. The regular group consisted of Amis, Braine, Robert Conquest, Bernard Levin and Tibor Szamuely. The Catholic creator of Joe Lampton, working-class lad who demurs at lunching at the Con Club, was heard to say: 'The Pope's a bloody lefty.' It was only right that Amis should turn Braine into a highly reactionary pope, supping Yorkshire stingo and despising *vino* as foreign muck, in his novel *The Alteration*. These former radicals had fulfilled Marx's thesis about economics being at the bottom of everything. A struggling author does well to favour socialism and dream of art as being useful to the state; to prosper with one's books brings capital, and the state had better leave it alone. Amis and Braine had to be virulent against the left. But the literary conservatism that Amis and Conquest were adopting seemed to be based on the false premise that literary revolution and political progressivism grow from the same roots. This was never so: the literary innovators have always been bourgeois with a tendency to fascism. Amis was, is, more of a modernist than he seemed to realise:

his prose style represents as important a breakthrough in the management of récit as that of Hemingway. But the new literary canon called for the exaltation of Kipling and Housman, the putting down of Pound and Eliot. I was not quite in my depth.

1967 passed, and with it much of my fifty-first year. It was time to take stock. I had written hard and paid my way, though not with my fiction. There was a little money in the bank, and I had to consider whether it might be possible to go into hiding and concentrate single-mindedly on the damnable craft of the novel. But then came the call that all authors dream of and at the same time dread. After Christmas Hollywood was on the line.

I HAD so far had a very marginal connection with the film world. In Etchingham Dr Gordon Sears, a consultant and author of a bestselling nursing manual, had a weekend cottage, and there I met his daughters, who were both film actresses. Heather Sears had played, among other rôles, Miriam in the film version of *Sons and Lovers*, against an American Paul Morel; Anne Sears had been the only woman in *The Bridge Over the River Kwai*. Both were handsome, charming girls who denied the glamour of the profession and emphasised the hard work. This was very British. I had met Shirley MacLaine in New York, and she had not been charming; she had spent most of the evening refuting my denial of her syllogism that all Englishmen were fags and I was an Englishman, *ergo*. A cinema director, formerly small stage actor, named D'Arcy Conyers had commissioned from me for a hundred pounds a script of *The Doctor is Sick*, which he wished to film though he could not find financial backing. I had grown fond of him. He had made a silly war film called *The Night We Dropped a Clanger*, which satirised RAF heroism, and was earning his living by making television commercials that promoted a brand of washing-up liquid. I had dedicated *Inside Mr Enderby* to him. A copy of this had been bought at a railway station bookstall by the great Father D'Arcy SJ, who had written to me to ask who this D'Arcy Conyers was. He was not a member of either the D'Arcy or the Conyers family, the two being consanguine, and was evidently a nonentity named Bloggs or something trying to push himself in the world of the theatre. This was shrewd. D'Arcy Conyers sounds like a stage name, quite as much as Winchester Lymington or Wantage Charlbury. I never discovered what D'Arcy's real name was. His widow is still trying, without success, to get a film made of *The Doctor is Sick*.

There had been an attempt, in which I was not at all involved, to make a film of *Honey for the Bears*, with David Niven and Kim Novak in the main roles and a script by John Mortimer QC. I was so removed from this project that I never quite understood why the film was never made. Apparently it was to be shot in Leningrad, and a dummy script had been prepared to show the Soviet authorities: in this, I gathered, the Western sellers of black market dresses were brought to Soviet book. The authorities discovered what happened in the real script and withdrew their permission to film on Russian soil. The mocking up of a convincing Leningrad at Denham Studios was beyond purse and ingenuity, and the enterprise failed.

There had been an attempt, in the middle sixties, to put *A Clockwork Orange* on the screen, with a singing group known as the Rolling Stones playing the violent quartet led by the hero Alex, a rôle to be given to Mick Jagger. I admired the intelligence, if not the art, of this young man and considered that he looked the quintessence of delinquency. The film rights of the book were sold for very little to a small production company headed by a Californian lawyer. If the film were to be made at all, it could only be in some economical form leasable to clubs: the times were not ripe for the screening of rape and continual mayhem before good family audiences. When the times did become ripe, the option was sold to Warner Brothers for a very large sum: I saw none of the profit. There had also been attempts to make a film of *The Wanting Seed*, and I had written several scripts for it. Script-writing can be a relief from the plod of fiction: it is nearly all dialogue, with the récit left to the camera. But it is a mandatory condition of script-writing that one script is never enough. There can sometimes be as many as twenty, with the twentieth usually a reversion to the first. In any event, scripts tend to change radically once they get on the studio floor.

I was summoned to Hollywood, or rather Burbank, to discuss the creation of a script on the life of William Shakespeare. My novel *Nothing Like the Sun* had at least been heard of in the film capital, and it was considered that I could produce something sensual and violent enough to be called *The Bawdy Bard*. I could not, however, adapt my own novel, as a theatrical option had been taken on it by a New York producer, and even to lift one of my own lines from novel to script would be rank plagiarism actionable at law. The madness of the show business world was already beginning to impinge on my innocence. I had to think out an alternative Shakespeare, not too difficult in respect of somebody Coleridge called myriad-minded. The film was, moreover, to be a musical, a hard-ticket one like *My*

Fair Lady and *Camelot*. Warner Brothers Seven Arts had done well with these adaptations of stage successes, but now a singing Shakespeare was to go straight to the screen, riding on a British glamour that had to yield the rest of the available profit before taste changed. The hard-ticket movie was one of the more pleasing innovations of the late sixties. Lasting at least four hours, with an intermission, it turned a visit to the cinema into a major occasion, like suffering *The Flying Dutchman*. It was solid entertainment, and the solidity was fancifully attached to the ticket one bought. There were non-musical hard-ticks, as they were called, like *Doctor Zhivago* and *Lawrence of Arabia*. These had in common British actors and a British scenarist. Though *Doctor Zhivago* was about Russia, it was a Russia with British accents. What could be more British-accented than a musical life of Shakespeare? I forbore to say that the real Shakespeare spoke like an Irish Bostonian.

I travelled in great luxury to Los Angeles and was met at the airport by a film star who had just turned producer. This was William Conrad, unknown to me although he had made a name in the Hemingway film *The Killers*. He was a bulky man from Kentucky with a Genghis Khan look. This Shakespeare venture was his own idea, his first attempt at a major production and, it proved, his last. He was to become famous as a television performer in a series about a private eye named Cannon, and then in another series about the Rex Stout character Nero Wolfe. He was a true actor in that he knew Shakespeare, which was more than most film stars did, and when he quoted, 'Like Niobe, all tears,' tears welled briefly into his handsome dark eyes. Though I had been seen off from Heathrow by an Egyptian functionary of the Warner Brothers London office, I did not yet have the cachet that entitled me to a suite at the Beverly Wilshire, so I was put up in the Manhattan Hotel opposite Grauman's Chinese Theater. There I dined on fat lamb and stewed tomatoes, which rhymed with theaters. I could not, of course, sleep, but television all night long flashed its used car commercials. I did not dare walk the night streets, since roving police cars mistrusted all pedestrians, especially those with foreign accents. 'This ain't Piccadilly Square, my friend.' Even strolling the dawn streets was dangerous, for the invisible knives of Los Angeles smog tore at the lungs.

The Warner estate at Burbank was dominated by the Arthurian castle built for *Camelot*, which a superstitious devotion to profitable British mythology forbade to be torn down. Rank Californian grass aped British lawns perpetually watered. I expected to be installed at once in the Writers' Building, but those days were over. I was here only to discuss the content of the script and then go home to write it, or rather a ten-page treatment together with the lyrics of the songs. Bill Conrad had a palace of an office with bathroom and well-stocked bar. His secretary, Katie, had been vetted by Bill's wife, a beauty given to horoscopes and astral bodies; she was found satisfactorily plain and even old, having worked for British films in the ancient Nova Pilbeam days. She said 'All righty' much of the time. She had already typed and xeroxed Bill's plan for the film, which was based on outmoded Shakespeare lore like the Charlcote deer-poaching and the holding of horses outside the Curtain playhouse. I had nothing much against this: the aim was entertainment not exact scholarship. For that matter I had nothing against a singing Shakespeare, being only too pleased that anyone should want to put the man Shakespeare on the screen at all. Some sound theatrical instinct was telling Bill that we were into a phase of popular music closer to the Elizabethan idiom than, say, the songs of Cole Porter's *Kiss Me Kate*. The groups that twanged guitars found modal progressions like C major D major E major easier than the old tonic and dominant. We were hearing a lot of Dorian and Mixolydian on the radio. Bill annoyed me only when he tried to improvise a song that began, 'To be or not to be in love with you,/ To spend my love being hand in glove with you'.

If there was British glamour briefly around, there was also a sort of black or Negro renascence which I thought justified making Shakespeare's dark lady into an unequivocal African in a farthingale. I wanted Diana Ross being bussed hungrily on her fair black shoulders while she played John Bull on the virginals. But Bill was a man of Kentucky and demurred. He was at that time discreetly supervising an all-black film being shot by a black man who would have nothing white in it except money. The black man called himself producer and director besides scenarist and originator of concept, composer as well, since his monody was to be heard on a harmonica, presumably played by himself. It was not a good film, since its maker was deficient in all the necessary talents, but it was undeniably, though in colour, a black film. If it did not succeed, that would be the mysterious fault of Whitey or the Man or Mr Charley. Bill was quietly and Kentuckianly shocked at the idea of Shakespeare, a very superior WASP, in thrall to a really dark lady: like Dr A. L. Rowse, he would be satisfied with a Sicilian. We argued about this over a commissary salad, Bill being greeted occasionally with the 'Hi' of stars and starlets who were pallid and shrunken. The age of the homegrown giants was over, and the Robert Redfords and Faye Dunaways were only just coming in. The British, with their strong stage tradition and flourishing television drama, were dominant, though also a pain in the ass, what with either their Julie Andrews prissiness or their Peter O'Toole hellraking. The militant blacks were a pain in the ass too, but one did not dare say that.

The major trouble with the devising of a plot for the Shakespeare film, which I now insisted be called *Will!* and not *The Bawdy Bard*, was that it did not seem to have any clear motivation according to the Hollywood prescription. It was just about a Stratford lad making it in the big time and getting laid by a black bitch. Of course, there was the Essex rebellion and the desertion of his wife and the death of his son Hamnet, but how could these be merged into a single theme you could write on the back of a four-cent postage stamp? A functionary was brought in who, I supposed, had to exist, though his office did not seem to be credible – the motivation man from the script department. He was very fierce about motivation: a movie was like a locomotive, running on predestinate rails to a depot on whose platform all the luggage of past action was deposited: everything had to tie up with everything else, even if historical truth was violated. This was probably sound, even Shakespearean. The motivation man was impatient with the deficiencies of past time and thought that Shakespeare in London could get news of his dying son in Stratford by Western Union or its archaic equivalent. He ended up with a grenade he hurled across Bill's huge office – guilt. It was all about guilt. Poor Will was a guilty man. Rub in the guilt and you had your motivation, though it made what was to be a musical entertainment kinda tragic. Having dealt us the gift of guilt he went on his way, to throw other one-word grenades at other script conferences.

Apart from a plot problem there was a structural problem. A hard-ticket movie fell, like a paranged coconut, into two halves, but Shakespeare's career insisted on dividing itself by three – segment one ending with the young Will fleeing from Stratford and Lousy Lucy law while the beacons of victory over the Armada flared on the back-projected hills, segment two ending with the death of Queen Elizabeth and Will at the peak of gentlemanly prosperity and guilt, segment three bringing in James I, witchcraft, *Macbeth*, the traduction of Will's daughter Susanna for being nought with Ralph Smith, Anne Shakespeare's admission of adultery with Will's brother Richard, all Will's fault for whoring around in London, Will's gloomy drinking bout with Ben Jonson (leave Michael Drayton out of it), pneumonia, death. Not a very inspiriting finale, but at least the credits could roll over a gentleman's coat of arms, *Non Sanz Droict*, and very defiant music. I had better go home and work it all out on paper.

Bill gave a farewell party for me at his mansion in Bel Air, its number, in the Los Angeles manner, astronomical, fifteen thousand and something. Bill was one of those music-lovers who seemed to believe that surrounding himself with musical instruments would osmotically also make him a musician. There was a piano in his office, and in his house a three-manual organ and an Erard harp, though with nobody to play them. I had always wanted to try out the glissandi at the beginning of *L'Après-Midi d'un Faune*, and I spent too much time unsociably learning how to tune the harp pedals. But there were no great star guests to defer to – only Joe E. Brown's former agent, the Miss America of 1949, and one or two dithering shelved bit-players. I warmed to Bill, who made his friends out of has-beens and film technicians and despised the egomaniacal big names, what there were of them before *Easy Rider* and *Midnight Cowboy*. He was hospitable with his two-stone turkey and fixings and his desire that I be laid before flying home. The quondam Miss America was a suitable lay for one of my age, but I was not in the laying mood. So we all played word games till the smoggy dawn rose over the Californian hills. Then I flew back to London in great luxury and travelled by stopping train to Etchingham in rather less.

Lynne was remarkably well, so much so that I ought to have been frightened. Her eyes were sharply blue, her complexion was rosy, the ascites looked like mere matronly roundness. She had not been drinking much – a little gin, well-iced, the odd pint of cider from the kitchen barrel. Relieved but vaguely disturbed, I got down to the making of a film treatment and the composition of twenty song lyrics. Writing the lyrics, I thought I might as well write the music too, in short score with hints as to orchestration (shawms, sackbuts, a chest of recorders, tabors). The Queen's Men arrived in Stratford with Dick Tarleton and Will Kemp and sang who they were:

> The Queen's Men,
> The Queen's Men,
> Not beer-and-bread-and-beans men
> But fine men,
> Wine men,
> Music-while-we-dine men.

Shakespeare's father sang a song about loving life, and the Mayers chorused about bringing the maypole home (though perhaps Mayers might be the property of MGM). Anne Hathaway warned Will against ambition:

> Will-o'-the-wisp, do not desire
> To follow fame, that foolish fire.
> Better by far
> The fire at home –
> Fresh dawn on waking
> And fresh bread baking.
> A will-o'-the-wisp should not aspire
> To be a star.

Will sang to little Hamnet in the Stratford snow, with a counter-pointed Christmas carol (Bill Conrad had insisted on Christmas; he was a sucker for Christmas, he said):

> Little son,
> When I look on thee
> I am filled with wonder
> Such wonder can be –
> Part of me, yet no part of me,
> Wholly good, yet the wood of my tree.

Ghastly, I see now, diminishing the theme and the characters, yet it was the sort of thing that was wanted. There had been talk in Burbank of commissioning the Beatles to write the score, but I feared their idiom. The truth was that only Shakespeare could write the lyrics and John Dowland the music. But, as the drama of the treatment developed, the irrelevance of song became all too clear. Plenty of singing in rural Stratford but not much occasion for it when Essex was executed or Will, if the Hays Office or the Catholic League of Decency allowed, handled his hard chancre. You could hardly enclose the man Shakespeare in grand opera even. What was needed was a wholly serious non-musical hard-tick that told as much of the truth as we knew and aimed to lose money. This would never be made.

We often assume that organisations which make money are officered by men of wisdom, cultivation and plain common sense. I began to hear a distant warning voice telling me of the madness of involving myself in the cinema. This voice sounded louder when I was called to London to meet a distinguished American producer who wanted to make a film of Aldous Huxley's *Brave New World*. I remembered that Huxley himself had once wished to make a Broadway musical out of it, and might have done so had Leonard Bernstein not been too busy to collaborate. That would have been a diminution of a serious and prophetic work, but not so profound as the one that was now proposed to me in a London hotel suite. For, the producer said, the brave new world Huxley dreamed up was really this present British one, with all those chicks in miniskirts. Cut out all the Huxley crap of producing kids in test tubes and get down to presenting the final solution of a world of flower children and rock and miniskirts and all these kids having a great time screwing. The producer had found out that I was writing *The Bawdy Bard*, a great title, and assumed I would have a delicate hand at showing endless screwing. There was no point in my protesting that *Brave New World* was about the importance of free will and the degradation of conditioned happiness. Crap, the producer said, we all got to be conditioned, this guy B. F. Skinner says so, a professor some place, so there'll be no war and a world made free for ripping off miniskirts and screwing. I had to decline the commission he offered. He was disappointed, saying that I was evading the responsibility of putting Huxley right and showing a courageous new world of chicks having their miniskirts screwed off. This producer was older than I, but he had taken a rejuvenation course in a Swiss clinic.

I returned to sad Will and the completion of the treatment and the songs. They were sent off and, as in a libel suit, the project settled into a long sleep. Lynne and I left Etchingham with Haji and the cats and took breath for a vigorous season in London. For the management of the Phoenix Theatre was to present my *The Eve of Saint Venus* as the stage comedy it originally was, and there was talk of filming not merely *A Clockwork Orange* but a great deal of my work. A clothing store tycoon in America, movie-struck since he was a kid, was establishing a production company. He had read all the books I had written and found them cinematic, even the brief study of James Joyce. He would begin by setting up *A Clockwork Orange*, which the age of screwing and miniskirts was at last rendering acceptable for the screen, frontal nudity, rape and all, and he had his eye on various directors who would help me to write a script which should not reproduce the book too exactly. This was an aspect of film-making which bewildered me, the unwillingness to stick to the book. My four delinquents were variously to be turned into miniskirted girls and violent old age pensioners. The serious music crap was to be eliminated and hard rock substituted.

I was learning a great deal about the film industry, though not quite enough. One thing I was slow to learn was the importance of having something vaguely creative on paper which could be brandished in the hard faces of film financiers. An independent producer would prefer to have a first draft screenplay to wave, but scripts cost money. If he could get a treatment for nothing he considered that he was in business. There was an independent producer around who wanted to persuade MGM to back a hard-ticket film of *The Canterbury Tales*. He gave me an elaborate lunch with much cognac after and begged me to write him a long letter outlining a possible treatment. I approved of the project and still do, cursing Pasolini's homosexual travesty of Chaucer, and gladly wrote ten pages of single spacing, suggesting among other things that the Nun's Priest's Tale be done as an animated mediaeval cartoon. My enthusiasm was, as most enthusiasms are, unbusinesslike. My letter was really a ten thousand dollar treatment given for nothing. I have been more careful since, though not careful enough. Anyway, MGM disapproved of Chaucer, some old Shakespeare type guy who garbled God's plain English. The films actually made are an iceberg tip. The cinema seethes with unrealised projects.

This was not only a season of mostly aborted show business (*The Eve of Saint Venus* was never produced in the West End; a musical version of Nevil Coghill's translation of *The Canterbury Tales* seemed likely to run for ever at the Phoenix, giving the lie to MGM scepticism. Only *A Clockwork Orange* was filmed, and that not yet) but of heavy social drinking. Some professors from Amherst College, in London with their wives, made contact and, in their rented flat, vermouthless martinis. The British Council used me to entertain, at my own expense, visiting Hungarian and Finnish writers who soaked up whisky as parched earth rain. In February 1968 the *Time-Life* London bureau arranged a kind of definitive party in its Bruton Street premises. Lynne looked well in golden wig and caftan, knocking the gin back, quarrelling with Lady Snow and Edward Heath. Everybody was there, including the photographer Lord Snowdon. 'Hi, Tony,' greeted the *Time-Life* men.

I deserved well of Lord Snowdon. The *Daily Mirror* had decided to divest him of his title and refer to him as plain Armstrong-Jones. This was an aspect of a populist policy which called the Queen's consort 'the gabby dook' because he was loud in his denunciations of impertinent journalistic questions. It was a policy that could find no wrong in the enactments of the Labour government. When sterling was shamefully devalued, the *Daily Mirror* had a joyful headline about the 'perky mini-pound', presenting Britain's thinned currency as a pert teenager who would seduce Continental markets. As for the un-ennobled husband of Princess Margaret, I spent a good deal of my spare time writing to the editor in the person of an invented Pakistani named Mohamed Ali, who expressed bewilderment at the marriage laws of Great Britain, which permitted a royal princess to have two husbands. 'For, dear mister editor, she have Lord Snowdon and Mr Jones at one and same time which is bigamy. How this possible me and undersigned friends would sincerely wish to know.' There then followed thirty Muslim names, headed by Mohamed Ali, all in the impeccable Arabic script I had learned in Malaya. The editor replied to the effect that the husband of Princess Margaret had two names, and the *Daily Mirror* preferred to use the more demotic of them. 'I think you lie, mister editor, because no man have two names if he is not criminal. I ask again why royal bigamy permitted,' and so on. This went on for a long time, my waste of which on a frivolity must be blamed partially on the ethos of the sixties. I learned later that the editor was very annoyed. Eventually the *Daily Mirror* permitted Mr Armstrong-Jones to be Lord Snowdon. There he was at the *Time-Life* party, apologising that the missus could not come.

This was Lynne's last party. She had two more long sessions with me in pubs, both of which ended in violence, mine not hers. In the Antelope off Sloane Square she met an old wartime friend, Zenka Porteous, and was animated with her. Both were accused of lesbianism by a loud stranger whom I squirted and then clonked with a soda water siphon. The police were not summoned. In a pub on Villiers Street, she began to shake with dengue, which the landlord interpreted as delirium tremens, ordering us loudly out. Him I ineffectually hit and was hit back. Back home Lynne complained of nausea. She tasted, she said, strong meat extract in her throat. Then she turned pale, knowing what it was. A massive portal haemorrhage started while she lay in her bed: there were not enough pots and pans in the kitchen to hold the tides of blood. We had no London doctor, but I telephoned the first Chiswick one I found in the directory. He examined her and then called the general hospital in Ealing, saying: 'She's sitting on a volcano.' She and I were driven in a clanging ambulance: she was leaving home for good.

Neither of us realised this. She was given a blood transfusion and prepared for the excision of the spleen. She turned grotesquely yellow and it was left to a visiting clutch of Singapore nurses to remark on this with loud yelps. Lynne cursed them in Kuo-Yü, astonishing me with a sleeping knowledge of the language I never knew she had. After the operation she believed she was cured. She vowed never to drink again, though not to forsake pubs, which had been so much part of her life. She would take tonic water with a slice of lemon and a dash of bitters. She might conceivably add the odd glass of chilled light white wine. I foresaw a repetition of the old routine, a gradual augmentation of alcohol intake culminating in another portal haemorrhage. But she had suffered the statutory two, after which there was no recovery. I read up her ailment for the first time in Henry Letheby Tidy's *A Synopsis of Medicine* (an onimous name, suggesting a neat trip with Charon). Few of us want to face reality: we had kept her trouble vague, not really diagnosable.

I read that alcoholic or portal cirrhosis was a chronic degeneration of the liver due to the prolonged ingestion of alcohol, characterised pathologically by increased interlobular fibrous tissue and degeneration of the liver cells, and clinically by obstruction to the portal circulation. The external symptoms Lynne had shown were revealed to be classic: tongue heavily furred; breath foul; distended abdomen contrasting with wasting elsewhere; skin (the hepatic facies) dry, sallow and icteroid; 'when ascites occurs, very bad: this is almost a terminal event'. One would have had to be a St Julian to embrace that body, engage that breath. Ascites was the accumulation of serous fluid in the peritoneal cavity. The origin was Greek *askos*, a wineskin. That was all too appropriate. I settled to guilt. What nonsense I had preached about free will: I should have snatched tumblers from her hand, emptied bottles down the sink. That, of course, would have been cruel. I had taken her to the tropics, where shortage of vitamin B is hard on the liver. I had always persuaded her to drink drink for drink with me, ignoring the truth that women's livers are not men's. At the beginning of our relationship she had hated pubs; I taught her to love them. The attack in blacked out London had produced dysmenorrhea and a need to take in much liquid to replace the steady trickle of lost blood. She had opted for beer by the pint, which, on her recovery and modest Malayan prosperity, she had abandoned for gin, a more compact way of feeding the alcoholic need that beer, more or less on doctor's orders, had induced. And yet I hugged the blame. It was right for me to feel like a murderer.

I was not a murderer yet. Lynne had been admitted to the Ealing hospital a few days after my fifty-first birthday, 25 February 1968, itself an occasion for much gin while we watched on television a study of the eventful summer on Lake Leman when Mary Shelley wrote *Frankenstein*, her husband the *Hymn to Intellectual Beauty*, and

Byron, in the intervals of fornication, *The Prisoner of Chillon*. I had written the script for this. She was still alive, though growing languid and comatose, three weeks later, when a conclave of doctors met me and looked at me like a bench of hanging judges. 'How well do you know your wife?' I was asked. I said that I had been married to her for twenty-six years. There were no further questions: I had condoned her slow suicide.

Works of fiction which present dissolution and death rarely show the outside world, and the trivial affairs which sustain it, going brutally on, perhaps rightly impatient with the snuffing out of the universe that a single obscure death represents. My life had to go on: I had certain professional commitments. One of these – a trip to Australia to open the Adelaide Arts Festival – I had cancelled. The pop singer Adam Faith wanted to turn actor and was toying with the notion of playing Christopher Marlowe in a play I should write for him, though he was uneasy about Marlowe's being what he termed a queer. There was a kind of serial literary anthology for the BBC Overseas Service, in which Michael Redgrave, already terminally ill, read poems I commented upon. News from Burbank said that my treatment of the Shakespeare project was accepted and now I had better start on the script. I had better, also, see what films I could, learning something of those new techniques which now, with the sixties long gone, seem so outdated – jump-cuts, dialogue begun in one scene and finished in another, flash-forwards. I went to Leicester Square to see *Camelot*, which debased the Arthurian legend as *Will!* was to twist the Shakespearean truth. Life had to go on, and it was, we both tried to believe, to go on for Lynne. Keats lived without lungs and she was surviving without a spleen and with a liver that was a pure mass of fibroid tissue. I came home from drinking in a Leicester Square pub to telephone the hospital and learn that Lynne was sleeping peacefully and normally. I went to bed.

I was awakened at 3.41 by the ringing of the bedside telephone. A Pakistani voice said that my wife was sinking and that I had better come at once. It was the black rainy morning of 20 March, which my Snoopy calendar, a present from his creator, told me was the first day of American spring. I telephoned for cabs, but none were available. I called for over an hour, wondering what sub-Huxley treacle I could feed to a dying wife ('Let go, darling. Don't fight. Enter the bigger reality'). When, at about five-thirty, with the rainy night still sitting heavily over London, I got to Ealing, I found Lynne behind screens in her final coma. There was nothing I could say that she could hear. Her breath was a mere wisp and faded altogether five minutes after my arrival. It was as though she had hung on to a parody of life till then. All one could say was that it was a painless death.

I would have to return to the hospital in the true morning to collect her rings (the breaking of a finger which the American deserters had proposed would now cause no pain) and the death certificate. I found a minicab to take me home. Its radio played loud music, redolent of life, screwing, miniskirts. When a singing group named the Grateful Dead was announced I demanded that it be switched off. The driver demurred, saying that he had his sodding rights. The Grateful Dead sang me home. The cats and Haji slept. In my typewriter was an unfinished review for the book section of the *Washington Post*. It was about a new American dictionary of quotations. There was nothing else to do till dawn except finish it. I was glad, I wrote, that the lines of Sir Henry Wotton on the death of Sir Albertus Moreton's wife had not been neglected:

> She first deceased; he for a little tried
> To live without her, liked it not, and died.

That was shameful showmanship, a sly demand for pity. Letters would eventually arrive, blaming my transposition of the pronouns on an instinctive male chauvinism. For the moment, however, I was ready to bury my dead and then blot out my future.

THERE WAS no burial. Lynne had long been haunted by some story of a woman awakening in her coffin and had insisted that, when her time came, she should be cremated. The cremation took place at Mortlake, with taped music (Brother James's Air) and a brief non-denominational homily from the resident clergyman. The resurrection of the body, he almost laughingly said, was so self-evident a truth that no argument against it held, even when the body was vapourised. The only mourners except myself were Lynne's sister and the Amherst professors and their wives. Lynne's niece Ceridwen did not attend, though she had come with her mother from Leicester: she tried on Lynne's clothes and was delighted that a fine pair of leather boots fitted well. I was offered the ashes in a canister but refused them. The thing to do was get rid of all physical appurtenances: let the local predatrices, mostly Irishwomen, ransack the wardrobe; give to Deborah Rogers the lynx fur coat she had coveted; fill a cab with size three shoes and dump them at the Salvation Army depot. In the bathroom a single false tooth on a plastic palate lay in a glass: she had died with all her teeth save one that had been punched and loosened by her American assailants. In a day or two there was nothing of her left, but it is not easy to be wholly rid of the dead. Haji, with his mad psychic talent, cocked his head at her ghost coming down the stairs, barked at her silent voice. I heard her creak in the rocking chair, her nervous cough in the room above. I wept; I was damnably alone. Neither of us had made close friends: the closed circle of the culture that is marriage somehow forbade it; it had always been so.

The poet Martin Bell had left his wife and run off with a young girl: I had no drinking companion in Chiswick. Christine Brooke-Rose and her husband Jerzy Peterkiewicz invited me to dinner in Hampstead: Jerzy had been in the Ealing hospital at the same time as Lynne with a stomach complaint; he had emerged with a dietetic restriction – champagne and potatoes. Olivia Manning and her husband R. D. Smith went further: they arranged for me to meet a charming woman of thirty-eight who was willing to cohabit, though not in marriage. She had parted from a wealthy husband who left her with a Park Lane flat, a chauffeured limousine, and several thousand a year on condition that she not remarry. I preferred to savour a drunken loneliness, cracking hard-boiled eggs over the kitchen sink. I contemplated my own physical decay and then pulled myself together. I bought a bottle of Marsala and cooked some slices of veal in half of it; with the other half I made myself a zabaglione. I was being drawn to Italy but could not understand why. Lynne, I remembered, had insisted on pronouncing 'zabaglione' with a bag in it. She was always impervious to correction; correction made her angry; she always knew best.

Immortality makes sense only when the individual soul can be thought of as merging into a great collective mush of sainthood. If we take anything with us into the next world, it is not what survives in the memories of our relicts. Lynne survived in fragments which could be shuffled together to form abstract virtues and vices – her utter fearlessness, except of dentists and the dark; her devotion to animals and plants; her inability to grasp that there might be a morality of sex – but the fragments themselves were signatures of an inexplicable reality, closer to poetry than to God – her pronunciation of 'screw', her slightly deformed little finger which a pony had crushed, her inept performance of 'Gunga Din', her graceful if drunken hula. What could such fragments mean? Presumably the humanity which was irrelevant to the theologians. T. S. Eliot had wondered at the meaning of an old white horse galloping over a meadow. I wondered at the meaning of her story about the Welshwoman who said to her neighbour: 'All the colliers do laugh at your drawers on the line, you elephant-arsed old bugger.' We all survive as bits and pieces.

To the British state Lynne was an inert body to be filched of cash. I was surprised by the state's generosity in granting eighty pounds towards the cost of the funeral; I was horrified by the state's immediate closure of our joint bank account with a view to assessing death duties. The state is never so efficient as when it wants money. I received an official letter coldly informing me that my wife was dead and now had to pay for the privilege. I had heard that the functionaries who sent such letters were protected from abuse by a special department of the inured or insensitive well-versed in coping with execration. I therefore execrated. A monstrous amount of money was taken: the assumption seemed to be that my life as well as my wife's was now ended, that I had no future to finance. There was even a demand that the value of my copyrights be immediately assessed. They turned out to be worthless. If I married again, which at the moment seemed improbable, it would be without the resources appropriate to setting up a new ménage. I would have to emigrate to a low-tax area.

One week after the funeral, at 3.41 in the morning, the bedside telephone rang. I woke and lay petrified: the film was going to be re-run, I was being summoned to the hospital again to witness the final breath of my wife. I could not answer: I let the telephone go on ringing. An hour later it rang again: this time I thought I might be safe. It was California on the line, the hunters were up in America. A woman's voice like frozen orange juice said that Mr Conrad wanted to speak to me. And then Bill Conrad told me that he had read what had happened, that death was crap, that I was to come over there ostensibly for a script conference but really to get laid, pissed, inducted into a new life. Jack Mohamed of the London office would make all arrangements. It was as if America was trying to make amends for that lost tooth, symbol of so much else lost.

I was free to travel, I had no wifely permission to obtain, but I was responsible for three animals, all of whom accepted my widower status, Haji barking less now at the unseen and unheard. I arranged for my local cab-driver, Terry Sutton, one of a charming breed of Cockneys with little Anglo-Saxon blood, mostly Jewish and gipsy, to take over both house and animals in my absence. The evening before leaving for Los Angeles I took Haji on a round of the pubs. In one with low tables Haji expressed pleasure at the entrance of an Irishman and his women, but the Irishman, a young but bald navvy, fearful that his pint would be knocked over, said: 'Stop your fucking dog wagging his fucking tail.' I told the Irishman not to be stupid and he said: 'I'd bash you if you wasn't an old man.' I said: 'I've got more hair than you anyway, you baldheaded bastard.' This was very unseemly. Outside the pub I struck out unhandily, while Haji looked on with interest. The navvy punched me in the mouth and loosened the four bottom incisors. This was an interesting fulfilment of a fictional situation. In my novel *Honey for the Bears* the hero has lost his four front bottom teeth and wears a very loose prosthesis. This was precisely what was to happen to me, though not just yet. The practice of fiction can be dangerous: it puts ideas into the head of the world.

I had a bizarre TWA flight as far as Chicago. The airline was trying to attract custom by attaching a rotation of regional cuisines and fanciful regional ambiences to its first-class cabins. TWA's public relations department spelt out the scheme in a tasselled pamphlet: there was oo-lah-lah French, with the stewardesses dressed as for the can-can; there was Italian ('you like-a da music of Giuseppe Verdi, Joe-a Green to-a you?'); there was Manhattan penthouse, which might or might not have been more genuine. I had the British style imposed on me ('the new swinging Tom Jones Britain, not the fuddy-duddy what-what-old-fellow dead scene of Basil Rathbone and Dr Watson, don't you know'). The stewardesses wore mini-skirts and tunics of Beefeater design, with union jack knickers. They served Milwaukee beer in pint plastic tankards and what was termed a pub lunch – mild shrimp curry with Thousand Island dressing on the obligatory salad. I grew drunk and condemned the banality of the image: the captain was brought in from his cockpit to quieten me down. I feared another punch in the teeth; I slept. Still, I was being reintroduced to life, such as it was.

Life in Los Angeles now meant a suite at the Beverly Wilshire Hotel, dinners at Chasen's, and a visit to Forest Lawn, where, Bill Conrad assured me, I would see very clearly how much crap death was. This was over a hot pastrami sandwich in an eaterie close to the cemetery gates, its name The Last Chance. Bill was right. If this Californian way of death was its most up-to-date, that was to say American, version, then death was crap. Evelyn Waugh's *The Loved One* exaggerated nothing. An oleaginous voice oozed a commentary on a stained glass reproduction of Leonardo's *Last Supper*; there were statuettes of little girls displaying their knickers in a high wind; there was a Poets' Corner where Mrs Adelaide Schultz and other literary dignitaries were inurned. The sales talk of the hostesses was so persuasive that I nearly put down a hundred-dollar deposit for my own little nook under the cypresses, but Bill said: 'Don't do it, boy. You gotta real Poets' Corner in Westminster Church. Wait a bit and you'll get in there for free.' Bill had great confidence in my literary talent. Damn it, I was writing a script on the life of Will Shakespeare.

Waugh had described a script conference as a session of coffee house chatter. We had some of these, but we also had performances of the music I had written for *Will!*, fully orchestrated and with mixed chorus, stereophonically recorded. I spent a lot of time in my Beverly Wilshire suite composing more. I was going to do well for credits, Bill said: script by, lyrics by, music by. The project was growing sufficiently to encourage discussion of casting: Robert Stephens as Shakespeare; Maggie Smith, his wife, as his wife; James Mason as Philip Henslowe; David Hemmings as Christopher Marlowe; Peter Ustinov as Ben Jonson ('because he looks like Ben Jahnson'). The Earl of Southampton? The Earl of Essex? The Queen herself? Time enough to think of those; get the script started. At least we got the story line developed over gin and bourbon as far as the Essex rebellion. Bill had a good idea about that. The day before the execution of Essex, let the Lord Chamberlain's Men be summoned to Whitehall to present *Richard II* before the Queen. This play, after all, triggered the rebellion. Poor Will, as John of Gaunt, sees the Queen signing papers. Is he, the author of a play about regicide, to be beheaded? No, he is merely made to suffer a nightlong vigil, be escorted to Tower Hill at dawn, witness the Earl's beheading, and then submit to a tongue-lashing from the Queen: stick to your fairy stories, little man; don't meddle with history; history is an undying fire, and fire burns. My later examination of the facts showed that the Lord Chamberlain's Men were indeed ordered to play at court on the eve of the execution. It was Shrove Tuesday, and the Shrovetide revels went ahead as usual. What the play presented was we do not know, but it would have been like the Queen's sardonic humour to insist on *Richard II.*

I did not get myself laid on this visit. I seemed to be keeping myself pure for some profound venerean event of the future, not yet defined, unguessed at. I accompanied Bill's wife to a great astrological dinner at which a lecture was given on the horoscope of the beached *Queen Mary.* I had my own horoscope plotted: it afforded no hint of a coming major event in my life. I went home to Lynne. No, I did not, but I went home. Deborah Rogers had decided that I must change my publishers on both sides of the Atlantic – from Heinemann to Jonathan Cape; from Norton to Knopf. Friends of hers, bristling with Jewish know-how and panache, headed the houses – Tom Maschler in London, Bob Gottlieb in New York. Gottlieb was in London when *Enderby Outside* was published: he conceded that it showed talent but he checked any tendency to overpraise; after all, he had edited *Catch-22* into a bestseller. In New York at this time both parts of the Enderby story came out as a single volume entitled *Enderby*, to a fair measure of critical praise but no hope of high sales. Jonathan Cape was preparing a volume of my essays, mostly written for the *Spectator*, under the title *Urgent Copy*. My life was changing a little.

It seemed to be changing a lot when John Bryan, a producer who had made his initial name as a cinema art director, proposed making a film of Enderby inside and outside. He, I, and the chosen director Joe McGrath, were each to exhibit two talents in the production – John would produce and design; Joe would direct and devise film trickery; I would write both the script and the music. Bryan had already, with Alec Guinness, filmed Joyce Cary's *The Horse's Mouth* – a movie that honoured a visual artist whom the goddess of material success rejected; the Enderby film, doing the same thing for a poet, would be the other panel of a diptych. I wrote the script and was paid. Albert Finney was to play Enderby and Anouk Aimée all the women. All that came of the project was that these two married. It would have gone ahead if John Bryan had not dropped dead of a heart attack at the Cannes Film Festival of 1969. But I was already having doubts about the viability of putting poets on the screen: who wanted poets, even if one of them was Shakespeare? I heard rumours from Burbank that Bill Conrad was now fighting with the Warner Brothers studio chiefs about *Will!* Bill telephoned to say he was coming over to London to continue the fight. This seemed to me to be like fighting for Rome at Philippi, but apparently all Hollywood was at the Ritz or Claridge's at that time. It had something to do with all the money that had been made out of *My Fair Lady*, *Camelot*, *Lawrence of Arabia* and *Doctor Zhivago*.

Meanwhile, in extreme loneliness which unhappy local married women, mostly Irish, tried to assuage, I worked on the script for *Will!* I had to educate myself in a new technique, even a new grammar, learning how to clip dialogue, move cameras about, when to use two-shots and long shots and close-ups. I worked hard but with a kind of hopelessness, knowing that the first script would be unacceptable simply because it was the first. After about thirty minutes of screen time the maypole was brought home in Shottery, and drunken Will woke in the arms of Anne Hathaway. How many more hours would have to elapse before he left her his second-best bed?

Bill Conrad arrived in London in a spring well-advanced but rainy. He shared a Mayfair apartment with Sheldon Reynolds, a Europeanised American producer, and it was possible to convince both that I knew a little about writing for a visual medium, for the BBC showed a sixty-minute film I had helped to make on the life and work of the Czech composer Martinú. This was the kind of television documentary, conveying as much dramatic tension as straight information, that could not be made in America. It certainly could not be made on a thousand-pound budget. Hollywood's mad spending was a phenomenon to which I found it difficult to adjust, and it was figured in the London lifestyle of these Americans who took over our capital without diffidence, dragging me with them to restaurants with an indigestible cuisine and night clubs where expensive whores clung to them. In one of these lavish clipjoints Bill paid a hundred pounds to a large-breasted strumpet he favoured: this was the fee for getting me laid as he had been laid. I declined the gift, rightly: Bill was later to complain that she gave him a dose.

When Bill had missed being knifed by the Mafia in a Soho *trattoria*, had admired Harold Wilson's oratory in the House of Commons, had furnished his yacht, then at anchor in Santa Barbara, with solid British equipment, and had been soundly clipped in Paris, it was time to meet the head of the Warner Brothers studio at an exclusive club in Park Lane. This was a kind of extraterritorial enclave where bills were paid in dollars, where dark Levantine men with many rings stroked asthenic starlets, and all the items on the menu, even the spring vegetables, had been imported from the United States. The head of the studio was a very young man to whom Bill almost tremulously deferred. We put the Shakespeare project to him succinctly and he said: 'Great. You got all you want here in London – Westminster Church and St Paul's Cathedral and, yeah, you even got that river.' I had to point out that St Paul's had been built in the Restoration period and that Elizabethan London was best found in York or Strasbourg, but he was impatient with these niceties. London, though it swung, was kinda old, like Shakespeare himself: as with those youths of the Berlin *Moby Dick*, this young American distinguished no degrees of antiquity. The point was that we could go ahead with the project: front money would be at once available, a budget of several million dollars could be compiled, *The Bawdy Bard* was a great title. Bill shut my mouth quickly on that. Afterwards he was calmly elated: my British voice, which breathed a sort of Shakespearean authority, had convinced Benny or Bunny or whatever his name was that we had a great enterprise on hand, a new *My Fair Lady* with bosoms in it and old-time screwing like in *Forever Amber*, to say nothing of plague and fire. We were made, boy. Bill bought me, at the studio's expense, a very large brandy of great though vague antiquity.

Bill remained around, and it was my duty to take him by river to Richmond, show him Hampton Court, regale him with old-time music hall at the Players' Theatre, disgust him with belching and farting Chaucer at the Phoenix Theatre. But somebody more important than Bill had just re-entered my life. This was the Italian lady I had made love with in the empty Chiswick house in late 1963. Her name was Liana Macellari, lately divorced in Boston from the black Ben Johnson, at present working in Cambridge on projects of applied linguistics. She had, all those four years back, entered my life very briefly and then disappeared to Paris, but not before giving birth to a child in a London hospital on 9 August 1964. The child was mine, a boy named, though not baptised, Paolo Andrea. She announced this fact almost incidentally. She had known I had a sick wife, had heard that I had become a widower, commiserated, now assumed that I could acknowledge fatherhood but made no other proposals. She was living with a man in a house on Victoria Road in Cambridge, and the house was full of rent-paying Iranians. She must, I said firmly, leave that man and the Iranians, bring my son to Chiswick and at once marry his father. But she did not approve of marriage, since this was a Christian sacrament and the Church was the enemy of all women. She was deeply radical and wore a kind of Mao outfit. My Californian horoscope had said nothing of this cataclysmic change in my life. She was piquantly beautiful in her Mao outfit, had a bigger appetite for life than either Mao or Marx would endorse, and filled my heart at once and for ever.

Being willing to give birth to my child did not necessarily indicate a devotion to the father. A child had to be given birth to to fill the emptiness in the soul of her mother, who was grieving over the death of her other daughter, Grazia. Grazia, whose photographs I was to see, had been a girl of great beauty, and a fine scholar and a notable athlete, a representative of Italy in international sports and a devoted climber of mountains. She had been on an Alpine expedition in an early spring when the slopes were still icy and had slipped to her death. The authorities responsible for the expedition could be blamed entirely for this: in an obscure way it was the fault of the Christian Democrat party, who would prefer the risk of a girl's being killed on a mountain to her being seduced by sports like dancing, physically safe but morally dangerous. The Christian Democrats being Liana's great enemy, she could turn only to the Italian Communists, who promised a diminution of the power of Catholicism and a better deal for women. I, the father of a son I was still to see, could probably be loved for myself, but that might take time. Moreover, Liana was committed contractually to a research position in Cambridge, was looking after a man on the fringes of the theatre but at present without work, and was finding it convenient to · have her son looked after not only by the man but by the female Iranians, who had names like Fatimah and Shireen and fed the lad on powdery sweetmeats.

I was adamant in my demand that she break her contract, leave the house, move in with me and Haji and the cats, and prepare for marriage. I refused to allow my son, still an abstraction, to grow up illegitimate. Matters must be regularised, and soon. For the moment Liana was prepared to lunch with me and make love on free days but no more. Bill Conrad, meanwhile, fretted at my neglect of him and went back to Los Angeles. Joseph L. Manciewicz was willing to be appointed director of *Will!*, so Bill telephoned me in the middle of the night, but would not be able, because of another commitment, to discuss the project until November. By then the script should have been delivered, photocopied, and passed around. Bill commented, before catching his TWA flight with its Manhattan penthouse fantasy, that I looked thinner.

When the calendar, in bitonal counterpoint with the weather, had just announced summer, Liana walked out on Cambridge and in on me. She brought my son with her, a child not quite four with something of my nose but otherwise a beauty that combined the Celt and the Italic. He was a well-made vigorous climbing boy who preferred to engage the streets naked. He was officially a Cockney, having been born within the hearing of Bow bells, but spoke Cambridge English with no Italian accent. He could say '*Ciao bambina*' and often did to elderly ladies, but he called spaghetti 'boschetti'. Fish he called 'shif'. He ate raw bacon and drank milk by the quart and was imperious in demanding his dinner. Liana came of a family which had maids and a cook and hence had never learned the Welsh arts of housekeeping. I had to take to the kitchen very seriously and cooked more than I wrote. Shopping with Liana for basic foodstuffs became a more operatic experience than Chiswick was used to, and it disclosed that there were more Italians about than I could ever have suspected: a Cockney butcher was revealed to be from Calabria, and a red-haired girl at a cash register spoke the language of Goldoni. The Chiswick house was now a shambles less through neglect than through its becoming a miniature Naples filled with tough children, black and white, who followed the naked lure of Paolo Andrea. They made ambushes of the furniture and climbed the curtains. As making love took up much of the day as well as the night, these children were not easy to control: only the smell of burning enforced a closer watch.

Liana's desertion of Cambridge was not all that pacific. The man she had lived with raged on the telephone but eventually gave in. He even hired a truck to convey Liana's library to Chiswick, though he dumped it viciously on the doorstep. I kept out of his way with the prudence of a victor in love. I kept out of the way of Eric Swenson of Norton of New York, who arrived in London enraged at my treason. I did not understand the rage: I had brought a little prestige to his publishing house but absolutely no money. Liana and Paolo Andrea and I kept escaping to Etchingham, whither, for some reason, *Time-Life* photographers pursued us. The American press, romantic at heart, seemed moved by the turbulent happiness that was rewarding my devotion to ill-paid literature. Alvin Lee, the Australian head of *Time*'s literary section, promised me a front cover, but he died before this could be implemented.

We escaped in a 1930 Morgan tourer which I bought for Liana. Italian women are natural drivers, fast and with animal reflexes, and they have a sense of style which disdains the orthodox family saloon. Liana had had a 1924 Sunbeam which she sold to Lord Montagu's automobile museum; soon she was to have a Bedford house on wheels. The Morgan meanwhile was cheered by truck drivers and frequently broke down, but that apparently was one of the joys of motoring. My life had been utterly transformed: I had a young and beautiful mistress or betrothed of exotic origin, a son who, in the Bristol fashion, called me Antoniole, and a new mobility. I needed to earn money to support this ménage, but I was writing little except reviews for the *Spectator* and *Country Life*, usually surrounded by loud children who treated the typewriter as a piano for several hands. There was also Haji, much louder, delighted with the perpetual play in which he joined. He was very much a dog for play. An attempt had been made to breed from him, and he had been shut in the Etchingham cellar with a collie bitch on heat, but he had insisted only on play. He was known in the dog trade as a bad doer.

In the country and London alike I began to see how much the British disliked children. Britain is the only country in the world which needs a society to ward off cruelty to them. Where could one take a child in the long summer evenings? Even pubs with gardens were barred to them; in restaurants their careless elbows swiped dishes from the table. Paolo Andrea's preferred nakedness appalled most adults. Only in the Café Royal, with its Italian waiters, did he seem welcome. I beguiled his restlessness with stories – after all, story-telling was supposed to be my trade – and he always wanted Germans in them, whom he confused with germs. As for professional story-telling, I was too much preoccupied with living my own life to invent lives for others. But a living had to be earned, death duties had eaten at my capital, the prospect of writing furiously in a low-tax area was less an attraction than a necessity. Italians, however, all love London, and Liana demurred at the prospect of an exile for me which would be more like a repatriation for her, since I proposed setting up house on the Mediterranean.

Malta, to be exact. Cyprus, Gibraltar and Malta were all in the sterling zone, but the Rock was overcrowded, Cyprus was discontented, and Malta was inviting the retired British to come and pay a tax of sixpence in the pound. Liana and I decided to inspect Malta. Paolo Andrea was sent back to Cambridge and his adoring Iranians, the cab-driver Terry Sutton moved in with his wife on Haji and the cats, and we flew to Luqa and took a hired car to Mabel Strickland's hotel in the Mdina. We registered as man and wife, but on the morrow of our arrival the *Daily Mail* had a brief romantic item, a laughing photograph, and the headline BURGESS TO WED AGAIN. This was embarrassing: the Stricklands, an old Malta British family and the owners of the *Times of Malta*, were respectable. The response to the revelation of our living in temporary sin was, however, minimal: the double bed was removed and twin beds substituted.

We were impressed with several things in Malta – the Caravaggios, the baroque architecture, the blue clean waters, and the language. Maltese was, we discovered, a kind of Arabic in Romic script, with a number of Romance loanwords. Liana and I had in common a concern with linguistics and especially toponymy, place-names being visible and often bizarre history. But, Liana said, Malta had a Sicilian smell. And there were too many priests around. Vendettas were allowed, but not sex. Since she had translated Thomas Pynchon's *V*, which has Malta among its settings, she was anxious to see Strait Street, or the Gut, in Valletta, where sailors picked up girls. This place did not officially exist, any more than did the Maltese Mafia that worked in London: there was a lot of hypocrisy around, and there were also two archbishops, one for Malta and one for the island of Gozo. Because St Paul had got to Malta before getting to Rome, the Maltese clergy prided itself on professing a more genuine Christianity than the Vatican retailed. It was a highly repressive Christianity and, as if to prove this, there were a lot of fireworks. Firework manufacture seemed to be a cottage industry, like the potting of shrimps in Morecambe, and there were many unpurposed explosions. It was possible, though, that some of these were all too much purposed, an expression of vendetta. Vendetta was the theme of most of the films shown: sex was taboo.

In the small township of Liji, in the geometrical centre of the island, we inspected a rather fine house built in 1798, the year of Napoleon's invasion. It was floored in marble, had an impressive *piano nobile*, three bathrooms and four toilets, and a garden with its own artesian well and many lemon and orange trees. It had a bad reputation, so we heard in a local bar, because its former owner had hurled himself from the roof in a fit of depression. Liana and I, not being Maltese, were not put off by the talk of a screaming ghost. The house seemed to me the sort of place where a writer could set up his books in the kind of clear light that was lacking in London, and work in moderate comfort. I was entirely wrong to purchase it, as I was to discover, since it committed us to an ambience we learned to dislike and even fear. It proved not to be resaleable. It would have been better to rent more humble premises and see how we got on. But I had always regarded the purchase of property as good investment. Only in Malta was the value of property to go down.

I put down my deposit with Cassar and Cooper the estate agency in Valletta. Certain brown faces lightened with what I ought to have interpreted as relief. Then Liana and I drank, ate, swam, drove, noted the African quality of this parched land which had no trees, except in private orchards. The story in Acts of St Paul's being bitten by a snake when gathering wood was not to be believed: the island had been treeless even under the Romans. There was the bay where Paul was certainly shipwrecked. It was a queer-sounding Pauline Catholicism they had here: since the vernacularisation of the mass you could hear Allah praised in the churches, and Lent was known as Ramadan. Liana with bare arms was not admitted into one of these churches. But perhaps, in those late sixties, liberalisation was on its way. A miniskirted Maltese girl who had evidently lived in

Manchester struck out in Valletta at a soutaned priest who tut-tutted at her gear: 'You get some trousers on and look more like a bloody man.' Whatever the nature of life for the Maltese, we could be above it. No more English winters for me: Malaya and Brunei had thinned my blood and I had suffered in icebound Etchingham. On a London street I had slipped and fallen. I proposed a permanent Mediterranean exile.

We flew back and talked about marriage. There would be no church wedding: Liana hated the Church while loving its art. George Dwyer, Archbishop of Birmingham, having read in the press of my forthcoming Italian marriage, assumed this would drag me back to the faith, but non-Italian Catholic clerics do not know the naturally atheistic Italians as well as they should. He telephoned me and said: 'She'll butcher you, lad.' This was a reference to Liana's surname Macellari, which may be cognate with *macellaio*, meaning a butcher, but probably goes back to the butchering of the battlefield. And then, from Liana, as so often: was marriage necessary? Yes, because testamentary rights had to be fixed and Paolo Andrea had to be legitimised. First, though, there had to be confirmation that she had genuinely been divorced on grounds of desertion, and this meant contacting the appropriate legal department of the Commonwealth of Massachusetts. Ben Johnson, the son of a black Boston lawyer, was believed now to be living in Rome with a new wife. Being American, he had the right to a universally valid divorce, but Liana did not. Married to me, in Italy her state would be bigamous. This was something that had to be risked. For that matter, according to the registrar at Hounslow, there was a certain risk in regarding as viable under British law the act of divorce now confirmed on paper from the Commonwealth of Massachusetts. But, law being a matter of precedents, one was taking risks all the time. In the autumn of 1968 Liana and I had our registry office wedding, while Paolo Andrea played outside, not naked, with children of the streets. He was no longer a bastard, but that was all one to him.

We now bought new furniture and arranged for its dispatch, along with the old furniture of both houses, to a Malta warehouse. I proposed letting the Chiswick house, complete with Haji and cats, to Terry Sutton and selling the Etchingham house to the daughter of Mills the grocer: this disposal of the houses had, in the event of our leaving England again, always been Lynne's intention, though it had never been put in writing. Then came the purchase of a Bedford Dormobile, in which we were to travel through France, Italy and Sicily to Malta. The Morgan was to be crated and sent. The Bedford

Dormobile was a handsome vehicle that, through an ingenious arrangements of shutters and convertible seats, could be transformed into a house with two bedrooms. There was a gas cooker, a toilet, a sink, even a bar. There was a steady table that could be set up with a typewriter on it. It seemed possible to live for ever in this compact rainproof dwelling, with its chintzy curtains shutting out the night. Was the nomadic life possible in an age when governments wanted to know where their citizens were so that they could be soundly taxed? Gipsies were gipsies, citizens of their own traditions, a mercifully illiterate people to whom letters never came. Hitler had killed off as many as he could; the post-Hitlerian state had been taught to disapprove of them. Matthew Arnold's scholar gipsy was a romantic figment. The life of the road was a tempting idea, but a professional writer had to have an address.

A nightingale had sung in Chiswick throughout the summer. What woke me more was my first wife as a revenant, slim, smart, very blonde, very blue-eyed, announcing that a mistake had been made in the Ealing hospital, it was not she who had died but another: there had been a confusion of documents. Now she was back and we could resume our life together. But, I stammered, I have made new arrangements. You *have* to be dead: another woman had taken over my life. I woke groaning and sweating. This nightmare recurred even when we were at anchor on the roads of Europe. My sleep is still not wholly free of it.

In articles for the press, British and American, I announced my intention of leaving England for good. It was a kind of Jeffersonian declaration: a decent respect for the opinions of mankind required that I should declare the causes which impelled me to the separation. I was not being disloyal to the land that had bred me: that land rather had been disloyal to the faith of my ancestors; it was the land of the Test Act and the Gordon riots. I would be more at home where the Angelus sounded at noon and people made the sign of the cross in public. Anyway, the British, before the dissolution of their empire, had regarded exile as a kind of patriotism. I had gone abroad twice to serve that empire, or what was left of it, and now I proposed serving something bigger – the language which had united it and had produced a great but mostly disregarded literature. I could serve that language best by considering it against the foil of other languages.

There were other reasons for exile – my marriage to a European, my need of light, my disgust with British taxation. This last was presumed to be the one and only reason. To make the declaration at all was pretentious, but it proved to be a kind of anticipatory answer to an attack made on me in the *Daily Mirror*. I was a rat leaving a sinking ship, it said. Rats are wise to leave sinking ships, but Britain did not seem to be sinking more than usually. There was a kind of rage at a writer's presuming himself to be free, which he is. The only guilt I have felt at leaving England is the guilt of not missing England more.

THREE

OUR TYRES were filled with air near Wingham, but the caps were not replaced. Our petrol tank was brimmed before driving on to the packet at Dover, but the cap was not replaced. A customs officer bullied us and made us display our money. A car-turntable-manipulator on the boat sold us a cork bung for a pound. So much for England's farewell. It was, of course, raining heavily.

The state's limitation on the export of sterling was a problem. Once in sterling Malta we would be in a free-spending zone, but there was a great non-sterling stretch of Europe to cover. My official abandonment of Britain was not yet accepted. We drove off at Calais to find October France as wet as October England, glum at the prospect of having to count every sou and live off loaves and cheese and swigs of *vin ordinaire*. The French hate waste on principle, and French motorists kept stopping us to show how much essence we were spilling: that cork bung fitted badly.

The Bedford Dormobile, which looked like an ambulance, was permitted to park anywhere, even on a bridge over the Seine while unaffordable Paris pulsed in lights without. There was something voluptuous about turning the vehicle into a two-bedroomed hotel and lying naked while rude youths tapped at the windows. And so south-east towards Provence. I took the opportunity, while Liana was sleeping, to baptise Paolo Andrea in rain-water: '*Ego te baptiso Paulum –* ' did *Andrea* take a Latin or a Greek accusative? – '*in nomine Patris et Filii et Spiritus Sancti, Amen.*' At need any layman was permitted to do it. It was best to be on the safe side.

We were not robbed until we got to Avignon. The old papal town was full of mean-eyed Algerians. Liana had a great leather bag which contained all our documents and money as well as the gold trinkets of a dead wife. After an evening in which Paolo Andrea pranced naked through the streets ('*Il est fou,*' muttered the Avignon crones), his mother laid the bag down to open the Dormobile door and put the inert child to bed. It was whisked off immediately by an Algerian who had been skulking in the shadows. The money and traveller's cheques were loss enough, but the theft of an Italian passport was devastating. In those days there was a British consulate at Nice, and the news of the theft of two British passports was greeted with no surprise: Avignon and Algerians had bred a new version of an old song: '*Sur le pont d'Avignon on y vole, on y vole.*' I had evidence of my own identity – *Urgent Copy*, just out on our departure, with my name, age, birthplace and photograph on the dust-cover. This did not impress the officials: there will always, to the British, be something shady about a book. There was much secret telephoning of London, chiefly – so I was told at day's end – to find out if I was kidnapping this child. At dusk a joint passport was issued to father and son: this made more sense than Paolo Andrea's own filched document, on which the photograph was of a generic baby. I was even allowed to draw francs to the tune of a hundred pounds from the Nice branch of a British bank. Liana's case was very different.

At the Italian consulate in Nice it was regretted that a passport could be issued to an Italian citizen only in Rome, and then only after exhaustive enquiry. As a travel document Liana was allowed to have a sick green provisional form of the kind usually issued to criminals travelling under escort. Paolo Andrea, with no retaliatory intent, locked the consul in his office. Sadly that night we ate a bouillabaisse outside Monaco and then drove in apprehension to the Franco-Italian border at Ventimiglia. The apprehension was justified. The brutal official, in a nest of armed men from the Italian south, inspected Liana's document, crashed the table with a stonebreaker's fist, and cried: '*Criminale!*' My Italian then was more of a Dantesque than a colloquial order, and the best response seemed physical: I hit out and guns were drawn. I said loudly and slowly: '*Questa situazione è proprio fascista.*' I was told, rather mildly: '*No, è regolare.*' The chief of frontier control, *il dottore*, was summoned and there was a fine operatic scene in which Liana granted herself only the odd *arietta*. She had an attitude of controlled amusement, as in confrontation of an old enemy whose every move was foreknown. What was the relationship between herself and this violent *inglese*? Whose was that child sleeping in the front of this probably stolen vehicle? Where was proof of ownership of anything? The *inglese* was an *amico* and the child was his. Where then was the mother of the child? Dead, dead, dead in childbirth. I got the impression that the British, long deprived of the financial means of foreign travel, were now an unknown race on the continent of Europe. My passport was pored over like a stone of the Hittites. The scene ended with an admirable male duet, tenor and baritone, with odd mezzo-soprano interpolations. Then, as in *Otello*, the storm calmed and all was peace and the dandling of sleepy Paolo Andrea. We were allowed to enter Italy.

I now began to appreciate what Orwell had written of the major differences between Britain and the continent from which it had sundered itself. Once you form a police state it is very hard to dismantle. The bullying and hectoring were indeed *regolare*: Liana's defiance represented a hopeless attempt to change history. She had refused, on her marriage, to become a British subject: she clung to her Italian passport, made out in her maiden name, in order to retain the right to fight her own government. Orwell had written of the gentleness of the British police, who shared the mild knobby faces of those they protected rather than persecuted. Italian police faces are not like that. Unseducible by the charms of a woman, they melt when great hairy hands handle a child. In that too they are different from the British.

Despite the servants of the state, whom all Italians cordially detest anyway and are adept at cheating after two millennia of misrule, I began myself to melt as we wheeled along the Ligurian coast. This was not quite *la douceur de vivre* one was entitled to in middle age, but I had grudgingly to admit to an improvement in health, a loss of weight, days that ended in love and began without hangover. I had left behind the north of gin and animal fat and had entered the land of olive oil and garlic and cheap wine. The Genoese women adored Paolo Andrea but were prepared to strike out at parents who allowed him to run around without the protection of *la maglietta di sanitá*, a kind of D'Annunzio name for the undervest. Paolo Andrea could spill *caffé* milk or smash glasses with impunity. All the hope of the Italian future lies desperately with children.

We crossed Emilia into Veneto, and in St Antony's own cathedral in Padua I prayed (O saint who findest lost things) for the recovery of Liana's passport by the Avignon police and its delivery to the Questura in Rome. But St Antony would find it difficult to comprehend exactly what a passport was (a little book, dear saint and patron, to tell the disbelieving world who we are). Paolo Andrea knelt too before the gaudy statue, gazing up at it in awe: he had never been inside a church before this. Our prayers proved ineffectual. We continued our grand or little tour, my senses overwhelmed but, since this was not Ireland, my religious doubts unassailed. As for the Grand Tour of the past, I had written a long essay on it for a gorgeous coffee-table book published by Paul Elek, pretending to know all about it. There had been altogether too much pretence and lying in my literary career. Now I promised my patron saint, or any other heavenly body that had ears, to live a life of total honesty and absolute fidelity. I would be loyal to my wife and son. I would work hard and try to tell the truth. I have, I think, kept my promises. And so to Venice.

On the road to Venice, in a tiny town whose name I have forgotten, the Bedford Dormobile or Bedmobile sustained its first injury. The narrow street clasped the wide white moving vehicle with loose finger and thumb. But from the offside wall two ancient hooks protruded. One scored the fibreglass body from front to rear, the other shattered the open frosted glass louvres of the tall but narrow lavatory. The noise was of doomsday. We got out to raise arms to unhearing heaven, while cars honked mercilessly behind. There was nobody to complain to: the history of Veneto alone was to blame with its left-overs from a far past, rusty hooks of great length perhaps for hanging chines of bacon. The malign fates had robbed us and were now attacking our home. A glasscutter cut ordinary plate glass to fit into the louvre slots. When we got to the dry-land area west of the Piazza di Roma, from which one embarks to engage the water-city, we met an Australian and his wife who were touring Europe in a pantechnicon with showers and spare bedrooms called, with dangerous optimism, The Happy Wanderer. They had sustained no scratch. Life was clearly being unfair to us. In a Venetian *trattoria* Liana and I had our first quarrel.

It was about nothing really. She had ordered as a special treat for me a plate of *polenta*, to be eaten with the sauce of stewed rabbit. But to me this yellowish pudding seemed apt to be taken only with raspberry jam. I was, she complained, insulting the cuisine of her country. Her country? Veneto was not her country: she belonged to the Marches. All our quarrels were to be reserved to the kitchen: olive oil and garlic confronting suet dumplings and boiled spuds. She adored fennel and endives; she devoured chicken gizzards and lightly fried brains. I did not. Her inner economy was a European one, mine all too insular. Paolo Andrea was ready to live on what he still called boschetti, followed by ample and multicoloured *gelati*. He howled for *gelati* on a *vaporetto* proceeding along the Grand Canal and, slapped by his mother, howled again. Slapping a child was an aspect of public life in Italy: everybody was involved in the justice or injustice of it. We disembarked near San Marco and Paolo Andrea was bought a *gelato*, though not by his parents.

In a bookshop I was surprised to see my name on an elegant

dust-jacket over the title *Un' Arancia a Orologeria*. Einaudi of Turin had at last published *A Clockwork Orange*, ill-advisedly translated by Floriana Bossi into the Milanese dialect. It was appropriate that my marriage into Italy should be so celebrated. It was my first but far from last experience of meeting a book of mine in public whose appearance had not been announced to me in private. Liana haggled with the bookseller and brought the price down: this was something to give to Liana's mother in San Severino, whither we were circuitously bound. Her surviving daughter had married a genuine author, meaning one translated into Italian. One in love with violence, judging from the content of this Italian début. But Paolo Andrea, whom she had still to meet, would be the best present.

My visual education was belatedly beginning. I needed it, a northern Catholic who, like James Joyce, had been brought up on sounds. Liana had studied the history of art in Bologna and Rome; she was a tireless ciceronessa, making me drunk on Giorgione and Titian. I made no move in the direction of becoming Ruskinian. I was not over-impressed by the manipulation of space. I could not deny the beauty of the Venetian skyline, but it was unframed by time. There it all was, Tintoretto in the autumn sun, but it was not music: it had no rhythm, no beginning nor end. Beautiful, yes, but what did one do with it? It did not perform, it just was.

And so south towards Bologna. The Bedmobile was looking weathered, battered, lived-in. It was often too much trouble to demolish the double bed in the rear each morning, reconverting it to a couple of facing cushioned benches: it lay, all rumpled sheets, for the night's repossession. The seven-feet-tall lavatory plywood door refused to close, swung, stuck so as to impede the driver's vision of the road behind. British workmanship, the old complacent complaint. A cupboard piled with British crockery grew bored with its burden and decided to consider gaping and disgorging, but I was just about too quick for it. The engine remained loyal, but the flimsy fittings conspired to rebel. The little cargo of Italian cheeses gave the impression that we were carting a corpse. Still, there was nothing really to complain about. We were free as the air, though letters and obligations were piling up in London, Hollywood, Valletta. We reached Bologna, one of the scenes of Liana's youth. In the main post office there a majestic ageing lady named Eleonora Laderchi was in charge, married to a retired colonel named Oscar Pioli: being in charge meant being on call, though calls seldom came, in the crammed flat above; it also meant carrying the same army rank as her husband. I was now meeting the outlying flanks of Liana's family.

It was a complicated family, and I had decided to shut my eyes to it as far as I could. The Laderchi branch had married into the Pasi branch, and the Pasi branch was noble and of immense antiquity. Liana's mother was the Contessa Maria Lucrezia Pasi della Pergola, and she had married Liana's commoner father for love. He had been an actor, and his voice was still eerily to be heard on television in dubbed films. He had been violently anti-fascist, but cancer had got him before the executioners of the party. He had also, while resting from the theatre and cinema, been a photographer, and it was while photographing the Pasi family that he had met the young contessa. Aristocratic blood was thus tempered with peasant, which in England would have been lower middle-class like my own, though the name Burgess pointed to something higher. Antonio Borghese sounded better than Maria Lucrezia Macellari, the burgher higher than the butcher. The Pasi family, which had spawned counts and barons all over the north of the peninsula, still cherished its family trees and its coat of arms; there had been one count who claimed descent from Attila, who has always been popular in the north-eastern cities he ravaged. Liana could thus, if I wished, in temper be called a Hun.

Anyway, a kind of family contact had been made in Bologna, and a closer contact could be postponed till we had visited Faenza, another of Liana's girlhood towns, and Florence. Meanwhile I had a quick sample of Bologna, which had the flavour of Central Europe and, in the winter that was approaching, would have a Central European cold. This meant sampling the Bolognese cuisine, a cuisine adopted by the French when Maria de' Medici, daughter of Francesco, grand duke of Tuscany, married Henry IV of France. This is not a history book, and I will not go into the connection between Tuscany and neighbouring Emilia, where Bologna stands. *Spaghetti alla bolognese* traduces Bologna, which is not keen on pasta, a gross southern diet. The Bolognese restaurants served delicate meat dishes and feathery desserts. And Florence I remember for its T-bone steaks, called *fiorentine*. I resented having to worship Florentine art and architecture, perhaps chiefly because a brand of aesthetic Englishman proud to call itself Anglo-Florentine had already besmirched the canvases and façades with its stroking fingers and epicene cooings. That was always the trouble with trying to approach Italian art with the eye of innocence: the eye was not permitted innocence; too many sophisticated appraisers had got in already. Giotto – wonderful, yes; the Michelangelo David – exquisite if blatantly pederastic. And now let us eat a *fiorentina*, eating being a temporal process, like music. Let us leave the spatial arts to Sir bloody Harold Acton.

Back east in the *Marche* or Marches, we ate oysters on the windy quay of Ancona, visited Macerata, and then anchored for a while in the small town of San Severino. Here, on via Leopardi, Liana's mother, the old contessa, was renting a couple of rooms from a peasant woman named Oliva, shrewd, analphabetic, a keeper of hens. The castles and *palazzi* of the contessa's branch of the Pasi family had long gone, sold cheap to Milanese speculators in a bad time; Italian inflation had turned the *lira*, once a solidity like the English pound, into a ghost. In her dark room the contessa, whom I had now to call *mamma*, painted abstract compositions in water-colour, read Samuel Beckett in Italian, and re-read with tears the elegy she had written on her daughter Grazia and published at her own expense. Well, here was a kind of substitute in Paolo Andrea, who had some of the looks of the aunt he had not known. '*Paolo mio,*' his grandmother cried, enfolding him, '*amore.*' The Paolo was for her, the name she had wanted. It could now be detached and left wholly in her possession, and his *mamma* and *babbo* could call the child simple Andrea, the most generic of names, meaning only a man. It would in time be Gallicised to André by schoolfellows but finally Anglicised, Scotticised rather, to Andrew, appropriate for the blood he had inherited from his grandmother on the British side. Kilted and bagpiping, he would become a Scot, rejecting the Italian and Irish and the seasoning of Sassenach. But for now he was Paolo to one and Andrea to the others.

Liana's mother was a handsome old lady with fine feet and ankles, whose Italian had a touch of the Slavonic: she would talk of *Evropa* and *avtomobili*. She had been headstrong rather than decently courageous during the Nazi occupation. When an officer of the SS presumed to enter her house she tried to drive him off with a broom, as if he were a straying goat or goose. SS men had stolen a pig from the peasants, clubbed it to death and then ordered Liana's mother to perform the disembowelling. She refused. They took out their pistols. She refused. Liana had stepped in with a volunteer knife, a mere schoolgirl who openly read Heinrich Heine and Henry James. The SS men had holstered their guns. This family had known too much oppression – from Mussolini, from the Germans, from the bureaucrats and the priests. There were ancestral memories of the Austrians and even the Turks. I began to understand Liana's reluctance to throw newspapers away. Starved of the freedom of information, which the Russians call *glasnost*, she found, and still finds, the democratic press too precious to be used for wrapping old boots. After a year in New York we were to sail back to Europe with three japanned tin trunks crammed with the *New York Times* and its supplements.

The contessa lived a frugal life on a small pension and minimal dividends, eating little because she had never learned the arts of the kitchen. Her voice was loud, apt for spacious *saloni* and the hectoring of servants. A youngish and most elegant sister-in-law, Rosetta, lived in a flat in the same town with her retired husband Tarcisio. She cooked exquisitely in the Bolognese manner. The contessa spent some of her time in the local *circolo*, where bridge was played and the piano unplayable. There was another Contessa Maria there, whose husband had been in the diplomatic service in Singapore. She cooed passable Malay: '*Tabek, tuan. Apa khabar?*' I did not expect to find this in San Severino. As for myself, I seemed to be acceptable, bad Dantesque Italian and all. Liana's mother had not liked her daughter's being married to a black man, despite his proficiency in the translation of Italo Svevo. She had, in her confused way, feared that Paolo Andrea might be black. But he was white enough, brown anyway, naked in the San Severino streets, gorging on hundred-lire *gelati*. And I was certainly white, tall too, a Britisher. The Contessa Maria said that I was *un uomo molto semplice ma simpatico*. Nice enough, though simple. Neither my Italian nor her Malay was conducive to postures of sophistication.

A telephone call to London disclosed that I was expected in Burbank on a date in early November and, the day before flying to Los Angeles, in the Hilton hotel on Park Lane for a conference about the Enderby film project. Looking back, I am not able to understand how I managed to complete two lengthy shooting scripts in that period of turbulence and change. I do not boast about the quality of my work, but I may be permitted to pride myself on the gift of steady application. I will get things done somehow, as D. H. Lawrence did. I fade out of the life of my loved ones to work, even while in their presence, and to them I do not seem to have been working at all. I will even compose music in front of a television film that is blasting music of its own. I do not like my work to get in the way of other people's lives. I do not call for silence or cups of tea. In the Bedmobile, jolting through Italy, I would type at the rear table, having made myself a pint of strong tea on the stove fed by nether gas tubes. The gift of concentration stays with me, and it is perhaps my only gift.

As for now, there was not all the time in the world. We had to get to Rome to secure a new passport for Liana, then to Naples to take ship to Palermo. On the other side of Sicily, at Syracuse, a ship would arrive to take us to Valletta. An air ticket would, I hoped, be waiting for me at Luqa. And, before I left for London and beyond, deliverymen would appear in Lija with furniture and a crated Morgan; electricity and water would have to be turned on. Our stay in San Severino had to be brief, but at least contact had been made. Contessa Maria Lucrezia Pasi della Pergola had a palpable grandson called Paolo, and I had Italian relatives. I learned something of small-town life in the Italian Marches. It was essentially an open-air life, centred always upon a delectable piazza – the cup of *espresso* or *cappuccino* at the café with its outdoor tables, gossip, the *passeggiata* of the late afternoon with the young of the two sexes eyeing each other, the new film with Gassman or Mastroianni at the Virgilio or Orazio. The *ristorante* was for the posh, the *trattoria* for such as ourselves, with its limited bill of fare, housewifely cooking, waiters more like younger brothers than disdainful paladins. The true art of Italy was urbifaction: they knew how to build towns. Wordsworthian nature meant little, for only as a civic being did man or woman fulfil him/ herself. We made now for the primary city, seat of the greater bureaucracy, where the triple tyrant displayed himself on occasional Sunday mornings.

I was beginning to understand why most Italians, including my new wife, felt about the Catholic Church as they did. It was just one more source of repression. God had played a great joke in allowing Jerusalem, the true Christian seat, to fall to Titus and implanting the papacy in Rome. Italy was essentially pagan, like Constantine the Great himself. There was one reality in the flesh, a substance to be rejoiced in, and another in the intellect, expressible in a language which could still be Ciceronian, but the soul was an unknown quality. Catholicism was meant for one country only, and that is Ireland, with its Lancashire outposts. Arriving in Rome, I found the gust of its paganism hitting me as before, a city for the flesh, for the devious compromises of cardinals who kept mistresses, where the intellect found its best play in the machinations of the bureaucrats. We went to the Questura, where, on the sight of Liana's travel document, the cry of 'Criminale!' went up again and I bunched my fists.

What Liana had to prove was that she, Liliana Macellari, existed, that she was an Italian citizen, that she proposed moving to Malta, and that she required a stolen passport to be replaced. She was blamed bitterly and multiply by the sour men in uniform for her carelessness in allowing it to be stolen. There was absolutely no possibility of her obtaining a replacement, a passport being a precious state document which it was criminal to lose. For, even if the state were to decide of its goodness to issue a replacement, what proof was there that she was who she said she was? There was, Liana said, the matter of a birth certificate in Macerata, her own copy of which had been stolen with the other documents in Avignon. Avignone, Avignone, we are sick of hearing about Avignone. All this was a matter of great astonishment to me – the brutality of the officials, the refusal of fascism to die, the assumption that there was something criminally unpatriotic about claiming the right to travel. Nor could I invoke our marriage, the right of a wife to range the world with her husband, citizen of a democratic state, for our marriage would be held to be bigamous, and, if not, a wife should partake of her husband's nationality and claim a passport from the appropriate state department of her husband's nation. I went to see the British consul. Liana did not wish me to: she wanted to continue the fight, a slight dark-haired girl facing blustering officials. But, I said, we could not stay in Italy for ever.

The British consul shook his head with deep regret at my request that my wife's name be added to my own passport. If we had been travelling the other way this might have been possible. But for an Italian national to claim British citizenship otherwise would be a long business with much waiting, months perhaps, and much filling in of forms. I left the consulate in deep depression. My country had let me down. The particular depression primed a deeper one: I was surprised to see Stephen Ward walking through my dreams in the Bedmobile, parked in Piazza Santa Cecilia. This sacrificial victim had affected me more than I knew. The depression was such that I took out the phial of fifty barbiturate tablets that had belonged to Lynne and looked long at it. It was all that was left of her. Having it in my pocket had ironically staved off the desire for suicide that had hit me periodically in the first months of my widowerhood. Now I considered that I had been misled in believing that a new life was possible, with a young wife and a young son and a permanent sunny exile. I had killed a woman and had to be punished for it. Liana came to the café table where I sat over an empty espresso cup and snatched the phial from me. She threw it into a drain.

Our task now was to seek out old friends of Liana's who might vouch to the Questura that she was who she said she was. Bruno Micconi, for instance, who lived in an apartment with his Scottish wife high above Piazza Santa Cecilia and taught economics at the

University of Rome. Liana had known him at Cambridge. One wall of his flat was entirely covered by a blown-up portrait of Karl Marx. There were others – the writer Giuseppe Berto, whose novel *Male Oscuro* I had reviewed at some length in the American magazine *Commonweal*; another writer, Giorgio Manganelli; the Italo-Jewish critic Paolo Milano, friend of Saul Bellow's. There was a little session, organised by the Rome branch of Einaudi, to introduce my *Arancia a Orologeria* to the Roman literati, and Berto, Manganelli and Milano were there. There was a discussion about *liberum arbitrium*. Milano quoted Hans Sachs in *Die Meistersinger*: *'Wir sind ein wenig frei'* – we are a little free. That summed up Liana's and my position: I had to disavow a legal marriage; we were stuck helpless and without much money in Rome. The Questura did not want witnesses to Liana's identity: it had become interested in her relationship to this Englishman and this child. It summoned the three of us to sit daily from eight in the morning on in the cold marble halls where Roman citizens were hectored and not quite beaten. Giorgio Manganelli had an ominous name: *manganello* means truncheon.

Desperately Liana sought help from her uncle, her father's brother, who had been a wholehearted fascist and disclaimed his allegiance just in time. He had done well out of both the war and the period of reconstruction. He was nicely settled now in some Christian Democrat sinecure. He was an unpleasant little grey man who invited us to lunch at the *Circolo Militare*. The dining-room was all cold marble and its only adornment was a huge statue of Giulio Cesare. Andrea, remembering St Antony in Padua, asked me if he had to kneel in front of it. Then, responding to the vague unpleasantness of his great-uncle, he got under the table and stayed there, occasionally calling for *gelati*. The uncle was a poet: he was bringing out at his own expense a little volume dedicated to *lo spirito umano*. This had become a very fascist concept: under fascism rubber truncheons and castor oil had to be tempered with abstractions like progress, divine beauty, the human spirit. Poems were to be written not about inscapes and instress, dogroses and a particular old horse with a bruised fetlock; they were to honour *luogi nobili* where *uomini illustri* unspecified had been whelped. The minestrone was cold and the veal was tough. He could do nothing for his niece: he did not want to be mixed up in a shady marriage which was no marriage; matrimony, even to a black American, was for keeps, so spake Holy Mother Church. We had to buy a chemical for our chemical closet: he would willingly take us in the rain to a shop that served the outdoor life, but he would do no more. He left us in the rain outside a door which said: *Tutto per la Caccia*, everything for the hunt. '*Tutto per la cacca*,' he quipped, driving off. Shit to him too. The shop sold no chemical.

The Questura, after a week of fruitless attendance, established that this woman was living in sin with this man, and that this child was of the brood of sin. Sin was for the Church to deal with; the Questura, in its various electronic quests, discovered that a woman called Liana Macellari had been issued with a passport at the Italian consulate in Reading. Interrogations of some length, full of tricks that did not fool the interrogated, led to the conclusion that a passport might in time be issued, but it would take many weeks. Liana flew at the beasts with strong white teeth exposed. *Calma, calma*. She got her provisional passport. It cost a lot of money, but Liana fortunately discovered she had a few thousand lire in a Roman bank.

Only Andrea had enjoyed Rome, whose baroque statues, especially those over the Fontana di Trevi, he saw as immense toys to be climbed over. The poet Clough had called Rome 'rubbishy'. Its virtues lay in miraculous twilight and a free steady spurt of mineral water from the fountains. The baroque was a joke, all extravagant musculatures. The Romans were coarse with a huge vocabulary of abuse. Andrea picked up *cazzo* from them and *vafnculo*. We made for Naples. He, who was scared of nobody, learned true fear when he saw Neapolitan children, the most exquisite little rogues and expert thieves in the world. I clung tightly to our passports and money. On the bay our Bedmobile was hoisted aboard the ship plying to Palermo. This was done with operatic panache and much laughter. The Neapolitans are a cheerful people, despite the oppression of thieves and the Camorra, the corruption of local government. When, after a night's sleep on deck, we arrived at dawn in northern Sicily, we met the obverse of the Neapolitan temper in the gloomy, well-nigh tragic, faces and bearing of the Palermo dockers who clumsily swung our vehicle to the quay, inevitably smashing the plate-glass substitute louvres. We were in brutal country, the land of the Mafia. Taking coffee in a side-street, we heard a young man, swarthy as an Arab, tell his friends of his forthcoming marriage. He was going to paint his penis purple, he said, and if his bride evinced surprise he was going to cut her throat.

This island had always taken a kind of grim pride in its destitution – not really supported by waters jumping with fish and soil of a volcanic richness – and on destitution had been built rigid codes of hypocritical honour, the suppression of women, vendetta, the knife flashing in sunlight. Liana, the northern Italian, short-skirted and open in manner, was looked on slyly in lust and detestation. For God's sake let's get to Syracuse. We passed small townships set high on hills, miniature mounts of purgatory. Mist swathed us on the narrow dangerous passes. As we drove through night-time Catania, Andrea decided to take against me, the disciplinary stranger who had lurched into his life. Pitching his voice high, he kept telling his mother about a legendary time 'when we was little boys together and Antoniole was not with us'. We parked on the moonlit quay of Syracuse and I cooked spaghetti and canned *sugo*. I comforted myself with strong tea. This was very alien country.

The ship for Malta was a day late in arriving. I had my hair cut on the quay. We visited the aquarium, whose denizens represented a sort of decent non-Sicilian normality. We looked at the ruins of the Greek amphitheatre. A little man in spectacles, who had visited and even worked in the remote land of the peninsula, praised Sicilian intelligence – 'the brightest people of the whole Italic race' – and affirmed that Columbus had found Sicilians waiting for him when he reached the New World. They were so bright that they were led either to art or to the higher criminality. He sang from *Cavalleria Rusticana* – 'Turiddu hath stolen mine honour' – and deigned to dine off fish soup in our mobile dining-room. He was right about the art, the literature anyway – Pirandello, Piccoli, Lampedusa, Scascia. As for the Mafia, Mussolini had effectively crushed it but the American occupiers reinstated it. Liana was troubled by the look of Sicily. It reminded her of something. That something was Malta.

The ship came, the Bedmobile was gloomily hoisted, we sailed south. We were taken ashore at Valletta in a felucca with an eye painted on its prow. Our moving home followed in a lighter. Now our home was to be all too static. We rested for the night in the Corinthia Palace Hotel, where we saw Lucille Ball on television. In English. I was back in a colonial situation, though Malta was now an independent state. D. H. Lawrence, packing his 'kitchenino' for the Sardinian trip, had made sandwiches of 'good British bacon from Malta'. Eggs-and-bacon territory, strong tea, imported Bass and Guinness, the nostalgia for the days of British rule which lingered all over the dead empire. 'I have many good English friends,' the official at Valletta who was processing our vehicle through customs boasted. 'They sometimes invite me to dinner at their homes.' After breakfast we faced a long and difficult day. Lija had narrow streets which even the local buses had difficulty negotiating. The pantechnicon which carried our furniture and the crated Morgan set off agonised honkings. I was disturbed to note what I had not noted before: our house faced the Lija police station, and I had never got on well with colonial or post-colonial police. I foresaw that they were not there for my protection but for that of the staider British retired – General Fanshawe, for instance, who lived a few yards away, and whose wife I heard, as our goods were cluttering the street, complain loudly: 'It's a disgrace. All sorts of low moneyed people coming here now.' The General was later to dispose of me as 'a writer fellow – made his money out of dirty books, I suppose – with a wop wife'.

I took a taxi to the offices of the Electricity Board in Valletta and asked the ancient weary Maltese in charge if he would be good enough to turn on my supply. His response was similar to that of the Roman Questura at the request for a passport. 'The provision of electricity is a business that requires much lengthy negotiation. Why do you want electricity?' I told him. He said: 'Let us consider the nature of electricity.' Time was wasting. I had a flight to catch. Back at the house in Lija I found a number of local Maltese, the Borg and Grima families, adjusting bare wires at great peril to themselves and even connecting a dusty telephone. An old man named Joseph Grima had already appointed himself gardener. A fat girl called Mary Borg said she was the maid. Seeing lights go on, she said: 'Is good like that.' Naughty children coming home from school at lunchtime rang our doorbell. These I slapped. At day's end, an hour before flight-time for London, an uncrated Morgan and the Bedmobile stood at rest outside General Fanshawe's house. The furniture was in place.

There was no time to consider a profound problem that had arisen. When I had announced in the British press that I was emigrating to Malta, a young student of Valletta University had written to me care of my publisher with a questionnaire: 'Why are you coming to Malta? What do you like about Malta? What is your opinion of the Maltese people?' I gave guarded replies but stressed that Malta seemed a fine place in which to conduct my work as a writer. The cunning youth had published questions and answers in the *Times of Malta*, announcing to the Maltese government that I was not settling there in decent retirement, which was the condition for being what was known as a 'sixpenny settler', that is one who paid a tax of sixpence in the pound for the privilege of doing nothing in the Maltese sun. There was, in the mound of mail that was waiting for us, a letter from the Maltese Prime Minister's office informing me that my request for immigration was denied, since I was a writer who proposed to write. Like any tourist I was permitted to stay in the country for only three months at a time. This meant that I was still domiciled in Great Britain and liable for taxes there. I groaned. One thing at a time. Let me get to London and then to Los Angeles. Liana drove me to Luqa, where an air ticket but no place on the London plane awaited. 'You are on stand-by,' a Maltese functionary said with satisfaction. I was too weary to argue. A minute before take-off I was granted a seat. It seemed wrong somehow to be glad to be leaving Malta. Leaving Liana, even briefly, was of course a different matter.

AFTER THE gipsy life of the Italian roads it was strange to be suited and urban again, staying at a Hilton hotel, dining with John Bryan the producer at the Mirabelle, fine-tooth-combing the shooting script of the Enderby film, which might conceivably be called *A Blast from the Smallest Room*, that review title rejected by the *Yorkshire Post*. John Bryan was fit and eating quenelles, knowing not the day nor the hour. After his death at Cannes the contract was annulled though the script-money paid: nobody since has wanted to put Enderby on the screen.

I got myself new inoculations at Heathrow, the old certificate of jabs having gone with my old passport at Avignon, and flew from a bitter London November to Los Angeles sun and smog. Joseph L. Mankiewicz and Bill Conrad were waiting for me at the Warner Brothers studios in Burbank. (Katie the secretary said to Bill: 'How thin John is,' and Bill replied: 'Yeah, he's getting fucked.') The script for *Will!* had been xeroxed and Joe, as I had to call him, found it promising but too long. The estimate on running-time had worked out at something like six hours: there was an invaluable old lady around who read scripts with a stop-watch and had never yet been more than ten minutes out. It was not after all to be a musical, which was something of a relief, nor was it really a waste: some day I could write a novel about the making of a Shakespeare musical. The exclamation point after the title also had to go: it was too reminiscent of the Dickensian travesty called *Oliver!* Joe was an Anglophile who knew his Shakespeare. He had made an acclaimed *Julius Caesar* with Marlon Brando saying 'For Brutus is an honorabubble man'. His *Cleopatra*, which substituted the poetry of vision for that of language, had cost much and been a box-office failure, and Joe's star had been temporarily clouded. He was entrusted with Peter Shaffer's *Sleuth*, which had only one set and two characters. A hard-ticket film on Shakespeare's life would restore him to the costly world of spectacle. He would build Elizabethan London and, I feared, make it too clean. What I wanted was dirt, and plenty of it: greasy farthingales and black half-moons on the fingernails of the struggling Bard. What I wanted also was sex, the lustful untying of points. Joe promised me bosoms.

I trusted Joe, though I mistrusted his cleanliness. He was a fine director, and his *All About Eve* I considered a masterpiece. It had recently been turned into a stage musical for Lauren Bacall, and Joe was not getting a red cent out of it. That was showbiz, with its swindling contracts thick as doctoral theses, in all of which there was deadly small print that one's eyes grew too weary to read. As for *Will* without the exclamation point, Joe took it for granted that I would be screwed to the limit. But, as MGM blazoned hypocritically under its snarling lion, art was primarily for art's sake. Joe gripped his pipe between strong Hollywood teeth, held the script in gloved hands (some Hollywood allergy or other had brought out some Hollywood rash or other), and went through it scene by scene. Cut this, cut that. He could not fault the dialogue, which admitted no anachronisms but went easy on the thee and thou. The big problem was structural, the screwing of tension towards the end to produce a thrilling dénouement. Biography had to yield, as always, to dramaturgical need: Shakespeare would have nodded.

What was to happen at the end was this. News would reach Will in London that his daughter Susannah was being arraigned not by a regular court but by a synod of black-suited Puritans on a charge of adultery with a certain Ralph Smith. Will, hating and hated, would arrive to find that it was all his fault: Susannah and Smith, who was ill in bed, had been reading *Romeo and Juliet* together, Susannah following her physician husband's behest to shake Smith out of a lethal melancholy. Nosy Puritans had heard words of love coming out of Smith's bedroom. Anne Shakespeare took the opportunity of confessing a real misdemeanour in the presence of the scowling Brownists: if they were looking for adultery they would find it in her, who had slept with Will's brother Richard during her husband's over-long absences in London. Could an erring wife be blamed for seeking elsewhere comfort her husband was unwilling to give? The point was that everything was Will's fault. Play-making was in itself sinful and the occasion of the sin of those who else would never dream of committing it. Will would stagger out of his own house, converted into an irregular court of morality if not law, find Ben Jonson pausing awhile in Stratford on his weight-reducing walk to Drummond of Hawthornden in Scotland, get drunk with him, see in delirium his dead son Hamnet transformed into Hamlet, catch cold, die.

It looked as though we had a workable script. Joe was more confident that the film would go ahead than either I or Bill Conrad. Bill had heard rumours of changes at the top in the Warner–Seven Arts organisation, with the consequent scrapping of all existing projects; I just did not believe that I would ever see Shakespeare's life on the wide screen. But Joe was enthusiastic. It was revealed that the casting I had already heard about emanated from him – Robert Stephens as Will, Maggie Smith as Anne, Peter Ustinov as Ben Jonson (because he looks like etc.), James Mason as Philip Henslowe, Somebody of the David Niven type, though younger than Niven, as the Earl of Essex. Jessica Tandy, whom I had not seen act since the old days when she had been Ophelia to John Gielgud's Hamlet, was to be Queen Elizabeth. We dined with Jessica Tandy and her husband Hume Cronyn, and her flesh and blood presence seemed an earnest of her taking the queenly role. Now what I had to do was to fly home and cut the script down to four hours or so. So I flew, having first sent a cable to Liana of the time of my arrival at Luqa. There was the ambulance-looking Bedmobile waiting.

I was home, meaning in a Malta that would not, for the moment, accept me as a non-working, bridge-playing, boozing settler. Andrea was very much at home; he was even speaking Maltese. There was a small grocery shop across the street run by a man called Grima, and their quarters behind the shop swarmed with children. Andrea was sleeping there more than in our mansion, which had plenty of room. Liana had bought him a rocking-horse to keep him home, but he preferred other children. He also preferred the diet of the poor Maltese to the meaty dishes I cooked for him – bread and conserve of tomatoes, with ample potatoes on the side. I set up a study looking out on the orange and lemon trees and began to work on a thinned *Will*. But first I wrote a verse-letter to Vladimir Nabokov, who was about to celebrate his seventieth birthday:

> That nymphet's beauty lay less on her bones
> Than in her name's proclaimed two allophones,
> A boned veracity slow to be found
> In all the channels of recorded sound.
> Extrude an orange pip upon the track,
> And it will be a pip played front or back,
> But only in the kingdom of the shade
> Can diaper run back and be repaid.

Such speculations salt my exile too,
One that I bear less stoically than you.
I look in sourly on my lemon trees,
Spiked by the Qs and Xes of Maltese,
And wonder: Is this home or where is home?
(Melita's caves, Calypso's honeycomb.)
I seek a clue or cue. Just opposite,
The grocer has a cat that loves to sit
Upon the scales. Respecting his repose,
One day he weighed him: just 2 rotolos.
In this palazzo wood decays and falls;
Buses knock stucco from the outer walls,
Slam shut the shutters. Coughing as they lurch,
They yet enclose the silence of a church,
Rock in baroque: Teresan spados stab
The Sacred Heart upon the driver's cab,
Whereon, in circus colours, one can read
That *Verbum Caro Factum Est*. Indeed.
I think the word is all the flesh I need –
The taste and not the vitamins of sense,
Whatever sense may be. I like the fence
Of black and white that keeps those bullocks in –
Crossboard or chesswood, Eurish gift of Finn –
The 'crossmess parzel'. If words are no more
Than *pyeoshki*, preordained to look before,
Save for their taking *chassé*, they alone,
And not the upper house, can claim a throne
(Exploded first the secular magazines
And puff of bishops). All aswarm with queens,
Potentially, that board. Well, there it is:
You help me counter the liquidities
With counters that are counties, countries. Best
To read it: *Caro Verbum Factus Est*.

Nabokov read my work and seemed to like it. The sourness of this
letter had much to do with my having read a review of my *Urgent
Copy*, waiting for me in the mail, published in the *Listener* and
written by the poet Geoffrey Grigson. This denied me either critical
ability or the basic capacity to put words together with any elegance.
It also called me 'coarse and unattractive'. As for the palazzo Liana
and I and, occasionally, Andrea were living in, I was perhaps being
too hard on it. It was old and peeling but very roomy. The trouble

was not the house but Malta itself. There was too much religion in it: it dominated even the buses that slammed shut our open shutters in the narrow Triq Il-Kbira or Street the Big: these had, as I told Nabokov, votive lamps burning before an ill-painted Sacred Heart in the cab of the driver. It was repressive religion and one of its expressions was a censorship that was to affect profoundly my attempts to earn a living at literary journalism. Certain books were not allowed in; at Luqa airport a team scrutinised the British newspapers and cut out or inked over underwear advertisements or bathing beauties which might inflame Maltese youth. One could sometimes buy a *Daily Mirror* that collapsed into scissored tatters. A few yards away from our house stood the small palace in which Prince Philip, on naval duty in Malta, had lived with his bride Princess Elizabeth, now in the possession of Desmond Morris, author of the bestselling *The Naked Ape*. Forbidden by the Malta censors the proofs of its sequel, he had had to go to England to correct them. In that late autumn of 1968, my novel *Tremor of Intent* appeared almost simultaneously in Danish and French. The Danish version was entitled *Martyrenes Blod* and had a blood-dripping crucifix on the cover. The Maltese allowed me to have this. The French version was called *Un Agent Qui Vous Veut du Bien* and sought to attract readers with a dusky nude. This was sequestered. I smelt terrible trouble.

Liana and I decided to spend Christmas outside Malta. This was partly so that could buy another three months of residence on re-entry while the Prime Minister's office deliberated on my request to live permanently there. Not that we thought of genuinely settling, like the boozers, bridge-players and party-givers who lived on pensions, dividends, or remittances. Our aim was some day to leap north into Italy when I could, probably illegally, secure enough dollars to buy property there. Our other aim was to travel: during Lynne's long illness this had been denied me. Meanwhile I proposed finishing the film script, on whose delivery Warner Brothers had imposed a sudden deadline which, perhaps deliberately, was made near-impossible to fulfil, on an Indian ship, the SS *Uganda* which was to cruise between Malta, Naples, Ajaccio, Tunis, Barcelona and Mallorca – probably not in that order. Andrea loved the *Uganda*: it was another massive toy, like the Trevi fountain. I kept mostly to our cabin, clacking away.

I had an artistic shock in Barcelona, of a kind that, in Italy, had not been severe enough to make me take either painting, sculpture or architecture with the right seriousness. I was aware that my aesthetic tastes were too time-bound, that I would never be able to produce the kind of fiction that women write – full of the visual world as well as the motor and auditory. Only a woman born blind could write like James Joyce. It was the architecture of Gaudí, seen in the Barcelona cold and rain after vomiting the fried cow-heels of Los Caracoles, that provided the shock and the revelation. Gaudí had begun his cathedral dedicated to the Sagrada Familia in 1884 and it was still being built when, in 1926, he was run over by a street-car and killed. It was far from finished in late 1968. There had never been any plan. Gaudí had worked on the structure like a novelist, letting new ideas effloresce as he built. The towers of the Sagrada Familia were more than an unfinished novel; they were a meal – foraminated like waffles, crunchy, with pinnacles of crisp sugar. I was told to think of *art nouveau* on a fantastic scale when viewing the Casa Batlló, with its balconies like carnival masks, lizardy roof-tiles, roughcast walls stuck all over with fairy money, pillars like limbs, stone dripping like stalactites. I thought more of an eccentric negation of the rectangular, genuine frozen music of a rhapsodic kind, and, in an obscure manner, I saw a reflection of my own brain in it. Gaudí had gone his own way in the manner of an antinomian Catalonian, scorning the four-square critics: he was an encouragement to any artist. I was desperate to be done with the film script and at work on a Gaudiesque novel.

Nothing much else that was inspiring came of that winter cruise. Brown Indian hands served turkey and Christmas pudding. Andrea had to be prevented from tightrope-walking on the taffrail: he had not inherited my imperfect sense of balance. Fighter planes skimmed over the sea in Tunis, tanks crunched along the streets, Americans were drunk in the bars as though expecting doomsday. In Napoleon's birthplace in Ajaccio I felt the pricking of a historical novel and groaned at the prospect of research. The little house, to my half-drunken sense, reeked of Buonaparte libido. We sailed back to a drenched Malta and my decision to evade writing a novel – whatever it was to be, I knew it would be difficult – and produce instead a brief biography of Shakespeare which should be sumptuously illustrated. This was a mode of using up research for the film which I was sure now would otherwise be wasted. Desperately trying to finish the script, I yet knew it was not going to reach the screen. The book itself, being highly visual, would be a substitute for the film.

This was not what Jonathan Cape, or rather its head men, Tom Maschler and Ed Victor, really wanted. They were trying to give me what they termed a 'breakthrough'. I had written hard and produced novels of some worth, but these had not sold. This was so blatantly announced that I felt embarrassed, as though there were holes in my underpants. Cape wanted to put me on the map as a selling novelist, but here I was producing a volume of essays which Geoffrey Grigson hated and proposing a book on Shakespeare. Still, Tom and Ed were kind: they recognised that I had been through a bad time. They had, during the first month of my widowerhood, commissioned me to write the preface to a reprint of Joyce's *Stephen Hero* and then rejected it as ill-written. It had to be ill-written since I was going through such a bad time. Now they recognised that I had to let the turmoil of the deeper levels of my mind subside before I could get back to serious or comic (which is also serious) fiction.

Tom Maschler and Ed Victor were remarkable young men. They were not the slow-going amateurs of traditional British publishing; they were pushers, go-getters, with no debilitating Anglo-Saxon blood and an energy that could only be termed transatlantic: Ed Victor, indeed, was, is, American. I had first met them when they invited me to an exordial luncheon at a new go-getting essentially smart restaurant. The taxi-driver said he knew where it was, guv. But then he proved not to know, and Tom Maschler emptied obscene wrath upon him, expressive of disgust at amateurism. Tom Maschler, who had published *The Naked Ape* to acclaim and profit, came to Malta to urge Desmond Morris in his palace to finish *The Human Animal*: he was full of energy and temper. He came again with his wife, a famous culinary columnist, and I cooked for them: it was as though there were holes in my saucepans. When Ed Victor came to Malta to discuss the illustrations to my Shakespeare book he was equally formidable. He stayed on Triq Il-Kbira and asked for one slice of toast for breakfast. I made him two, and he emptied obscene wrath upon me. I cowered. A vendor in the street called 'Haxxix!', pronounced hashish, and Ed Victor was quick to rush out to buy some. It turned out to be only vegetables. Ed Victor was to become a literary agent with a Rolls-Royce. Tom Maschler remains a whiz-kid legend. I could not write the sort of fiction they thought they could sell. I was unworthy of their energy.

The office of the Maltese Prime Minister now decided that I could stay if I promised not to earn money by working. This was a promise I could only partially keep, but Malta did its best to make me keep it wholly by holding back books sent to me for review. Getting journalistic commissions was difficult anyway, since the telephone installed by the Grima and Borg amateurs, having no listed number, could not receive incoming calls. Messages from the foreign (meaning British and American) press had to come through the Cable and Wireless Company, meaning men on loud motor-cycles. I was told I would have to wait ten years for a regular installation. When I was cabled as to whether I would review a particular book and cabled back yes, further cables would impatiently ask when the review was coming, and I had to cable asking when the book was coming. The book, of course, had already been sent, but it was being held for inspection in the censorship department of the Valletta General Post Office. I was summoned there one day to stand before an official's desk and asked to show good reason why I should be permitted to have the collected poems of Thomas Campion.

'He's a great English poet, this collection is of considerable importance, a review of this collection will announce its importance to the literary world. Moreover, reviewing is one of my trades.'

'You would review a book of dirty poetry?'

'It is not dirty.'

'Oh yes, it is. You have not read the book and I have. You think because I am a Maltese I do not understand English. There are filthy poems in this book.'

'No, there are not.'

'Do not contradict me.' And then a qualified radiance replaced the bureaucratic frown. 'Ah – now I remember. Campion was an English martyr and is now a saint. He must have written these dirty poems before becoming a holy man. You may have the book.'

He had got hold of the wrong Campion but I did not enlighten him. I took the book and ran.

When the completed pentateuch of Doris Lessing, *Children of Violence*, had to be reviewed at length for the *Sunday Times*, four of the books slipped through the censor's net (as did, bafflingly, at the same time, Legman's monumental *Rationale of the Dirty Joke*), but one did not. This was *Landlocked*. I took the sacred-hearted bus to Valletta and barged roughly into the censorship office, where two old men, not too literate, were at their gleeful work of dirt-sifting. The number of books they had yet to vet made my heart sick. 'I want that book there. It has been sent to me and it is my property.' But I could see from the cover why it had to be dirty: the fingers of a man clutched the fingers of a woman, and the woman's arm was bare.

'You must wait till we get to it.'

'When will you get to it?'

'Oh, in one or two months.'

'A review of that book has to appear next Sunday. I have to write the review. I am taking the book.'

'Oh no you are not.'

I took it. At the same time I swept their pile of putative dirt to the floor. They did not know my name; they could only report on a disruptive foreigner. This censorship business was absurd, and my fight against it was to render me *persona non grata*. I wrote to the Head of Censorship asking if he had an *index librorum prohibitorum*. He had. He sent a copy, very thick. Voltaire's *Candide* was on it, and not only Rousseau's *Confessions* but St Augustine's. *Lucky Jim* and *The Heart of the Matter* joined the novels of Marie Corelli. Oscar Wilde, Sigmund Freud, Marie Stopes, Havelock Ellis – these were to be expected, but it was surely going too far to ban Dickens's *Hard Times* and Thackeray's *Vanity Fair*? Most dangerously there were several textbooks on obstetrics and one on diseases of the bladder, forbidden to the medical students of the Royal University.

The Church of Malta, founded by St Paul before he got to Rome, considered itself to possess an authority the Vatican could not override. The colonising British had not been interested, as Napoleon had been, in liberalising the island. In this post-colonial epoch, there was not one British resident prepared to join in my fight against censorship, not even the author Nigel Dennis. The Maltese Jesuits, with the subtlety of their order, suggested that I give a lecture on pornography, thus bringing the whole issue of the bannable into an open forum. I acceded, prepared my paper with care, and eventually faced an audience of three hundred in the main lecture theatre of the university. In that audience there was not one layman or laywoman: there were nuns, monks, priests and bishops, though neither of the two archbishops (one for Malta, the other for Gozo). I threw my lecture, as I had thrown my books, into a large silence. I quoted *Areopagitica*:

As therefore the state of man now is, what wisdom can there be to choose, what continence to forbear, without the knowledge of evil? He that can apprehend and consider vice with all her baits and seeming pleasures, and yet abstain, and yet distinguish, and yet prefer that which is truly better, he is the true warfaring Christian. I cannot praise a fugitive and cloistered virtue, unexercised and unbreathed, that never sallies out and seeks her adversary, but slinks out of the race, where that immortal garland is to be run for, not without dust and heat. Assuredly we bring not ignorance into the world, we bring impurity much rather; that which purifies us is trial, and trial is by what is contrary. That virtue therefore, which is but a

youngling in the contemplation of evil, and knows not the
utmost that vice promises to her followers, and rejects it, is but
a blank virtue, not a pure; her whiteness is but an excremental
whiteness . . .

Few understood, and, if any nun there did, Milton must seem, in the
manner of a heretic, to be attacking virgin vows. I argued, perhaps
unwisely, that if the didactic had its place in print, so the pornographic might also as a device for refocillating sleeping passion, but
the important thing was not to confuse one category with the other,
nor either with a third category which might be termed that of pure
art. To ban a book on obstetrics because it showed diagrams of the
uterus and ovaries was to confound the didactic and the pornographic; to ban *Othello* because supposed sexual infidelity is its theme
was to misunderstand both pornography and art. Decisions as to the
possible depravity of a book, film or picture were to be made by the
individual, not by uninstructed bodies of state hirelings. Any
questions? There were no questions, but a fat Franciscan made a
throat-cutting gesture. .

Whether this lecture was taken to heart or not, I noticed a quiet
relaxation of censorship on the books that were sent to me for
review. *A Long Time Burning*, by Donald Thomas, *Books in the Dock*,
by C. H. Rolph, and *The End of Obscenity*, by Charles Rembar, all
got in and into an article called 'Swing of the Censor' in the *Spectator*.
This, for me certainly and probably for other writers living in
illiberal countries like Australia and Ireland, was a great year for
thinking about the allowable limits of sexual frankness. *Last Exit to
Brooklyn* had won its obscenity battle in Britain, and Philip Roth's
Portnoy's Complaint was to cause trouble, especially in Australia, for
presenting masturbation in all its sticky detail. Eric Partridge's
Shakespeare's Bawdy was reissued and his *Dictionary of Slang and
Unconventional English* now spelt out 'cunt' and 'fuck' boldly. The
old taboos were vanishing, but new taboos were coming in: one was
not allowed to say 'kike' or 'nigger'.

Those British expatriates in Malta who had heard of me as a writer
assumed, because of my shrieks against censorship, that I was
advocating the wholesale dissemination of dirt. This was not so: I
was and am too puritanical for that. In that lecture to the silent clergy
I had praised *Ulysses* for its reticence and its strategical placing of
mindless obscenity to mirror mindless violence, and I had condemned *Lady Chatterley's Lover* for using an obscenity in a context of
love and tenderness. What was needed was a grateful acceptance of

the new literary freedom and at the same time a willingness to use verbal discipline and restraint. But the sixpenny settlers were not interested in the arts. They gave parties which were reported in the *Times of Malta* by the social editress; they exhibited a superiority to the 'natives' very little different from what I had been used to in Malaya and Borneo. A lady called on us with no social intent: she merely wanted a contribution to the Maltese Society for the Prevention of Cruelty to Animals. She spoke patricianly. When Liana opened the door she demanded to see 'the lady of the house'. Liana said she was she. 'Oh, you speak English awfully well for a native, but I think I'd better give you a leaflet in your own language,' handing one over in Maltese. To have a wop wife was like being shacked up with a Chink or a Rock scorpion.

Well, we were certainly closer to the lower-class Maltese than to the disdainful settlers. Andrea made sure of that, growing tubby on bread and conserve of tomatoes. Maltese had become his language. I had always wished to learn a foreign tongue at the same rate as a child, and I strove to keep up with Andrea. It was impossible. While I was struggling with irregular verbs he was cutting a swathe through grammar, amassing idioms, not giving a damn about correct plural formations. When, later in 1969, the moon landing was announced on television, an image of the Maltese Prime Minister, Borg-Olivier, was flashed on to the screen for an inordinate time while the speakerine said: 'The head of the Maltese state was among the world leaders who sent congratulations to the President of the United States on this amazing achievement.' Andrea ran round the house crying: '*Borg-Olivier fuq il-qamar*' (on the moon). The moon in Maltese obsessed him. He was taken by his young friends to a religious class and taught the Apostles' Creed in Maltese. Confusing *il-qamar* with *il-kabar*, he said: 'The third day he rose again from the moon.' What he had learnt was very useful Moghrabi Arabic, but he was to forget it totally. To children language makes sense only in terms of immediate ambience.

If Andrea could make no linguistic contact with me, he achieved communication at a very morbid level: he caught and gave me chicken-pox. To a child this is nothing; to an adult it is an inducement of change in the neural chemistry. Something seemed to go wrong with my synapses. I found myself making ethical judgements on physical sensations, so that the smell, texture, whole concept of breakfast bacon became not merely gross but somehow immoral, even evil. I had bought an electronic piano and, while playing Debussy's *Arabesques* on it, I experienced gastric revulsion at the innocuous notes. Reading Ezra Pound's *Hugh Selwyn Mauberley*, I found that the images of the poems were starting up from the page and impinging like visual and tactile objects. I was frightened. I saw how fragile were the walls between zones of judgement. It had not been like that in the old days when I smoked opium. Chicken-pox had brought me into the new drug age, when the young jabbers and snorters actively desired the collapse of cerebral barriers.

Though now officially resident in Malta, I was, in 1969, more out of it than in, and it was with the American young, children of the new anarchy, that I mostly consorted. In the spring I was lecturing in western Canada and the state of Washington. The educated young were behaving absurdly. In Seattle I observed a burnt-out college library. The arson was the work of a candidate for a PhD in English literature who demanded a blessing on his proposal to write his thesis on Herman Hesse, a writer at that time very popular with the young. He was told, very reasonably, that Hesse was an ornament of German literature and inadmissible in a department of English. So he destroyed the whole fucking fascist library. The black students were as absurd as the whites. They demanded departments of Black Studies and were initially satisfied if an empty outhouse could have BLACK STUDIES chalked on its door. I wrote in the *American Scholar*: 'A course that encloses St Augustine, Toussaint l'Ouverture, Coleridge-Taylor, Paul Robeson and Papa Doc, because they were all black, is as ridiculous as one that deals with Robert Louis Stevenson, Joseph Stalin, Mark Twain and Salvador Dali because they all had moustaches.' The Seattle blacks wanted to learn Swahili, though I insisted that their ancestral language was Ibo or Krio, but rejected the only Swahili teacher available in the state of Washington because he was a white motherfucker. One black student of music rejected all white musical instruments, though, as I told him, Achimota College had a piano keyboard as its symbol, denoting the need for both black and white notes to achieve full harmony. A black student of nothing in particular, since he was virtually illiterate, insisted on his right to a general BA: he got it through bongo-playing, soul cookery, and a halting recital of black wrongs. I foresaw, and said so, that student indiscipline, victimisation of the faculty, and the elevation of racial rights above the demands of scholarship were going to degrade the study of the liberal arts, kill the departments of humanities, and leave the real work in the hands of the students of computer engineering. America was becoming one of my concerns.

Liana and I, leaving Andrea with his Maltese family, went to Canada in the early summer. At Heathrow, when the final call for boarding the flight to Toronto came, I found that she had disappeared. She was, and is, very good at disappearing: she is there, and then she is not there. Her flights are more than snipelike: they are akin to the teletransportation of the SF writer Alfred Bester. It is essential, when a flight is called, to capture her with a lariat. Not that she ever misses flights. I, in my Freudian way, am much more likely to do that: arriving three hours too early at the airport, I have ample time to lose my boarding card or overnight bag. She is efficient as well as beautiful. I am ugly and neurotic.

We flew to Toronto and then took a limousine to the little town of Stratford in Ontario. This had its Avon and cobs and cygnet-chivying pens upon it. It was where Tyrone Guthrie had set up first a tent and then a theatre for annual Shakespeare festivals. The theatre I found magnificent, open-staged, no proscenium arch, no scenery, no curtain, apt for the Elizabethan-Jacobean productions which were the staple offerings. This year *Hamlet*, *Measure for Measure*, *The Alchemist* and Richard Wilbur's translation of *Tartuffe* were being presented, as well as an adaptation of Petronius's *Satyricon* with music by Stanley Silverman. Meeting Silverman was to be important to me: later we were to work together on a production of *Oedipus Tyrannus* in my translation; more than that, he encouraged me to get back to musical composition. The Stratford (Ontario) summer festival was combined with a kind of vacation course in theatre, to which mostly Americans, mature and moderately well-heeled, came to hear lectures and join in seminars as well as see plays. I lectured on Elizabethan pronunciation and on the implications for Shakespeare biography of Hamlet's address to the skull of Yorick. I was not scholarly, except in ancient phonology, but others were – Robertson Davies, for instance, whose silvery Oxford cadences reminded me that British speech was acceptable in Canada, and that Canada's dominion status conferred a cosmopolitanism not really acceptable south of the Great Lakes.

I put my foot in things, as I often do. Asked why Polonius was so named, I begged my audience not necessarily to associate drivelling sententious stupidity with Poland, or to think that Shakespeare would have appreciated the quip about the Poles having the highest intelligence quotient in the world, though they had to share it among the entire population. The mere voicing of a negative was enough to convert it into a positive: 'not' cancels nothing out. A beefy Texan complained that he had not come all that way to hear Polack jokes, and then reeled some off to show how detestable they were. Otherwise the Canadian visit was a great refreshment, a genuine honeymoon, and a confirmation that the British Commonwealth worked. Even the haired barefooted Canadian young were civilised, courteously asking shoed dignitaries like the Mayor of Stratford to put their foot on smoked-out reefers. At the other theatre of Stratford, one with a curtain and a proscenium arch, Hume Cronym took the lead in a dramatisation of Fr Rolfe's *Hadrian the Seventh*. He half-confirmed in his dressing-room what I already suspected: that Jessica Tandy would not be playing the Queen in *Will*, for there would be no *Will*. I could say goodbye to hopes of a Hollywood success: if I wanted to lift words off the paper into the air I had better work in the theatre. This was what I was to do, though not in Stratford, Ontario.

Liana and I went to Montreal, where separatism was already smouldering. We ate well and expensively of the imported French cuisine and found in the French language bookshops that I was *un écrivain très peu connu*. It was strange to hear waiters and shopmen switching from Anglic colloquial ('You was fucking wrong there, fella') to rapid French with Norman phonemes. The Holiday Inn restaurant served *coq au vin* and *boeuf à la bourguignonne*. General de Gaulle had discreetly cried '*Vive Le Québec libre!*' and the French Canadians looked to a France they did not know, except for its exports. It seemed to me that what would make for a united Canada (though could so vast a territory ever be properly united?) was an importation common to both the Anglophone and Francophone regions – the commodities, culture and technological patterns of the United States. *Chiens chauds* would still be hot dogs, and Coca-Cola was already in Esperanto. The great issue was purely linguistic, and the growing attempt to outlaw English from Quebec would only be met by a brutish monoglottism among the Canadian Anglo-Saxons. It was all a great pity. Canada was, I thought, the country of the future, and both its opposed territories were trying to burrow into an unworthy provincialism. What Canada needed was a great poet who, like Whitman, would celebrate the totality of the land. It already had a considerable novelist in Robertson Davies. Perhaps a great composer, a Canadian Sibelius or Kodály, would better bridge the blood-gap. I worried about Canada, and still do.

It was not up to me to worry about anything except the procuring of dollars, US or Canadian, which could buy our way out of Malta. I was strictly bound to convert what dollars I earned into Maltese sterling, but I paid them into a newly opened account in the Chemical Bank in New York and wondered, not for the first time, why the ethics of the private life always had to contradict those of government. Liana and I entered the United States briefly from Montreal, so that I could lecture to a summer course in Harvard: this brought in an easily earned thousand dollars and made me consider giving up altogether the tapping out of ill-paid words. I could consider my literary career as a short interlude: my real vocation seemed to be that of a teacher.

We went back to Malta, but not for long. In high summer we took Andrea to Mallorca, not to meet Catalonians but to encourage him to speak English again, for the town of Deyá was full of expatriate Anglophones, the greatest of whom was Robert Graves. Dowling College in New York State was running a course in European studies, which meant, on the basic level, learning how to subsist on fresh fish, coarse bread, and harsh red wine. The young Americans on the course were very ill and cried for the hamburgers and Coca-Cola they could not get. Though Deyá was ennobled by the presence of a very civilised poet it was not in itself highly civilised, if by civilisation we mean garbage collection and water and electricity supplies that work. Liana, Andrea and I were put into a house built by a German who had installed his own power supply and hydraulic system. I woke in the middle of a moonless night, impelled to vomit, and groped for dead switches, not knowing where the toilet (was there a toilet?) was. There is little in the world more degrading than being copiously sick in total blackness on to one knows not what, and, at queasy dawn, being debarred by the absence of water from swabbing.

The one hotel, where the students were put up, was owned by one of the sons of Robert Graves: like most of the Graves ventures outside the literary field it had been a financial failure. Deyá had little to recommend it except the Graves magic, a literal magic apparently, since the hills were said to be full of iron of a highly magnetic type which drew at the metallic deposits of the brain and made people mad: Graves himself was said to go around spluttering exorcisms while waving an olive branch. I did not see him, and I did not want to see him. The bad blood between us went back to my undergraduate days, when I had trounced his collected poems in a review and he had responded with lofty insults. With the publication of his translation of Omar Khayyam I had, much more recently, renewed the attack and he had been disgruntled. I had never thought him much of a poet, but Deyá was full of his worshippers. In his biography of Graves, Martin Seymour-Smith mentions what he calls the Mediterranean Institute of Deyá and says that it had 'a number of regular instructors, of whom the least undistinguished and certainly the least drunken . . . was the overcredulous but personally likeable Colin Wilson.' Life is short, and I will not take that as a libel on myself. However undistinguished I was and am, I was never drunk in Deyá, though some, Ruthven Todd for instance, said that, liquor being so cheap, they could not afford not to be drunk.

As for Colin Wilson, whose *The Outsider* and various works on the irrational in human culture had made him a kind of guru, he was indeed likeable, though he made, in public, embarrassing statements: 'A major author like myself,' he would say, and 'My own system of thought differs from that of Bernard Shaw in certain respects' and 'Kierkegaard and I are at one on that particular point'. His presence among the impressionable American young was perhaps dangerous, because these were only too ready to throw over the rational. A group of students of so-called Creative Writing could evade the discipline of syntax if Colin told them to compose out of their synapses. I sat with a number of these neophyte writers who considered that all they needed to produce masterpieces was a little time, their beards wet with the local *gazeosa*, munching with distaste but on a point of student defiance sandwiches of the local *jamón*, while I gave them a lesson in elementary linguistics. They had, I said, to know the difference between a synsemanteme and an auto-semanteme. Colin came in and implied that what they primarily ought to know was the works of Colin Wilson.

There were some young Americans in Deyá who were not students. They were what in those days were known as hippies, meaning unworking youths in torn shirts, jeans and espadrilles, whose task in the great urban world was to mock the vanity of toil. But here, lounging and coffee-cadging in the sun, they unkindly though nesciently mocked the poor hard-working fishermen. Liana turned on them for their lazy slovenliness and asked why they did not smarten themselves up. Like that's not our scene, and so on. Spain was still Falangist, and the Guardia Civil naturally considered these hippies to be a blot on the peasant landscape, though comparatively harmless. They were satisfied to have one of their number sent every weekend to be ritually beaten up. This was always a half-wit named Mike. Like he's like Jesus, man. Like he's like what the shit you call it a scrapegoat, man.

My late response to the Deyá magic and sloppiness was to give a lecture I entitled 'Shakespeare the Great Bourgeois'. I gave this in a suit with a collar and tie, perhaps the first ever to be seen in Deyá. Colin Wilson was in the audience and he had something to say about the pity of history's unkindness to Shakespeare in not allowing him to be born late enough to benefit from reading the works of. A black American whom all Deyá had at first feared because they took him to be a harbinger of the returning Moors, said that he had a cousin named Shakespeare who could prove he was of the Stratford stock. As for the bourgeois urge to work hard and become a gentleman, which I presented as an ambition wholly laudable if it meant throwing off great literature on the side, this had to be rejected and Shakespeare's work correspondingly revaluated. He was not like Jack Kerouac, man. He was also a fag with his thee and thou. The fag revolution which was to debase gaiety had not yet begun, so there were none there to defend his faggery. The meeting ended in disorder and an attack on my collar and tie.

The night before we left Deyá for Barcelona, Rome and Malta, there was a full moon and an open-air party under it. An expatriate Irishman with a handsome Icelandic mistress had built on a hillside a house all of concrete. Most of the furniture was concrete too, except for a home-carpentered table which was brought out to the hillside to hold the bad wine and cheap gin of Mallorca. An American voice growled: 'Now we gotcha.' There were attempts to throw both Liana and myself down the hillside into the sempiternal garbage dump below. The reason for the rough handling of my wife was that she had grabbed from the American with the growl a little doll representative of some enemy into which he had been sticking pins. This she had thrown into a smithy fire. So she was told: 'You burnt my dolly, baby. Now you gonna suffer.' To young Andrea it was the use of 'baby' that was the true violence: he could imagine no worse insult to himself nor, by extension, to another. Liana was thrown and broke a little toe. I used the table as a shield and weapon. Women screamed. The Gravesian white goddess looked down, unmoved. A decent bearded composer whose life was dedicated to the setting of Graves's lyrics recited a sort of cantrip. It did not mend Liana's toe.

Falangist Spain was an appropriate place for toe-breaking: now in its dying phase, it dealt minimal violence but was strong on lack of information, preferring to put kittens in ribbons and cooing babies on the covers of its periodicals. So at Barcelona airport there was no information about flights to Rome and I waxed loud in my complaints. A Spanish official called me '*perro*' and I tried to lash out, somewhat drunk on Fundador. A flight was eventually whispered rather than called, and the aircraft limped east. The stewardesses spent the entire flight changing into flamenco costumes and then back again into uniform, granting the benison of duty-free cigarettes only to a few favoured clients. When the plane landed the passengers cried '*Olé!*': the bull of a crash had been overcome, but only just. The whole trip had not been worth it. I had made few dollars and Liana had to hobble round Rome with a plastic bag on her bare foot, elegantly secured round her delicate ankle with a silver bracelet.

Taking deep breaths before returning to Malta, we stayed at the Senator Hotel near the Pantheon, and Liana said we were to have dinner with Milton Hebald, the American sculptor. I did not want to have dinner with anyone. Andrea lay in naked ease on a bed and spoke wise words: 'Why you marry her if you not do what she say?' I went out to dinner with Hebald and his wife. Hebald had been long in Italy, sculpting and making money out of it. He was responsible for the James Joyce statue on the grave in Zürich and also for the signs of the Zodiac at the Pan American terminal of Kennedy airport. He had property in Bracciano, including a small house he was ready to sell. Liana had known him for some time, and he had painted a nude of her with no funny business. Liana wanted the house in Bracciano: I had to do something about earning dollars, and quickly too. In the autumn I did a rapid lecture tour of the American west coast at five hundred dollars the throw, starting in Vancouver and finishing in Los Angeles, though skipping the state of Oregon. Bill Conrad flew up to San Francisco to spend a weekend with me. He had bad news that I had long expected. The Warner Brothers–Seven Arts organisation had acquired a new head, and this entailed the cancellation of all projects initiated under the old one. Bill himself was going back to acting: there was to be a television series about a fat private eye named Cannon. Cannon was to be fat because Bill was fat. Bill was always a fine trencherman. We ate clams on Fisherman's Wharf and steak and kidney pie at the Francis Drake Hotel. We drank ramos fizzes and mai-tais and champagne. 'We'll get that fucking movie made some day,' he swore. We ended the weekend like Niobe, all tears.

In Monterey an ageing Henry Miller came to hear me talk on *Finnegans Wake*, but he did not stay to the end. The lady who introduced me was much fatter than Bill Conrad, a genuine scholar whose speciality was *Handlying Synne*. She talked very loudly about the importance of *Handlying Synne* in a bar with a girl organist, and the clients listened with interest to this fat broad who had never handled sin in all her fucking life. In Los Angeles my suitcase was ￼lamented this to a little adult audience that filled the front ￼of a cinema. 'That's America,' they said, and sent shirts ￼y hotel. I saw now that the great lesson of travelling light had been forced on me. An airline bag on the shoulder was enough. Pants pressed overnight in a motel, shirts washed in the hand basin, no underwear: that was the way for a sort of scholar to wander the United States. I went back to Malta via London, but was not permitted to leave the transit lounge: that was one of the conditions, for six months at least, of my deserting my native land.

THERE WERE still not enough dollars. A semester spent in the State University of North Carolina at Chapel Hill might help. We left Andrea with the Maltese family opposite: his command of their language was now very adequate; he did not confuse genders or verb-endings; his English was full of Maltese idioms, such as 'I kill you by knife'. He had to be forced home occasionally to eat something more substantial than tomato *conserva* and bread. When he became fractious about the egg I proposed boiling for him, I lost my temper and broke the egg on his head. He never forgot this. He has never forgotten it. He waited several years for his revenge, and the revenge was a thorough one. Our house, the key left with the Grima family, became in our absence a toy for innumerable Maltese children. Out of love, Cicco Grima, the father, began to paint all our furniture brown.

Liana and I stayed a day or two in Manhattan in the brownstone house of my editor at Knopf, Bob Gottlieb the publishing maven, who had made *Catch-22* publishable and was to become the editor of *The New Yorker*. His father-in-law, Niccolò Tucci, had long been a contributor to that rather boring and very provincial magazine, and his wife, Maria Tucci, was a beautiful young actress. I felt guilty towards Bob Gottlieb, since all I had given him so far was the illustrated book on Shakespeare, and what he wanted was a novel. But the need to earn rapid dollars militated against novelising. Knopf was making money out of books like *Catch-22* and the works of John Updike (a good author in that he did not exact large advances), but I did not see how the house could ever make a profit out of my involuted and very British creations. I had a novel in mind, one based on the structuralist theories of Claude Lévi-Strauss, but Gottlieb grew gloomy when I gave him an outline. It is unwise ever to give a publisher an outline, unless that outline is a catalogue of modes of fornication: it is like playing the proposed themes of a symphony with one finger. Gottlieb was the cleverest kind of New York Jew. He had sailed through Harvard and Cambridge, never sufficiently stretched by his tutors, had actually read the entire New York edition of Henry James that rested on his drawing-room shelves, and was an acute spotter of literary worth that was also profitable. He had been married before and had a big hulking son named Roger. He had suffered in his time and begun a course of psychoanalytical treatment with a long session of salty howling. Like Tom Maschler and Ed Victor, he was too good for me. Deborah Rogers, still my agent, admired this trio, and Bob Gottlieb admired Deborah, who he saw as the kind of imperturbable British aristocrat who would walk into a den of cut-throats to procure the autobiography of a thief and murderer.

Liana and I flew from La Guardia to Raleigh, where cigarettes were cheaper than elsewhere in the United States, and took a cab to the Carolina Inn in Chapel Hill. The other guests at this motel were policemen of a distinctly southern brand, with dangerously empty eyes, fat bottoms, guns with the safety catch off, and caps on in the presence of ladies. I pointed out that even in Western films cowboys doffed in a woman's presence, but I had a gun jocularly, or not so, poked at my guts in response. These policemen were there to patrol the Chapel Hill campus and pre-empt student riots of the Kent State University kind. They also shot at any automobiles they did not like the look of, meaning mainly foreign cars, and I was glad that we had not travelled by ship with our Morgan or Bedford Dormobile. The manager of the inn seriously assured me that they did not shoot to kill, 'only to maim'. In the inn cafeteria they would say: 'My my, just shoot me some of them lil ole carrots.' We took to eating at a hashjoint called Bill and Lew's. Bill was black and big, Lew white and little. One morning I asked for ham and eggs. The charming black waitress said there was no ham and eggs, honey. You got eggs? Sure we got eggs. You got ham? Sure we got ham, but we ain't got no grits. That was an exceptional morning. Normally grits were not merely in good supply but compulsory. Get 'em down, son, they'll do you good. Chapel Hill was brown bag territory. You could get beer at a saloon run by a very imperious black called Mr Jackson.

The blacks were very charming, especially the women, who possessed a kind of epic radiance. I was greeted ebulliently in a bank where I went to change some traveller's cheques. Then, on sight of the traveller's cheques, issued by the Midland Bank in Sliema, Malta, the atmosphere cooled. The white manager was called on, and he said he had never seen traveller's cheques like them before. He added: 'You just passin' through, stranger?'

I was not passing through. I was a visiting professor at the oldest state university in the Union. Thomas Wolfe had been educated there, and to my shock I found, on my campus wanderings, a plaque dedicated to him buried in the long grass. He had been forgotten. When I enquired about him at the bookstore it was thought that I meant Tom Wolfe, the white-suited initiator of the new, or higher, journalism. The jeaned and maxiskirted students of Chapel Hill did not want mammoth romanticism; they wanted Vonnegut and Brautigan and, of course, Hesse. They also wanted drugs, but they had been subdued somewhat by one of their number who, high on LSD and in a sixth-floor apartment, had taken off like a bat and bloodily crashed on the sidewalk. While I was lecturing on Milton, a squad of armed police drilled noisily outside: they meant to be provocative, restive as they were at the lack of student violence. I protested, but my chaperon professor affirmed that scholarship had to enter the modern world. And vice versa? That too.

Making John Milton enter the modern world was not easy. The most I could do with *Comus* was to present it as an allegory of the northern-southern divide. The lady was clearly from puritanical Massachusetts and Comus stood for a kind of sybaritism, sustained by a slave-maker's wand, that was subtropical and magnolia-scented. Look, he even offers the lady juleps. What was meant to be a brief sinecure, an exotic writer showing himself occasionally on campus, turned into passionate hard work. The past, whether it was Chaucer or Walt Whitman, had to be made alive for these young people who, with drugs and sex, thought they could subsist in an eternal present. The faculty was only too ready to hand over its students to me, especially at eight in the morning. Denied the right to teach in England, I had become a teacher of Americans. I see myself grabbing a quick cup of coffee and, raincoated against the morning squalls, threading my way among the busy squirrels in the long damp grass to await yawning tousled students who had crawled out of bed to hear some long-dead guy vigorously celebrated. I ended up with seven lectures a day, which was considered going too far.

If Liana decided to give a talk on Dante, this was acceptable, because Dante was Italian and she was Italian, and he was drawn into the world of contemporary Italian elegance: he was no more distant than Federico Fellini. Besides, she was also ready to talk to the film group on Jean-Luc Godard, who was known to be avant-garde. Liana was exotic enough to seem able to subsume past and present Europe in an image as spatial as a film. She might even have got away with a course on elementary Latin, which would be seen only as another kind of Italian. I was exotic too, but not exotic enough. I was temporally exotic, a kind of ancestral American.

I was turned into a genuine American, though one from the hateful north, on the occasion of Thanksgiving, which ought to have cancelled for a day the barbed wire of the Mason-Dixon line. Thanksgiving was awkward for us, since all the restaurants closed, and every member of the faculty assumed that some other member of the faculty had invited us to turkey and pumpkin pie. But young Ben Forkner, who was unmarried though engaged to a French *assistante*, knew of a restaurant some way outside Chapel Hill which would be open, divined that we were guests of no home, so drove us out for a slap-up celebration. The restaurant, however, proved unpatriotic and served only crab patties with the deep-freeze ice still in them. The waitress asked: 'What will you folks drink – milk or tea?' so Ben drove off to find an open liquor store and came back with a bottle of Roma Rocket, which seemed to be a mixture of grape juice and raw alcohol. It was an atrocious meal, and I tried to soften Ben's chagrin by turning myself into the host. I put down a twenty-dollar bill and was given change for a fifty. Naturally I said nothing. Driving away in the car we heard a shotgun fired at us and a voice calling: 'Come back, you goddam Yankee chisellers.' So I was a Yankee now, and Yankees too were a French girl, an Italian matron, and a son of Mississippi.

Tom Stumpf, a young professor of English with children he taught to sing Purcell, kindly laid on a post-Thanksgiving turkey dinner for us. He did more. He arranged to give an evening lecture on my work. I was embarrassed at this and decided not to attend, though I was impelled to stay close to the hall where it was given, perhaps in the hope of at least hearing occasional laughter. The rain was heavy as I patrolled the perimeter, so I went in. I was in time to hear Tom dealing with my first hero, Sgt R. Ennis of *A Vision of Battlements*. The name R. Ennis, Tom said, was a palinlogue of 'sinner'. I was surprised to hear this, since I had chosen 'Ennis' because, signifying an island, it pointed at the loneliness of the possessor of the name. But I could not deny that what he said was so. The best literary insights were coming from the Americans. They were prepared to look at a writer's unconscious. They were ready too to take contemporary literature with academic seriousness, thus helping contemporary authors to understand themselves. British universities shut us entirely out.

Chapel Hill was, despite its policemen, a good place, with a genuine dedication to scholarship, which overflowed into beery discussions in Mr Jackson's tavern. North Carolina itself was amiable and tolerant, though the Baptist writ ran here. But there was no establishment like the Bob Jones academy in South Carolina, where the fundamentalism was rabid and the King James Bible was the word of God. Duke University, however, seemed a dangerous place. Experiments in prevision and extrasensory perception were said to go on there, and an ex-Nazi *Gruppenführer* was alleged to run a tyrannical course in banting. I met the author of *The Godfather*, Mario Puzo, who came regularly to Duke to have his weight reduced on a diet of puffed rice. He would then take the road north, gorge pizza in every joint in Virginia, Maryland, Delaware, Pennsylvania and New Jersey, and be back, ready for more puffed rice. I was not invited into the English department of Duke, but a group of faculty members and their wives, who ran literary cocktail parties, asked me to talk on my work while they grew steadily glassier. At the end of the session the hippy lifestyle was extolled, and a woman said that we all ought to be hippies. Nonsense, I said, you cannot have parasitism without a host. I was then hipped and elbowed into a corner and clawed at. Liana got me out alive.

We went back to New York and Bob Gottlieb's brownstone, and Frederick Morgan, editor of the *Hudson Review*, to which I had contributed a regular 'Letter from England', gave a party for me. At this party I learned that, in 1970–1, I was to spend a whole academic year at the University of Princeton. It was like being back in the army, with news of a posting coming through over gin in the mess. The snow was coming down heavily over New York and New Jersey as Liana and I took a bus from the Port Authority terminal to the Princeton restaurant where we were to be lunched and inspected by Theodore Weiss and Edmund Keeley. Elizabeth Bowen, my predecessor in the post of Visiting Fellow, was there too, smoking cigarettes and coughing her way to a premature death, elegant though, with the unkillable beauty of an Anglo-Irish aristocrat, just off to spend Christmas with Eudora Welty. It dawned on me that this was Christmas Eve and, for the first time in my life, the day of the Nativity was to be like any other day, only rather worse – nowhere to be except Bob Gottlieb's empty house, nothing to eat, no presents, the shops closing early. Liana did not mind, the Macellari *Natale* always being an occasion for bitter family quarrels, but I could be forgiven the odd tear for the obliteration of a feast that Lynne had loved, celebrated with readings from the *Pickwick Papers* and *A Christmas Carol*, ribbons round the necks of the house pets, turkey and trifle, presents about the tree. My exile, in this New York

Dickensian weather, seemed to be to a cold region unblessed by lights. I sloshed into a just-closing supermarket and bought two pork chops in plastic. I cooked them badly. It would have been an insult to Christmas to cook them well.

Back in Malta we found that the Maltese government had begun its vendetta against us. The Morgan had been taken out of its hired garage by one of the Grima sons and driven about the island without a licence. The car, blameless enough, was confiscated. There was talk of confiscating the Bedford Dormobile too, for the pedantic reason that we had dismantled the gas cooker in it and this converted it into a vehicle different from the one we had imported in 1968. If one could no longer cook in it one could no longer live in it; ergo, it was no longer a mobile home. But it was a mobile home we had brought in with us: we were, in some mystical way, cheating the government. Liana's nails were ready to claw at the face of Maltese bureaucracy, so I bought her a guitar for their better employment. I wrote little minuets for her in E minor, a key whose three principal chords are easy on the guitar. I also wrote a novel, or a good deal of one. It was entitled *MF* or *M.F.* or *M/F*, I have never been sure which.

Bill Conrad, back at Warner Brothers, had facetiously suggested putting on a black *Oedipus* and calling it *Mother-Fucker*. The initials of my book were a homage to that idea, but they also stood for the hero, Miles Faber, who summed up man by being both a soldier and an artificer. The plot was based on incestuous relationships, but as seen through the lens of Lévi-Strauss's Structuralism. The book was to be published in Britain by Jonathan Cape, who had already published Lévi-Strauss's *The Scope of Anthropology*, his inaugural address to the University of Paris when assuming his chair there, and facetious critics were to see a kind of incest in the fact of a mother–discourse and a son–novel lying in the bed of a common publisher. That mother–discourse on the relationship between incest and riddles moved me a great deal: it was one of the three major revelations of my later life, the others being Gaudí in Barcelona and Belli in Trastevere. Lévi-Strauss had discovered that the incest–riddle nexus was to be found not only in the Oedipus myth but also in the folklore of the Iroquois and Algonquin Indians. There was one Algonquin legend he recounted, in which a boy finds his sister being sexually assaulted by his own double. He kills the double, only to discover that he was the son of a very powerful witch who has taught owls to talk. She looks for her lost son, now buried, and the brother has to pretend to be that son. The witch has her suspicions, which can be allayed only by the boy's marrying his own sister: no one would be so mad as to fracture the incest taboo. But even after the marriage the witch is not quite convinced, so she sets her talking owls to ask the pseudo-son riddles: if he gives the right answers, as Oedipus did to the Sphinx, she will know that he has committed the unpardonable sin and hence is not her son. The brother and sister escape when he unwittingly answers the riddles correctly, and they fly into the heavens, there to become the sun and moon in eclipse.

It was the structural relationship between riddle and incest, not the morality behind the taboo, that interested Lévi-Strauss. What I saw in the legend was the possibility of composing a contemporary realistic novel in which all the structural desiderata were fulfilled without the uninstructed reader's needing to know or care. The book was to have disguised talking animals in it – a Mr Loewe and a Mr Pardaleos and a Dr Gonzi (named for the Archbishop of Malta) with the lion-face of a leper. The hero, Miles Faber, was to have the riddle-answering gift, which would ineluctably lead him to the commission of incest with his sister. The filial incest implied in the title was to be an inherited family crime, if crime could be applied to an act performed, as with Oedipus, in total ignorance. Miles Faber, deliberately shifting from mother to sister, committing the crime only for the sake of self-preservation, would exorcise the family curse.

Sophocles, in *Oedipus Tyrannus*, does not invoke the riddle, and later literary versions of the myth, or film ones like Pasolini's, also ignore it. But *Pericles, Prince of Tyre* and *Finnegans Wake* make the ability to solve a riddle a condition for committing incest. In my own novel *Tremor of Intent*, written some years before reading Lévi-Strauss, the decoding of a secret message precedes a sexual act which the participants perceive to be incestuous in a proleptic manner, since the man later becomes a priest and the girl has to call him father. Clearly, the nexus had deep psychological roots difficult even for Lévi-Strauss to explain. Why the talking animal – Sphinx in the Oedipus myth, owls in the Algonquin? Was this nature warning man of the danger of knowing too much? Clarification of a mystery leads to the disruption of the social order. Why? It was not my task as a novelist to explain, as in the dénouement of a detective story. It was my task to load the plot with structures, chiefly binary oppositions. A binary opposition is implied in the title – male versus female (the title of the Brazilian translation was to spell this out over-explicitly). This, I said in effect, was a valid opposition, whereas the opposition black–white was not: at the end of the novel we discover that most of the characters are black; we have naturally, following the Western fictional tradition, assumed them to be white. One of the epigraphs to the novel cites Simeon Potter's 'There is no isogloss corresponding to the 49th parallel', meaning that American speech is a continuum but a political division suggests otherwise. And so on. The novel was the toughest I ever had to write and, of all those I have written, it is the one that displeases me least. The critics, as we shall see, were mostly contemptuous.

A literary commission, as opposed to a literary urge, got in the way of a fierce concentration on this, the first novel of my new life or *vita nuova*. It was proposed by the Tyrone Guthrie Theatre in Minneapolis that I translate Rostand's *Cyrano de Bergerac* for a new production there, probably with Christopher Plummer in the lead. He had already played in the Hooker blank verse version which, for various reasons, was not considered satisfactory. The artistic director of the Tyrone Guthrie Theatre (the Minneapolitans accepted the British spelling) was Michael Langham, a follower of Guthrie's directorial philosophy, and he had been brought up on a sharper, wittier approach to drama than could be fulfilled in Hooker's dreamy Georgian translation of *Cyrano*. There was no wit in it, and the lack of rhyme precluded the epigrammatic brilliance of the original. *Cyrano de Bergerac* may not be the greatest play in the world, but it usually packs an audience in. The Tyrone Guthrie Theatre was in the red: it needed a financial recovery, and a new *Cyrano* might help. Hidden structuralist engines drove me to the making of one only in order that I might follow it with a new *Oedipus*, one in which I could plant the 4–2–3 riddle (what animal goes on four legs in the morning, two at noon, three in the evening?) which Sophocles had left out.

Work on both *Cyrano de Bergerac* and *MF* (or *M.F.* or *M/F*) had to be intermitted in the early spring of 1970 so that Liana and I could go to Australia. An invitation to open the Adelaide Arts Festival in 1968 had had to be rejected because of Lynne's dying and death; now I could accept and also show myself, under the aegis of the British Council, in Singapore, Perth, Melbourne, Sydney and various towns in New Zealand. We would lose money rather than make it, for the Council would pay expenses only for myself, and I insisted that Liana travel with me. But Italians are always expert at fiddling, and in Rome Liana fiddled a massive fare reduction with Alitalia. Before starting our journey I learned that the American director Stanley Kubrick was to make a film of my *A Clockwork Orange*. I did not altogether believe this and I did not much care: there would be no money in it for me, since the production company that had originally bought the rights for a few hundred dollars did not consider that I had a claim to part of their own profit when they sold those rights to Warner Brothers. That profit was, of course, considerable.

When we landed in Bombay, Liana insisted on buying a huge toy bull elephant smothered in scraps of coloured glass. I did not know what was inside its soft cloth body but I feared the worst – discarded snotty rags, bandages off lepers with running sores, ancient chapattis and crusts of poppadom. Singapore let it in, which was surprising: it had become an over-clean town, a sort of tropical Geneva, and its Prime Minister Lee Kuan Yew had imposed a sub-fascist hygiene on most aspects of life in the lion-city. Dirty literature, filthy films, and clean long hair were alike forbidden, but I was happy to see that Bugis Street at three in the morning was as soiled and hoicking as ever, with *sateh* made of doubtful meat grilling over smoky fires. The rest of the city, though, no longer reeked of wet dish-rags and cat-piss. It was still a free port, the trading paradise that Sir Stamford Raffles had intended (Liana loaded herself with photographic equipment), but the old humanising shabbiness, an endearing property of British colonies, had been expunged. How much Mr Lee was in control was revealed when we met D. J. Enright, now resigning, along with other expatriates, from the university. The new vice-chancellorship was to be a political appointment, and the technocratic philosophy of Mr Lee, which his friend Harold Wilson shared, was to diminish the importance of the humanities. Literature had already become (Wilson's words) a minority sub-culture.

Any lecturing I was officially invited to do in Singapore had to be restricted to the purely technical region of applied linguistics. ESL – English as a Second Language – had its South-East Asian head-quarters here, under a Singapore Chinese lady whose appointment was undoubtedly political. The ESL taught, and taught how to be taught, still had a British accent – a long back 'a' in 'bath', no terminal 'r' – but it was clearly understood where the true linguistic prestige lay. Exercises in minimal pairs (sit/seat; bid/bead) and variable question-tags (everybody east of Suez, as west of Offa's Dyke, wants to say, 'He's dead, isn't it?') came out of American or American-inspired textbooks, since the home-staying British were slow to recognise, despite the evidence on their own doorstep, that ESL existed.

My *Malayan Trilogy* (called *The Long Day Wanes* in the United States) was known to some, though I gained the impression that it was not officially approved. It prophesied racial tension and even race-war in an independent Malaysia, and the prophecy was being fulfilled north of the Johore Straits. But Singapore was not Malaysia, though it had a nominal Malay ruler. Here the Chinese were in control, and a Malay in a sarong and songkok was a rarity. Lecturing on the book, I was aware that it was remote, historical, even exotic, as well as intelligible only in terms of the Wilsonic minority sub-culture. I was lecturing under the aegis of a dying academic tradition, though my heart lifted on the street outside the lecture-hall when I saw hordes of Chinese apparently anxious to hear me. But they were waiting for the live appearance of a Hongkong film star at the cinema next door. My audience was meagre enough.

There were, and are, Singapore and Malaysian writers of great talent who have brought new tonalities to English – Ee Tiang Hong, Lee Tzu Pheng, Goh Poh Seng, Wong Phui Nam, Edwin Thumboo, Wong May, Chandran Nair, Arthur Yap, Omar Mohamed Noor, Hilary Tham, Robert Yeo, Chung Yee Chong, others – but the literary cultivation of second language English is so far limited to the smaller forms – poetry and short stories. What needs to burst out of Singapore is an Asiatic *Ulysses*, if Lee Kuan Yew will allow it. The sad thing about the great city was the official fear of a free culture. The chic and beauty of the women, the incredible variety of the cuisine, the stimulation and soothing of the senses, as well as the vigour of commerce, seemed to be regarded as enough. Mr Lee should have been perturbed by the departure of a major poet and critic, but he was evidently not.

We flew to Perth, and Liana's Indian elephant was at once confiscated. My unspoken worry about its stuffing was made all too articulate by the customs officials – syphilitic bandages and all. Liana was prepared to leave Australian soil before properly stepping on it, clutching her elephant, and the immigration officers would have been quick to escort her to the departure lounge, since she did not have the visa that Italian citizens needed. But to her and the officials I pointed out that there was a major job to be done, namely the opening of the Adelaide Arts Festival, and what God had put together let not immigration regulations put asunder. Talking of Australia, Enright had said: 'You've been to worse places.' That was an understatement. This was the country for young Andrea to grow up in, bare brown toes splaying on the beaches under the sun. It was cosmopolitan too: Liana could have spoken nothing but Italian, starting with the fishermen at Freemantle and ending in the restaurants of King's Cross. Europe had entered the continent and begun to plane its tough wood.

But the chip on the Aussie shoulder was still there, and I wondered why. It was hard for this Pom to say the right thing, and, opening the Adelaide festival, I angered by trying to please. I quoted Drayton's verses to the Virginia pioneers:

> And in regions far
> Such heroes bring ye forth
> As those from whom we came,
> And plant our name
> Under that star
> Not known unto our north.

This, for some reason, sounded condescending, and my commendation of Patrick White's achievement aroused snarls about the 'Keep Australia Patrick White Society'. Meeting White later in Sydney, I could see what the lesser Australian writers meant. He gave Liana and myself dinner, exquisitely cooked by his Greek companion, and this was the first occasion in my life when the ladies had to withdraw, leaving the men to circulate the port. White spoke highly patrician English and made no secret of his homosexuality. He was not Aussie enough for the Aussies, and yet *Voss* was the supreme Australian novel. As for homosexuality, the digger prejudice was so strong that one had to suspect an occult vein of it in the most ostentatiously virile.

Australian women were well-built and beautiful: they had to be in that climate and on that protein-stuffed diet. If they were gauche, aggressive and dissatisfied, it was all the fault of the men, who were disinclined to woo and considered the sexual arts dirty. At parties, I noticed, the sexes remained separate, the women discussing dress and obstetrics at one end of the room, the men content with beery mateship at the other. The comparative indifference of the men to the women was summed up for me in a Perth restaurant. A very beautiful waitress, with sumptuous long legs exposed in a miniskirt, leaned over a table to collect a plate and displayed those legs to the limit. Only I was unholily moved; the rest of the male diners went on stolidly with their tucker. What sexual culture was to be discerned among Australian men seemed derived from literally camp situations – work, army, prison. 'Les Girls', men who put on a transvestite show in Sydney, were pure army or prison concert party. The homo-erotic was sublimated into mateship. But this was an outsider's view.

An Australian woman confirmed the outsider's view in a little book called *Now You'll Think I'm Awful*, which merely presented, with inevitable antipodean facetiousness, the facts of the matter. There was a lower midde class shame about sex. Philip Roth's *Portnoy's Complaint*, which I had read the previous autumn in San Francisco, was forbidden entrance into Australia, though copies could be bought in New Zealand. Censorship, which I had inveighed against in Malta, was of necessity the theme of the public lecture I had to give in Adelaide. The Australian Broadcasting Commission recorded the talk and was to transmit it on a Sunday evening, but it took fright at the last minute. I summed up the censorship situation in such of the countries of the world as I had visited, and attacked Malta as the most oppressive state of them all. I had forgotten that the Maltese population of Australia was many times bigger than that of the island itself; I should have been ready for the blistering counter-attack that awaited me back there, with the *Times of Malta* headline THE PRICE OF GRATITUDE.

Anti-intellectualism and sexual prudery both seemed to be British colonial legacies. The moral and mental climate of Australia did not do justice to the land itself, vast, with bewilderingly rich flora and fauna. The politicians could have been respected if they had made their philistinism an aspect of a policy, as in the fascist state that D. H. Lawrence had falsely foreseen in *Kangaroo*, but it was an aspect of power without enlightenment. Anti-intellectualism was to be met even among the writers. 'I'm a lowbrow,' one said, 'and I write for lowbrows.' Frank Hardy, a very considerable novelist, trembled with resentment of Patrick White, who had let Australia down by viewing it through the prism of a Pommy education. He spoke in a debate which I chaired, but the chairman, being a bloody Pommy intruder, could be ignored; nor could I, a guest, enforce with safety the rules of debate.

Even in an amicable drinking session the chip on the shoulder would be presented for knocking off. 'We don't want whinging Poms like you here,' said a literary girl. 'We want blokes like Yevtushenko.' You understand his Russian? 'That's not the bloody point.' It was best not to argue. It was best not to take Australia as other than a country pleasingly antinomian, crammed with sensuous delights (fine oysters, thick steaks, excellent white wine), blessed with wonderful light and piquant birds and animals. Lawrence, leaving the country after writing what is still the greatest novel about it, shrewdly lamented that the land had been used but not loved. Perhaps it was easier for a mere visitor to adore kangaroos and budgerigars than a farmer who could only curse their destructiveness, but it was not easy to forgive the total massacre of the kangaroos and joeys in a small Sydney zoo the night before I flew to Christchurch. There was a brutality of muscle as well as thought.

But it was an innocent brutality. Patrick White presents Australian evil in his *Riders in the Chariot,* yet I had no sense anywhere of genuine malevolence. Australia rather seemed a country that was doggedly determined to honour no-bloody-nonsense rather infantile masculinity, refusing to grow beyond the pioneer virtues despite the progressiveness of its universities, the work of its artists – who had to go to Europe for recognition – and a true democratic spirit against which its democratically elected politicians were disposed to fight. Australians saw themselves as despised by the motherland – and London-based Australian entertainers were dedicated to disparaging Australia as a mere comic turn – and exploited by America, a sister country with no chip on its shoulder. Things have changed since 1970 but not changed enough.

One is always looking for symbols. In the Sydney Zoo I thought I found one. A gorgeously plumed cockatoo fixed me with its eyes, humorous and all-knowing, and kept saying 'Hellow, cocky'. Then it would converse with its own kind in brilliant trills and roulades, a highly sophisticated bird-speech which emphasised the vulgarity of the greeting it had been taught. Australia was vulgar. I'm a lowbrow and I write for lowbrows. In the Sydney airport bar a schooner-downer asked me the riddle 'Why is the Colosseum rahnd?' Don't know. 'So the dygoes can't do a tomtit in the johnny orner.' My wife happens to be a dago. 'Good on yer, missis. Ave a schooner.' One could not take offence. The Indian bull elephant with its glass encrustations had been promised to Liana on her leaving Sydney. But it had obviously been incinerated, and quickly too, back in Perth. We took the plane to Christchurch. On it was a returning victorious rugby team which scolded us for not joining in the chorus of 'If I was a marrying maid, which thank the Lord I'm not sir'.

Christchurch seemed grim and, the world here being turned on its head, dourly northern. A foul wind blew in from the Antarctic. At the university I addressed a group of students on Samuel Butler and said that he was a great enough writer to draw scholars to the Canterbury settlement to discover more about his sheep-farming days, and a student not unlike Badcock in *The Way of All Flesh* ('Not only was he ugly, dirty, ill-dressed, bumptious, and in every way objectionable, but he was deformed and waddled when he walked, so that he had won the nickname which I can only reproduce by calling it "Here's my back, and there's my back" ') struck in rudely with, 'And I suppose they'd come like you, on a fat British Council grant.' There was a fair amount of resentment down there, resentment of big Australia, which called Kiwis 'Poms without brynes', and of a distant Britain which was neglecting its Commonwealth, and New Zealand mutton, to become Europeanised. In the evening I gave the Macfarlane lecture, for which, despite its endowment, the university did not have to pay, since the British Council was supposed to have paid for it. After the lecture we were given tea and raw carrot sandwiches.

One of my engagements was the opening of a national booksellers' conference at Rotorua on North Island. Rotorua was all bubbling mud and a motel. The booksellers and their wives cordially invited us to strip and join them in a jolly bubbling mud bath. Liana, always ready to try anything, plunged into the healthful filth, but I remained aloof and drinking. For dinner there was ill-roasted hoggart. The waitresses were glorious Maori girls, genteelly condescended to by the booksellers' wives (awfully nice girls, despite their lack of advantages). Over the thin coffee in the lounge (it cost more if you had it at table because of some trade union regulation) the booksellers from Palmerston, Hamilton, Masterton, Napier and Hastings exulted in their thriving greeting-card, paper doily and Barbara Cartland businesses and disparaged literature as a nuisance – hard to sell and it got in the way of the doilies. This made me mad. The next morning I thundered about booksellers' responsibility and attacked suburban philistinism. New Zealanders are politer than Australians: they took all this with good grace. But while Liana and I were waiting to take the little aircraft for Palmerston and paying for excess luggage (Liana, fretting at the loss of her elephant, had been buying tikis), two men from the conference arrived heatedly in a car. I had neglected, they complained, to declare the conference open. 'It is open,' I said, and boarded.

I do not wish to seem to disparage New Zealand. Wynford Vaughan-Thomas was being unjust when he wrote

> A Maori fisherman, the legends say,
> Dredged up New Zealand in a single day.
> I've seen the catch, and here's my parting crack –
> It's undersized; for God's sake throw it back!

I saw too little of South Island to be able to judge it, and the carrot sandwiches stuck in my craw, but I was impressed by Gisborne, Hawke's Bay, Taranaki, Auckland. Nature is green and the whole land geologically very young, so that bubbling mud and street tremors obviate boredom. I had seen nothing of the Australian aborigines, save for one old lubra of spectacular ugliness crossing the street in Melbourne, but I saw plenty of the Maoris, handsome, vigorous, integrated – at the higher social levels – with the white settlers. I liked the Maori giantess who brought me tea in the bedroom in Palmerston wherein the Queen had slept (I will never get closer to royalty) and said: 'If you don't like sugar don't stir it.' In faintly tremulous Auckland it was possible to buy books banned in Australia and to see films banned there too – *Easy Rider* and *Midnight Cowboy*, which showed me the way the contemporary cinema was going and how old-hat and prissy *Will* would have been.

I knew now that *A Clockwork Orange* was definitely being filmed – Stanley Kubrick was sending urgent cables about the need to see me in London on some matter of the script – and I feared, justly as it turned out, that there would be frontal nudity and overt rape. In Chapel Hill Liana and I had seen Scandinavian pornography freely on show, and some of the films of the new American wave considered themselves antiquated and reactionary if they did not use 'fuck' and show fucking. I foresaw a dangerous situation for myself and I was right to do so. Meanwhile I could be soothed by the blandness of Wellington, though that blandness was merely the thin surface of a bubbling muddy unrest among the young. It was as the author of a novel they considered subversive, though it was merely theological, that they tried to force drugs on me, affirming that I would write better stoned. There were a lot of drugs getting into New Zealand, many of them mild and green from the Polynesian territories, some of them crystalline and fierce. There was frustration around, but none were more frustrated than the New Zealand writers. Where was their readership? Where were their commercial outlets? Katherine Mansfield had turned herself into a European, and even Janet Frame had gone to America to be friendly with Saul Bellow. A grass-smoking young author with a glass-beaded headband that made Liana mourn the loss of her elephant, sitting tailorwise in a hut near Hutt, spoke of his intention to write a novel about James Joyce and Lenin and Tristan Tzara in Zürich. Europe had the great themes, New Zealand paper doilies. Alas for him, Tom Stoppard was composing a play, a wordy and facetious one, on the same collocation. The young man might yet be forced to write about New Zealand.

I listened in on a rehearsal of the very good symphony orchestra in Wellington. It was playing Vaughan Williams's London Symphony, drawn, like the writers, to the maternal centre. The French ambassador, who seemed to like the place, drove Liana and me back from a party to the Waterloo Hotel in Wellington: the *morne plaine* was far. At the airport we drank cocktails called Death in the Afternoon while waiting for the afternoon flight to Fiji. A girl named Helen Bradshaw, one of the New Zealand secretaries in Brunei, appeared in hail and farewell to mourn Lynne's death. 'She had death in her face. It always seemed to me that she wanted to die.' Too much death altogether before a flight to Fiji. We flew to Fiji and then to Hawaii. We expected to be processed into an American state by slender Polynesians decking us with leis, but the immigration and customs officers were fat, grouchy, specially imported mainland specimens to remind travellers that this was the US of A and aloha and hula-hulas were for the movies. We drank mai-tais and swam in the treacly waters under Diamond Head. We flew to San Francisco. We flew to London.

Stanley Kubrick had arranged that we lunch together in Trader Vic's, a worldwide mock-Polynesian concessionary restaurant that, in London, brooded beyond cinema-dark corridors in the Hilton Hotel. Liana and I, now seasoned mai-tai-drinkers, drank mai-tais. Kubrick did not turn up, despite the urgent cables crossing the International Date Line. It appeared later that he was worried about the copyright situation as regards a pair of lines sung by a drunk in *A Clockwork Orange*:

> O dear dear land I fought for thee
> And brought thee peace and victory.

Were those lines mine? Those lines were mine. Liana and I, after a lunch of mai-tais, went to Oxford Street to buy Burberry raincoats. Identically raincoated, though hers was much smaller than mine, we faced each other in the rain and she announced with much bitterness that she was not going back to Malta.

'To live, you mean?'

'To live, I mean. We collect Andrea and the Bedford and we take a boat to Italy.'

'The books, the furniture, the cats, the *fenech* and the *anfut*?' It was natural to give a rabbit and a hedgehog those names: they were native Maltese while the cats were ship's cats. 'We leave everything behind?'

'The animals can go to the Grima family. They will be a substitute for Andrea. We have enough dollars to buy the house in Bracciano. I beat Milton Hebald down.'

'When did you do that and how? By cable from New Zealand?'

'When we were in Rome before taking the plane to Bombay. You were asleep or something.'

There was some dubiety among the immigration officers at Luqa as to whether we were to be allowed in or not. I had said terrible things about Malta in Adelaide. I was in the little book, a mere ghost of the big book at Kennedy airport, wherein the undesirables were listed. But we were allowed in. Cicco Grima had painted most of the furniture a sick brown, and we had to pretend to be pleased. Andrea spoke no English at all. An official letter announced the forthcoming confiscation of our Bedford Dormobile. We had to get out quickly. Fortunately, a cargo boat bound for Naples was leaving Valletta in two days: there was room for twelve passengers and our mobile home. We stealthily drove on at dawn.

Arising from a siesta and coming up on deck, I found very small Andrea addressing three very tall Africans in what to them was fluent Moghrabi Arabic. He was telling them about Malta, now invisible, while pointing in the opposite direction. This was another symbol of something, I could not tell what. As we rounded Cape Granitola, Andrea was chattering in recovered English with a Cambridgeshire accent. By the time we were easing into the Bay of Naples he was peeling away Maltese like the skin of his breakfast orange. He said goodbye to his three tall Africans with a *Ciao, ragazzi*, like dubbed Gary Cooper striding out of a Wild West saloon. We landed, and our Bedmobile was cheered. We had to turn left near the *Mercato Ittico*, but the Neapolitans had forgotten their Greek: they called it the *Mercato Ittico del Pesce*. So we passed the Fish Market of Fish and took, like the Paolo after whom Andrea was named, the road to the pagan capital.

BRACCIANO IS a small town north of Rome on the lake that bears the same name – or it may be the other way round. There are three other towns on the lake shores – Manziana, Trevignano and Anguillara – but Bracciano has the most history. Here there is the Castello Orsini, which Napoleone Orsini started to build about 1470 and his son Gentile Virginio finished about 1485. One of the Orsini dukes visited England's Elizabeth I and witnessed the first night of *Twelfth Night*: Shakespeare, singularising his name with his usual bardic carelessness, made him the languishing hero of the play. The house we were buying from Milton Hebald dated from about 1485 and was probably one of the dwellings of the ostlers or scullions who served the castle. It was up on the *sentinella*, with a fine view of the lake, and situated in Piazza Padella or Frying-Pan Square. To state that we were buying a house was an exaggeration: it was part of a house only – a bedroom with a kind of antechamber, a pair of bathrooms opening on to a corridor, ancient stairs leading to a long salon and a tiny kitchen, further stairs going up to a roof-terrace: here the eyes dazzled with laky light. The house was already furnished minimally – an iron bed, a table, a stove fed by gas-bombs, ragged easy chairs, an old couch that was to be Andrea's temporary bed. The topography of the house, which had been less built than allowed to accumulate, was difficult to visualise: the Signora Elena who occupied part of it was known only as a pair of thundering feet above the bedroom; a single cave at ground-level seemed to house a whole growling family that came and went in a seasonal cycle.

The Braccianesi lacked the southern grace that Forsterians expect from their Italian visits. They mostly called themselves communists, and the hammer and sickle of the Partito Communista Italiano glowered from innumerable posters. They had not seen an Englishman for a long time, and they assumed that I was German. Because Liana spoke English they called her *l'americana*. A travelling vegetable-vendor refused to be disabused of my imposed teutonism and regularly called: '*Lei è tedesco, no? Guten Morgen, Deutschland kaput.*' It was no good my protesting '*Sono inglese*'. I was disguising myself as a Briton to evade punishment for wartime crimes. Still, all that was forgotten now: history was a burden Italians were only too ready to unshoulder. Guns were not for fighting but for shooting inedible little birds.

Andrea was speaking fluent but foul Italian of the local dialect in a very few days. His first song was *La Bandiera Rossa* – the Red Flag – which he turned into

> Avanti popolo alla riscossola
> Bandiera rossola bandiera rossola.

Sense was not for singing, and it was not for insults either. He did not unscramble *vafnculo* into its go-fuck-your-arse components. The children he played with had no innocence. They knew what a *cazzo* or prick was for, as also the complementary *fica*. They had no pets and they preyed on cats. The adults were gross and bulky. Black-clad grandmothers sat at the doors of their hovels on the narrow street that led from the *sentinella* to the town, hoping that our wide vehicle would graze them and enable them to claim insurance money. Still, I had come at last to a real country after too much travel and a wretched oppressive island that had not been colonialised into a civilised polity. The priests were thick on the ground but conventionally denounced as lackeys of capitalism or else warded off with the *malocchio* sign – two pronging fingers and a fist on the testicles. I sat at the table by the window in the laky light and wrote the last chapter of *MF* or *M.F.* or *M/F*. It is set in Bracciano.

I was not set, except physically, in Bracciano. I had not applied for Italian residence and I officially had no Italian money. There was sterling, soon to be a new kind of very insular sterling, with cents and mils, in the Midland Bank at Sliema that Malta was to nationalise. I had to write to the Maltese Treasury to request permission to convert £2000 into dollars in view of a forthcoming year's residence in the United States: I had, I said, to buy a car there. Permission was reluctantly granted, but I would have to furnish a receipt for the car and an eventual bank statement showing whatever dollar balance there would be, this to be reconverted back into Maltese sterling. Back in London Deborah Rogers was holding money for me which, for some arcane reason, could not be exported. This money was earning interest which was attracting British tax. I ought now to apologise to the reader for being so concerned with finance, for seeming to write more of a *biographia fiscalis* than a *biographia literaria*. But the British freelance writer has to be obsessed with money. He is not in the position of an American writer like, say, Saul Bellow, who is subsidised by a university appointment. His situation is best exemplified by the later life of T. H. White, author of the Arthurian tetralogy *The Once and Future King*.

Tim White, living with his dogs in a lonely hut on the moors, had written hard for little money when Messrs Loewe and Lerner decided to convert *The Once and Future King* into a Broadway musical called *Camelot*. This brought in a great deal of money which the British fiscal authorities wished to tax at the highest possible rate. Tim protested that the money represented the belated reward for a lifetime of steady and ill-paid writing and, spread over the writing years, amounted to comparatively little. The Department of Inland Revenue was not impressed and forced Tim to take his dogs to the Channel Islands (he tried Sark first, as I had very nearly done, only, like me, to discover that the Dame of Sark had the monopoly of bitches). In Guernsey he discovered that there was no reciprocal tax arrangement with the United States and had to pay American tax in full. He was forced to try to earn money by undertaking American lecture tours: he died of a heart attack on the ship going home.

I, unlike Tim White, had made no big killing nor was likely to do. I was merely trying to fulfil the basic human right of living where I wished to live and to convert a steady output of words into the means of subsistence. I could do this, for the moment, only by cheating. I was in the right country for cheating. The Italians, after two thousand years of bad government (except for the odd interludes recorded by Gibbon), had no respect for *la legge*. *La legge* got back at them with an oppressive bureaucracy. It seemed to me, and it still seems, that there should be more to life than fighting governments. And Liana and I lived in Italy with the prospect of more than a mere fight: legally divorced in the Commonwealth of Massachusetts, legally married to me in Hounslow, she was legally a bigamist in her own country. The fact that we had caught, in a Roman restaurant, a glimpse of her former husband with a new (black) wife did not affect her bigamous status. We had to hope that that former husband did not display vindictiveness and invoke Italian law against her while sitting comfortably behind the palisade of an American marriage.

I tapped away in Bracciano on the sunny roof, becoming lobster-red and peeling while the Braccianesi, brown as Arabs, swilled, belched and sang '*Domani non ci sono, domani vado via*', the theme song of the weekly television extravaganza *Canzonissima*. I needed to protect myself from *l'italianità*: after all, I was a British writer. I needed the English language; I needed books. But, though the house would fill in time with unsaleable review copies, the comprehensive library I had built since the war would never leave Malta. The lesser Elizabethan playwrights were there, a complete Gibbon, the Sussex collection of Kipling, a first edition of Swift's *Modest Proposal*. I had to start relying on an unreliable memory, failing to verify quotations, paraphrasing where I should literally cite. I could not sit on the sunlit roof with a well-thumbed favourite and a panatella. This was cigarette-smoking territory with the odd foul Tuscan cheroot to discourage the *zanzare*. Occasionally a small consignment of Mercator, a Belgian cigar with a strong smell of lavatories, got into the shop that sold salt and tobacco, the two state monopolies, but my days were spent mostly in nicotine hunger. A character in Aldous Huxley's *Eyeless in Gaza* says rightly that the small distresses never get into literature: it will have nothing to do with the pains of menstruation and the empty cigar-case. I was uneasy at a nagging set of small cultural frustrations, the sensation that, to survive here, I would have to turn myself into a kind of Italian.

But, like all the British abroad, I became too British, grumbling at the lack of smoked bacon, sausages with bread and herbs in them, Andrew's Liver Salts, Lea and Perrin's. Liana was not quite on home territory – Bologna, Rome, Ancona – but she was at least in the abstraction called Italy, happy with fennel, spinach, *zuppa di verdura*, chicken gizzards and calves' brains, fresh lake fish. But the lake fish were so fresh that they leaped desperately in the last throes of life on the market stalls. They were just about resuscitable, and I would buy them, rush them to a filling bath where they swam unhappily until flopped into a bucket and driven back to the lake. One could not be doing this all the time. Inveighing against cruelty to fish did not make me *simpatico*. Liana importuned me to make myself more *simpatico*, but I would not. Had Dante made himself *simpatico*? I read a lot of Dante; there was not much else to read.

I spent some of that summer in the Bracciano studio of Milton Hebald, learning to sculpt in clay. But my figurines were top-heavy and toppled. It was best to watch Hebald at work and, as if the back of my brain suspected that I would one day have to write, for Radiotelevisione Italiana or RAI, a television series on Michelangelo, question him about the technique of stone-cutting. You needed a huge block, he said, to make something as slender as the David in Florence: you had to keep cutting back all the time, chipping away your errors: there was never too much stone. An image was imprisoned in the marble of Carrara (better than the Sanpietra muck that was imposed on Buonarotti by his patron): it had to be released, as from the sonnet-form that it was natural for a sculptor to use if he turned poet. Clay was different. To make clay heads was like inventing characters in a novel. How about portraits? Portraits were inventions. Hebald invented me in clay. My fired image still stands in the neglected Bracciano house, brooding, unhappy, as *simpatico* as the Emperor Galba.

In the autumn we had to leave Bracciano for New York, *en route* to New Jersey, and this meant visiting the American Embassy on the Via Veneto in Rome to be equipped with a working visa. The Rome embassy, unlike its northerly sisters, insisted on thorough medical examinations before granting permission to work in that land that so jealously guarded its salubrity, moral, political, physical. Italy now seemed a double country, in which Milanese wealth and elegance lived with exportable dirt and syphilis. I refused to be examined: I said that both of my last medical examinations had concluded in prognoses of approaching death. If this meant reneging on a contract with a great American university, then so be it: there would be at least material here for an interesting article. I was let through unexamined, but only just.

The tourist flight to New York by Alitalia, not on that day on strike, had the flavour of a passage from a Third World capital – old women mopping their tears with dirty handkerchiefs and dribbling in their sleep on to rusty black; the swarthy moustached pinching the stewardesses like poultry; small thugs who ate with claspknives. The Mafia naturally travelled first class. In the immigration line-up at Kennedy the old man in front of me had no passport, but a family from Mulberry Street welcomed Zio Giuseppe with shining teeth. 'Okay, Giuseppe, you get yourself a passport tomorrow, okay?' To me it was: 'Now, mister, what makes you think you're gonna enter the United States?' We expected Andrea to be overwhelmed by the Manhattan skyline, but he said he preferred Birkirkara. We stayed a day or two in the Gottlieb brownstone, less guiltily than before: I had at least delivered the typescript of a novel. Then we took a bus from the Port Authority depot to Princeton, New Jersey. Our rented house there was on Western Way, near the football stadium, the property of a Chinese professor of mathematics on sabbatical: he had left behind his six-toed Chinese cat for us to look after, a very vicious beast that refused to wash and refused to be bathed.

My rank at Princeton was that of Visiting Fellow, and my task was to instruct students in Creative Writing. I was part of a subcultural sideshow, but I had expected to play at least a small role in the central academic work that led to a degree: I was, after all, a graduate in Eng Lang and Lit. But the English Department did not want me, except once, towards the end of my tenure, when I was invited to give a lecture on the history of literary criticism. I gave this gladly, though puzzled at the absence of the regular professor, who might at least have had the courtesy to present me. It turned out that he had a distant engagement that day and had merely used me as a fill-in: a single session from an outsider like me could not do much harm. Princeton was very exclusive, as the novelist John O'Hara had found out. There was a certain pathos in his spending his last years in the town, where he expected to be cocktailed and dined by the faculty as a distinguished author. He was snubbed as I was, though with less cause.

Dr Frank MacShane has written the life of O'Hara, and it was he who mitigated the boredom of my undergraduate Creative Writing by inviting me to instruct postgraduate Creative Writers at

Columbia. These mature students were serious: they proposed making a living out of fiction or, if that failed, becoming teachers of it. At that time a bestselling novel called *Naked Came the Stranger* had been revealed as the corporate work of a group of academic cynics who had written a chapter each. The chairman of the group, finding the book at Number One on the *New York Times* bestseller list, sat down on a bench in Central Park and quietly wept for America. I suggested that I and my Columbia group of a dozen attempt a similar collective roguery, with a leggy photograph of the best-looking girl there on the back cover. My students were shocked: they were too serious to wish to make money out of the debasement of a great art-form: they wanted to be Flaubert or, if women, Virginia Woolf. They were not quite American, and indeed one of them was Nigerian. He called me a white bastard, though chortling, and I called him a black one. This too shocked: colour, like the novel, was a serious business.

The Princeton Creative Writers were not serious. The relegation of Creative Writing to an extra-academic region where carpentry and photography were also taught did not encourage seriousness. There were girls at Princeton now, and they, and a sole black male, comprised my poetry-writing class. The girls did not require my patronage of doggerel about cutting the balls off men, nor did the black man, whose verse had the same theme, though it was more limited – white castration only, with the penis occasionally thrown in as a kind of *bonne bouche*. The recital of an unhandy expression of the new female vindictiveness would be greeted with 'Wow, that's great, Janice' and my strictures on form and syntax shouted down. Poetry, said the black man, hating me with hot eyes, was essentially emotion, but I said it was essentially words. And now came the great unanswerable question: what did I know about poetry anyway, since I called myself a novelist? I suggested that the management of language, whether in verse or prose, called for basic skills that were better pursued if one forgot about the term poetry. Too much mumbo-jumbo had become attached to the word, anyway: there was imaginative writing only, and it did not matter a damn whether it was set solid or chopped up into lines. This was not a romantic enough view for Janice and her cronies. I lost students and was not sorry to lose them. But the black stayed on till the end, exerting himself to the limit in the devising of new oneiric tortures and humiliations for the white man. As a white man myself, I suggested that my own feelings might be considered a little, but he did not see why. The black experience was the only valid literary theme of the age. How about the female experience, I ventured. Women, he said solemnly, were a kind of black.

This was madness. There was less madness in the short story group that came to my office in the evenings, bearing six-packs and ice and helping themselves to the vodka in my filing cabinet. Less madness but more sex. One blonde shapely angelic girl, the daughter of a police chief in Nebraska, recited, in weekly instalments, what I hoped was a purely imaginary saga of a girl's sex-life. Everything was there, in the grossest detail, from anilingus to multiple fellation. I saw swellings at the crotches of the jeaned males and heard groans. I was not above whimpering myself. And if the police chief dad ever got at her springback files? I could see the headlines in the Nebraska press: 'Dakota City Girl Corrupted By British Prof'; 'Princeton Porn: The Whole Story'. I feared that she might be raped, gangwise, by her brother students in the boiler-room. But when her first-person narratrix was ravished by the entire passenger-load of the train known as the Princeton Dinkie, her audience grew sick. Detumescence without ejaculation, except for my 'For Christ's sake, that's enough. Write us a sonnet to a mountain daisy.'

One of my students was Nathaniel Wouk, a son of Herman Wouk, a popular novelist for whom I have always had a strong affection. His *The Caine Mutiny* had won the Pulitzer Prize, but *Youngblood Hawke* was not rated highly. Though its theme, presented at almost Tolstoyan length, was the agony of the modern American writer, the book was not considered to be literature. Yet I know no novel that presents in such detail and with such honesty the war between art and commerce, the failure implicit in success, and, to use Orwell's metaphor, the prolonged illness which is the labour of writing a book. Being American, *Youngblood Hawke* is inevitably about money, but it tells the truth about a fiscal system which penalises the rare rewards of art and shows no mercy when the writer falls into the trough of indigence. It is a book I continue to recommend strongly as the only one I know, other than Gissing's *New Grub Street*, which shows what it is like to be a writer. When Wouk's son entered my class, the first volume of the massive chronicle of World War Two, *The Winds of War*, had just appeared. This, with its sequel *War and Remembrance*, seems to me to be the most thorough fictional account we have of the whole world conflict. If, in order to accommodate a multiple view which takes in everything from the rise of the Nazi party to the revelation of the death camps, with the London blitz, the fall of Singapore, and the battle of Midway as fully realised items in which Wouk's characters are involved, the work looks arbitrary and over-full of coincidence, this is a price that has to be paid for comprehensiveness. The Tolstoyan (and it is clear how much Wouk has studied Tolstoy) makes its appearance in modern American fiction in work denigrated for its lack of 'literary' qualities – word-play, avoidance of cliché, psychological subtlety. Wouk will never win the Nobel Prize, but his fiction exemplifies what Fielding, Dickens and Balzac thought the novel was about. Here I lay myself open to charges of middlebrowism. But probably the novel is a middlebrow form and both Joyce and Virginia Woolf were on the wrong track.

When Nathaniel Wouk came to me to learn how to write, I had a sentiment of referred reverence, of the kind I felt when first meeting Joyce's grandson. I even gave him a Schimmelpenninck panatella, which, in his innocence, he auscultated to gauge its quality. But he had no literary gift: he was no Martin following Kingsley. He considered that, as Herman Wouk's son and a Princeton tiger, he ought to be successful in something, but my failure to ignite a style, a movement, a fluency showed that it would never be in writing. He made me wonder what precisely my function was. To discourage, perhaps. But then I would have no classes and be forced to resign. Nathaniel came to me with a fellow-student who, a graduate already in French, had to achieve a piece of high-class translation as part of a master's requirement. I set him to render Mallarmé's *L'Après-Midi d'un Faune* into heroic couplets. He tried hard:

> These nymphs – I would perpetuate them. Clear
> Their luminous flesh upon the atmosphere
> Hovering, by tufted sleep oppressed. Was it a dream
> I loved? My doubts, fruits of old night, now seem
> To branch in many a subtle twig . . .

The task nearly killed him, literally. He collapsed, distressed, in my office, and I had to take him in my arms, offering fatherly comfort. I had let women and blacks get away with versified hate, a nice girl become an expert pornographer, the son of a prominent novelist discover that talent was not inheritable, a neurotic detest Mallarmé and wish for death. I was doing no good at Princeton.

The workload was oppressive but did not consume much time. In the house on Western Way I worked at my own translation from the French. Rostand was easier than Mallarmé, since I was dealing with the solidity of a nose, not the insubstantiality of nymphs:

Insolent: 'Quite a useful gadget, that.
You hold it high and then hang up your hat.'
Emphatic: 'No fierce wind from near or far,
Save the mistral, could give that nose catarrh.'
Impressed: 'A sign for a perfumery!'
Dramatic: 'When it bleeds, it's the Red Sea.'
Lyric: 'Ah, Triton rising from the waters,
Honking his wreathed conch at Neptune's daughters.'

But I had to do more than translate. Liana, Andrea and I journeyed to Minneapolis to see and hear the Tyrone Guthrie company and to confer with Michael Langham. He approved of rhyme but had his doubts about various aspects of the plot of *Cyrano de Bergerac*. We were now very much in the age of director's theatre, when a text could be refashioned according to what the director considered to be the taste of his audience or, more brutally, the dramaturgical inefficiency of the author. Langham thought that the character of Roxane had to be developed in order that she seem less of a fool, and that the scene in which the Gascon officers gorge the unexpected gift of a dinner before fighting the Spaniards was gross and unsoldierly. Also, since Americans had recently landed on the moon, Cyrano's fantasy about space travel would have to be radically altered, so that its technological infantility should not promote contempt in the audience. I had to rewrite about half the play, which was easier than translating it. This redaction was eventually published by Knopf, but it is contradicted by the version published by Hutchinson, which restored the entire original for the Royal Shakespeare Company. Thus, I have two translations of *Cyrano de Bergerac* in print, which is going too far. Encouraged by my transformation of Rostand, some of the Tyrone Guthrie company later wanted me to rewrite *The Taming of the Shrew*. A bad precedent had been established.

Liana and I had seen and admired the prototype of the Guthrie Theatre in Stratford, Ontario. Minneapolis had a playhouse to be proud of but was unwilling to let it have licensed bars. This was because the theatre was surrounded by churches and there was some law against the defiling of the Word of God with alcohol fumes. The citizens supported their theatre, drinking Coca-Cola in the intervals, but it could not quite pay its way. The heating bills must have been enormous in that arctic territory. This new, rhymed, witty *Cyrano de Bergerac*, to run in tandem with *The Taming of the Shrew* the following summer, would, it was hoped, restore solvency. The company was a good one, helped out by distinguished guests to play the leads, and it had its quota of black actors, who were to look awkward as Gascons. What I dreamed of in connection with the Guthrie Theatre was a dramatic academy with a three-year course: there was no equivalent to RADA either in Canada or the United States. But any dream I had in the realm of show-business was always to go unfulfilled.

Back in Princeton there was another arduous commission to work at. This was the treatise to be called 'Novel, The' in the macropedia of the new *Encyclopaedia Britannica*. The pay was small but the specifications of the work so fantastic that I was led in horrid fascination to see if the task was viable. For I had to consider Impressionism in exactly 401 words, and Chinese fiction in 623. I presumed that, when my typescript reached the Chicago head-quarters of the Encyclopaedia, arithmeticians fell on it but editors not, since the article was published totally without change. I had got the figures right (Pastoralism 208; German Novel 1,174) and that was all that mattered. Meanwhile the snow came heavily down. I had left England to avoid the northern winter, and here I was in the thick of it. The snow nearly killed Andrea.

Andrea had been sent to the John Witherspoon School, where he was not happy. He was sneered at as both a wop and a limey, set upon by blacks as an exotic white, and was not, as a British subject, convinced that he ought to be saluting the American flag and singing 'My country, 'tis of thee'. A good deal of remedial work was done on his accent, and in a month or so he had been fitted with an authentic New Jersey snarl ('Leame alone wilya' and so on). After a fight with a black whom he refused to consider as a brother, he went out into the snow and fell asleep. Frozen, he was picked up by a police patrol car and resuscitated. An American Christmas reconciled him to the brutality of New Jersey manners and weather – twenty parcels to open under the tree, kids' television flashing and blaring long before dawn. American commerce had swallowed Dickens whole, but a sincere feeling for the season seemed to warm New York and New Jersey. It was at Christmas, with its Thanksgiving rehearsal, that I wanted to be an American. Liana did not, for that would make her an Italo-American, a species not much admired. At Christmas she studied modern Greek, while Andrea and I watched *A Christmas Carol* and *Holiday Inn* on television.

I had already become partially American, in that the four lower teeth battered by the Irishman in a London pub had been removed by a Princeton dentist and, in time for the roast turkey, a prosthesis of solid pink American workmanship had been fitted. There had been

an intermediate time, however, when I had had to travel down to
Atlanta to address three thousand English teachers on the decay of
our common language with a gap in the lower jaw. I seemed to be
demonstrating the decay of the consonants. It was before this trip
that Arthur C. Clarke, who had written *A Space Odyssey* with
Stanley Kubrick, telephoned me to report progress on the film of *A
Clockwork Orange*, which, Clarke said, was visually exciting. He also
said that, if I wanted an image of the future, I would find it in the
Regency Hyatt Hotel in Atlanta, with its astonishing external
elevators like space modules. Andrea spent all his waking time riding
on these, and I was interested to note that there was a kind of genetic
adjustment to the technological age in his generation: he was six
now. I mean that, while I would fumble with the switches and
buttons of an advanced television set, an air-conditioning panel, and
the keys of a Moog synthesiser, his small fingers would hit out
without error. Perhaps he was meant to be an American.

But not a Princetonian. The Burgess family was not wanted in
Princeton. Retired Mafia dons might sit comfortably with the
university (in a sense they were as much concerned with the
organisation of the United States as the hidden departments of
astrophysics and Middle East diplomacy) but I had publicly
displayed disloyalty, and this could not be forgiven. There was a
very popular talk show on television run by a Nebraskan named
Dick Cavett, witty, erudite, eloquent, an alumnus of Yale. His
popularity did not seem to accord with the mechanical ratings, and
he was later to be relegated to the Public Broadcasting channel. As a
Yale man he encouraged me to say hard things about Princeton when
I appeared on his show, and I deplored the snobbish exclusiveness of
the place. My appearing on television at all let the side down, but I
was still an author, a book had come out, and both Knopf and I
needed publicity. The book was my illustrated biography of
Shakespeare, which looked well on the coloured screen. I understood that the true Shakespeare scholars of Princeton thought little of
its text, but that was to be expected.

The *Yale Review*, in which presumably Dick Cavett had no
editorial or financial interest, thought well of the book, and so did the
Virginia Quarterly Review and up-market periodicals like the *Atlantic*
and the *Saturday Review*. Disparagement came from my native
country. The *Tablet*, for instance, found 'the captions . . . coy,
clever-clever, or muddled. Plain factuality would have helped
matters. Burgess plainly does not know the religion of Shakespeare's
home and district, and his groundless attack on Shakespeare's wife

leads you to think that the biographer had known and hated her most of his life. One gets a strong feeling that Burgess had little heart for the work.' Unjust. The *Economist* said: 'His scholarship is defective, and the chronological order of the plays is either based on outmoded, or crankily hypothetical theories. The literary opinions are wilfully odd and coarse; they suggest that Burgess is carelessly writing down for an ignorant public.'

Perhaps inevitably, my Shakespeare novel *Nothing Like the Sun* kept coming up, and its deliberate fantasy became confused with the all too painfully amassed factuality of the biography. In 1970 Samuel Schoenbaum produced his massive *Shakespeare's Lives* and perhaps said all that there was to be said about my novel: 'An absurd gallimaufry of invention and (to put it mildly) dubious biographical theorizing, but Burgess has a redeeming gift of language . . . Normal syntax dissolves; the effect is Elizabethan yet the spirit modern . . . One may also discern in the sexual degradation of the protagonist a working out of the author's obsession rather than the fictionalizing of fact . . . Through the alembic of his sullent craft Burgess transmutes the dross of his data into the impure gold, grotesquely shaped, of his fiction.' He added that *Nothing Like the Sun* was the only Shakespeare novel that really worked. This was enough for me. The critics could denigrate the Shakespeare biography as much as they wished: it was only a portable version of the film that would never be made, a means of clearing a preoccupation out of my system.

Before 1970 ended there was another author to honour, and only Yorke University outside Toronto seemed prepared to honour him spectacularly. This was Charles Dickens, the centenary of whose death I helped to celebrate with a talk on Dickens as a playwright and an actor. Yorke laid on a Dickensian banquet, at which Andrea, in the role of Tiny Tim, was raised to the table on four telephone directories, and Robertson Davies spoke with silver eloquence. There was something deeply moving about this transatlantic devotion to the poet of London spectaculars and English grotesques. There was, after all, a unity in the empire I began to call Anglophonia, and the unity had more to do with Shakespeare and Dickens than with the language that was their raw material. I wanted to write for Anglophonia, not for Bloomsbury or Hampstead.

Spring came to New Jersey and with it the publication of *MF* or *M.F.* or *M/F*. I had clearly not written for much of Anglophonia. Critics on both sides of the Atlantic were bewildered. Frank Kermode, in the *Listener*, showed that he had read his Lévi-Strauss and saw that the novel was perhaps not fully intelligible without a knowledge of the riddle–incest nexus. 'What . . . is one to make of it? It is a puzzle and on its own terms forbids solutions. But Burgess is rather movingly putting to use the self-begotten system of his own imagination and language to protest against spurious disorder in art and life. This is too solemn an account of a book so bewilderingly funny . . . Its fertility is fantastic, and so is its ingenuity . . . Perhaps all one ought to do is to characterise the book as a riddling Sphinx, and abstain from guessing further, but it should be added that it is a work of astonishing narrative and intellectual energy, and that everybody who thinks the English novel lacking in those qualities should read it, twice. Anthony has earned his place among the birds.' That last statement refers to my naming the riddling birds of the sorceress after contemporary novelists – first names only, though it ought to be possible to guess the rest when given Iris, Kingsley and so on. I included an Anthony, who could have been Powell, but many reviewers assumed I meant myself and attacked my presumption. Kermode admitted me to the company of the novelists, but the *New York Times* saw me only as a 'brilliant literary machine, a Teletype tapping all of English literature.' The novel was 'a mechanical bird, technically marvellous but secretly dead'. *Newsweek* termed it 'a ragbag of murky linguistic riddles about incest uttered by a dessicated sphinx to a trivial Oedipus'. That term 'ragbag' is always turning up, usually when my work is at its most structured. A review whose author and provenance I have forgotten said that there was more intellectual fantasy in Bob Dylan's 'The Circus is Coming to Town' than in my book.

The trouble with *MF*, let us forget the other variants of the title, was that it became readable only ten years after publication, when the intelligent young, for whom it was chiefly intended, had had time to digest some of the elements of Structuralism. By that time the novel had been driven out of print. The subsidiary group of readers I had had in mind were all French – after all, Structuralism was their property – but Lévi-Strauss became outmoded and the problems of translation seemed insuperable. Georges Belmont said that he would devote the last years of his life to it, but he said it when he was approaching eighty. Let me drive it out of my mind with the dismissal of Jonathan Raban in the *New Statesman*: 'It's too pygobranchitic: meaning, roughly, that it breathes heavily through its hinder parts.' This is what British literary criticism had descended to.

At the end of the academic year Liana, Andrea and I crept out of

Princeton, settled for a week in Manhattan, and then – loaded with copies of the Sunday supplements of the *New York Times*, which Liana refused to discard – boarded the *Leonardo da Vinci*, a ship of the Italia Line. I could see why travellers to Europe preferred to fly: that way they evaded the blackmail of the luggage-loaders of New York and the luggage-unloaders of Naples, who were, usually literally, brothers, cousins and sons. 'You wanna I should trow dese in a da water?' a loader asked, ready to do it too, when I handed over our bags and a ten-dollar bill. For twenty dollars he was even willing to give me a receipt. When the Mafia boarded, the loaders' voices had a more timorous sound.

I had had the Mafia much in mind during our Princeton stay. The retired dons and their wives were respectable citizens of the town, and one of Andrea's teachers had actually married on to the outer rim of the Tagliaferro family, of whom only a moribund grandmother was left. The old lady was the last surviving speaker of a Sicilian dialect that Andrea's teacher had had to learn. Liana could not understand it. I had made marginal contact with the Mafia after performing a daring act on the *Dick Cavett Show*. A writer in the *New York Times* had said that only a person suffering from terminal cancer would be so foolhardy as to suggest that there were homosexual mafiosi. I took up the challenge and told the television audience that the violence of the Mafia was undoubtedly a compensation for sexual insufficiency, and that pederasty was a common practice in the New York *famiglie*. I received shortly afterwards a discreetly worded letter from a firm of lawyers with WASP names, admitting that my generalisation, though foolish, was not actionable but warning me against particularised allegations.

I had had a different kind of Mafia fantasy in mind also – a novella, complete with the title *A Princeton Romance*. A visiting British author, teaching Creative Writing at the university, comes home one day to the rented house on Western Way to find his Italian wife in tears. She has had a visit from two Sicilians, bearing a message from their don: his admiration for the cinema performances of the Italian wife's actor father, now dead, has always been considerable. He wishes to pay vicariously for his enjoyment by putting a Studebaker, complete with chauffeur and bodyguard, at the disposal of the daughter, and, if necessary, to wipe out any enemies she or her husband may have in New Jersey or New York. But there is a catch. A convent-educated daughter of the eldest son of the *padrino* has poetic ambitions: she has even written a volume of poems which no reputable publisher will publish, and the *padrino* and his *consigliere* recognise the futility of putting the strong arm on firms like Knopf and Simon and Schuster. The Visiting Fellow, husband of the daughter of the great Italian actor, must engage in regular editing sessions, thuggishly chaperoned, with the young poetess, and render her poems publishable. The wife of the Visiting Professor, made hysterical by the constant lurking of Mafia thugs in the bushes, insists on going home to Italy, but her husband cannot afford to break his contract with the university. The poems are ghastly, all about the hovering angel of a dead mother, the presence of the infant Jesus in the daffodils, and pink dreams of romantic love. They have to be changed radically and filled with explicit sex. They are published, but the *padrino*, horrified at the intrusion of sexual scandal into a respectable Mafia family, wishes for a contract to be taken out on the Visiting Fellow. But he cannot be found: he hides himself in his office in the bowels of the university, shacked up with a glorious blonde girl, daughter of a Nebraska police chief. Take it from there. Stories are always the very devil to finish.

The mafiosi on board the *Leonardo da Vinci* were respectable and old-fashioned in their concern for the chastity of their women, who were ringed, jewelled, elegant, seductive, but discreetly guarded by swarthy gorillas who shaved thrice daily. I was discreetly escorted by two of them from the ship's cinema because I offered a large handkerchief to a raven-locked daughter who was weeping at *Random Harvest*. From then on I distanced myself from all shipboard activities, except for the midnight *spaghettata* – a superfluous meal after the five of the day, but there was always magic, even for the mafiosi, in the mound of sauced pasta that recalled a devoted *mamma* and an innocent childhood. It held the body down to the bed: the corridors rang with the snores of the surfeited. I re-read my *Honey for the Bears*, in which I had exactly prophesied the loss of my four front teeth and the discomfort of a loosening prosthesis. Novel-writing was dangerous. Liana and I started to translate *Finnegans Wake* into Italian. Andrea wanted to know the story and I told it. He was impressed: Joyce's monster is fundamentally for children. He even drew HCE. Later, that year in Rome, when the British Council had put on a jejune film of *Finnegans Wake* and Andrea was kindly asked how he had liked it, he said: 'I prefer the book.'

At Naples the unloaders said: 'You wanna I should throw dese in de water?' and were paid too many lire. We were met in two cars by Edoardo and Muriel Cappolino, a fat couple, the wife American, who made money in the modes current in Italy – running a film dubbing studio, developing real estate, dabbling in such branches of local politics as were profitable. The two cars were necessary because of Liana's tin trunks crammed with the *New York Times* Sunday edition. Edoardo Cappolino was called Edu, like Elgar in the finale of the Enigma Variations. Because I had settled in Bracciano, he proposed to its electors that, if he were made *sindaco*, he would turn the dour town into a nest of the arts. Our Bedford Dormobile had been garaged in our absence, but even so it was a miracle to find the petrol tank unseasoned with sugar and no PCI slogans scratched on the bodywork. We got into it almost at once and drove to Trieste.

We made the trip in order to be in on the last sessions of the international Joyce congress, which, in those days, varied its venue between Trieste, Paris and Dublin. Cathy Berberian, the remarkable singer who has no entry in the new *Grove*, was performing Joyce songs, as well as the ingenious *Sprechgesang* setting of a passage from *A Portrait of the Artist as a Young Man* composed by her former husband, Luciano Berio. Her singing techniques were avant-garde, and they made much of gulps, hockets and seeming to vomit into the body of a grand piano. I had written a setting of a Malay *pantun* for her, with alto flute and xylophone accompaniment. She and Berio were prepared to try anything, and he demanded from me an opera libretto in which all the characters should be enclosed in boxes but somehow, in six pages or so, blend the plots of *Rigoletto*, *Il Trovatore* and *Don Carlos*. This was beyond me, but little was beyond him, or her. They made me nostalgic for the musical career I was temperamentally fitted for but technically insufficiently equipped. We were too late for even the closing session of the Joyce congress, meeting various returning professors on the road, including Richard Ellmann at Venice. Dick had upset the delegates by relating the false blood of Buck Mulligan's blasphemous transubstantiation, at the beginning of *Ulysses*, to the real blood of Molly's menstruation at the end. He had also pointed out, which nobody seemed to have noticed before, that the 'Stately' of the opening is balanced, as in a fragment of a mirror fugue, by the 'yes' of the close. This too made me nostalgic – for a scholarship for which I was fitted neither temperamentally nor technically.

All I could do in Trieste, which now had a Viale Joyce and a Via Svevo, was write about the place for the *New York Times*. Trieste is in Italy – whatever Italy means, other than RAI, Brandy Stock, and the ice cream confections of Alemagna – but it was, at the end of the war, *uno stato Topolino*, or Mickey Mouse state, hovering between the opposed claims of Italy and Jugoslavia; before that it had been the great eastern outlet of the Austro-Hungarian Empire. The girls had

the Titian hair of Veneto, and the dialect was close to that of
Goldoni: I saw a postcard written by Lucia Joyce to her father – '*Go
una bella bala*', where the initial '*g*' is a transformation of a dead '*h*',
very Slavonic. Liana and I saw that the translation of *Finnegans
Wake* into Italian entailed a translocation: it would work only if
Dublin were changed to Trieste. No Italian publisher wanted the
work anyway: we regretfully gave it up. We could see why Joyce
had felt at home in the town: it was a Dublinesque port un-
oppressed by baroque architecture, a great place for talk over drink,
irredentist in Joyce's time, Catholic but full of Jews. Dubliners
worry about the hero of *Ulysses*, saying, 'He's a bloody Jew, and
my father says he never saw one Jew in the whole bloody place,'
but Leopold Bloom is in the book because he was, and still is, in
Trieste. *Ulysses* is, in a sense, the last great artistic product of the
Austro-Hungarian Empire.

Andrea walked, flipper in hand, with the penguin Marco in the
Trieste Aquarium, and then we crossed the border into Jugoslavia,
having first had a fight with one of the Italian frontier guards, who
objected to Liana's taking photographs, tore out the roll, and said, as
if it explained something, '*Sono Napolitano, io.*' Neapolitans,
especially when exiled to the north of Italy, give themselves airs
solely on the strength of their origin. They will sometimes even
apologise for being in Cremona or Padua, as though they have let the
Neapolitan side down. Civic pride is a substitute for talent, probably
vocal. They will sing, usually badly, at the drop of a hat. It is hard to
see what there is to be proud of in Naples, a derelict city whose public
utilities are always breaking down, run by the Camorra and corrupt
officials. But Neapolitans declare Neopolitanity as though it were
learning or wealth: they are probably proud of the criminal ingenuity
which is their response to inveterate poverty. The guard at the
frontier did not sing but he shouted, and he had to be punched. Then
he brought out his gun, which was unloaded.

Jugoslav border officials, although they are properly sons of St
Mark, pretend not to speak the dialect of Veneto or any other brand
of Italian, preferring to say: '*Alles ist in Ordnung.*' Jugoslavs are petty
thieves when they are not petty liars, and they are wary of giving
information. I generously blamed their shortcomings on communism, and I saw how wrong Wordsworth was in supposing that
the beauty of nature, of which Jugoslavia has much, especially on its
coastline, attached itself to the souls of men surrounded by it. All
Liana and I wanted was the town of Pulj, formerly Pola, and the site
of the Berlitz school where Joyce had taught. But Pulj was first not

on the map and then, when found, disclaimed its topographical features. We went home.

I WENT home only to leave home again. *Cyrano de Bergerac* was in its final stages of rehearsal at the Tyrone Guthrie Theatre in Minneapolis, and I had to try out and conduct the incidental music I had written. Stanley Silverman, who had composed the music for *The Taming of the Shrew*, was also there, and he had given a professional verdict on my score, which was playable enough for me to be paid $500 for the theatre's sempiternal right to perform it. This was the first money I had ever earned for composing music, and it thrilled me far more than the far more substantial earnings that would accrue from the play. My little backstage orchestra consisted of a clarinettist, a trumpeter, a keyboard performer, a cellist, and a very beautiful girl who played percussion. For the scene in Ragueneau's bakery I specified a set of metal kitchen utensils hung on a wooden frame, these to accompany a kind of mock march-theme, and she struck them with the right seriousness. She also taught me useful tricks with a cymbal – striking it on the head of a kettledrum pedalled in a rising glissando, so that the tones became attached to a toneless instrument; lifting a cymbal rolled with kettledrum sticks from a tub of water, with a consequent rise in pitch. I became more interested in these inarticulate noises than in those being made on the stage, but I noted script changes that did not please me.

The new directorial liberty allowed Michael Langham to mix up bits of the old Brian Hooker translation with my own, on the grounds that some of his lines were more effective than mine. Thus the line 'I am too proud to be a parasite' found its way into a set of impeccably rhyming couplets and, because of its rhymelessness and its prosodic woodenness, stood out embarrassingly. This, and other Hooker borrowings, made the critics leap in glee on what they called my plagiarisms. Otherwise, except for those of the Gascon cadets who had to be supposed to be freed slaves from Senegal, the production caught the spirit of Richelieu's France and American accents were discreetly Europeanised. The lead was to have been played by Christopher Plummer, whom Liana and I had briefly met in London to see if he trusted me, but Plummer was busy on a film and the role was taken by Paul Hecht, who had been successful in the Broadway musical *1776* (a work too chauvinistic ever to be presented in London). He had, as Langham had foretold me, big balls and a great gut. Christian was played by Len Carriou, later to take the lead in Stephen Sondheim's *A Little Night Music*, and Le Bret, whose part now absorbed that of Carbon de Castel-Jaloux, was given to James Blendick. Jimmy had been a cabaret singer and was inspired to turn actor by the example of Christopher Plummer: he was to play, and sing, with Plummer in the musical version of the play that was, a year or so later, to bomb on Broadway.

The musicalisation of *Cyrano de Bergerac* into *Cyrano* had been, from the time of my translation commission, in the mind of Richard Gregson, an agent turned producer. He, and his former agential partner Gareth Wigan, the husband of Georgia Brown and the eventual head of Twentieth Century-Fox, seemed to be in control of the Tyrone Guthrie enterprise in a way I was too unbusinesslike properly to understand. Gregson was, in that summer of 1971, still married to the film actress Natalie Wood, who turned up, glamorous but a little cold, to the first performance of *Cyrano de Bergerac*. The following year she was separated from him for an alleged act of infidelity on Gregson's part, and Gregson's distress was to generate tensions which made the development of the musical, already unhappy, unhappier still.

Hubert Humphrey, the Minnesota senator and presidential candidate, was present at the first night of *Cyrano de Bergerac*, and I sometimes wonder if the audience's response to certain lines in the second act was not stimulated by his presence. Christian loves Roxane but is too inarticulate to woo her in poetry; Cyrano has the right eloquence, and Christian envies him.

CYRANO: Well, why not borrow it?
          And, in return, I'll borrow your good looks.
          There's promising algebra here: you plus I
          Equal one hero of the story books.
CHRISTIAN: I don't think I quite –
CYRANO: So I don't see why
          I shouldn't give you words to woo her with.
CHRISTIAN: You – give – me – ?
CYRANO: Call it a lie,
          If you like, but a lie is a sort of myth
          And a myth is a sort of truth.

Those last lines brought the house down and accorded to Rostand a political sophistication which was really mine, since there is nothing at all of Rostand in that whole passage. At least, I take it that the audience, sensitised by Humphrey's presence, sniffed something political there. The actors were disconcerted by the unexpected applause. Neither in London nor on Broadway was there any exceptional response to that quip. Audiences are the real authors of plays, since, in the manner of great art, they are unpredictable. But all the audiences of my *Cyrano de Bergerac* have been all too predictable with respect to a passage which is no more than a straight rendering of Ronsard. The poet-pastrycook Ragueneau is appalled to find that his wife has been using his friends' poems as wrapping-paper for hot buns:

> But to do *that*, with *those*!
> It makes me wonder what you'd do with prose.

Even when Ragueneau moved upstage scratching his bottom not a titter was raised. Perhaps this proved something – the good sense of the popular mind in not accepting that the prose–verse antithesis of the classical tradition has any validity today. Whatever the critics may say, the audience always has to be right.

The ending of the play is a problem to the translator, since Rostand's last word is *panache*, which is only literally rendered by Hooker's 'white plume'. I felt that the French word, with its cluster of moral and cultural associations, had to be retained, and that it had to be inserted throughout the play in various clarifying contexts. Thus, when it came at the end, the audience would meet it as an old acquaintance:

> You take everything – the rose and the laurel too.
> Take them and welcome. But, in spite of you,
> There is one thing that goes with me when, tonight,
> I enter my last lodging, sweeping the bright
> Stars from the blue threshold with my salute –
> A thing unstained, unsullied by the brute
> Broken nails of the world, by death, by doom
> Unfingered – See it there, a white plume
> Over the battle – a diamond in the ash
> Of the ultimate combustion – My panache.

It worked. Paul Hecht received regular standing ovations, and so did Jimmy Blendick when he took over the part in a revival. There was standing room only every night, and the finances of the Tyrone

Guthrie Theatre moved towards the black. I may be forgiven a small smirk of triumph: such have not been conspicuous in this chronicle.

Richard Gregson committed the error of supposing that, since this version of the play was a financial and, though not great art, artistic success, it would be an even greater success when converted into a Broadway musical. After all, the strength of *My Fair Lady* lay in the original Shaw text: a Broadway failure was usually blamed on a weak libretto. But *Cyrano de Bergerac* already had plenty of music in its speeches, and a lot of this would have to be eliminated to make room for song – inevitably more banal than a sweep of rhymed rhetoric – and for the 'production numbers' which drove a song home. In my innocence, I thought I could shrug off a truncated version of the play and a dozen or so song lyrics, collect what money was offered, and then get on with more serious work while awaiting my nightly Broadway percentage. I should have read my contract more closely and seen that the lyricist-librettist of a musical is as much an existential participant as an actor-singer, that this peculiar Broadway genre is less a product than a process. In other words, the making and remaking of *Cyrano* would continue till its closing night.

Gregson now had the contractual right to assume that I was a hired employee of his. He summoned me from Bracciano to meet the man who was to compose the music, Michael Lewis, a Welshman, Welsh-speaking, who had emigrated to a suburb of London. Having been long married to a Welshwoman, I foresaw what one of the problems would be – the inability on the part of a native speaker of an unstressed language to understand the prosody of English. There would be no point in my writing lyrics for Lewis to set, for he would get the stresses wrong – putting 'the' on the first beat of a bar, for instance, or coming down with a thump on the last syllable of 'sausage'. This prediction was more or less correct. Lewis had to write his tunes first and leave it to me to fit words. In the later stages of the production there would be transatlantic telephone calls, with 'Ready, *bach*? Key B flat. Common time. Anacrusis F. Dotted crotchet D. Quaver C. Minim low F. Got that?'

Michael Lewis was an amiable young man, ebullient in the Welsh manner, uxorious, successful in the sphere of film music. I envied him: he had actually heard his music played on a more or less full symphony orchestra. He had been a client of Gregson when Gregson had been a show business agent, and Gregson had confidence in him. Lewis had the Celtic gift of being able to knock out a tune, so long as he had a piano for the knocking. This was not composition as I understood it: in my own amateur writing of music I had seen the whole process as a cerebral one, with the keyboard kept at a distance. Only thus can one inwardly hear vocal or orchestral sounds. Lewis was also cavalier about alto and tenor clefs and transposing instruments – write your stuff in the treble or bass clef, at pitch, and leave it to the copyist underling to make the right professional adjustment. Lewis also preferred his singers to have the gift of absolute pitch, which is a rare one, except in the novels of D. H. Lawrence. There was lordliness in his professionalism, which I presumed to be that of the cinema and the recording studio. What, as *Cyrano* was to prove, was quite beyond him was the crass kind of inspiration which would produce a popular song.

I was allowed to go back to Italy with a number of 'top lines' – that is to say, tunes with chord indications underneath. I knew now who was to sing some of these tunes – Christopher Plummer in his first musical role, since his rendering of 'Edelweiss' in *The Sound of Music* could not really be called musical. I got down to work in Rome, not Bracciano. Rome had been Liana's long-term aim, with Malta and Bracciano as Mediterranean stepping-stones towards it. She was a city girl, as she was always saying, and Rome, with all its faults, was the archetypal city. Her Cambridge friend Bruno Micconi, the lecturer in economics at Rome University, had now transferred himself to the University of Siena, and his flat in Piazza Santa Cecilia, Trastevere, was available to us. Our tenancy would be shaky, since landlords knew no legal barrier to either rent increase or summary eviction, but, with the house in Bracciano to fall back on, we would never be homeless. There was a lot to be said for even a precarious existence in Rome.

The apartment was at Number 16A, on the third floor, and it had a salon, two bedrooms, a workroom, a bathroom, and a cold water kitchen. In the 1970s Italian, or Milanese, furnishings were at their best, and the flat soon became a model of chic, what with wall bookshelves in the shape of a half-globe, a huge metal light-picture with beaten bronze doors to shut off or open up individual luminous patches; a great Italian *letto matrimoniale*, of the deep wide kind in which the wives of Mafia bosses dictate midnight policy; tables, chairs and desks of lucid cream or crimson; floor lamps in body-shaped parchment of the kind called ghosts or *fantasme*. The elegance was unabetted by tidiness: Liana said that life was not the making of beds but the unmaking of them. The untidy life of the *piazza* and of the narrow abutting lanes, car-honks, song, the labour of the makers of fake antiques, was answered by the baroque beauty of the *basilica* of Saint Cecilia, where the bones of the patroness of music were said to lie. We looked out on the flaking golden *putti* who guarded her church, some of whom made minute obscene gestures at such rulers of Rome as would pass or enter. There was a baroque organ within, and on this I was occasionally to play, though not the tunes of *Cyrano*. Gazing out, I felt happiness stirring like a threat.

Andrea was fitted out for the autumn term at the *Scuola Regina Margherita* with a *grembiulino*, following the charming custom of the schools of Italy. The *grembiulino*, which Andrea grumbled at and termed a grumbelino, was a kind of painter's smock, blue for a boy, white for a girl, with a floppy mock-cravat attached. It kept the clothes clean and was a junior version of the scholar's gown. At the school Andrea turned into a Roman and spoke Roman, which is not the dialect of Dante. Roman looks like this:

> *Vedi l'appiggionante c'ha ggiudizzio*
> *Come s'è ffatta presto le sscioccajje?*
> *E ttu, ccojjona, hai quer mazzato vizzio*
> *D'avé scrupolo inzino de la pajje!*

The double consonants mean what they say. Roman has resisted the diphthongisation of Tuscan, so that *buona sera* goes back to the Latin as *bona sera*. 'L' turns readily into 'r', so that *il calcio*, football, becomes *er carcio*. The dialect is crammed with obscenities, and there is a phone, not a true phoneme, which comes up like a belch and sounds like *booooh*. It is a gesture of indifference or nescience. The poet Giuseppe Gioacchino Belli was the great master of the dialect and a scholarly recorder of the filth and blasphemy. He wrote 2,279 sonnets in Romanesco, and one of my tasks became the translation of some of these into Lancashire English. I translated one in the intervals of writing love lyrics for *Cyrano*. It is over-free, but it reflects something of Belli's anthropological seriousness.

> The orchidaceous catalogue begins
> With testicles, it carries on with balls,
> Ballocks and pills and pillocks. Then it calls
> On Urdu slang for goolies. Gism-bins
> Is somewhat precious, and superior grins
> Greet antique terms like cullions. Genitals?
> Too generalised. Cojones (Español)'s
> Exotic, and too whimsical The Twins.
>
> Clashers and bells – poetical if tame.

Two swinging censers – apt for priest or monk.
Ivories, if pocket billiards is your game.
I would prefer to jettison such junk
And give them Geoffrey Grigsons as a name,
If only Grigson had a speck of spunk.

Grigson is now dead, but I abate none of my resentment at his allegation of my coarseness, even though Belli encouraged it to develop. A statue of Belli stands at the entrance to Trastevere, just by the Ponte Garibaldi. He left great verse unto a little clan.

Rome was full of thieves, thus proclaiming itself to be a true Catholic city, and a lot of the street-stealing was done by *scippatori*, pairs of young men on Vespas or Lambrettas, with the pillion-rider grabbing American mink stoles, handbags, Gucci cases with legal documents or literary typescripts inside them. Liana was to have a bag with her passport in it stolen three times: the response of the Questura was a Roman scolding for being a victim. As in most modern states, it is the victim who is the criminal. When, much later, I wrote a book on the language of James Joyce, I carried it in its Gucci case towards a Xerox shop to be copied, but it was *scippato* on the way. The typescript was presumably fluttered into the Tiber or Tevere and the case sold for a few thousand lire. I had to write the book again, not with too much resentment: it was probably better the second time. These *scippatori* were never caught by the police, who probably shared in their proceeds: their little motor-cycles were not legally obliged to be fitted with a *targa* or number-plate. Petty crime is excused, or even exalted, by the greater crimes of the *Quirinale*.

Despite the thieves, the streets and piazzas of Rome were a joy. We ate our evening meal in open-air *trattorie* and went to the seasons of old films at the *cinéma d'essai* on the Campo dei Fiori, where the statue of Giordano Bruno – a victim of papal obscurantism honoured by the anarchic Romans – broods on the reconciliation of opposites in heaven. The Romans loved cinema, and their off-duty lives were more cinematic than operatic, what with the colour and gesture of the evening *passeggiata*, the background of piazza and fountain for an assignation or a quarrel, the sense of an invisible camera recording everything, the border between the genuinely filmed and the potentially filmable not always easy to descry. Liana and I spent part of a summer evening tearing down fascist posters from the streets of Trastevere, to the rage of the film director who arrived with his team the next morning: we had defaced the décor of a historical drama.

The dramatic instinct of the Romans was best expressed in the concept of *la bella figura*, an innocent ostentation of the body, even when swollen with pasta, and a harmless boasting about sexual conquests (mostly fictitious), as well as hyperbolic honorifics. All men, even bartenders, were *dottore*, unless they were street-cleaners: these were merely *capo* or boss. I was always addressed as *professore*. To be a writer in Rome was no small thing: one was creating art or scholarship, not, as a disdainful British MP had said when opposing library lending rights, scribbling on a pad before the fire. It was a pity I was only writing a Broadway musical. It was a pity too that the literary fame I was to gain in Rome should be of a sub-Belli order: he had merely described filth and violence; I was to be a *padrino* promoting it. In the autumn of 1971 Liana, Andrea and I were ordered by Warner Brothers to go to London, there to stay at Claridge's, and be ready for a private showing of Stanley Kubrick's film *A Clockwork Orange*. Not Andrea, of course: he was to be granted the less gamy treat of *Bedknobs and Broomsticks*.

I KNEW Kubrick's work well and admired it. *Paths of Glory*, not at that time admissible in France, was a laconic metaphor of the barbarity of war, with the French showing more barbarity than the Germans. *Dr Strangelove* was very acerbic satire on the nuclear destruction we were all awaiting. Kubrick caught in a kind of one-act play, trimmed with shots of mushroom clouds, the masochistic reality of dreading a thing while secretly longing for it. I felt, though, that he over-valued the talent of Peter Sellers and made the *tour de force* of his playing three very different parts in the same film obscure the satire by compelling technical admiration. *Lolita* could not work well, not solely because James Mason and Sellers were miscast, but because Kubrick had found no cinematic equivalent to Nabokov's literary extravagance. Nabokov's script, I knew, had been rejected; all the scripts for *A Clockwork Orange*, above all my own, had been rejected too, and I feared that the cutting to the narrative bone which harmed the filmed *Lolita* would turn the filmed *A Clockwork Orange* into a complementary pornograph – the seduction of a minor for the one, for the other brutal mayhem. The writer's aim in both books had been to put language, not sex or violence, into the foreground; a film, on the other hand, was not made out of words. What I hoped for, having seen *2001: A Space Odyssey*, was an expert attempt at visual futurism. *A Clockwork Orange*, the book, had been set in a vague future which was already probably past; Kubrick had the opportunity to create a fantastic new future which, being realised in décor, could influence the present.

So, once the reception staff of Claridge's accepted that Liana was my wife and not an Italian-speaking nanny, we were given a suite suitable for an oil-sheikh and I feared the worst: I feared that I would have to work for the film; film companies give nothing for nothing. Liana, Deborah Rogers and I went to a Soho viewing-room and, with Kubrick standing at the back, heard Walter Carlos's electronic version of Henry Purcell's funeral music for Queen Mary and watched the film unroll. It was typical of Princeton's exclusiveness, I thought, that Carlos's score should be contrived at Princeton while I was there and I knew nothing about it. After ten minutes Deborah said she could stand no more and was leaving; after eleven minutes Liana said the same thing. I held them both back: however affronted they were by the highly coloured aggression, they could not be discourteous to Kubrick. We watched the film to the end, but it was not the end of the book I had published in London in 1962: Kubrick had followed the American truncation and finished with a brilliantly realised fantasy drawn from the ultimate chapter of the one, penultimate chapter of the other. Alex, the thug-hero, having been conditioned to hate violence, is now deconditioned and sees himself wrestling with a naked girl while a crowd dressed for Ascot discreetly applauds. Alex's voice-over gloats: 'I was cured all right.' A vindication of free will had become an exaltation of the urge to sin. I was worried. The British version of the book shows Alex growing up and putting violence by as a childish toy; Kubrick confessed that he did not know this version: an American, though settled in England, he had followed the only version that Americans were permitted to know. I cursed Eric Swenson of W. W. Norton.

The film was now shown to the public and was regarded by the reactionary as the more dangerous for being so brilliant. Its brilliance nobody could deny, and some of the brilliance was a film director's response to the wordplay of the novel. The camera played, slowing down, speeding up; when Alex hurled himself out of a window a camera enacted his attempted suicide by being itself hurled – a thousand-pound machine ruined at one throw. As for the terrible theme – the violence of the individual preferable to the violence of the state – questions were asked in parliament and the banning of the film urged. It was left to me, while the fulfilled artist Kubrick pared his nails in his house at Borehamwood, to explain to the press what the film, and for that matter the almost forgotten book, was really about, to preach a little sermon about *liberum arbitrium*, and to affirm the Catholic content. The Catholic press was not pleased. I told the *Evening Standard* that the germ of the book was the fourfold attack on my first wife by American deserters, and this was summarised on news-vendors' posters as CLOCKWORK ORANGE GANG ATTACKED MY WIFE. Maurice Edelman MP, my old friend, attacked the film in the same newspaper and I had to telephone through a reply. I was not quite sure what I was defending – the book that had been called 'a nasty little shocker' or the film about which Kubrick remained silent. I realised, not for the first time, how little impact even a shocking book can make in comparison with a film. Kubrick's achievement swallowed mine whole, and yet I was responsible for what some called its malign influence on the young.

There was, certainly, an influence that could not be wholly malign, and that was the musical content of *A Clockwork Orange*, which was not just an emotional stimulant but a character in its own right. If the pop-loving young could be persuaded to take Beethoven's Ninth seriously – even in its Moog form – then one could soften the charge of scandal with the excuse of artistic uplift. But the film, and perhaps the book, seemed to deny the Victorian association of great music with lofty morality. There were still musicologists around who alleged that Beethoven opened up a vision of divinity. Alex gets something very much opposed to that out of the scherzo of the Ninth, which sets ikons of Christ marching while making a communist salute. Still, the music remained the music, and the *Clockwork Orange* record that was all over London only invited to violence on its cover.

At Kubrick's home, where I went for dinner, I met first his guard dogs, then the daughter, now grown, who had been the lisping infant on the blepophone screen in *A Space Odyssey*, and then the delightful wife who had been the singing German girl at the end of *Paths of Glory*. I met also Kubrick's concern with music. After Alex North had crippled himself with the rushed writing of a score for *A Space Odyssey*, Kubrick had decided to draw his music out of the existing concert repertory. He set a bad example to some of his followers. John Boorman's *Excalibur*, for instance, uses music from *Tristan und Isolde* and *Götterdämmerung*, whose non-Arthurian associations are blatant. But Kubrick has usually chosen right. I showed him, on his piano, that the Ode to Joy and 'Singin' in the Rain' (which Alex sings while thumping the husband of the woman he proposes to ravish) go in acceptable counterpoint. I could see the gleam in his eye of a commercial exploitation, but he let it go. What he gave me of value was the idea of my next novel. This was all to do with music.

I had for some time past toyed with the notion of writing a Regency novel, a kind of Jane Austen parody, which should follow the pattern of a Mozart symphony. There would be four movements – an allegro, an andante, a minuet and trio, and a presto finale – and the plot would be dictated by symphonic form, not by psychological probability. So in the first movement, at a country house party, the characters would be introduced in an exposition, become involved in a violent fantasy in the development section, and then be as they were before in the recapitulation. There was an obvious problem: music admits exact repetition, but this is impossible in narrative prose. The problem might be solved by inexact repetition – characters recapitulating their actions in a changed prose-style, or doing new things in a style which recalled, in rhythm and imagery, what had already been stated. The project presented such difficulties, and so large a promise of unreadability, that I let it lie in a drawer. I mentioned this to Kubrick in a discussion of narrative techniques, and he suggested what I should have already thought of – namely, the imitation of a symphony which already had narrative associations and, for plot, the filling out of the theme which had inspired the symphony. He meant Beethoven's Symphony Number 3 in E flat, the 'Eroica', which began by being about Napoleon and ended by being about any great military hero. Where were these narrative associations? The first movement was clearly about struggle and victory, the second about a great public funeral, and in the third and fourth the hero was raised to the level of myth – a specific myth, that of Prometheus, which Beethoven spelt out by drawing on his own *Prometheus* ballet music.

Kubrick was not presenting this idea in a generous void. He wanted to make a film on Napoleon, using techniques denied to Abel Gance, and he wished Napoleon's career to be contained in a film of moderate length. He needed a script, but the script must be preceded by a novel. The musicalisation of Napoleon's life, from the first Italian campaigns to the exile on St Helena, would be an act of compression, and it would suggest compressive techniques in the film. Thus, if the battle of Waterloo came with Beethoven's scherzo, then the cinematic narrative would be justified in speeding up the action to an almost comic degree. Exile and death on St Helena would have to follow Beethoven's technique of theme and variations – perhaps recapitulated film styles from Eisenstein on – and Napoleon's death would have to be followed by his mythic resurrection, since Beethoven says so. The financing of such a film –

with helicopter shots of the major battles, all reproduced in pedantic detail – would run into more millions than *A Clockwork Orange* had cost, but the film had to be made some day and Kubrick was clearly the man to make it. Meanwhile, the writing of a novel called *Napoleon Symphony* (the only possible title) would cost only time.

I left for Rome with film money much on my mind. The men who had originally bought the film rights to *A Clockwork Orange*, Max Raab and Si Litvinov, were prominently featured in the closing credits as joint executive producers, whatever that meant. It meant probably little more than that they were entitled to a percentage on the film's takings. They would be doing well, if the queues and the lengthy initial bookings were any indication. I was doing badly. I had received a single small payment for the release of my rights and there was no talk of royalties. A bad contract had been drawn up. It was not long before I was forced to take Warner Brothers to court at a cost of several thousand pounds in legal fees. I was eventually granted a percentage smaller than those of Raab and Litvinov, to be available when the film was 'in profit'. It takes a long time for the films that make a profit at all – few do – to reach that state. When my first cheque came, it came naturally through my agent, who had deducted a ten per cent commission. This was not balanced by any contribution to my lawyer's fees. I began to wonder about the wisdom of having an agent.

Back in Rome, I discovered that the Maltese government, now a socialist one, had deleted me from the list of residents and wished to confiscate my house. I was given a bald order to deliver up my keys to such a department on such a date. George Armstrong, a charming American who was Rome correspondent for the *Guardian*, made a news item out of this, and other newspapers followed him. MALTA GOVERNMENT GRABS AUTHOR'S HOUSE. It sounded bad, perhaps even to the Malta government. The house was speedily deconfiscated, but neither its sale nor its lease was permitted. It was to stand empty, and still does. I was not organising my new life very efficiently. I was exiled from Britain but not to any particular territory. I was not in Malta and had no residential status in Italy. I expected the Questura to knock at the door of the Rome flat and escort me to jail or to the airport. One night a plainclothes policeman arrived and I put out my wrists for the handcuffs. But he merely wished to know whether the blaring of the band at the nearby restaurant *Da Meo Patacca* was causing annoyance. Of course not. Most certainly not.

Other foreign writers in Rome had put their lives well in order.

Muriel Spark, for instance, who lived with her cats in a kind of palazzo; Gore Vidal, the scourge of America, who resented having to pay full United States tax and was trying to get a Colombian passport; George Armstrong himself, whose flat in the Piazza Rienzi was tended by two imported Bengalis. It was through an invitation to dinner from Armstrong – curry, naturally – that I learned how powerful was the Italian fear of the *malocchio* or evil eye. Mario Praz was a guest, and Liana turned pale when she saw him. She would not even utter his name, which she distorted to Zarp. It was not his fault that he turned milk sour or killed with a glance newborn infants. The *malocchio* falleth where it listeth. Pope Pius IX, a kind and holy man, was a powerful *iettatore*. 'Then he visits the column to the Madonna in the Piazza di Spagna,' said a contemporary, a workman, 'and he blesses it and the labourers, and of course one of them falls from the scaffolding the same day and kills himself. There is nothing so fatal as his blessing.'

Priests in general have the *malocchio*. They have given up sex and are neither men nor women. They swish by in skirts and turn the meat on the butcher's stall bad. The right response, an apotropaic gesture, is a clutching of the testicles and a pronging of two fingers in the direction of the *iettatore*. Mario Praz, to my knowledge, never notably harmed with his eye, but there was always the fear that some day he would. He was a great scholar of English literature but was interested in evil – the influence of the Marquis de Sade on Victorian poets like Swinburne, the kinship of sex and death. He is dead now, but Liana still fears that he may cast the *malocchio* from the grave. She still calls him Zarp.

Christmas came to Rome, and the jewelled holy *bambino* lay in his crib in innumerable churches, surrounded by candles which drove out the dark and the cold. Rome has a palpable winter of chill winds and dull light which tourists rarely come to experience. In the Piazza Navona stalls were set up for the sale of trinkets and unripe bananas coated in chocolate; the dismal bagpipes of the Abruzzesi imitated dying pigs. Babbo Natale, a northern importation, chortled under his white beard. Liana's mother, the ageing Contessa Pasi, came to 16A Piazza Santa Cecilia, accompanied by the daughter of the other San Severino contessa, the Maria who had cooed, '*Tabek, tuan*' to me in greeting and informed her bridge *circolo* that I was *un uomo molto semplice*. They had to sleep on the floor of the salon, which was no way to treat aristocrats. Liana's detestation of *Natale* as a season of family vendettas was justified. There was some fine operatic vituperation between mother and daughter, over what was not clear, but Andrea gleefully reported: 'She call her an *assassina*.' Who called whom? 'They both call.' I cooked. I had much on my mind.

I was worried over my over-willingness to sign contracts without reading them. I had signed a contract with Richard Gregson, and there was fine print in it which entitled him to call on me to perform my writing services at any time and in any place he designated. Now I had to go, immediately after Epiphany or the feast of the witch Bifana, to Minneapolis, so that presumably he could stand over Michael Lewis and myself while we concocted songs for *Cyrano*. I did not like this: a writer is a free being, unsupervised. Nor did I like the prospect of a January in the coldest city of the Union, with the probable exception of Anchorage or Fairbanks. I had left Britain to seek warmth, and here I was off to freeze in a town where the television newscasters greeted the morning with 'Heat wave today, folks – we're up to minus 33'. I was not sure that I much cared for Gregson. He had been involved in two reputable films – *The Angry Silence* and *The Planet of the Apes* – and presumably knew something about the financing, to his profit and mine, of a Broadway musical. But his manner was cold, and he had cultivated a disdainful patrician accent which Hollywood probably admired, but it reminded me of the kind of army officer who was eventually killed in the field by his own men. There was a certain Hollywood vulgarity under the veneer. He had written to me to say that we had the makings of a great success but he advised me to 'keep my spaghetti crossed'.

I made a gesture of independence that harmed only me: I insisted on paying my own air fare. But at Rome airport I was put into first class and told that Warner Brothers had arranged my ticket: my cheque would be returned. Why Warner Brothers? What had they to do with Gregson's *Cyrano*? I discovered, once I had landed at Kennedy, that Warner Brothers were relying on me to boost *A Clockwork Orange*, which had just opened in New York. My life was always being arranged for me behind my back. I flew to Minneapolis, and blood that the tropics had thinned screamed in appalled disbelief at the cold. One could not go out into it. I left the Holiday Inn on my first morning to walk to Jim and Joe's (or Fred and Jack's), the best tobacco store in the world, but I was driven back by the knives that were thrust into my lungs. A poor dog howled bitterly at the corner. He had started to micturate, but the stream had started to freeze at once, and he was ligatured to the wall by an icicle. What happened here when the heating broke down? Were strikes of fuel-deliverers possible? I took a heated taxi to Tom and Bill's and equipped myself with Schimmelpenninck Duets. I would only survive this Minneapolis spell by drugging myself with tobacco.

The year began badly for Minneapolis and poetry with the suicide of John Berryman. His unquiet ghost, the ghost of a serious and despairing poet, would hover over this sub-literary labour of lyric-writing. Lewis was ready with the tunes, and I coaxed words out of his rhythms:—

> Love is not love that looks for grandeur or grace,
> Haunted by handsomeness of form or of face.
> That is no love but just a shell on the shore –
> Time will erase it, and you'll see it no more . . .

That was Roxane's last song. I could not foresee any great popularity for it. The period setting forbade the perky colloquialism of Lorenz Hart. Turning Cyrano's nose speech into a number called 'Cyrano's Nose' meant losing the sweep of the couplets and pattering like an inferior W. S. Gilbert:

> If my nose ever burgeons
> To that hypertrophic state,
> I'll call a team of surgeons
> In to am—pu—tate.

Gregson and Michael Langham sat unmoved while Lewis and I performed, a duo at an audition, desperately wanting applause. If nothing went right, that was probably because nothing ever could, not with this adaptation. Song did not push the action forward; it slowed it down. Only when the nuns of the final scene could be imagined singing their autumn carol did a little warmth creep into the chill rehearsal room:

> Around comes the autumn. The swallows are leaving,
> The year is unweaving her garments of red.
> Out of his hiding the winter is riding,
> So nature lies still and pretends to be dead.
> Aspen and yew
> Will be quivering and bare.
> What will we do?
> We'll be shivering the air with –
> Around will come Christmas, the feast of the stranger,
> The beasts in the manger will fall on their knees –

Green in the cloister and green on the altar,
A promise that green will return to the trees.

The song was a round, and it was a round that the nuns would shiver
the air with. Tovah Feldshuh, a regular member of the Tyrone
Guthrie company, tried it out, unrounded, to her own guitar
accompaniment. Michael Lewis, with Welsh lability, broke down in
bitter joy. Tovah was to play no more than her old role of
refreshment seller, but she deserved better. She deserved the role of
Roxane. Gregson scoffed when I suggested this casting, not having
divined the talent which was to charm Broadway in the Singer
adaptation about the girl disguised as a yeshiva student and the skill
with which she was to play Katharine Hepburn in a television series.
He was to spend a long time looking for a Roxane.

While Lewis and I were chained to the songwriting craft in
freezing Minneapolis, the devising of numbers which would please
Gregson as producer and Langham as director grew to be a recessive
process. Indeed, the inability to please presented itself as a kind of
talent. The show required about ten songs, but nearly ninety would
be written before the end of the run. I informed Gregson that I was
leaving for New York since I seemed to be doing no good in
Minneapolis, and he swore very nastily at me in the kind of
bloodfilled tones I had not heard since my army days. Then I said I
would resign and he softened. The trouble with Natalie Wood was
eating at his heart, though he was seeking consolation, on the level of
courtship only, with a Miss Solomon who worked on the Tyrone
Guthrie staff. She was a charming English girl who, when I gained
permission to fly to New York, saw me off at the airport. She told
me not to be too surprised at what or who awaited me at La Guardia,
then she went off in her car, waving. At La Guardia it was she who
awaited me. I nearly collapsed. Then all was explained – the
charming Misses Solomon were identical twins, and the one at the
New York end worked for Warner Brothers. American show
business was all hostile symbiosis mitigated by clan-ties, like the
Israelites in the desert.

Warner Brothers put me up in the Algonquin Hotel and they put
Malcolm McDowell, who played the lead in *A Clockwork Orange*,
into the Pierre. These two allocations subtly designated our separate
métiers, for the Algonquin remains a literary hotel and the Pierre is
for movie stars. That Malcolm was now a star, indeed a superstar,
was proclaimed by all the critics. He had been previously known for
his part in *If*, directed by Lindsay Anderson, which had a cult

following. It had been so poorly financed that it had run out of colour, but the alternation of colour and black and white was taken for a deliberate artistic effect and had been praised for its boldness. Now Malcolm had risen above cult to the big time. He and I, in a kind of father–son mockery, were to appear on radio and television and publicise the film. The relationship was apt, for in the film the hero is named Alex Burgess, though only after he has been named Alex Delarge (a reference to his calling himself, though only in the book, Alex the Large, or Alexander the Great). The cinema gets away with inconsistencies which no copy-editor would stomach in a novel. Also with factual errors and sheer solecisms that the extravagant finance should obviate. In *The Great Gatsby*, the great poster with the eyes of God is labelled OCCULIST. In *The French Lieutenant's Woman*, and not in that alone, men wear coat-shirts, which were not invented till the 1930s. In *Brideshead Revisited* (and its being merely a film for television is no excuse) a company quartermaster sergeant is addressed as sergeant-major. I could go on.

Before embarking with Malcolm on a publicity programme which, since Kubrick went on paring his nails in Borehamwood, seemed designed to glorify an invisible divinity, I went to a public showing of *A Clockwork Orange* to learn about audience response. The audience was all young people, and at first I was not allowed in, being too old, pop. The violence of the action moved them deeply, especially the blacks, who stood up to shout 'Right on, man,' but the theology passed over their coiffures. A very beautiful interview chaperon, easing me through a session with a French television team, prophesied rightly that the French would 'intellectualise like mad over the thing', but to the Americans the thing looked like an incentive to youthful violence. It was not long before a report came in about four boys, dressed in droog style copied from the film, gang-raping a nun in Poughkeepsie. The *couture* was later denied – the boys had not yet seen the film – but the rape was a fact, and it was blamed upon Malcolm McDowell and myself. Kubrick went on paring his nails, even when it was announced that he was to be given two New York Critics' awards. I had to collect those at Sardi's restaurant and deliver a speech of thanks. Kubrick telephoned to say what I was to say. I said something rather different.

We are all movie-stricken, however much we may deny it, and the Sardi's ceremony gave me the opportunity to kiss, chastely enough, an elegantly ageing Paulette Goddard, whom I had always admired, and younger stars like Mary Ure, who did not long survive my kiss. It was with stoic fatalism that I saw myself, a writer, being both promoted and demoted. Fame was coming through my tenuous connection with the film medium; the book I had written was the mere raw material for cinematic processing. Paulette Goddard sympathised, for she had been married to Erich Maria Remarque, and so did Robert Shaw and his wife Mary Ure: Shaw had written good novels and a good play. It was this damnable glamour of the silver screen, a glamour less apparent to the actors and actresses whose images were up there than to the popcorn-chewing gawpers.

Malcolm McDowell remembered too well, and was still sore from, the physical and psychological pains he had endured while making *A Clockwork Orange*. He was terrified of snakes, but Kubrick had announced one morning: 'I gotta snake for you, Malc.' His ribs were broken in the scene of humiliation where a professional comedian is brought on to demonstrate the success of the conditioning: the comedian had stamped on those ribs too hard. He had nearly suffocated when, with no cut-away, his head had been thrust for too long in a water tank. Kubrick was an imperious director, too imperious even to work with a script: script after script had been rejected. The filming sessions were conducted like university seminars, in which my book was the text. 'Page 59. How shall we do it?' A day of rehearsal, a single take at day's end, the typing up of the improvised dialogue, a script credit for Kubrick.

Tired out with explaining the title of the film and sermonising about *liberum arbitrium*, I found it a relief to obey a summons to return to gelid Minneapolis. Lewis was still working away at tunes whose dumb eloquence had to be focused into words. He had, he thought, something for the end of Act One, when Cyrano, emboldened by a mistaken belief that Roxane loves him, prepares to fight a hundred men at the Porte de Nesle. I did my best.

> I breakfast with princes,
> I banquet with kings,
> I swoop down on eagles –
> Defeather their wings.
> As swift as a whirlwind I leap and I run,
> The stars are my bullets, the thunder my gun,
> I hunt and I eat the red meat of the sun
> From now till forever is done,

'From Now Till Forever' being the title. These were not Broadway words; they belonged rather to European musical comedy, closer to Lionel Monckton than to Rodgers and Hart. Hart had got away with 'period' lyrics in *A Yankee at King Arthur's Court* only because he was granted the double vision of the Middle Ages seen through modern eyes. He could write

> Thou swell, thou witty
> Thou sweet, thou grand –
> Wouldst kiss me pretty?
> Wouldst hold my hand?

which is both tender and mocking to verbal archaism. I had to pretend to be expressing the late seventeenth century. It dawned on me that the only way in which a musical *Cyrano* could work would be in a Mark Twain style, with a big-nosed bank clerk transported back to Richelieu's France to enact Cyrano and, at the end, win his girl in modern America. But it was too late for that. When Michael Langham began to call *Cyrano* 'a play with music' it was evident that we were apologising for a hybrid, sidling on to Broadway rather than crashing it.

After a day's hopeless work I went back to the Holiday Inn to find it on fire. Some disaffected waiter or boilerman had enflamed the floor I was staying on, and firemen were dousing the stricken area with a grey chemical that ruined my luggage. I had to get out, and it seemed reasonable to go back to New York. There *A Clockwork Orange* was still being denounced by the conservative as one of the causes of enhanced juvenile violence and at the same time praised by the progressive as liberating. At the Algonquin I received notes and telephone calls about equally divided in praise and blame. A New York Indian threatened me with a tomahawk, and a striptease performer, enclosing her photograph, offered to come to my bed. A former Jesuit priest named Tom Collins actually reached my bedroom and offered to make me rich. He knew all about books, and he showed me one he had published – a theological work about the Holy Ghost as God's thrust into human history. If I could write the outlines of three novels on, respectively, George Gershwin (*The Rhapsody Man*), George Patton (*The True Patton Papers*) and George III (*The Man Who Lost America*), he could guarantee advances totalling a million dollars.

What was he, an agent? No, not an agent; I already had one of those. Had I? Did he mean Deborah Rogers in London? No, Robert Lantz in New York. Surely not. And then I remembered the night of the Sardi's ceremony and a nightcap at the ornate apartment of this Robert Lantz. Lantz was a film man who looked after Malcolm

McDowell as well as established stars like Elizabeth Taylor and Richard Burton. He had offered to look after my books as well as my commitment to *Cyrano*. How did Tom Collins, former SJ, know about this? New York, the biggest city of the free world, was also the smallest. In respect of the arts it was a village. As for one particular art, I gained the impression that the reality of a book was less important than the idea of it. Write the outline of *The Rhapsody Man* and sell it to Hollywood, then get some hack to work at the literary spin-off. And what precisely did Tom Collins do in this sphere of book-making? Book-making was right. If authors wrote books, he made them. Try one out now before tackling the million-dollar trilogy. Write a small book and leave the rest to me. He would arrange format, typography, illustrations, taking his cut of course. Near dead with fatigue, I said I would think about it. Tom Collins seemed disappointed. I could at least give him an outline there and then: there was a desk, here was a pen. I fell asleep and let him find his own way out. But that was very far from being the end of him.

I STOPPED off in London on my way back to Rome. I had to deliver the two plaques confirming that the New York Critics considered Stanley Kubrick the best director and script-writer of the year. I also had to appear on a BBC radio programme to defend Stanley Kubrick's art and the apparent depravity of a book that few had read. This programme was one of a series put out on the most demotic of the BBC's channels, in which discussion on serious topics with a live audience was justified with breaks for pop music. The seriousness was thus mitigated and the final effect was cynical. The anchorman of the programme was a former disc-jockey named Jimmy Savile. He had been noted for bipartite hair-dyes and his love of the young. He had boasted of the 'quids' he had earned in his promotion of musical garbage, but he had the reputation also of a philanthropist who used the media – newspaper, radio, television – to help the suffering, unite the sundered, and be admitted to the Order of the British Empire. His name now never appeared without the OBE appendage. He was taken, with hair decently greying, clad in an orthodox suit, not a disc-jockey's motley, to be the finest type of Yorkshireman and paid to promote the virtues of British Rail.

The attacks on the film of *A Clockwork Orange* were bitter. One member of the audience cited the Poughkeepsie rape of a nun, ignoring the disclaimer that the film could have no influence on the ravishers. I stuck to one point – that the events of real life are anterior, naturally, to their representation in book or film, and that neither cinema nor literature can be blamed for the manifestations of original sin. A man who kills his uncle cannot justifiably blame a performance of *Hamlet*. On the other hand, if literature is to be held responsible for mayhem and murder, then the most damnable book of them all is the Bible, the most vindictive piece of literature in existence. The audience was not convinced. Savile maintained the right objectivity, but he ended the session by asking a man in the audience to stand up. This man admitted he had served a long jail sentence for Grievous Bodily Harm. He was asked by Savile if his reading had influenced his criminal behaviour. Without doubt, the man replied, and the programme came to an end.

This weighting of what was meant to be a free discussion with a dramatic conclusion that confirmed the prejudice of so many made me boil and wish to inflict GBH on Savile. I was also sickened by the manner in which a book that, all of ten years before, had made very little impact on the reading public was now becoming a kind of invisible primer of evil. It was not to be invisible for long. Deborah Rogers sold the paperback rights to Penguin, and a reproduction of the American edition soon appeared on the market, with the final, regenerative, chapter omitted and a stupid glossary of the nadsat slang added. Kubrick filed the nails of the other hand in Borehamwood and left me to be the target of vile accusation. It was clear that I would never be awarded an OBE.

So going back to Liana and Andrea in Rome was returning to Europe in a more than geographical sense. Any trouble I was to have in Italy would, much later, be for alleged blasphemy more than the fathering of youthful violence. Europe, being more or less Catholic, saw what both the book and the film were really about. Roman journalism was to play up my status as the *padrino* of sin, but it was also to accept that sin was not my invention. The French and Italian terms for free will were close to St Augustine's *liberum arbitrium*, and to speak of *libre arbitre* or *libero arbitrio* was automatically to invoke theology. *A Clockwork Orange*, whatever Protestant Britain might say, was theologically sound.

Italy had to wait some months for the completion of the dubbing of *Arancia Meccanica*, so I did not have to wander Trastevere or climb to the Gianicolo with a mist of notoriety around me. The Italian film industry, however, knowing the film of *A Clockwork Orange* well in advance of the general public, saw that I might be useful in supplying a tang of evil to its products, so I began to be called on for additional dialogue and, soon, whole scripts. The Italians were still a filmgoing people: they liked company and crowds and were claustrophobic enough not to relish watching a small screen in the garlic-scented dark of a living-room. Italy had a large domestic market for films, but it naturally tried to sell these abroad and, to that end, dubbed them into English in the recording studios of Rome. Sometimes an internationally known actor would be imported to enhance the chance of foreign sales. Thus, Dustin Hoffman had appeared in a film called *Alfredo Alfredo*, and I was commissioned to improve the English of his voice-over passages. I saw the film at a stage in which Hoffman alone spoke English while the other actors spoke Italian. He would be Italian-dubbed for the domestic version and the others English-dubbed for Anglophonia. It was remarkable to see Hoffman pretending to understand what was clearly to him unintelligible. It was too late to improve his dialogue, but the linking VO sections could be gorblimeyed into acceptable, almost literary, English. I liked the way the Italian film-makers did business. A man came round with the written commission and, the following evening, collected my work and handed over an envelope crammed with ten-thousand-lire notes. No nonsense about cheques or contracts. The Italians knew the value of non-taxable cash.

I had a much more serious dramatic commission to fulfil in the spring and summer of 1972. *Cyrano* was not to be cast and go into rehearsal till much later in the year, and Michael Langham, though granting that its out-of-town première should be held in the Tyrone Guthrie Theatre, had a whole season to fill before this somewhat marginal event: though the director of *Cyrano*, he was primarily a director of legitimate drama. After the success of *Cyrano de Bergerac*, he wanted another new translation of a classic play, and he first proposed *Peer Gynt*, with the film star Paul Newman in the lead. I began to work on my Norwegian, but Newman grew shy. Langham then decided that *Oedipus Tyrannus*, with Len Cariou playing his last serious role before appearing in Sondheim's *A Little Night Music*, could well do with a brand-new translation and even an unclassical approach. Not only a translation but an adaptation.

While Britain and America were either howling against or fulsomely praising the modernism, nay the futurism, of *A Clockwork Orange*, I plunged into the Attic antique and worked at Sophocles. With a rusty scrapheap of Greek behind my eyes and, on the desk, a Liddell and Scott dictionary that fell to pieces with fingering, I worked in no spirit of precise scholarship but solely out of a desire to create a version suitable for a particular theatre and a particular director. It is always a comfort to know that theatrical effectiveness is the best answer to the screams of outraged purists. In terms of a tradition that still works in the study but is, I submit, shaky in the theatre, I made Oedipus blind himself in full view of the audience. The Attic aesthetic forbade the presentation of violent action, but it was not easy for a modern audience to pretend that *King Lear* had not yet been written.

There was another reason too for meddling with Sophocles, and this had to do with the claims of reasonableness. Men whose eyes have been put out do not, unless they are still under a local anaesthetic, talk reasonably, or even unreasonably: they do not talk at all. It seemed to me that the agony of Oedipus's witnessing the death of his wife–mother was enough agony to sustain him through one long passage of dialogue; his self-mutilation should properly bring all his capacity for speech to an end: thereafter other forces could take over.

As for meddling with Sophocles's lines as opposed to his action, nothing that he wrote was taken away, but something was added. What was added related chiefly to anterior action – Oedipus's solving of the riddle of the sphinx. Most people, though not all people, know what the riddle was, and few, knowing the riddle, find it easy to understand why only Oedipus could solve it. It is a very easy riddle, as one of my child-characters (not to be found in Sophocles) points out, and I had to find a plausibility for Oedipus's success following the lethal failure of so many others. The point made by one of my 'elders' is that the riddle was not meant to be answered, since answering it might prove more dangerous than not answering it. It is presumably better to be eaten alive by a monster than to kill one's father and marry one's mother. The riddle, I tried to show, has a particular applicability to Oedipus in arithmological terms. We can separate out from four legs, two legs and three legs a figure of resurrection, since 3 leads on to 4 and resumes a cycle. Oedipus, seeing himself as a creature of unknown parentage, exults in being a sort of creature of nature, an animal–human member of a family which is itself the cycle of the seasons. But he ends as a kind of mutilated god who helps to keep that cycle alive. In both images he is not unlike the sphinx.

The adaptation of *Oedipus* solved, or seemed to, the riddle I had been asking myself while writing *MF*. Why this association between three disparate-seeming elements – the act of incest, the riddle, the animal–human destroyer? The sphinx or, in the Algonquin legend I had used, the talking bird ought to symbolise the cursed or holy (sacred, etymologically, meaning both) product of a forbidden union. The riddle might stand for the intriguingly easy but inexplicably forbidden (boy-child and girl-child in bed together, love-play, punishment, why?) or for the knot which holds natural or social order together, untied at our peril though so tempting to untie. For order had both to be and not to be challenged, this being the anomalous condition of the sustention of the cosmos. Rebel becomes hero; witch becomes saint. Exogamy means disruption and also stability; incest means stability and also disruption. Oedipus is the cause of the state's disease and disruption but also, through his discovery and expiation of sin, the cause of its recovered health. He is a criminal but also a saint. In other words, he is a tragic hero.

Stanley Silverman came to Rome to discuss the writing of the music for what was to be called, not for the first time, *Oedipus the King*. Langham wanted the chorus to sing, not just recite, and had the idea of their singing in a language very remote, to suggest the antiquity of the legend. The remotest language possible was Indo-European (which Langham's typist rendered as 'indoor European'), and this meant dragging out of the more scholarly etymological dictionaries those hypothetical roots marked with an asterisk. There was to be a lot of music and a number of strange instruments – a shawm, a bull-roarer, ancient drums. There was so much music, indeed, that eventually Stanley and I were able to present *Oedipus the King* as a cantata.

The wounds inflicted by *A Clockwork Orange* were being soothed by immersion in the waters of the past. Vincenzo Labella came to me with another ancient myth and a larger project – the creation of a script for a television series to be called *Moses the Lawgiver*. This was to be financed jointly by RAI or Radiotelevisione Italiana and Sir Lew Grade and to be filmed in Israel and Cinecittà. There had to be script collaboration with Italian writers – Vittorio Bonicelli and Bernardino Zampone – but the work was to be primarily an English language production and I would get top billing. My first task was to write the script as a book – a kind of epic poem which would generate rhythms neither antique nor contemporary. This, as *Moses*, was eventually to be published in both Britain and America, but both publishing houses collapsed and copies of the book are very rare. The Napoleon novel which I had already started had to gather dust.

It was put about by Roman gossips that Vincenzo Labella was the son of Pope Paul VI, officially called *nipote* or nephew, chiefly because he carried a Vatican passport, but the truth was that his father had been a lay Vatican official and Vincenzo had been born a Vatican citizen. He became a professor of Roman history at the University of Rome, but the producer of *Ben-Hur* had called him in as historical adviser. Fascinated by film, as we all are, he had now himself become a producer, especially of projects that required historical knowledge. He would not permit the kind of solecism that Hollywood producers, believing history to be bunk, impose upon an ignorant public: he believed that historical accuracy was no impediment to mass entertainment. He was brown and claimed Etruscan blood, wore smart Italian suits, and was charming in both the modern and ancient languages. He was separated from his Italian wife and living with an American girl whom, when civil divorce came to Italy, he proposed marrying. He had two beautiful legitimate daughters, the elder of whom was to be shot dead by her lover while Vincenzo and I were working together on another biblical project called *Jesus of Nazareth*. He was to suffer professionally from the ignorance of colleagues and stupidity of actors but was ready to use his fists, even on the set and in the Israeli desert.

How was I to be paid for the script I had to write? Not in the orthodox manner of a cheque or cheques, but through the expansion of the house in Bracciano. Signora Elena still stamped about on the ceiling, but our lateral neighbours had departed, and we could now buy their property and attach it to ours. The corridor with its two bathrooms could have a door cut into its thick mediaeval wall, and this would lead to a lower salon and, by means of ancient stone stairs, to a lower one again, this in its turn leading to a cellar which could contain a heating apparatus. Italians saw nothing eccentric about paying in kind. When, later, Vincenzo wanted me to adapt a novel called *Il Fascistibile* into a film script, I asked for a Broadwood piano. Federico Fellini was to pay me for work on his *Casanova* with a leather-bound tome on Florentine antiquities, a magnificent Gucci satchel, and a cine-camera. But when I translated a script for Antonioni he gave me nothing.

Orange Mécanique, shown in Paris to highly intellectual plaudits, got in the way of my Bible studies. *Le Nouvel Observateur* was stupefied by the originality of Kubrick's dialogue, which was all mine, and I had to complain to its editor, Olivier Todd, about the assumption that the entire concept was Kubrick's own. Despite their disdain for English, the French intelligentsia ought at least to know that my book existed. After all, Christine Brooke-Rose, who had beaten the *anti-romanciers* at their own game, had written on it at length in one of the French literary reviews. There then arrived in Rome from the publishing house of Robert Laffont two remarkable editor-translators – Hortense Chabrier and Georges Belmont. They proposed making me better known in France. The only novel of mine that had so far appeared there was *Tremor of Intent*, turned by Michel Deutsch into *Un Agent Qui Vous Veut du Bien*. The house that had purchased my Malayan books had, I remembered, eventually discarded them because they had no confidence in my future. *Tremor of Intent* had been difficult to put into French, but not so difficult as my other works. Hortense and Georges were bilingual and foresaw few problems. Hortense, one of whose ancestors was the composer of *España* and *Marche Joyeuse*, had been brought up in a château with an Irish nanny. Georges had taught French at Trinity College, Dublin, and Samuel Beckett was an old colleague and friend who maintained that Georges's English was better than his French. Georges was a poet, and he had translated James Joyce's poems, though not to Joyce's satisfaction: Joyce had wanted his stanza-forms and rhyme-schemes to be retained, and this had not been possible. Georges had also done some work on the French translation of *Finnegans Wake*, with Joyce groaning in his chair about *un calembours juste* to be found in Rabelais: 'Och, I can't see it what with me eyes, but it's on an odd-numbered page about half way through the second volume.' Georges would have no difficulty with me.

The summer of 1972 was, then, a busy one. Warner Brothers sent me to the Cannes film festival to promote Kubrick's film. This was *hors de concours*, since only a film not previously shown could compete for the prizes, but Cannes, with the entire cinema world present, was the place for the, so to speak, ultimate press conference. For me the high point of the visit was a meeting with Groucho Marx. A luncheon was given for him, but the guests were mostly intellectual Parisians, the majority monoglot, who were more concerned with the structuralist and semiotic content of *A Night at the Opera* than with the rollicking fun that had never aroused their laughter. Groucho was shy and bewildered, though Mordecai Richler and Louis Malle eased him into reminiscence of the old vaudeville days with hookers at two bucks a throw. I asked Malle if he was acquainted with the work of Messrs Gilbert and Sullivan, and then Groucho's blue eyes opened wide and he sang:

> Taken from the county jail
> By a set of curious chances,
> Liberated then on bail
> On my own recognizances . . .

From then on things went well. Groucho had come with the notorious girl who was to claim, four years later, the bulk of his estate. She kept saying 'Aw, cut it out, Grouch,' whenever he sang bawdily: this was to show that she was in charge. It was clear that Groucho's great days had been the penurious ones on tour in the sticks: the films were no more than inadequate spin-offs. He quoted T. S. Eliot ('Aw, cut it out, Grouch'). His French and German were rusty but adequate: after all, the Marx family was from Alsace-Lorraine. He gave me a Romeo and Juliet cigar which I kept till it fell to pieces. He was spontaneously witty, but not above filing away the occasional unpurposed crack. It was on this occasion that a lady was mentioned who had ten children because she loved her husband. 'I love my cigar,' Groucho said, 'but I take it out sometimes.'

An imperious summons came from Richard Gregson to meet Christopher Plummer in London and to write for him the sort of song that he wanted. Plummer was a star and was to become, though briefly, a singing star: he was above the kind of rubbish that Lewis and I had been turning out in Minneapolis. With Groucho Marx I had met artistic humility; with Plummer I met self-consciousness about stellar rank and large pride in hard-won techniques. Lewis's melodies were disparaged as banal, and my lyrics were not much better. I resented the postures of servitude into which I had betrayed myself but had to accept that I was there to feed an ego. It was probably salutary to have to revert to a kind of military situation in which orders and rebukes were to be humbly swallowed, but I felt that the whole *Cyrano* project was a war that could not be won. In the army I had been in trouble for saying unguardedly in a lecture: 'If we win this war – ' Now we all had to be totally confident of a box-office success: it was the only way in which we could be paid for time and energy lavishly expended. But I did not believe that even an 'if' was viable.

I was too much in the paws of producers and directors. I needed my old status of a novelist threatening to renege on his contract if an editor proposed changing even a punctuation mark. But the current novel *Napoleon Symphony* needed more work and research than I could give to it. When the City College of New York invited me to spend a year as Distinguished Professor I seized at once the chance of that temporary elevation. If I had to be in the United States for the rehearsals and openings of both *Oedipus the King* and *Cyrano*, at least it would be under an aegis nobler than that conferred by show business. Bertrand Russell had once held my professorship, though City College had expelled him for immorality. Distinguished was right. The title soothed my regret at being an extinguished novelist.

FOUR

WE BOARDED the Bedford Dormobile and took the road for Naples, where we were to embark on the *Leonardo da Vinci*. A tall beautiful black girl named Francesca drove us: this was to give her practice in driving the heavy exotic thing back. Francesca was Ethiopian. She had been brought up on Italian but spoke some English. We had first met her selling walkie-talkies at a huge Christmas fair in EUR, the futurist suburb of Rome that remained the most solid relic of fascism. We persuaded her to become our secretary, or, rather, to join the complex that was beginning to surround us on the initiation of the television *Moses* project. This meant chiefly keeping Italian script-collaborators, religious and historical advisers, speech coaches and would-be actors out of the Roman flat. We were travelling to New York by sea so that I could work on the script undisturbed.

In Naples the face of Malcolm McDowell glowered from posters advertising *Arancia Meccanica*. A fundamentally nice boy had been transformed into the pattern of all hooligans. Naples did not require cinematic instruction in the best modes of violence. Only Americans expected that Neapolitans could be taught efficiency in other spheres of action. The *Leonardo da Vinci* did not appear, and nobody in the offices of the Italia Line knew where it was. A beef-red American intending passenger grew apoplectic to the admiration of the shipping clerks and collapsed with a heart attack. An ambulance was very slow to arrive. The slogan 'See Naples and die' was now disclosing its meaning. A day or so late, the *Leonardo da Vinci* was hailed on the horizon like a vision of a *Terra Promessa*. The returning New York Mafia was the first to get aboard.

I sat in the first-class salon not with the *Moses* script but with a pen and a wad of music manuscript paper. I had to write a sonata for harmonica and guitar. This had been commissioned by an American harmonica virtuoso named John Sebastian. He lived in Rome with a French mistress but made money by travelling the United States

with his harmonica and a pianist, soon to be a guitarist if he could get
enough arrangements and original compositions to fill up the two
hours of recital time. He had a son also named John Sebastian who
was better known than he, since he was a rock singer, but he was
damned if, having already changed his name from Rabinowitz or
something to one with a more musical aura, he was going to change
it again. People rolled up to his recitals in the belief that they were
going to hear his son and then clamoured for their money back. This
was a pity, because he was a fine musician. Villa-Lobos had written a
concerto for him but had got the cadenza all wrong.

It was strange that, as a sort of musician, I was learning to compose
for the most awkward instruments in the world. Berlioz said that
nobody could compose for the guitar without being able to play it.
The same was true of the harmonica, which, if one were to play Bach
or Vivaldi or Burgess on it, had to cease to be the suck-blow solace of
soldiers on the Somme, alternating wretched triads and dominant
ninths. It had to be a four-octave mixture of flute, oboe and clarinet,
capable of only a few chords, equipped with a key that raised the
entire compass a semitone, activated by a little breath and a tongue-
point thrust into the aperture adjacent to the sounding one, so that
the melancholy suck-blow harmony should be warded off. As for
the guitar, I knew what could not be played on it, and this was
probably enough. As I penned my notes, a drinking mafioso told me
that you not a write a music a that a way, you use a pianoforte, so I
told him to stick to his killing business and I would stick to mine. A
Jewish lady New York concert manager informed me that John
Sebastian was a genius; I was whatever I was, which was nobody she
had ever heard of. I had been spurred by that last infirmity of noble
minds to wish to be, if not famous, at least a little known. But, as it
turned out, I was known only to the immigration officers who got
on board in New York harbour. They said: 'Welcome back to New
York, Mr Burgess.' There was no welcome for the Jewish lady
concert manager.

There was time to worry about Andrea, who did not seem to wish
to be worried about. I was worried about his education, or lack of it.
He spoke coarse Roman, with occasional deviations into refined
Tuscan: he had inherited an ear. His English had been relearned in
New Jersey and was now to be rerelearned in Manhattan. His
schooling lacked continuity. This was all my fault. If I had been a
bank clerk in Ealing there would have been continuity enough, but I
had elected, or had forced upon me, the role of a sort of international
author in a kind of negative exile: I knew where I no longer lived but

was unsure of the place of my expatriation. I felt at home only in the Bedford Dormobile, which had no address. But now I was to become an adoptive New Yorker.

We were to take over the tenth-floor apartment of the poetess Adrienne Rich on Riverside Drive. She, a famous feminist and man-hater, was to assume a year's residence in a Mid-West university. We were not permitted to enter her flat until we had been examined by the committee of the apartment block, and this did not propose to convene a meeting until after Labor Day. So, very expensively, we occupied a suite in the Algonquin Hotel, and I faced, with a kind of hopelessness, the commitments of the coming academic year. I would have to teach Joyce's *Ulysses* for the first semester and Shakespeare for the second, and I would have an unchanging Creative Writing group for the whole year. I had also committed myself to a lecturing tour of the United States, travelling to Florida and Louisiana and Colorado and Maine on the days when City College did not require my services. Then there were rehearsals of *Oedipus the King* in Minneapolis, to say nothing of work on *Cyrano* which had to be re-engaged almost from scratch. Vincenzo Labella, producer of *Moses*, threatened to bring over my Italian co-scenarists at regular intervals. But my major problem was a lack of money.

I would not see a salary cheque from City College until the end of September, which had only just begun. I cleaned out my Chemical Bank account in paying the Algonquin and a deposit on the tenancy of the Riverside Drive apartment. I had traveller's cheques, but no Manhattan bank was willing to cash them. I had lost the right to use a credit card because of a prolonged postal strike in Rome, during which my cheques to the American Express company failed to arrive and its computer system – which fed the news of my defection to the computers of other credit card companies – was not programmed for explanatory correspondence. As usual, Liana found a way out. She dealt with a Sicilian wine-shop on Broadway which was glad to exchange lire cheques for cash dollars. The vintners sent the lire back home to Catania, and they would rather see Liana mugged for the dollars than themselves be burgled for them.

Manhattan was violent enough, but not to Italians. When Vincenzo Labella brought over my co-scenarists and their growing sons, as well as the proposed director, Gianfranco de Bosio, our loud Italian on Broadway was as good as a defensive weapon. In restaurants, discussing artistic problems in the making of *Moses*, we would seem to be planning a gang war. Not even Italian intellectuals are weeds: there is a breadth of shoulder and a hairiness of hand, as well as a dangerous eye-flash, which do not attract black or Puerto Rican muggers. Gianfranco de Bosio was no weed. My fellow-scenarist Vittorio Bonicelli proudly referred to him as a genuine Moses in his own right, one who had smuggled Italian Jews over the Swiss border during the Nazi occupation. But he had made his name as an avant-garde director of films and plays. The trouble was that he knew no English and would be in charge of a television series to be shot in English. I would have to meet that trouble after the academic year in New York.

We moved into Adrienne Rich's flat, which was dark but roomy. A bank of television screens and a couple of armed black porters, in a uniform designed by a Mrs Rapaport of the block committee, guarded the main entrance on Riverside Drive. It was pointed out to us that we had joined a community and I might even be expected to contribute to the block magazine. It was a community sealed off from the dangerous city outside, sufficient for the door-to-door visits of the block children at Hallowe'en, who, if they trick-and-treated on the street, might be given drugged cookies or chocolate bars with razor blades in them. I was asked by the *New York Times* to write an article on my impressions of life in a quarter which was more Hispanic than Anglo-Saxon or Jewish, and I made much of the cockroaches or *cucarachas* which infested the kitchen. I compared them to a Latin American community, poor but lively: if they would leave me alone I would leave them alone. After all, Don Marquis's Archy might be among them. The block committee was not happy about this: I had disclosed a shameful family secret to the outside world.

The *New York Times*, perhaps being short of local news at the time, seemed intrigued by the fact that an author made notorious by a dangerous movie was blandly performing an academic job. Cameramen entered the classroom where I was trying to explain Buck Mulligan's 'And going forth he met Butterly'. Cameramen even followed me on to the subway and snapped me holding on to a metal pole. One reader wrote in to say that I looked like a visitant from Mars. A reporter shrewdly commented that Liana seemed more at home in the urban world than I. This was true. The city girl knew how to use the city, fighting overcharging greengrocers with vivid Italian, a language which even New Yorkers north of Mulberry Street seemed to know, haggling even in Fifth Avenue boutiques. As for Andrea, it was not safe for him to engage streets where drug-pushers caught their clients young and black rogues castrated whites if they were small enough. A bus came every morning to take the block children to school; it brought them back in the evening. Andrea went to the Dalton School on Park Avenue. Here he was taught the Algonquin rain dance and the tonalities of Newyorkese. But his Italian was kept alive at home.

I suppose, by the time Christmas came, I felt myself to be more of a New Yorker than I had ever been a Londoner, a Roman, even a Mancunian. My British accent was no handicap; in a town with so many varieties of immigrant English it seemed even to approach a decent American eastern seaboard norm. New York is an accepting city, and I was accepted. My face became known because I appeared on television talk-shows; at New Year I joined Mayor Lindsay to deliver a greeting to the boroughs. New York became the more home because I left it so often. Taking a taxi back from La Guardia airport, after a lecture in Oregon or South Carolina, to the familiar dirt of Riverside Drive, what could I say except that I was coming home?

Manhattan had all too recognisable features. The university towns I flew to tend, in memory, to merge into one. The students too unify into an image of innocents desperately trying to understand the modern world that was being fashioned behind their backs and, more particularly at that period, to work out the morality of their position as regarded the Vietnam war. The fact that I had become associated with the film of *A Clockwork Orange*, which put theology as well as violence on the neighbourhood or campus screen, gave a kind of authority to what became a regular homily. I emphasised the importance of moral choice, saying that we were defined as human beings by our capacity to choose. It did not matter which make or automobile or brand of cornflakes we chose, but the choice between good and evil mattered a great deal. The definition of good and evil was difficult, but those two eternal entities did not always coincide with the community's loose and mutable moral dichotomy. In other words, what was right was not necessarily good, and evil and wrong did not have to be the same thing. The state professed horror at murder but was always ready to go to war. Whatever good was, evil was certainly the wilful impairment of the right of a living organism to fulfil itself. At the bottom of the scale of evil enactments, to fart loudly during the performance of a Beethoven quartet was reprehensible because a piece of music was an organic substance made manifest by its players, and the fart was a wound malevolently, or stupidly, inflicted. Stupidity itself could be classified as an aspect of evil, since intelligence was required to work out, to the satisfaction of the individual soul, a rough and ready guide to moral action. At the top of the scale of evil, torture and murder for their own sake, *actes gratuits*, were most damnable.

Who was to damn? Not God, who might or might not exist, and certainly not the state. The state could not be trusted, since its moral system was based on expediency and usually smelt of hypocrisy. My listening students had to make up their own minds as to whether or not it was evil to kill in Vietnam, but, having made up their minds, they must be prepared to take the consequences. If they evaded the military draft by crossing the border into Canada, they must expunge from their consciences any sense of failed patriotism or of cowardice. It was frequently on the grounds of courage or of love of country that evil acts were enjoined on citizens. That a visiting foreigner could say such things to audiences of a thousand or more was, of course, a proof that the United States was still a free country. There was too much of the muttered 'Like *Nineteen Eighty-Four*, man' from students who, if they had read Orwell at all, had not read him carefully. The point was that no young American had necessarily to acquiesce in an evil that was as much the fruit of stupidity as of an ill-considered moral righteousness. Communism in Vietnam threatened only American eastern markets; Vietnam itself might interpret it only as agrarian reform. Crusading America had not worked out its moral situation in terms of the great theological entities: its intelligent young citizens had to take moral judgement into their own hands and damn the consequences.

I have a false memory of flying to the homogeneous state universities in a perpetual blizzard, often in Piper Cubs as the only passenger, of arriving at airfields with shacklike terminals, usually at dawn, to discover that snow or fog was on its way and all flights were cancelled. Sometimes an aircraft was able to reach Boise in Idaho or Carson City in Nevada, only to become grounded indefinitely as the snow piled up. I would telephone the lecture agency at 666 (ominous number) Fifth Avenue and refuse to travel to a Hellfire Gap which would hold me till the spring. 'We'll sue you, Mr Burgess,' cried the tough old man in charge. Sue and be damned. I seemed to attract the snow. In New Orleans, where snow had not been heard of for at least a century, snow fell, cars slithered, the local blacks looked purple. Snow was getting its own back for my desertion of Charles Dickens's country.

In Milwaukee there was deep snow and no one to meet me and a failure of memory as regards the motel I was to stay at. In the airport concourse a pretty girl was crying bitterly and I asked if there was anything I could do to help. She yelled 'Leave me alone, wilya' and battered my chest with her tiny fists. The police grabbed me. They asked for an ID I did not have (my passport was at home, namely on Riverside Drive, NY), they contemned my foreign accent, they took me to a secluded corner for a salutary beating. I was saved by the appearance of my university sponsor. He did not like the police much. His father and mother had put on evening clothes to attend a Rotary dinner. Having left his latchkey in his day suit, the father tried to effect an entrance into his own house by climbing through a window. He had been shot from a passing patrol car. The police everywhere in the United States seemed less guardians of the law than agents of a kind of alternative criminality. A week before my Milwaukee visit, the New York police had gone on strike. This resulted in a diminution of street crime. It was as if, with one team out of action, the other team could not play.

I travelled far, wide and crazily. There was no geograpnical logic in the lecturing schedules the agency arranged. I would fly from Austin, Texas, up to Buffalo, New York, and then west to San Diego, California, all in the same two-day segment. The agency was above consulting the convenience of its clients. It fixed flights and motels and deducted from the cheques it received for lecturing services rendered the cost of the airfare. The client had to fork out on the spot for his bed and board. More important, it deducted thirty per cent commission, which it regarded as an insufficient profit. It was no wonder that the vigorous aged head of the agency bawled me out and threatened to sue when I refused to head into January snow or fall fog. Once or twice I failed to honour a lecturing commitment when ready to march on to the platform. This was when a sly document was produced at the last minute for my signature, over which I was to swear not to criticise adversely the United States Government, comment on its policies, find good in communism or bad in the American Constitution. If I refused to sign it was because, more than some Americans, I wanted America to be the land of the free.

I WOULD fly home, and then take the subway, the IRT on 96th Street, to my City College classes. An area defaced by dogmerds, occasional corpses, persistent muggings, and various gestures of black disaffection, was the major centre of Manhattan higher education, but, in the name of democracy, it was abdicating its responsibility. For no educational qualification was needed to enter the university: entrance was a democratic right. Fortunately, the Jewish students with their *yarmulkes* ensured a core of seriousness: they were ready to be taught, fulfilling an honourable tradition of their race, but neither they nor the gentiles seemed to have absorbed enough in their high schools to fit them for higher learning. They knew neither Latin nor Greek, and their foreign languages were immigrant tongues some of them were trying to unlearn. It had been my intention to run a course on the novels of Evelyn Waugh, which would introduce them, through easy, elegant and humorous English, to a foreign culture not too dissimilar from their own. But Evelyn Waugh was not available in paperback publication; nor, for that matter, was Ford Madox Ford, Henry James, or Joseph Conrad. Modern literary studies were suffering from the commercial limitations of New York publishing. Joyce's *Ulysses* was all too available in a cheap edition, and this, a kind of fount of modernism, could be appreciated by these young New Yorkers only in a context of culture they did not have.

Thus, it was necessary to teach them the *Odyssey* before engaging Joyce's parody of it. Before they could appreciate the 'Oxen of the Sun' chapter they had to know something of the history of English prose style. They had to have read some Edwardian novels in order to see precisely what Joyce's innovations were. For that matter, they had to be made to read *Dubliners* and *A Portrait of the Artist as a Young Man* to see the progress of his innovation. *Dubliners* disappointed them because nothing happened in it: they were uneasy about the whole point being that nothing happened. They expected literature to be didactic: they all knew, which no Europeans did, the novels of Ayn Rand. But perhaps it was enough, in a season lasting from Labor Day to Christmas, or Hanukah, that they should glimpse some of the possibilities of modernism. It might also have helped them to be taught by a practising writer who earned a living, such as it was, from the manipulation of language. It is the cash nexus that counts in the United States. That Milton only got five pounds for *Paradise Lost* is a powerful argument against taking him seriously.

The semester from New Year to the end of my year's tenure was taken up, in the aspect of mild scholarship, with a course on Shakespeare given at eight in the morning to two hundred and fifty students. The sessions were held in a large lecture hall on Convent Avenue, and outside this lecture hall was a cashier's office complete with *guichet* before which black students waited to receive a weekly subsistence allowance. Whether they were more than merely nominal students I never discovered; I know only that they waited with competing cassette recorders of the kind called ghetto blaster, and that their noise prevented me from making a start on my lecture. I rebuked them and received coarse threats in return, as well as scatological abuse which was unseemly in any circumstances but monstrous when directed at even an undistinguished professor. What would Bertrand Russell have done?

There are some institutions that cannot, except at grave peril, be democratised, and universities are among them. With an open admission system implying the right to a degree, City College could impose none of the disciplines that prevailed at Oxford or Cambridge — no gatings, no rustications, no harsh words from tutor or dean or provost. When a student entered my office to say 'What did you mean by giving us that shit this morning?' I was free enough to hit out, at least verbally, because I had nothing to lose: I was not a career academic hoping for tenure. The democratic spirit put the students above the professors: they were consumers questioning what they consumed. Towards the end of my year I was given two hundred and fifty pencils and two hundred and fifty printed forms, one for each of my Shakespeare students. The forms asked for an evaluation of their lecturer's professional skill and (this being America) personality. Who were these children to presume to judge? I tore up the forms but kept the pencils. As I say, I had nothing to lose.

My Shakespeare course was less concerned with the play texts than with their background. I asked the question 'Why was this play written at that particular time?' and tried to give an answer. But first I had to guess at the kind of man Shakespeare was and be beyond guessing at the kind of England he worked in. To the children of democracy ranks like Duke and Earl were for black band leaders. They had to be taught about a social structure that still nominally existed. They demurred only when I discussed Shakespeare's grammar school education, with its emphasis on Latin. I said: 'I am now going to write on the blackboard three lines from a play by Seneca. Their meaning counts less than their prosody. When we talk of the Senecan element in early Shakespeare we often mean the way he manipulates language. He learned a lot of verbal tricks from Seneca.' When I began to chalk my Latin up, a number of students began to walk out. I raced after them, dragged them back, then locked the door. I had often wondered why I had been given a key; now I knew. This revulsion from the ancient languages was, even for a modern democracy, pathological. But one of my students responded to Seneca, to his own surprise, with a germ of interest. He began to teach himself Latin. A year after, I received a postcard from him: '*Gratias ago*. J. Breslow.'

There was not much point in taking my students' written exercises seriously. There were too many of them, and they were all going to pass anyway. They were very direct when slangy, and totally evasive when written in gobbledygook. One had to take one's choice between 'Lady M. said she would pull the kid away from her tit and watch it croak on the floor' and 'Lady M. demonstrates an over-reactive syndrome when adumbrating a hypothetical infanticide'. These jeaned and T-shirted youths and girls of Manhattan, tousled and blear-eyed at eight in the morning (or usually eight-fifteen: they knew I had a fifteen-minute fight with loud and unruly blacks), were decent and honest but probably ineducable by the standards of my own studentship. They suffered from identity crises. I tried to demonstrate the futility of worrying about identity by giving a lecture on a non-existent Elizabethan playwright, complete with excerpts from his non-existent plays, who certainly had identity but lacked the property of existence. This trick did not go down well. My students wanted honesty. They also wanted relevance, whatever they meant by it.

The true students, who were not for me, were the paunched and bearded postgraduates who drank in the Library Bar and Grill on Upper Broadway or saw foreign movies at the Thalia. They were ready to discuss Herr Settembrini and Frau Chauchat in *Der Zauberberg* or dissect Hopkins's prosody. Late one night, walking home alone from a party, I found myself followed by murderous thugs who turned out to be bulky postgraduates anxious to argue about what really happens in the last two pages of *The Wings of the Dove*. Blacks lurking in the small hours would not be interested in Henry James. They would, I believed, knife me because of my magisterial rebukes on Convent Avenue. I usually carried my swordstick but only brandished it once. That was on Twelfth Street and my would-be assailants were white and feeble with drugs. Walking through Harlem I had no need of self-protection. The worst punishment the blacks could wreak on the formerly tyrannical whites was to make them invisible. It was Ralph Ellison's novel, which few of them had read, in reverse. Those blacks who had read *Invisible Man* and deigned to discuss it with me over City College coffee considered Ellison to be an Uncle Tom. He turned out to be a civilised man of great charm, charming also his wife, earning a high salary as holder of a United Nations chair, worried less about race than about writer's block. The best worries are always creative ones.

Joseph Heller, one of my two fellow Distinguished Professors (the other was Elie Wiesel), did not worry about writer's block. He had, he knew and frequently proclaimed, written a great book in *Catch-22*. Unfortunately it had been turned into a mediocre film, whereas *A Clockwork Orange* had not. Heller and I had to appear on the platform at a rowdy *table ronde* in which, to Heller's satisfaction, it was concluded that great books do not turn into great films. The best films, it was said, were always based on mediocre literary materials. Someone affirmed that I did not exist: I was merely an invention of Stanley Kubrick. The newspaper report of the debate said that Joseph Heller and Stanley Kubrick were on the platform. A man in New Orleans called after me with 'Hey – you Kubrick?' I ought to have joined my students to dither over an identity crisis.

My Creative Writing specialists had got over their identity crises, if they had ever had them. Their identities were proleptically writ large on blockbusters bigger than *Catch-22* and more violent than *A Clockwork Orange*. I got off to a bad start with them. I had foolishly arranged to give a lecture in the wilds of Wisconsin on the day of our first meeting and so conveyed a message that they must occupy the time in writing a sestina. The sestina is the most difficult of all verse-forms, and I fancied I could hear growls and knife-whettings pursuing me over the airways. My guilt was exacerbated by shortage of cash. Liana and I had travelled together to a concrete college some distance from Madison with enough money to pay for a night in a motel and three dollars over. We hoped that the students would give us dinner, but all they did was indicate a yoghurt automat in their union building. They all seemed drugged on Milwaukee beer. Liana crossed a perilous highway from the Holiday Inn to a neoned diner and came back with hot chicken and potato salad and fifteen cents change. The man in charge of the diner was probably hiding a Calabrian identity under his name of Joe or Nick and could be beaten down. We took a dawn flight to La Guardia, I both dyspeptic and guilty, and prepared a barricade against the sestina-writers. For Creative Writing was considered by its students to be an extra-mural activity and lessons in it had to be conducted in the instructor's own home. In fact the students arrived moderately unaggressive. One of their lot, inevitably a youth with a *yarmulke*, had written a very competent sestina, though all six key-words were obscene. If you're a real writer, he said, you can write anything. They did not really want to gainsay that.

If they had expected to be admitted to an imported British household, with a pipe-rack, warmed leather slippers, and a calfskin complete Jane Austen, they soon found they were mistaken. For Vincenzo Labella sent Francesca over from Rome to ensure that I

worked on *Moses*, and students were greeted at the door by a tall
Ethiopian beauty, as well as the aroma of frying chicken gizzards.
The rumour went around that I was conducting a *ménage à trois*, but
that was only two-thirds true. They heard Andrea being scolded in
cross Tuscan; they found the monoglot Gianfranco de Bosio anxious
for a new instalment of script, as well as an occasional Michael Lewis
with a new top line and a request for a lyric. They even found a Jesuit
Tom Collins encouraging them to think that a million dollars could
be forthcoming on the provision of three titles and three outlines. In
other words, they entered a literary household.

The black guards below assumed that anybody could go up to my
flat if the magic word student were mentioned, and I found myself
with a number of supernumerary Creative Writers who had not
enrolled, including a very handsome prostitute who wanted to write
romantic novels. On a day on which there was no class, the guards
unwisely, even criminally, allowed up a woman who intended to kill
me. She was the wife of a professor of English literature in South
Carolina whom I had met a year previously when she had
apparently been sane. Now she was clearly not. She alleged that I was
stuffing her brain with my works by remote control, and that I had
arranged for the Times Square ribbon news sign to be programmed
with extracts from my novel *Enderby*. She called me a bastard who
was trying to murder her identity. She had a large handbag with God
knew what weapon in it and was fumbling at this when Liana and
Francesca, who had been out shopping, returned. Francesca got her
reiterating her charge against me while Liana telephoned the police
from the kitchen. A couple of Puerto Rican cops came up, found a
toy gun but a real flick-knife in her bag, then took her away. I could
prefer no charge against a person evidently demented, and I heard no
more. But the black guards had to be more vigilant in future. The
block committee, with rabid loyalty, obscurely hinted that I had let
the black guards down. Ah well, this was New York.

What could I teach these sharp, wary, vigorous Creative Writers?
Only the grammar they should have learned in fourth or fifth grade,
only the professional trickery which shocked them with its insin-
cerity. They were terribly sincere, even when they divined that there
was money in this writing racket if only you cut out the
artsy-shmartsy crap. By professional trickery I meant and mean the
use of repetitive verbal tropes to fix a character in the reader's mind,
helped along by ocular tics and patches of alopecia (give the character
the name Fox, since he has fox-mange); how to describe a seething
party with everybody talking at once; how to convey a stormy sea by

raiding an arbitrarily chosen page of a dictionary (stairwells of foam, waves rearing in stalagmites, precipitating in stalactites, staminiferous in their stalwart stallion-balled stalling angles). Or I could concentrate on opening techniques, with reference to *The Good Soldier* or *Middlemarch*. What I could not evade was the dogged listening to dull work in progress. Wow, that's great, Janice.

What were their chances of publication by New York houses to which they cynically gave names like Loch-in-Knopf, Whorecourt Brace and Sonofabitch, Fucknam, Random Louse? Fortunately none of us knew what had happened in 1969, when, at the age of thirty-two, John Kennedy Toole had committed suicide after the final rejection of his brilliant *A Confederacy of Dunces* (Bob Gottlieb at Knopf was said, probably wrongly, to have provided the last straw). Nor did we know that at least two distinguished New York novelists had had long-published prize-winning novels retyped and sent around under pseudonyms, only to meet not merely rejection but total absence of recognition. Merit was the least of the guarantees of acceptance. Perhaps there was something in what Tom Collins said about selling a book on its title. One of my students wrote a quite unemetic novel he called *Vomit*, and at least one publishing house asked to have a look at it. Another attached the totally irrelevant title *The Philadephia Syndrome* to his work in progress and actually received a small advance. The one student of mine whose brief and quite elegant novel was not merely paid for but actually printed was uniquely unfortunate. When the print-run started some operative pressed the wrong button, the book turned left instead of right, and the entire edition was shredded and pulped. If these young people learned nothing else, they learned how heartbreaking the writing game was.

IT WAS a relief to hear my own words instead of other people's. Professionally delivered too, not rawly mumbled in the curiously unerotic tonalities of New York. *Oedipus the King* opened in Minneapolis and was such a success that the audience was scared of applauding at the end. Stanley Silverman's music, with its relentless sphingine rhythm (4–2–3), helped to stress the ritual nature of the production. People sat on the edges of their seats as though at a murder trial or a revivalist meeting. I had played for one laugh and got it, though the laughter was uneasy. Oedipus says to Tiresias: 'Ruin, ruin. Let us think of the city's ruin. I saved it once. I will again.

I am Oedipus.' Tiresias replies: 'And I am going. Give me your hand, boy.' During the interval a young lady seated behind me vigorously expatiated to her fellows on the nature of Sophoclean humour, a property I did not know existed. It was a good thing that there were no real Sophocles scholars in the audience: they would not have tolerated the hero's on-stage self-blinding, nor the dialogue that followed:

CHILD:	What has happened to his eyes?
CHORUS LEADER:	It is a long story. You will hear it some day.
CHILD:	Who did it to him?
	He had only one enemy. And that was the Sphinx.
	But he killed the Sphinx.
CHORUS LEADER:	Perhaps it was better to be killed by it.
	The riddle was not meant to be answered.
CHILD:	But he answered it. He saved us.
	That's the story we're told.
CHORUS LEADER:	It is dangerous to answer riddles,
	But some men are born to answer them.
	It is the gods' doing. They hide themselves in riddles.
	We must not try to understand too much.
CHILD:	Why?

That 'Why?' is the last word before the final (sung) chorus. I recognised that my adaptation and translation was not really Sophoclean at all, but, I say it again, in the theatre nothing matters except what works. The two ravishingly pretty little girls, daughters of high-class Minneapolitans, who led blind Oedipus off as Ismene and Antigone, were above pedantic considerations of fidelity to a long-dead Greek. They were anxious to meet the author, and they addressed me as Mr Sophocles. 'And which of you is Ismene?' I asked, and was told: 'Oh, I'm Ismene, and she's Antigone.' Thus to characterise, without even one line to speak, was to take the drama seriously in a Sarah Bernhardt way. She used to put make-up on her whole body, though only her face was visible.

The other theatrical venture of the year was painful not in a referred manner but all too damnably directly. The musical *Cyrano* was finally cast, with Christopher Plummer in the lead, Leigh Berry as Roxane (whom, with Daniel Defoe and indeed Alexander's mistress in mind, I called Roxana), Mark Lamos as Christian, Jimmy Blendick as Le Bret, Patrick Hines as Montfleury, Louis Turenne as the Comte de Guiche, Arnold Soboff as Ragueneau. An open audition was held in the Palace Theatre, Manhattan, and it was surprising how few turned up for it. A taxi-driver, who drove me, talkative in the New York hack manner, told me he was a resting actor, so I sent him along to be audited for Christian. He would have been given the part if Mark Lamos had not been better. The production got under way at the Guthrie Theatre, where it was to open in the early spring of 1972. The first scene promised well because it had two production numbers which gave the false impression that it was a genuine Broadway musical. Plummer, equipped with a chest microphone, sang the 'Nose Song', which was a virtuoso performance (inferior, though, as histrionics, to the original nose speech out of which the lyric was concocted), and, at the end of the scene, led the chorus in 'From Now Till Forever' towards the fight with a hundred men at the Porte De Nesles. From then on the songs were merely intrusive: one wanted them to be over quickly so that the story could proceed. There was a good deal of petulance among the actors. Plummer announced often that he was 'going home', and this refrain was taken up even by the orchestrator. Copyists of orchestral parts threatened strikes. Michael Langham, as director, insisted again that this was 'a play with music', not a Broadway musical at all. The final scene, with the broken Cyrano declaring his love and then dying, was harmed by song, but song had to go into it because Gregson the producer insisted on wrenching the whole project into a genre for which it was not fitted. And so, to my shame, Plummer, before dying, croaked:

> I never loved you –
> That word must fly
> And die like smoke in the sky.
> Be thankful for all
> The love that lives on,
> But sometimes let fall
> Just one lonely tear upon
> The memory of
> This truth or this lie –
> I never loved you, my dear love,
> Not I.

The little songs were inflated with grotesquely thick orchestrations. Lewis and I had wanted no more than a seventeenth-century combo, with three or four violins, a flute and oboe but no clarinet (an instrument not yet known in the reign of Louis XIII), preferably seated in near-darkness at the rear of the action, but the Musicians' Union insisted on a pit orchestra of at least thirty-five players. We were not obliged to use all these: silent trumpets and drummers would be quite willing to play cards in the pit so long as they were paid the statutory union rate. We were forced into having the regular brash Broadway sound, with three trombones, in order to justify paying out good solid dollars.

The Minneapolis opening was not quite a failure, except that the audience clearly wanted more play and less music. Songs that merely broke into the action without being built up into production numbers received no applause. It seemed necessary to continue writing more and more songs in the hope that one or other of them would be a show-stopper. Christian was entitled to a song in the first scene, so he was given 'A Man Without Words', which was taken out after one performance. A song for the Gascon cadets was intended to explain what the key-word *panache* meant:

> To follow your military calling
> While the Alps and the Pyrenees are falling.
> To pare your nails when the doomsday trumpets crash –
> That's panache.

This too fell flat and had to go. Desperately I penned a lyric for Cyrano in the style of 'Impossible Dream' in *Man of la Mancha*, which gave a more sentimental, self-sacrificing meaning to *panache*, but this had to go as well. Gregson was as good as ordering show-stoppers and telling us that we would lose our asses if we did not come up with them. I had to protest through my new agent, Robert Lantz, when the limit of eighty-odd songs, all used once, if at all, and then abandoned, had been reached. Enough was enough, or too much, already.

This was a strenuous time. I was commuting from New York to Minneapolis, since both Gregson and Plummer wanted their lyricist there on the spot, as well as fulfilling my nationwide lecture engagements. Our insufficient *Cyrano* would have to compete on Broadway with *A Little Night Music*, with lyrics and music by Stephen Sondheim and Len Carriou, who had been Oedipus, in the lead. The songs in this were said to be brilliant. 'Your show is sick,' pronounced Robert Lantz with Teutonic bluntness, 'and it is your duty to make it well. Your work at City College is of very secondary importance compared with that obligation. Your star is crying out for you, and you must bow to his wishes.' One of the star's wishes was for a really devastating show-stopper which should stand as the musical counterpart to Cyrano's virtuoso speech about his inter-galactic voyage. Lewis and I had already written an eight-minute number which was a kind of Holst's *Planets* in miniature, but this would not do. We ended with a nonsense song, very sub-*Finnegans Wake*, full of occult dirty meanings. The title, according to the double-record album I have before me, was 'The Thither Thother Thide of the'. I blush. I blushed.

I was not the only one to blush when Gregson decided that Michael Langham, the brilliant pupil of Tyrone Guthrie, the director of an exquisitely beautiful *Love's Labour's Lost* and a very notable Broadway *Andorra*, was not good enough for this ghastly *Cyrano*. He was dismissed in his own theatre and replaced by Michael Kidd, well-known as a dancer and a choreographer, who demanded wholesale rewriting of the libretto and took it upon himself to refurbish some of the lyrics. Kidd seemed to want the singing nuns of the last scene to be turned into Vietnam war widows, giving out their 'Autumn Carol' with stylised wistful march-steps. Odd flat quips were inserted about women's liberation. The period dialogue grew dangerously up-to-date. For no good reason Montfleury's comedy *Clorise* was turned into a tragedy, with purple vestments and minor chords. I had my name deleted from the credits as librettist, so that the book was now 'based upon Anthony Burgess's adaptation of *Cyrano de Bergerac*'. In its revised form *Cyrano* left Minneapolis and went to Toronto.

In merely geographical terms, Toronto is closer to New York than is Minneapolis, but it lies in another country. Commuting would have been easy enough if the immigration officials on either side of the frontier had let me whiz through on the brandishing of a passport, which was the procedure with Canadian and United States citizens. But, though a subject of the same queen, I was begrudged entry into the senior dominion. Entering Americans got 'Hi, Joe' and 'Okay, Stan' but not I. How long do you intend to stay in Canada? One night only. And then the same tomorrow. I don't think we can believe that, sir. On one occasion of trying to return home – that is, to New York – I met very stern opposition.

'Why do you wish to enter the United States?'

'I'm already there, along with my wife and son. I am a Distinguished Professor at the City College of New York. Indeed, in two hours' time I have a lecture there.'

'You cannot enter without a PJ3041. This you do not have.'

'I've never heard of a PJ whatever it is.'

'There's no call to be facetious, sir. You should have obtained one at the US Embassy in your country of residence.'

'How do I get one now?'

'You return to your country of residence.'

'Now? You mean now?'

'I'm only following regulations.'

And so on. I faced the prospect of being unable to enter either Canada or the United States, spending a lifetime in the no-man's-land of Toronto airport, where, insolently I thought, the United States Immigration Department had set up shop. I would have to beg dimes, unshaven, for a cup of coffee. But I got mad. I was already in the way of getting mad because of Christopher Plummer's madness. I had had to go to a recording studio outside Toronto to hear Plummer make a 45 rpm disc of two of his songs, accompanied by an orchestra of fifty. He swore that 'I Never Loved You' was being played a tone higher than at the previous day's rehearsal and threatened to go home. To which the only possible reply was: 'Jesus Christ, man, do you honestly believe that an arranger and copyists would stay up all night to transpose this silly song from C major to D major merely for your discomfiture? Have some bloody sense for God's sake.' Show business and the bureaucracy of immigration were showing a madness which made me mad. And then I had to go to my office in City College and be greeted with: 'What did you mean by that shit you gave us yesterday?' But it was an achievement to be permitted to do this. 'Okay. You'd better see your campus counsellor about getting an XY4298, which will do as a substitute for a PJ3041 but valid only for two weeks. Okay?' Not okay, not at all okay. 'You talk of a campus counsellor? Damn it, man, I'm a Distinguished bloody Professor.' And then: 'Your tone of voice is hardly conducive to making me believe that claim, sir.'

Cyrano went down moderately well in Toronto, which greeted Christopher Plummer as a distinguished native son. Poor Michael Lewis went on hammering out new tunes in his hotel bedroom, where a piano had been installed. When the show transferred to Boston, he was still hammering out tunes. But Boston took very kindly to *Cyrano*, and it had to be retained at the Colonial Theater for a further two weeks. Plummer came to life at the end to be granted a standing ovation. There was something supposititious about the cheers, however, as though he were being applauded for something he could have done if only he had been permitted to – namely, act Cyrano straight without the burden of the lyrics and music. Still,

Broadway, always sensitive to provincial successes (provincial? Boston provincial? The show business magazine *Variety* always called Boston 'the Hub'), tried to grab my services for other projects while I was still a New Yorker. A young man named Stephen Schwartz, responsible for *Godspell* and a new musical called *Pippin* (about Pépin le Bref), wanted to work with me on an adaptation of Thomas Mann's *The Transposed Heads*. The erudition of these purveyors of near-trash was always astonishing. I was commissioned to draft a libretto for a musical about Houdini, in which, improbably, Orson Welles was to play the lead. I actually completed the book and lyrics for a stage version of *Les Enfants du Paradis*, but Michel Leblanc, the elected composer, decided to declare that he would work only with the poet Richard Wilbur. Zero Mostel wanted to play Leopold Bloom, whom he had already played in Burgess Meredith's *Ulysses in Nighttown*, in a musical version of *Ulysses*. He was too old for the part, and he died shortly after. But I was to write this musical version, under the title *The Blooms of Dublin*, and hear on radio, instead of seeing on the stage, its first performance on 2 February 1982, to celebrate the centenary of Joyce's birth.

I had energy in 1972, and I needed energy. New York exacts every ounce – physical, intellectual, creative – but it feeds the nerves while trying to exhaust them. There was much more to do than I have already recounted – reviewing for the New York press, giving free lectures to local bodies, trying to cope with the demands of Tom Collins ex SJ, who, while waiting for the three books on the three Georges (Gershwin, Patton, III) which would bring in the million dollar advance, required something small and thoughtful to be written immediately. I ended up with a novella called *The Clockwork Testament*, which, as it dealt with the death of my poet Enderby, was subtitled *Enderby's End*. This recounted the last day in his life, which was not too dissimilar from the continuing days of my own. Enderby's beach restaurant in Tangier has been visited by a Hollywood producer-director, not unlike Kubrick, who gets on the cheap from the innocent poet a film scenario based on Gerard Manley Hopkins's 'The Wreck of the Deutschland'. This sublime mystical poem is converted, not by Enderby, into a farrago of clerical sex and Nazi violence; nevertheless, Enderby is blamed for being the father of a piece of pornography. He is blamed daily over the telephone, as I was for the film of *A Clockwork Orange*, in Adrienne Rich's flat, which he inhabits alone, masturbating and gorging on the wealth of the Manhattan supermarkets. He, like me, is a visiting professor under threat from black students. Like me, he carries a swordstick, though he bravely draws blood with his in a scene of attempted rape on the IRT. Like me, he is visited by a mad lady who threatens murder; unlike me, he is shot at but survives only to die of a heart attack. He leaves unfinished a long narrative poem about Augustinian predestination and original sin, contrasted with Pelagian free will and innocence. The work was written in ten days and made into a beautifully illustrated book by an artistic team brought together by Tom Collins. Knopf published this, and I received money for it, though not much. From the British publication I received nothing whatever. The five thousand pounds advance was paid to Collins in his agential capacity and he kept it all.

Robert Lantz was naturally annoyed about this intrusion of jesuitical sharp practice into my creative or (properly) commercial life, and so was Deborah Rogers, who, visiting New York on business, joined with Lantz in deploring my unprofessionalism, innocence, and treachery. Not that I was really robbing either of anything like a sizeable commission. Lantz, though he could occasionally rhapsodise about the beauty of Mann's prose in *Lotte in Weimar*, was inclined to evaluate literature in strictly financial terms. In those terms I was no asset to an agent who brokered the services of Elizabeth Taylor and Richard Burton at a million dollars a film, thus earning one hundred thousand on each deal. He told me, on the strength, or weakness, of my sales, that I was a failure as a professional novelist. This, of course, I knew, but I had believed that it was the duty of a literary agent to encourage his clients. Having been robbed of five thousand pounds by one go-between and made to hang my head before two others, I began to consider that the time must sooner or later come to make my own deals. The time came when the *Time-Life* corporation asked me to contribute to their series of illustrated books on great cities of the world. Naturally I, the brief New Yorker, must write about New York. When I achieved a polished and repolished typescript this was at once processed by *Time* staffmen into *Time* prose, which has what are termed corporate-level virtues. Liana took the photographs that were to illustrate the book, but *Time-Life* considered that her eye was too individual, insufficiently corporate. I made a bad deal – outright sale of property world-wide, no royalties – and wondered if I could ever make a good one. Still, I paid no agent's commission.

Liana was, when not eating the city alive with her cameras, recording its voices. This was an aspect of the dialectological concern inseparable from her old profession of teaching the teaching of

Italian. Happy the husband whose wife knows what a bilabial fricative is. She also turned Manhattan into an isle of fearful joy – so much to see, so much cultural variety, all to be noted with that extra alertness needful in a city of muggers. She also imported Italian chic. I recently came across a copy of *The New Yorker*, not previously seen, which reported my giving a luncheon talk on *The Ring and the Book* to the New York Browning Society. I am described as looking 'a bit bearish, but very modern', whatever that means. As for Liana, 'dark and beautiful, like Anna Magnani', she astonished. 'Wow,' a woman is reported as crying, 'Gucci pants at a Browning lunch. Now I've seen everything.' As for our son Andrea, whom New York was maturing like a forced plant, he fell in love with *Cyrano*, which he had seen in Minneapolis, Toronto and Boston and was now to see on Broadway. It was the pretty banal little tunes he fell chiefly in love with, though the sacrificial aspect of *panache* was to have a large influence on his love-life, and he yearned to play the tunes on a wind instrument. He went back to Italy to play them on a clarinet but, later, he played more exalted melodies on an oboe. He is still playing the oboe, and the cor anglais as well. His musical career may be said to have started with a theatrical experience which brought me little but distress.

Cyrano opened in the late spring of 1972 at the Palace Theatre. I attended the première but did not join the nail-biting company at Sardi's, dithering through the night while they awaited the reviews in the early editions. Clive Barnes in the *New York Times* could make or break a Broadway production. It was strange that a book could sell or a film draw queues in spite of atrocious reviews, while a stage show depended on the verdicts of journalistic hacks. Actually *Cyrano* did better than it deserved. Clive Barnes: 'Christopher Plummer triumphs in a great performance. In this *Cyrano* he is simply magnificent. The whole musical has drive and style.' Leonard Harris, on CBS television: '*Cyrano* is a big, romantic and melodious musical! A rousing addition to the season!' Allan Wallach in *Newsday*: '*Cyrano* is unabashedly sentimental and swashbuckling – great fun in its swordplay, horseplay and lovers' deceptions. Christopher Plummer is all that any Cyrano – musical or otherwise – should be: flamboyant, witty and filled with that indefinable quality Cyrano calls panache.' Martin Gottfried in *Women's Wear Daily*: 'Christopher Plummer is brilliant. One of the greatest actors alive.' And so on. But (I have quoted selectively; indeed, I have quoted the record album cover) there was always the reservation I had nursed from the beginning: why goldfoil the lily? The play itself would have

cost less, and Plummer, unchained to song, would have been twice
as effective.

Cyrano did not run long. It was too costly. Lewis and I had to agree
to forgo our nightly earnings so that the actors, and that thirty-five-
piece orchestra, could be paid. Then the Watergate scandal broke and
New Yorkers stayed at home to watch television. The New York
Arts Club gave me a gold medal for services to the New York arts,
the academic year ended, Liana began to pack her copies of the
Sunday edition of the *New York Times*. I reflected that only in this
remarkable city was it possible for a professor of literature to be
associated with a Broadway musical and a notorious movie. But
perhaps Academia was too tolerant of its defilement by the demotic,
as it was too eager to find virtue in Black English and beauty in
subway graffiti. I was invited to deliver the Commencement address
at Fordham University and expected noble music on the organ. But
the faculty and graduands were entertained by electronic instruments
and a black girl who sang out of *Godspell* into a microphone. She then
sang

> Reach out an' touch
> Somebody's han'.
> Make this a better world
> If you can

and cried: 'Come on, folks, touch.' So shamefacedly robed doctors,
masters and bachelors had to. I abandoned the speech I had prepared
and improvised a tirade against vulgarity and debasement. It was, I
suppose, elitist. It did not go down well. Fordham's dissatisfaction
with me even got into the correspondence columns of the *Times
Literary Supplement*. I was assured, as I had been assured before and
have been since, that never again would I be permitted to enter the
United States: the academic world, through the political, would
exert its clout.

And yet I had been offered the opportunity to become a permanent
New Yorker, in one of the most reputable university gifts the city
had to bestow. I could take over the chair of the retiring Lionel
Trilling at Columbia, rise above show business and the novelist's
craft and become a professorial observer of literature, a decently
withdrawn arbiter of its values. It was a terrible temptation that still
haunts me. Security for life, high status, the dignity of scholarship. I
think, however, I made the right decision in refusing the honour. It
was not really suited to one masochistically inclined to the hard

knocks of the Grub Street life, one not inclined to disdain vulgarity in the right place, one not averse to scandal. And I was more given to the mockery of scholarship than to the practice of it. For good or ill (ill, so the British critics mostly said) I was a novelist, unsure of my income, moderately sure of my vocation. My year as a New Yorker had ended, and I would not be renewing it. Francesca flew back to Rome to await our later arrival. Liana, Andrea and I took passage to Naples (you want I should throw these in the water?) on the *Michelangelo*. Andrea spent most nights away from his cabin, in the company of the granddaughter of the poet Ogden Nash. It was one of his rare literary connections. He was growing up now.

THE EIGHT sixty-minute *puntate* of *Mosè* or *Moses* were finished in the flat above the Piazza Santa Cecilia. There was too much material, but there always is. The novelist, writing dialogue, forgets how slow actors are in delivering it, and how they like to maintain meaningful silences with no particular meaning. I wanted the delightful episode of Balaam and his ass to be done as an animated cartoon for the pleasure of the Israelite children; I wanted the sad love story of Zimri and Cozbi to be given the full romantic treatment, with burning kisses in close-up, which Italian film-makers call *primo piano*. But Moses must not be too long off the screen, since he was to be played by Burt Lancaster.

Then we moved to Piazza Padella in Bracciano, where the work of expansion and reconstruction – payment for the script – was said to be coming to an end. The house was rather like a ship. One entered by way of B deck, went below to C deck and D deck, then mounted again to A deck and took the ladder to the windy top. D deck was an ancient cellar converted to a boiler room though the boiler was not to work. B deck was a saloon or *salone* with a doorless archway leading to a study and library. A door led to the corridor we already knew, with its two bathrooms and master bedroom. On C deck was another *salone* with a neighbouring bedroom for Andrea. We already knew A deck. The work in the cellar had unearthed various Etruscan artefacts, most of them appropriated (ostensibly on behalf of the Italian state) by the *muratore* or builder. The house was a roomy one, but I was removed from its wider spaces and its unfinished work. This was territory for Italian altercation. I, the foreign *professore*, was confined to the bedroom and ordered to write: the clacking of a typewriter might encourage the dilatory labourers to labour.

I wrote a book long commissioned by André Deutsch, who was building what he called a Language Library. It was about James Joyce's use of language, and it was permitted phonological and morphological technicalities. I called it *Joysprick*, which any reader of *Finnegans Wake* will see is a fusion of *Joycesprach*, joystick, the prick that brings joy and the prick of conscience or agenbite of inwit. This was the work I took in a Gucci case to be photocopied in Rome, only to be robbed of it by *scippatori*. I wrote the book again at once, since my brain had already photocopied it but cerebral photocopies are apt to fade. I then started drafting a musical version of *Ulysses*. I had no piano at the time – one was to come later as payment for the script of the unmade film *Il Fascistibile* – and had to rely on my inner ear to assess its tonalities. But, whatever Ernest Newman believed about the superiority of imagined to enacted sound, the outer ear needs the physical ictus, the gorgeous mists of harmonics. Liana and Andrea and I got into the Bedford Dormobile and toured the Italy north of Bracciano looking for somebody with a keyboard: all I wanted was a couple of hours with one, however untuned, to bring my short score to life. But Italy between Rome and Milan seemed to have no keyboards. So we examined Etruscan remains, having now a proprietary interest in them, and, in Etruscan tombs on the D. H. Lawrence route, heard erudite German tourists sneering at the small knowledge of the Italian guides. I worked away at the score in outdoor *trattorie* and had visiting mafiosi pointing the finger and saying 'You not-a write-a *musica* that-a way.' My bottle of ink spilled in the wind and obliterated a complex passage, but an Italian woman, pointing to the ink-pattern, said '*Che bello.*' The Italians are visually troped; music to them is only the tenor voice and its sexual thrust.

In a bar in Cremona, a town noted for its fiddles, we found a piano, long locked, the key lost, but hefty Neapolitans, in the joy of expecting to hear 'Santa Lucia', forced it open. They apologised, in the Neapolitan manner, for working in exile in an unvocal town like Cremona, thus letting down their city and their own talent. I did not get very far with the trying out of *The Blooms of Dublin*. We had ghastly tenor duets of a folkloric nature, with improvised tonic-and-dominant accompaniments, and fragments of the better-known Italian operas. I was getting to know Italy now. It is unjust that Italy should claim musical pre-eminence, even forcing Italian on music as its international language, when Italy's genius is so visual. No nation can build towns as beautiful nor claim a better right to regard nature as a shapeless substance to be redeemed by urbifaction. The Italians are not Wordsworthian. Man fulfils himself in the town. There is too much wild nature in music, and it has to be tamed into simple four-square patterns, as in Verdi and Bellini. The tenor does not proclaim Byronically to the woods and hills: he is a kind of sexy politician for the town *piazza*. The Italians would listen to Aaron, but not to Moses.

Moses took us back to Rome. The actors who were to film in Cinecittà had arrived or, Romans and Rome-dwellers, were already there. Burt Lancaster and the woman he was living with were fitted out with a *palazzo* outside the city. His son William was to play the young Moses. The French new-wave star Tertzieff, who was to be the Pharaoh, knew no English but, with commendable professionalism, had learned his English lines by heart so as to give no trouble with later lip-synchronisation. There was a huge press conference over which Sir Lew Grade presided. I approved of Lew Grade, who had admirable Cuban cigars and a no-nonsense attitude to the project. For the benefit of the more intellectual Italian journalists I stated why the Mosaic theme was important: here was the definitive establishment of monotheism, as well as the beginning of the alphabet and the theological contract which affirmed free will. Lew Grade merely said: 'We're doing it to show confidence in our two countries, which are still great countries though they've both being having a bloody hard time.' A journalist called: '*Quanto costa?*' Lew said: 'That's all I hear, kwanter coster. Well, it's going to cost a lot, but it's going to rake in a lot.'

How much it was going to rake in did not concern me. I had done my work and been paid for it. My responsibility as sole script-writer (despite the eventual credits, the contributions of the Italians had to be jettisoned) was, however, considered to be still going on: big actors ask for changes, demand explanations of lines meant to be ambiguous, discuss the Hollywood horror called motivation. Anthony Quayle, who was playing Aaron, had already telephoned from London to ask what I meant by the character's look of 'somewhat untrustworthy nobility'. Burt Lancaster, it was clear, was going to make his own changes and sneak them into the can – easy to do when the director knew no English. I had otherwise nothing against Burt, except his unwillingness to take women seriously: he admired my wife's body more than her intelligence. He had worked well with Visconti in *Il Gattopardo* and knew all about the bewildering polyglot mess of making films in Europe: different performers speak mutually unintelligible languages and have to pretend to understand each other. Hebrew and Arabic would be added to the Babel when the company got out of Cinecittà and moved to Israel. I kept out of Israel, though Andrea stayed a week at the King David Hotel in Jerusalem, complaining of the bland diet. There were warplanes zooming over the desert: this meant that all the dialogue had to be dubbed in Tel-Aviv or Rome.

I kept away from the whole project because I had a novel to write. This was *Napoleon Symphony*, which required the big architect's table I had in the Rome flat, since, as well as the typewriter and manuscript, I needed maps, battle plans, chronological tables, reproductions of the paintings of David, and the orchestral score of Beethoven's 'Eroica' Symphony. One of the problems of the undertaking was the proposed brevity of the book – 365 printed pages, as I gauged it: compression was a headache. Galdós had based a four-volume novel on the structure of the 'Eroica', but expansion fights against the essence of the symphony, which can be concise because it is able to say so many things at the same time. The regret of all novelists who have been brought up on music is that counterpoint, which mirrors the multiplicity of life, is not possible in verbal language. Prose and poetry are monodic, though poetry less so than prose: what William Empson had shown in his *Seven Types of Ambiguity* was that words as used by a poet can convey more than one meaning, and, in the seventh type, opposed meanings, as with the 'buckle' in Hopkins's 'The Windhover'. 'Buckle' means both to collapse, like a bicycle wheel, and to fasten for action, as with a military belt. But this is to turn a word into a chord, not a passage of words into a piece of counterpoint.

In *Finnegans Wake* the chordal technique goes to the limit – puns are chords. Shaun is 'mielodorous' – meaning that he is melodious, malodorous, and smells of honey. The Celtic twilight is also the cultic toilette, where a brief phrase more than a word suggests an elementary counterpoint, as does the 'abnihilisation of the etym' – atomic destruction is also (*ab nihilo*) the re-creation of meaning from nothing. In *Napoleon Symphony* I wanted extended fugal effects but I could only get them through juxtaposition. In the *marcia funebre* of the 'Eroica' there is a double fugue. Its parallel in my novel is the building of the two bridges – for the *fuga* or flight of Napoleon's army from Russia – over the Berezina. This is described alternately in soldier's low language and the chaste prose of a military chronicle. But there is no effect of simultaneity. Nor here, where the voices of Napoleon, Josephine, and her children Eugène and Hortense are raised after the discovery of Josephine's adultery:

O GOD TO THINK THAT ONE TO WHOM I

ENTRUSTED MY VERY INNERMOST HEART IN KEEPING but I swear it is all long over it was foolish but it is long done I have lived a life of solitary virtue there is evidence talk to Madame Gohier your whole family is against me they will say anything I WOULD HAVE DONE BETTER TO LISTEN TO MY FAMILY A MAN CAN TRUST ONLY HIS KIND O GOD GOD THE TREACHERY LET ME NEVER TRUST ANY WOMAN AGAIN I WHO SPENT SUCH TRUST ON A WORTHLESS WORTHLESS *let us speak for our mother let us speak for ourselves let us be a happy and united family she loves you we love you you love her* YES EUGENE YOU ARE A BRAVE FINE YOUNG MAN AND YOU HORTENSE ARE O GOD GOD GOD I was foolish God knows I was foolish but I learned my lesson long before these calumnies spread

I was doing my best but perhaps, as in the Sirens episode of *Ulysses*, the best of a musicalising novelist could only demonstrate that the art of narrative is not the art of the symphony. My concentration on literary parallels for musical concepts was to get me into trouble with the more naïve critics, who thought I was committing unforgivable errors when I misspelt the name of the Balcombe family on St Helena as Bascombe and gave *Volk* the wrong gender – *der* instead of *das*. I was, in these and other ways, trying to plant an S into the reader's mind – wrongly present or wrongly absent – because the key of the 'Eroica' is S or Es or E flat. When I looked for a structural opposition corresponding to a tonal one in Beethoven, I could find it only in an opposition of elements – earth versus water. This proved too banal for the reviewers. Napoleon fears water, unless it can be tamed into civic fountains: he feels himself to be in control of the land. I thought of earth as the home key of E flat and water as the distant (in terms of the tonal cycle) key of D flat, which begins the coda in the first movement of the 'Eroica'. My coda to the first part of the novel begins with Napoleon's brooding over the perfidy of water, the female element; an attempt at his destruction by a terrorist bomb immediately follows. If the D flat of danger can be read as C sharp, it will enable the coda to find its way back to the opening E flat theme, which contains C sharp, and a final assertion of triumph. England is the ruler of the perfidious element, and English-financed terrorism can be met with the rigour of greater police control in France. The enemy's D flat becomes Napoleon's C sharp, which will take him, through home-associated keys, to the E flat of his coronation and the end of the first movement. This goes further than the blind tuner's tuning-fork in Joyce's Sirens episode, which stands for absolute pitch and is expressed through the tapping of the blind stripling's stick. Joyce got away with it and hence sanctified similar tricks. I was to learn that I was living in the era of post-modernism.

In the last movement of the 'Eroica' Beethoven explicitly identifies his hero (once Napoleon; anonymous after the assassination of the conspiring duc d'Enghien) with the mythical hero Prometheus. He takes a theme from his ballet music *Prometheus* and weaves variations on it. I heard the first four notes of Beethoven's bass – E flat B flat B flat E flat – as singing INRI – *Interfaciamus Napoleonem Regem Imperatorem* – and made a blasphemous identification of Christ and Prometheus, Prometheus being Napoleon removed from history and transferred to mythology. INRI pounds away like four nails being hammered in (the cross is appropriate to St Helena, since St Helena found the cross). As a parallel to Beethoven's variations, I decided to present Napoleon's exile and death on St Helena in a series of pastiches of prose styles from Jane Austen to Henry James (shot through with tropes from Gerard Manley Hopkins in a last desperate attempt at counterpoint). As the dying Henry James thought he was Napoleon, it seemed in order to make Napoleon a brief Jamesian hero. I used verse as well – a pastiche of Wordsworth's *Prelude* and one of Tennyson's *In Memoriam*. At the very end, for Napoleon-Prometheus-Christ's resurrection, I merely, and arbitrarily, ransacked the dictionary:

> . . . the bellowing gnu, ships and clarinets and tempests,
> the Son of Sirach, hazel and witch moth, cuckolds and
> warlocks, sorrel and alexia, Sir Thomas and Breslau and
> all the flowing wine of the world rejoiced. Rejoice. And
> again I say rejoice. And I say aga INRI ng bells bells
> bells and rejoice. Rejoice.

Here Beethoven disappears and Henry Purcell takes over with his 'Bell' Anthem – 'Rejoice in the Lord alway'. The naïve saw, or heard, a final tribute to Joyce, but it is not really there.

The point about following the structure of the 'Eroica' was less the looking for verbal parallels to musical effects than accepting the non-linear presentation of the hero's life that seems to lie under, or over, Beethoven's score. The hero dies in the second movement, is resurrected in the third and fourth and, at the end of the finale, is seen on horseback leading his troops once more into battle. The orthodox novel cannot encompass death and resurrection – not even a novel about Jesus Christ – but music evidently can, and for this novelist to submit wilfully to musical form was a sly way of announcing victory over the grave. Joyce's way of denying death in *Finnegans Wake* is perhaps rather crudely cyclical: you finish the novel in the middle of a sentence, whose continuation and end you find by turning back to the first page. But, with a cycle, you can have no triumphant finale. It was Beethoven's triumphant finale I wanted and got.

The composition of this novel was arduous. Historical facts had to be checked, battle plans closely examined, but, in the modern manner, the reader had to be kept in doubt about the competence of the narrator. (This is a kind of bet-hedging: genuine auctorial errors can be blamed on an author the author has invented.) The work contains a number of anachronisms – Napoleon hears the Thought Police of *Nineteen Eighty-Four* speaking in French; the failed assassin Stapps quotes Hans Sachs's final monologue in *Die Meistersinger*. But the mere fact of writing in contemporary English imposes the duty of anachronism. When, much later, I wrote *The Kingdom of the Wicked*, which is about the struggle of Christianity to survive in the first century AD, I reflected that even to use the word 'assassin' was anachronistic. The Old Man of the Mountains employed *assassini* or hashish-eaters to kill Christians, but that was a long time after SS Peter and Paul. This discouragement about language became an encouragement to make willed historical errors: there are disguised references to Oscar Wilde and Freud and, grossest of all, Luke the physician has read Juvenal, who is yet to be born. But if Shakespeare could make Ulysses quote Aristotle and have clocks striking in ancient Rome, a modern writer on historical themes need not be too pedantic about exactitude. Human nature does not change, and human nature is what fiction is about.

Napoleon Symphony was published, on both sides of the Atlantic, in 1974. The reviews were mixed. Peter Ackroyd, in the *Spectator*, said: 'Mr Burgess employs a variety of styles in an excessively self-conscious way, with the result that any dialogue between recognisable human beings seems a trifle cracked . . . We are not particularly amused.' *The New Yorker* said that 'the substance and tone of this book and the Eroica Symphony are worlds apart. The music is noble and grand; the book, for the most part, is embarrassingly base.' It spoke of 'idle historical gossip' and 'soldierly bluster' and deemed the whole work a 'misguided venture'. The *Economist* found me 'too clever by half', gave me 'an Alpha for ingenuity', but complained: 'Dammitall, who can have the *Eroica* and the life of Napoleon filed in his head for ready reference?' The *Washington Post Book World* talked of a 'novel of Joycean virtuosity'. The sacred name was always coming up, as though Joyce were the sole fictional innovator: Galdós was not mentioned, nor Bely, nor even Sterne. Paul Chipchase, in *The Tablet*, called the book 'a rich vast growling narrative poem sometimes in prose' and added: 'The thought that wove it never dropped a stitch.' This pleased me, as it was a line from one of Enderby's sonnets: Chipchase had read something of mine other than the work under review. Women reviewers, as was to be expected, were appalled. Victoria Glendinning, in the *New Statesman*, said: 'The heart sinks, the eyes glaze when faced with the prospect of reading Burgess: his writing sets up an initial hostility because it is so noisy.' Lorna Sage, in the *Observer*, spoke of 'a wonderful deadness: which is really the paradox of Anthony Burgess, as it is with so many of the writers who currently get the best fun out of the novel – he is original, inventive, idiosyncratic even, and yet the ingredients are synthetic, ready-made. His own attitude to this, so far as one can extricate anything so direct from the novel, is determinedly, manically cheerful. Better the collective unwisdom of the verbal stew, he would say, than any tyrannous signature.' This last statement is probably profound. Emma Tennant, in the *Listener*, spoke of a 'vulgar-Freudian' touch and concluded that the book read 'like a nightmare future'. Frank Kermode, in the *Manchester Guardian Weekly*, said kindly that I was 'writing very serious comedy and doing it with extraordinary resource, variety and pace. And if his imagination must, in the last analysis, seem un-Beethovenian, those are still Beethovenian qualities.' And Peter Lennon, on 1 December 1974, picked it for the *Sunday Times* as the best book of the year.

I quote these reviews neither to qualify hostility with occasional praise, nor to damp praise with rejection, but again to show how useless the reviewer's craft is to the practising novelist. I knew better than anyone that the book was a failure – as, on a far superior scale, *Finnegans Wake* is a failure – but no art can progress unless failure is sometimes risked. Those who sensed that the book failed could not say why; they had to fall back on highly subjective responses, finding dirt and vulgarity and a general lack of gentility in the representation of a soldier's career which was, of necessity, dirty, vulgar, and ungenteel. The anonymous critic in the *Times Literary Supplement* said that the soldiers' 'lingo recalls the Home Guard more readily than the Old Guard', but, when the book got into French, that lingo was Old Guardish enough. It was apparently wrong to have

Napoleon's troops grousing: 'When do we get some fucking leave, how about our back pay, I've got this pain in the balls, citizen sergeant.' The critics of London and New York, especially if they are women, will always make *ça pue* gestures at the bad smell of the content if they cannot discover what is wrong with the form.

When, if I may anticipate by a few years, *Symphonie Napoléon*, in the virtuoso translation of Hortense Chabrier and Georges Belmont, was published in Paris, the critical response was interesting. The French intellectuals were, perhaps having read Peyrefitte's *Le Mal Français*, suffering a phase of breast-beating unusual in the land that invented chauvinism. They lamented that no French novelist had yet celebrated their great Corsican adequately, and that it had to be left to a British novelist to do their work for them with something like Rabelaisian verve. They could not, however, understand why *un romancier anglais* (the French do not much care for the term *britannique*) should want to write about Napoleon with a kind of comic sympathy. They had to be told, in interviews on radio and television, that my father had said, over my cradle, 'Perhaps he'll be a new Napoleon,' and that we North-Western Catholics were more European than British. My grandmother had sung, 'The French are on the sea, says the Shan Van Vocht'. The writing of the novel was, they had to learn, expressive of a social, cultural and religious division that still went on in the land of my birth.

Napoleon Symphony (the title, if I may make one last reference to a reviewer's response, was considered pretentious, as if a symphony, like an epic poem, were something more than a mere form) was not likely to make me much money. What money was coming into the *Casa Borghese* in Bracciano, where the novel was finished, was only obliquely earned by fiction. *A Clockwork Orange*, solely because of Kubrick's film, had appeared in many countries and in languages I could not read. The Bulgarian, Czech and Polish publishers sequestered the royalties, and the Israelis, who had produced both a Hebrew and a Russian version of the book, did not pay up. The Russian translation I read with interest. I expected that the translator would call *nadsat* something like *tin*, that *chelloveck* would be *man* and *groodies bresti*, but he had been delighted to find a good part of the lexis already Russian and his work partly done for him. This version was only for Russian-speaking émigrés: the book never got into the Soviet Union, nor did the film.

Film was my work in the hot Roman summer of 1973. Uncountable cans of *Moses* were sent from Israel to the International Recording Studio in Rome, and, in intense heat with no air, Michael

Billingsly, Andrea and myself got down to work with the moviola and the stern task of editing. The major actors had already post-synchronised their lines, but odd fighting Hebrews flashed into view mouthing nothing. Fresh dialogue had to be written to accommodate scenes that had crept in in defiance of the script, to be dubbed later by the hack actors of all races that infested Rome. The major performers had deviated from the lines I had given them. Burt Lancaster as Moses had a few final words with the Pharaoh before handing over as Israelite spokesman to his brother Aaron. I had written:

'You will not be hearing from me again.'
'Why not, cousin Moses?'
'Because I am slow of speech.'

Burt, for reasons of his own, had changed that last line to 'Because I am uncircumcised of lips,' accompanying the words with a kind of nail-clipping gesture in the region of his mouth. How did one make him revert to a statement that made sense, as well as having biblical authority? He could not be called back from California for less than a minute's work. We found a back view of Moses in another scene and Billingsly himself dubbed in the correct words. Billingsly was a young American who had come to Rome to study art and been drawn into the film industry. He was a fine cutter and patcher, and long experience with the poring over of visible but silent (or unintelligible) vocal organs on the moviola had turned him into a first-class phonetician. He knew what sounds the actors on the tiny screen were uttering, even when he was ignorant of their languages. If the sounds were hopelessly exotic, he could still fabricate an intelligible and relevant English out of them. Being American, he could contrive an acceptable imitation of the Lancaster voice. When we came to a close-up of Anthony Quayle as Aaron shouting to the Israelites: 'God has chosen people like you and I' (inexcusable in a classical actor), we had to find a brief close-up of the back of his head so that I could dub in the correct 'me'. I, like Quayle, was, am, British.

My own background as a teacher of phonetics began to prove useful, and not only in *Moses*. The films made at Cinecittà (one of Mussolini's more lasting gifts to the Italian people) were, and still are, of two kinds – those for domestic consumption which, hoping for sale in the United States as well, are shot in Italian and later dubbed into English, and the international productions, like our

Moses and the films of Fellini, which have polyglot casts and have to be dubbed into all the major languages when shooting is over. I wrote acceptable synchronisable English for a number of producers in Rome. Fellini's films were the easiest to dub. The master, reconciled to the impossibility of using microphone and camera in concert, used to insist that his actors justify the opening and shutting of their mouths by merely counting – *uno, due, tre . . . eins, zwei, drei . . . wahid, itsnayn, tsalatsa.* This would enable him to say: 'Take it back to thirteen' (or *tredici* or *dreizehn* or *tsalatsat ashar*). Anyone with experience of the teaching of languages could always look for the counting rhythm in the movement of the actor's head. When I dubbed some lines for Fellini's *Casanova*, I saw that the habit of post-synchronisation was imposing a limitation of techniques: there could not be too many close-ups. But in *Moses* there were a lot of close-ups of characters saying the wrong thing: it was all too evident that the director knew no English.

I said earlier that the occasional anachronism does not harm a historical novel. Spoken anachronisms of the grosser kind are instinctively avoided by the novelist, who tries to create a timeless language without idioms or slang. This applies too to the writer of scripts for historical films, but directors and actors, less sensitive, allow jarring modern colloquialisms to creep in. Few go as far as Franco Zeffirelli, who permitted 'okay' more than once in the script of a proposed film on the Emperor Hadrian. He also allowed a Zealot to say in our *Jesus of Nazareth*: 'We've had a damned sight too many of these fake messiahs.' In *Moses*, Burt Lancaster told representatives of the twelve tribes to scout round the countryside, saying: 'Your job is to find out what manner of people dwell there.' 'Job' was not acceptable. But, if it had been acceptable, could he really be permitted to pronounce it as 'jahb'? The problem of how far American phonemes can be allowed in cisatlantic historical drama remains insoluble, for British phonemes – in something biblical especially – are just as out of place. But at least British phonemes relate to a classical theatrical tradition and, perhaps more important, to a sempiternal class structure that was never transferred to America. The kings of Egypt can justifiably speak like the Queen of England, but not like the President of the United States. Moses, an Egyptian prince, should properly talk as though he had been to pre-war Eton.

The filming of *Moses* in the Sinai desert disclosed that some of the miracles of the Exodus were not extravagant legend but sober truth. The Nile was sometimes stained with red mud that looked bloody.

There was a shot of Burt, dissatisfied with a scene and visibly if inaudibly growling 'Fuck it', viciously hitting a porous rock with his staff. This immediately gushed water. The starving Israelites were fed on a miraculous draught of quails, which they caught in nets. The scene of this happening was no more than *cinéma-vérité*, with local Arabs doing the netting. Manna obligingly came down in the form of white tamarisk flakes. There was no need for Cecil B. de Mille trickery when it came to the passage out of Egypt. The Israelites probably crossed the Sea of Reeds, where a strong wind whips up the waters and presents a dryish bed. That wind kindly blew for the filming. We could have had Moses turning his staff into a serpent, but that was, to too many callers at Port Said, a banal entertainment put on by the gully-gully man – a snake drugged and rigid is thrown to the deck to wake up and writhe.

Having long had an ambition to write film-music, I inserted one or two little songs into the script. These, surprisingly, turned up in the workshop projection. One of them should not have turned up. I wrote it as a discardable obscene joke, but there it was, a marching song for the infanticidal Egyptian troops, trilled loudly in a variety of Palestinian accents:

> Here's the way we earn our pay:
> We've been ordered off to slay
> Little Jews so long as they
> Have balls between their legs.
>
> That's no way to earn your pay.
> We would rather, any day,
> Meet their mothers and then lay
> Our balls between their legs.

This is an instance of the ineradicable coarseness which lady reviewers deplore in me. I had a bigger and not at all coarse musical intention for *Moses*, and that was an entire orchestral score. I wrote a good deal of it, but the closed shop went into operation. Ennio Morricone composed the music, and Lew Grade tried to soothe me by commissioning words for the main theme, these to be sung by Barbra Streisand. It was decided finally that she had better not sing them.

Film is literally made, in the sense of put together by hand, in the cutting room. Cutting is the operative word: the floor becomes littered with miles of discarded action. Neophyte actors, proud to be at last in a movie, invite their friends to the first showing, only to find that they have disappeared. When Billingsly and I, with Andrea turning the lever that set the film moving, had finished our work, technicians arrived from London to complete the task of massive elimination with 'Anthony, we're going to cut down this half-hour of battle scenes to a montage of one minute. Would you write a voice-over for the narrator on the lines of "Over the years we fought many battles"?' When you hear a narrator in a film you can guess that the scissors have been sharply at work. The London technicians, in a lust of cutting, finally turned eight hours of television into a couple of hours of cinema entertainment. This was the *Moses* that the critics sneered at, saying: 'Come back, Cecil B. de Mille, all is forgiven.' They were right to sneer. The large screen showed up the insufficiency of the resources, less than epic. It was a sort of shoestring *Ten Commandments*.

But the televisual *Moses* was not as bad as the British critics had to believe, being convinced that anything produced by Lew Grade was bound to be vulgar and inferior entertainment. The Italians, on the other hand, were enchanted. They do not read the Bible, which is not good entertainment in its Italian version, a very uninspired one, and this story of persecuted and liberated Israelites came to them fresh and astonishing. None of the critics perpetrated the vulgarity of the *Sunday Telegraph* summation which, describing the wrapping of the foster-mother of Moses in her cerements, said, 'Mummy turns into a mummy.' Where the lofty British found the film laughable, they did not consider that parts of it were intentionally comic. Re-runs on European and American television show a kind of gawky classic quality, an endearing imperfection which has an acerbic European gust, far from the efficient blandness of American biblical epics. The film more than recovered its cost, which was not excessive. Emboldened, Lew Grade announced: 'Lads, we're going to do Jesus.'

As an earnest of his desire to have me write the scenario for this, along with Suso Cecchi d'Amico as obligatory Italian collaborator, Lew manifested Levantine generosity. A huge colour television set, as well as a Philips videocassette player (sadly soon out of date), arrived in Bracciano. When I made trips to the United States, a box of Lew's extra-long Cuban specials would be waiting at the check-in desk – always waved through by the US customs officials as obviously pure Tampa and hence not confiscable: Lew's influence seemed to go far. Visits to the Dorchester Hotel in London meant accommodation in Lew's permanent penthouse suite, with an overstocked bar in the corner. Publishers had never treated me like this.

RADIOTELEVISIONE ITALIANA was to collaborate with Lew's International Television Corporation in the financing of *Jesus of Nazareth*, but the big money was to come from General Motors. 'General Motors is going to buy Jesus,' Lew said. As he had not read the New Testament, he was not able to add: 'And for more than thirty bloody pieces of silver.' His ignorance of Christography was said to have been jeered at by Ted Willis, another lord of entertainment, who bet him ten quid that he could not even give the names of the twelve apostles. Lew said, allegedly: 'Right. There's Peter. There's John. There's that geezer Judas. I'll tell you the names of the others when I've finished reading the script.'

Vincenzo Labella was again to be executive producer. The director was to be Franco Zeffirelli. Franco was one of those men I should have disliked and mistrusted, but I could not. He had boasted that his Shakespeare films, *Romeo and Juliet* and *The Taming of the Shrew*, were the only ones to have made money: Larry's efforts, *Henry V* and *Hamlet* and *Richard III*, had been box-office disasters. But Franco had succeeded with Shakespeare at the cost of eliminating the Shakespearean. I had seen the script of *Romeo and Juliet*, where the blank verse had been turned into prose. In *The Taming of the Shrew* he showed what Shakespeare had merely wittily described. He was good at showing. He was a showman. The spectacle of his operatic productions was, and is, superb. I liked the man, with his northern Italian features and colouring and his bull-terrier frowns of concentration. I found him *simpatico*. I admired the total absence of intellectuality, with all life subordinated to the visual. A pupil of Visconti, he had learned from him an absolute mastery of the camera but had absorbed nothing of his tortuous sensibility. There was no decadence in Franco's art, no tinge of the corrupt. His sensuality seemed without guilt. He had done well in his trade, and the rewards were highly visible. There was the great house at Positano and the other great house outside Rome, with handsome young men in attendance. He had many dogs, and Andrea, who was becoming expert with his ciné-camera, made a little film entitled *I Cani di Zeffirelli*. The master would have appreciated the lack of cerebral content.

Before a line of the script had been written – or, more pertinently, a page of the preliminary novel which I had to compose before I could deal in stark dialogue and camera directions – a huge press conference was held in Rome. I said that we were not concerned with making a devotional film with a laundered misty Christ, but a highly realistic evocation of the Roman Palestine that produced him, with sweat, dirt, humanity, Jesus the man. '*E il figlio di Dio?*' came a voice from *L'Osservatore Romano*. He would be the Son of God, *certo*, superhuman, and Franco here would very competently recreate the miracles. My words about Christ the man struck too deeply home in Franco, and in the United States he was to stress publicly that we were dealing with humanity and not divinity. The response to this in the Bible Belt was drastic: we were perpetrating blasphemy, and General Motors was abetting it; no good fundamentalist would ever again contemplate buying one of the products of General Motors. General Motors took fright and withdrew from the project, but IBM took over. Christ came to bring not peace but a sword.

After the press conference there was a vast banquet at a villa outside Rome, to which almost the entire British episcopate was flown out. My step-cousin George was not there, but the Anglican Bishop of Birmingham conveyed his regards. There did not seem to be much Catholic clergy there at all, but the Chief Rabbi of Rome attended. Lew Grade was made a *Cavaliere della Repubblica*. There was no pledge of Vatican approval, unless that inhered in Franco Zeffirelli, who, as the regular television producer of great events at San Pietro, was cherished by the Holy City. And Vincenzo Labella, of course, had his Vatican passport. 'Get down to it, Tony,' Franco said, departing with a party of gorgeous Roman girls. Liana alone was not happy about my getting down to it. I was up to my neck in show business, and show business had never done me any good. She threatened divorce (not peace but a sword), and I feebly countered with: 'If I don't do it, who can?' I was not boasting; I was merely pleading the right background, a capacity for irony to offset Italian sentimentality, a certain competence in writing dialogue. There was also the question of money. She was not mollified, but she did not utter the dreadful word *divorzio* again, recognising that it did not fit into the context of what I was getting down to. But she foresaw accurately enough that there would be no smooth passage to Golgotha and beyond.

RAI had a team of religious advisers, and the chief among these was Dr Gennarino Gennarini. He did not trust British Christians, even Catholic ones. The Emperor Constantine was crowned at York, which is only a brief train journey from Manchester, but he did not pick up Christianity there. The British were natural heretics, and the greatest of these was Pelagius. He ordered me to attend a kind of First Supper, saying '*E molto importante mangiare insieme,*' and began to give me my orders. I evaded these orders and escaped from both Gennarini and a sweltering summer in the Italian lowlands by loading a typewriter and the New Testament into the Bedford Dormobile. We set off for the Alps. I took the New Testament in Greek, in order to get a fresh or original look at it. There are four versions of the life of Christ, and the most popular is the least reliable. This is the highly romantic novella written by St John, too long after the historical events, with a wedding at Cana and the resurrection of Lazarus, of which Matthew, Mark and Luke say nothing. These three evangelists are so like each other that they can be studied as a single book called the Synoptic Gospels. Papal encyclicals were always heavily footnoted with St John, and Zeffirelli could justify his own romantic preference for it on the highest authority. I foreknew that we would have a full-dress resurrection of Lazarus.

The gospels were not enough. I had to read Josephus's *History of the Jews* and manuals on the technique of crucifixion. The traditional image of Christ carrying the whole cross, dear to the fundamentalists of the American South, apparently flouted historical fact. He would have carried merely the crosspiece, which would then be affixed to a permanent upright at the place of execution. It was going to be dangerous to deny traditional iconography. The more I read Matthew, Mark and Luke the more I became dissatisfied with their telling of the sacred story. They remain fine propagandists but mediocre novelists. 'The devil entered Judas,' says John. How hopelessly inadequate. That man at Warner Brothers would have cried out against inadequate motivation for betrayal of the Son of God.

I had to remake Judas from scratch. I remade him first as a decent American college boy, well read in Latin, Greek and Hebrew, devoted to his widowed mother, charmed at first by Jesus, later wholly convinced of his divinity, but so politically innocent that he runs to the Sanhedrin and says: 'This man is the Messiah.' The Chief Priest nods and says: 'Ah, the Messiah, is he? The Zealots think he's a political activist come to free Israel from the Roman yoke. They'll kill him when they hear his true mission. Help us, Judas, to have this Jesus safely sequestered until the time is ripe for his instatement as the Promised One.' And so the arrest in the garden, Judas's shocking loss of innocence, his suicide following his awareness of involuntary betrayal of the one he would never wish to betray. That was my first Judas. The final Judas was a palimpsest of Judas as sweet innocent, as higher zealot, as indiscreet blabber, as disappointed idealist. But the devil did not enter him.

I found it necessary to invent characters who have no place in the gospels. Judas had to have a primary contact in the Religious Council, an old fellow-student of theology, believed to be imaginative and progressive but in fact highly reactionary. This character, whom I called Zerah, was, as the story progressed, revealed as a necessary wheel in the destructive machine: I even gave him the last word, a bitter and baffled one: 'Now it all begins.' Another character essential to the narrative was a deputy procurator willing to sign Christ's death warrant, a formality Pontius Pilate refuses. Barabbas's full name might have been Jesus bar Abbas: his name might have been set down in a portmanteau death warrant without the patronymic: 'Here we have a Jesus. It doesn't matter about the rest of his name – bar Joseph or bar Abbas. His Excellency has already signed. As long as there's a Jesus up there on a cross this afternoon the record will be quite in order.' And the deputy procurator receives a handful of shekels from the Jews.

The twelve apostles are not well characterised in the gospels. I tried to fasten individual traits to them: it was all too easy for them to blur into a dozen interchangeable bewildered artisans with beards and dirty smocks. I made doubting Thomas a dour Scot with the sour scepticism of a highland race. Thaddeus I made a fluteplayer, Bartholomew a physician with a queasy stomach. One had to be careful with the beloved disciple John, especially in a permissive age only too anxious to turn his special relationship with his master into a homosexual one.

As for Jesus Christ himself, I was haunted by T. S. Eliot's phrase in *Gerontion*: 'In the juvescence of the year/ Came Christ the tiger.' That 'juvescence' is wrong (it should be 'juvenescence') but the tigrine image seemed to me to be just. I feared that the cinematic Jesus might be a weedy Dustin Hoffman. I wanted him to be massive, muscular, with the big-chested capacity for hyperoxidation that made Napoleon the man he was. The voice that delivered the Sermon on the Mount must have been immense. One could upset the whole doctrine of the Resurrection by positing a pocket of air in Christ's lungs when he was taken down from the cross. A gigantic Christ got into the novel I rapidly wrote in the Bedford Dormobile parked in an Alpine valley. In the film we had Robert Powell. But Powell, I was later to hear from Vincenzo Labella, had his own magic. Leaving his hotel in Christine robes, a Rothmans between his lips, he unleashed a thunderstorm which had Arabs grovelling before him in the wet.

The first script which came out of the first draft of the novel was considered ludicrous by Franco Zeffirelli. I expected this. I expected the filling of a whole shelf with discarded scripts. But there was not only Zeffirelli to please. The RAI theologians, with Gennarino Gennarini at their head, could not find me among the Alps, but they tracked me down in Ansedonia and Siena. They told me what to write. 'Write it yourself, for Christ's sake,' I said with reverence. 'No, no, *tu sei lo scrittore*.' Note the familiar form *tu*, which I had never authorised. One suggestion was that Jesus, in formulating the Lord's Prayer, should stumble over the word *padre*, stuttering *papa papa* in homage to His Holiness. That meant he would say *fafa fafa* in English, thus honouring H. C. Earwicker, who is 'fafafafather of all things for to bother us'. But they had only an Italian viewing public in mind. Their horizon was too small to encompass a great international production with James Mason and Ralph Richardson and Laurence Olivier. Something small and devotional was required for small Italians who had forgotten their catechism; the film was to be a religious annexe of the Christian Democrat Party. These theological advisers were ten a penny; I would have traded them all for an adviser in carpentry.

Gennarino Gennarini and his colleagues never read the novel out of which the script was squeezed or hacked. They would not have been pleased by my presenting Christ as a married man. That he *was* married, though briefly, entering on his mission a somewhat embittered widower, seemed to me to be very likely: a state of bachelorhood lasting into the late twenties would have been unusual in a tight Jewish community. If there was a marriage feast at Cana, it may well have been Jesus's own. I did not expect Franco Zeffirelli to dare a married Christ, though he might have been willing to suggest a homosexual one (this could have accorded with historical truth; who can tell?). There had to be a middle course: there was enough shock in showing Christ carrying only that crosspiece. The middle course meant also cutting out the pedantry of my scene in which Jesus tells a young Greek that it is as easy for a camel to pass through the eye of a needle as for a rich man to get to heaven. He uses Greek to the Greek, and the Greek for camel is *kamelon*. But *kamilon*, which means rope, is the more plausible word. When Judas, who knows Greek, tries to translate for the other disciples, he is not sure whether he heard *kamelon* or *kamilon*. Jesus smiles and shrugs Jewishly, leaving the semantic problem to posterity.

The work of writing the novel, provisionally entitled *Christ the Tiger*, ended in Ansedonia, among bodies honeyed by the sun by the sea and black hair smelling of woodsmoke. Surrounded by animal calls of the pagans, I resuscitated the dead Christ. Zeffirelli was not quite orthodox in wishing to end the series with a great *Pietà* – camera tracking away from the wailing mother, arms held aloft to rainy heaven, her dead heavy son on her knees. In choosing Olivia Hussey, once his Juliet, for the Virgin Mary's role, he found the loudest wailer in the business. He had to be reminded, gently, that the Resurrection was the whole point of the death. Viewers of the film will note that the risen Christ makes rather a casual appearance, with no Easter trombones, but that the crucifixion and deposition are presented with all the stops out. It was with the screaming Hussey that the series really ended for Franco. I could see his point; artistically speaking, the Resurrection is something of an anticlimax.

Franco never really got a satisfactory script from me, or from the collaborating Suso Cecchi d'Amico, a gracious lady, of a famous artistic family, who had had a distinguished career in the Italian cinema. Credited as the third scenarist, Franco was entitled to go his own way when the film was set up in Tunisia. I proposed publishing my own novel at the time of the release of the series, partly to show what I had wanted on the screen, partly to cash in on the impact of a much ballyhooed popular event, but Vincenzo Labella was quick to get ready a literary spin-off from the script by a man named Barclay, and the cunning Franco brought out *Il Mio Gesù*, which sold heavily in Italy. The series, and film made out of the series, is generally known in Italy as *Il Gesù di Zeffirelli*. My book was published abroad – *Homme de Nazareth*, *Jesucristo y el Juego del Amor* – before it appeared in England. Even in England it was an American publication, limiting me to one advance and one set of royalties instead of two.

The filming was done in Tunisia, where there was a good exchange rate on the dollar, and where the Arabs, all eager to be extras, looked sufficiently like Jews. Many of these, ignoring the cameras, thought they were participating in the Second Coming. The scene where Christ feeds the five thousand is a good, hungry, bread-tearing scene. Anne Bancroft, as Mary Magdalene, can be seen weeping bitterly, and a fat decent Tunisian matron, seated next to her, takes the tears as genuine and pats and kisses her hand in comfort. This is rather moving. The elaborate Jerusalem set was not struck after filming but taken over by the Monty Python team, who made *The Life of Brian* with it. Franco was disgusted and spoke of blasphemy, but that comedy, which I have seen some ten times on videocassette, strikes me as being a very fair interpretation of the lot of the Jews under Roman rule. I wish I had written the script for it.

THE SCRIPT of *Jesus of Nazareth* was finished in a country house in Montalbuccio, outside Siena. This house belonged to Bruno Miconni, Liana's economist friend, who proposed spending a year in Cambridge with his Scottish wife and son, whose name was Fergus Micconi, a fine fusion. He needed a thousand pounds, and he suggested that we rent his house and pay that sum in advance. We needed to get away from Roman robbery and Bracciano sourness, and we could not spend all our time in a motor caravan among the Alps and on the cool coast of north-west Italy, so we set ourselves up in Montalbuccio and Andrea, poor child, had a new dialect to learn. The house was surrounded by a garden full of vipers in a bad year for vipers. These vipers fell from the trees and bit the cats and dogs that abounded, and much time was taken up in rushing to a pharmacist in Siena to buy antitoxins. The rest of the time, except for cooking in an ancient kitchen with the rough ingredients of village shops, was given over to work rather remote from literature. I was fulfilling the aspirations of my mother and father by climbing the ladder of show business. We cannot escape our heredity.

The Bedford Dormobile was not behaving well. It frequently stopped in mid-career and had to be pushed. I did the pushing, and the result of one uphill heave was a cardiac fibrillation a local doctor frowned at. The rumour spread about RAI that I was not long for this world and had better be rushed into certain televisual projects while there was still time. One of these was a series on the life of Michelangelo. Another came close to that failed Warner Brothers project about the man Shakespeare, though this time Shakespeare was to be seen from a specifically Italian angle, as indicated by the proposed title, *Shakespeare da Noi* – Shakespeare among us. Vincenzo Labella, as producer of both enterprises, was to get money from Lew Grade, who, now a knight of the Italian Republic, could not without discourtesy and ingratitude deny it. Radiotelevisione Italiana would put in as little as it could. Unlike the BBC, RAI had, and continues to have, ample resources. It has the best of both worlds, charging a licence fee and at the same time earning a large revenue from its commercials. It seems to spend most of its money on lavish spectacles featuring Rafaella Carrà and other blonde temptresses. In terms of choreography, special effects, and near-naked girls of painful seductiveness, these evoke the days of the old Hollywood musicals. For the rest, it buys as cheaply as it can or puts as little as it can into joint European enterprises.

The Michelangelo life was eventually made, though I never saw it. The Shakespeare project ended up as a shoestring abomination made with British money alone, with my script rejected and the Italian element wholly expunged. Vincenzo Labella's intention was that we show the great heretic Giordano Bruno in his English exile, making a contact with Shakespeare that may well have been made through the School of Night and Christopher Marlowe. Shakespeare's provincialism is modified less by London than by the whiff of an Italy where sun and visual glamour, the dangerous passion of revolutionary ideas, internecine struggles and hot love will provide his best dramatic materials. And, as a companion to the Earl of Southampton, who has been entrusted with a diplomatic mission in Veneto, he sees Padua, Verona and Venice. A visit to Rome recalls its imperial past. All this was fanciful, but it might make good television. A miniature London was to be erected on the shore of Lake Bracciano, and Vincenzo proposed that the Globe playhouse be a permanent structure there and that Bracciano itself become a site for a regular artistic festival. No place less likely than Bracciano for such a cultural flowering could be envisaged. Its materialism, endorsed by the local communist party, and its xenophobic philistinism were not what tourists think they mean when they burble about the glory of Italy. In the evenings its streets were full of sad recruits from the local infantry barracks, searching vainly for a dish of pasta like mother used to make and, equally vainly, for a bit of grumble and grunt. They mostly ended up in the Virgilio cinema, yawning at Disney's *Fantasia* and wondering when the action was going to start, or nursing frustrated *cazzi* at some film about a Calabrian priest falling in love with one of his parishioners and finding the essence of God the Creator (with an inadequate heavenly choir mooing in the background) in the act of fornication.

Anyway, *Shakespeare da Noi* never got beyond my first draft scripts, and all that remains of it is the music I composed, which, so Vincenzo Labella assured me with Roman, or Vatican, sincerity, would certainly get on to the soundtrack. This music I eventually turned into a ballet suite called *Mr W.S.*. The BBC broadcast it twice and then, in obedience to Musicians' Union regulations, destroyed the tape. I wrote it in Bruno Micconi's study, looking down on the writhing vipers in the garden, while the huge portrait of Karl Marx, transferred to Montalbuccio from Rome, looked down on me. I wrote it without the aid of a keyboard to check the harmonies, putting myself entirely in the situation of the deaf Beethoven (whose harmonies were simpler than mine and did not have to be checked). Then I composed a far larger piece of music. This had Shakespeare in it too, but not as a subject for dramatisation.

My novel *Napoleon Symphony* had been much appreciated by musicians, who applauded the attempt to attach musical form to the craft of the narrative, even though they knew it had to fail. One American musician wrote to me to say that he had enjoyed the book and that he divined I must be primarily a composer. His name was Jim Dixon and, if he had read me, he had evidently not read Kingsley Amis. He was in charge of the orchestra of the University of Iowa, and he invited me to compose an extended work for it. There would be no money in it, and I would have to pay out thousands of dollars for the copying of parts, but I would be assured of adequate rehearsal and a competent performance. The student orchestra was large and expert, and it had recently performed Scriabin's *Poem of Fire*, with the part for the colour organ transferred to a laser beam apparatus. I had, with some difficulty, to rehabilitate my notion of a student orchestra. One had to assume a technical brilliance which found no problems in Berg or Boulez and was young only in its lack of experience of life. In other words, it would have less expressive subtlety than the old bald-headed Hallé. Its wind soloists would read their notes exactly but they were too young to get behind the notes. Why a need to have lived life is essential to the proper playing of mature music remains a great mystery, but it is certain that musical notes are an analogue of human experience. One needs to know what sex is before playing *Tristan and Isolde*, and, though orchestral players call a certain work of Debussy's *An Afternoon on the Phone*, its first flautist has to be above jokes and know what Mallarmé was getting at.

I began to write a symphony for Jim Dixon's orchestra. I wrote it for a conventional Straussian ensemble, though adding parts for piano and mandoline and, in the last movement, for tenor and baritone soloists. When I say that the work had Shakespeare in it, I mean that these two soloists sang words by Shakespeare – the spring and winter songs at the end of *Love's Labour's Lost* – and that, from the same play, I took as a theme the six notes that Holofernes sings when expounding on the excellence of the poet Mantuan. Shakespeare scholars have never been moved by the fact that there are two musical phrases spelt out by the Bard in solmised form. As I say above, in *King Lear* we hear four notes taken up by Richard

Addinsell and turned into the opening of his main melody in the *Warsaw Concerto*. In *Love's Labour's Lost* Holofernes warbles: 'Ut re sol la mi fa.' This, better read as CDGAEF, is a very adequate motif that makes musical sense when sung or played backwards or upside down and, followed by itself transposed a tritone higher (or, of course, lower), makes up a *Grundstimmung* suitable for a serial composition. I was to base my finale on the theme and point its provenance in *Love's Labour's Lost* with the spring and winter songs.

Composing this symphony, I was not earning a living, but I was fulfilling an aspect of myself that had been too long dumb. It was a relief to be dealing in pure sound and pure structure, far from the fury and the mire of human veins. The human referents of music are too vague, general and, I suppose, Jungian to excite as sex and violence excite, and sex and violence, whether we like it or not, are the two main elements of fiction. There is also a certain calligraphic satisfaction in the setting down of musical notes, which trace visual patterns corresponding to auditory ones. I have always approached the writing of an orchestral score with a draughtsman's hand and a draughtsman's materials – ruler, black ink, sharp nibs. I have never used a pencil and an eraser, working out each measure thoroughly in my brain before setting it down in ink. Sibelius would work out an entire symphony in his head, finding its transcription on to paper something of a bore, since all the creative excitement was now spent. Scoring is physically hard work, and the time expended in filling up the twenty or thirty staves to the page can give the composer a false idea of the duration of performance. One spends five or six hours on a passage in *allegro vivace* tempo which takes something like twenty seconds to play. On the other hand, a page of typescript can take longer to read out than it does to write. Moving from the composition of fiction to that of music, one enters a different kind of time.

At Christmas 1974 I had nearly finished the first movement. But on Christmas Day I was ready to die of food poisoning. There had been a number of strikes of electricity workers, matching strikes in other fields, and, because of brief absences, I was not aware that some frozen Brussels sprouts in the deep freeze had thawed, decayed, re-frozen, thawed, decayed, re-frozen. Being the sole true northerner of the family, I ate these with the Christmas turkey while the others ate fresh spinach. Then death seemed to announce itself. Recovered, I composed the slow movement, which was a funeral march. The last, Shakespearean, movement celebrated, with winter and spring, my, or man's, resurrection. The scherzo was merely fast and noisy.

The work on two hundred and fifty pages of full score was still going on when I had to travel the United States on the last of my murderous lecture tours. At least, the intention of the lecture agency seemed to be lethal – Florida to Wisconsin, Sacramento to Vancouver, most flights pre-dawn, sleep reserved for a brief Easter break. I made the flight from Rome with Vincenzo Labella: he and I had to meet the princes of the ABC network in New York, along with a sort of cultural adviser to General Motors, to convince them that *Jesus of Nazareth*, which was now being filmed in Tunisia, would not harm the air-time of the one or the product of the other. The fact that contracts had been signed did not seem important: contracts were only paper. The Americans required the assurance of physical presence, personality, a scent of culture, commercial seriousness, even sexual vitality. Of this last Vincenzo had plenty. The head of ABC, who treated the General Motors man with a kind of disdain improper for a paying client, wanted the mature Christ to appear in the first instalment, so that American viewers would know the kind of character they would have to live with for the next seven. I wanted the first instalment to be a complete and separable celebration of advent and nativity, so that it could be used for all future televisual Christmases. The ABC man won. The meeting ended with an elaborate lunch and reciprocal assurances of liking and confidence. The contracts would not be torn up. Then I started my journey.

The symphony was completed in motel rooms and airports. Muzak in the latter interfered with the work of the inner ear. In Orwell's *Nineteen Eighty-Four* there are, presumably, state-employed musicians who compose hymns to the glory of Big Brother. Do they have to work with the telescreen blaring? Presumably. I have seen occasional composers and executants trying to write or examine scores in airport lounges and hotel foyers, with insidious muzak, which nobody knows how to turn off, seething non-stop away. There has to be a new breed of musician who can seal off those extraneous sounds and hear only what he wants to hear. If I am a musician at all, I belong to that breed. I draw on the motor as much as the auditory sense. I imagine my fingers moving on a dummy keyboard: their configuration suggests a sound. But if Beethoven had lived today he would have desired deafness earlier. The softening-up music of American government offices, the white noise of restaurants and hotel lobbies is a tyrannous imposition of which nobody complains. The next stage will be a kind of hypnopaedia of which nobody will complain either. There is only one civilised airport in America: that is Chicago's O'Hare, where the muzak is always baroque and usually Vivaldi. But surely any invasion of the ears is a kind of criminal assault?

I sent the score off to Jim Dixon in Iowa and proceeded with my travel and lecturing. I was accompanied by a memory of sexual excitement – the whole land to be figuratively ravished, its women, or girl undergraduates, not so figuratively. But I was a new man since my second marriage. I did not sustain fidelity out of duty. I was sexually, or amatorily, fulfilled. I could look on these delectable hip-swinging sirenettes with indifference. But indifference is a challenge. I was pursued by a rather mature undergraduate girl from Oshkosh, Wisconsin, to San Francisco. I was friendly, even hospitable, but inseducible. I was also overworked.

Returning briefly to New York from Vancouver in order to fly to a college in Troy or Antioch or Rome (all NY), I was met outside my hotel by Cubby Broccoli and Guy Hamilton. They handed over a wad of paper and a portable typewriter. Cubby Broccoli was the producer of the James Bond films and Guy Hamilton was one of their directors. The next scheduled James Bond film was *The Spy Who Loved Me*, but it was permitted to transfer only the title from the book to the screen. Ian Fleming had forbidden, and was still forbidding from the grave, any use of the material in the novel. The novel had been a failed experiment in shoving Bond to the margin of the narrative and making the protagonist an English girl looking after an American motel. The subjects of the story were arson, possible rape, and violent killing in the private sector, not the realm of SMERSH or SPECTRE. It would not do as a book – the critics condemned it wholesale – and it was not permitted to do as a film. Broccoli and Hamilton wanted a script from me that should be a totally original story. I found out later that they wanted scripts from a score of other writers, the intention apparently being to throw all these into a mixer and pull out a synthetic plot. So, on my travels, I hammered out my own contribution to the mélange.

I knew from the start that it would not work, but a horrid fascination drove me on. I followed the formal pattern of the Bond films as closely as I could. Before the main title sequence I had Bond in Singapore fighting a Chinese musical gong society and drowning one of its thugs in a tub of shark's fin soup, seasoning it with soya sauce as the thug goes under. But Bond is then shot and left for dead, though he is merely stunned. He recovers to find a Chinese surgeon ready to extract a bullet from his shoulder, using acupuncture as an anaesthetising technique. Bond learns about acupuncture and is given the two needles – one for *yin*, the other for *yang* – as a parting gift. Driving to Singapore airport he sees a Jumbo jet go up in flames as it leaves the runway. This is an apparent motiveless atrocity engineered by CHAOS – the Consortium for the Hastening of the Annihilation of Organised Society.

A plenary meeting of CHAOS – in a maritime location not clearly defined – shows an Orson Welles monster based on my own character Theodorescu, crippled and confined to a wheelchair, tended by a Scottish Presbyterian doctor. He is the chairman of CHAOS, and he announces a programme of terrorism for its own sake, not for financial gain. The consortium has made enough money and must learn the pleasure of pure power. Great figures of the world – queens, presidents, popes – must render themselves obscene or absurd in full public view as the price for not seeing a school, a sanatorium, an orphanage wantonly destroyed by CHAOS. That blowing up of a jet plane leaving Singapore was the price the Pope had to pay, somewhat vicariously, for refusing personally to whitewash the ceiling of the Sistine Chapel. The chairman-monster's terrorism is fired in part by his beautiful daughter, who, loved and then deserted by 008, Bond's colleague, vows revenge on the world. Her chagrin has manifested itself in a hideous facial rash which she covers with her raven hair. She does not realise that 008 has been killed by SMERSH. It is she who, in the first main scene, burns up millions of dollars in a huge baronial fireplace to indicate the worthlessness of money in comparison with vindictive power.

She is one justification of the title. Another is a beautiful Australian opera singer whom Bond thinks he loves. Bond sets out to discover by what means the seemingly inexplicable explosions which destroy innocent targets are operated. He finds out that people who have had appendectomies in a particular German clinic have been, unknowingly, fitted with a nuclear explosive device in the scar tissue which is activated by a distant radio signal. Infiltrating the German clinic he discovers the former mistress of 008 in charge. She devises delicious tortures for him but he comes through unscathed. More, he convinces her that 008 did not betray her. She sees something of 008 in 007, perhaps inevitably, since he was Bond's twin brother. They make love. Miraculously, as in Greene's *The End of the Affair*, the hideous facial rash disappears. He learns from her that her father is committed to blowing up the Sydney Opera House on a gala occasion at which the Queen and all the leaders of the British Commonwealth will be present. The alternative is for the American President to disport himself obscenely on international television. In

Sydney, Bond discovers that the lovely opera singer, who is to play the lead in Strauss's *Salome* on the gala occasion, has had an appendectomy at the German clinic. He performs an emergency operation, using the acupuncture needles to anaesthetise, and then pincers the explosive device out of her scar tissue. The 007- (formerly 008-) loving girl sees what looks like an amorous encounter. The hideous rash returns. She tries to kill Bond. Sydney, not just its Opera House and distinguished audience, will be destroyed by a nuclear bomb. I do not think I have to continue.

There had been a time in New York, when I was engaged on the *Cyrano* musical, that had shamed me with a sense of betraying a commitment to higher art. Henry James, with his dachshund Max, had appeared at the bedroom door to make an admonitory gesture – a raised moving finger in the manner of the Neapolitans. Clattering out the ridiculous script in a motel bedroom in Idaho, I found that the demons of literature or the lecture circuit had killed my voice. I had a lecture to give and could utter not one word. I stepped on to the platform dumb but hoping for a Graham Greene miracle. I prayed to St Antony of Padua, and he, who had failed to retrieve stolen passports, restored enough of the lost voice for me to give a sort of lecture. But other malign forces assailed me. After a morning lecture in a Quaker college in the Mid-West, the principal looked sternly at me and said: 'Anthony Burgess, thee are not well.' I agreed, by God, and collapsed. I came to on a bed to find students breathing kif-smoke down my throat. I had a black-out in Pittsburgh. I found myself alone at a table in the restaurant of the William Pitt Hotel. An aged waiter came along, seated himself in the chair opposite, and said: 'Well, my friend, what can I get you?' This was no way for a waiter to behave. My only salvation was to flee America.

America was behaving strangely, or it may have been my synapses. I had been given too many presents of smokable drugs by grateful students (grateful? What were they grateful for?). I lighted up at the end of a lecture in a small college near Los Angeles, and the reek excited the attention of the campus police. Being an innocent foreigner, I perhaps did not know what I was smoking and so was let off with a caution. In a college in Memphis, a young Soviet student abused American hospitality by rising in the middle of my lecture to denounce what he called American fascism. The Americans meekly took it all, breast-beating, masochistic. It was left to me to defend America. A remote motel in Texas had put up a lighted notice: WELCOME ABOARD ADMIRAL BURGESS. I made up to a girl student in Stetson who growled, 'I'm a guy.' I had better leave.

But Europe was preparing for me a deeper descent into madness. I was chosen as a member of the jury for the Cannes Film Festival. The Cannes event was preceded by one in Nice – the annual literary award made by a munificent municipality – and, as one of the judges, I was to be engaged in real culture before passing on to its debasement. The prize was given to Nadine Gordimer because this was *L'Année des Femmes*, and the French jurors, not knowing her, had nothing against her. This, I discovered, was how literary prizes were awarded – no unanimity as to merit; dissension based on chauvinism; a weary acceptance, after bitter logomachies, of a harmless name. This, I was to learn later, was pretty well why the Nobel Prize was, to the world's bemusement, given to obscure Montenegran poets and Finnish fabulists. The various awards of the Cannes Film Festival were accorded on a more positive basis.

The Cannes jury consisted of Jeanne Moreau, George Roy Hill, Fernando Rey, Lea Massari, Pierre Salinger, a Russian lady named Marya Smyslovskaya, myself, and a handful of obscure French film journalists who pronounced anything noisy (like Ken Russell's *Tommy*) *génial*. Madame Smyslovskaya was there only to vote for the Soviet entry, *Ils Luttaient pour la Patrie*, a noisy war film, hence *génial*, but not quite *génial* enough to get more than one persistent vote, that of Madame Smyslovskaya. Madame Smyslovskaya, whose French – except for her regular exordial *Voyez-vous* – was not really intelligible, was intelligible enough when she burst into tears at the final counting. She was to report back to Moscow that *Ils Luttaient pour la Patrie* had won no prize, despite its obvious superiority to the pornographic Western entries, and she would be in severe trouble. The jury kindly agreed to give a minor *court-métrage* award to a Soviet cartoon film, but she was not mollified.

The jurors were put up in respectable hotels but permitted to eat only of the *table d'hôte*. If *tomates à la provençale* appeared on the *à la carte* you were not allowed to have them. It was not possible to escape from some Brazilian exercise in sex and violence or from Sir Lew Grade's travesty of the Robinson Crusoe story: your name was taken by a haughty elegant French lady at the morning, afternoon and evening performances, and if your name was missing you were told to pack your bags and go home. There has always been something of the atmosphere of the *lycée* about French discipline. There is an ingrained pedantry in the French: waitresses will correct your genders and even prostitutes can sound like schoolmistresses. The discipline at the Cannes Film Festival was qualified by a certain failure of organisation. The jurors, in their immaculate obligatory *tenue de soirée*, were granted no special means of entry into the *salle*: they had to fight their way through crowds which the gendarmes did little to regulate. These crowds were not there to acclaim Jeanne Moreau or Lea Massari or Fernando Rey, great stars though they were. They were there to greet toothy little starlets who showed much bosom. Photographers were always ordering me out of the way so that they could get a good view of an exposed nipple. In wrath I eventually smashed a camera and was in grave trouble with the police. But I spoke up on behalf of the dignity of the land of Racine and Molière and against the debasement of art. The police, remembering their lessons at the *lycée*, let me go.

Most of the films were pretty bad. *Tommy*, the British rock opera, was *hors de concours* and merely the final noise. The sole judgeable British entry was a Lew Grade abomination which presented Robinson Crusoe as a white fool and Man Friday as the fount of natural wisdom. Lew met me as I was going in to an official dinner and enjoined patriotism on me: 'Get 'em to vote for it, Tone boy.' But it did not get one vote. An excellent Canadian entry, *Les Ordres*, was condemned by the French because they could not understand the French. The big prize went with little difficulty to the Algerian entry, *Les Jours de Braise*. We were given an anonymous warning that a bomb would go off in the great *salle* if it did not win. It was no worse a film than the others, though it raised an interesting moral question. George Roy Hill and I tried to leave the showing during a scene in which, lavishly and in close view, the throat of a camel was cut. We were not permitted to leave, since the doors had been locked. Pierre Salinger, in his fluent but very American French, alleged that, in aesthetic terms, there was no difference between the *coupage fictif de la gorge d'un chameau* and the real thing. In cinematic art everything depended on the effect. How the director got his effect was his own business. This, I thought, was dangerous philosophy. And then the fictive rape of *Orange Mécanique* was brought up. Was not its impact the impact of real rape?

How far Kubrick's film could be held responsible for the pure violence and the violent sex of so many of the Cannes entries it was not possible to say. Film pornography existed before *A Clockwork Orange*, but it was cheap stuff for underground showing, not for exhibition in the public cinemas. Now, at the Carleton Hotel, stalls had been set up by production companies and exhibitors to advertise pornography that pretended to be cinematic art. One film, called *Amour d'un Porcelet*, was about a man's regular copulations with a young pig, and the young pig had been brought as a kind of promising starlet to Cannes: it slept in the bathroom of the producer-director, a hairy Armenian. In one of the film magazines in the mass of promotional literature under which jurors were snowed, there was a detailed account of the making of a piece of sodomitic pornography: 'I'm sorry, Delphine, but in this shot you've got to have three men's pricks up your ass.' No pseudo-serious film could be shown unless it had its passages of nudity and sweating copulation. A Dutch entry showed a man kissing a bald head like a breast while he masturbated, but for the most part 'entry' was an operative term. I was queasy. Was I proving myself to be old-fashioned?

The erotic now meant the unsuggestive. Was there a kind of honesty in showing this writhing of flesh under hot lights? The films I had been brought up on in the nineteen-thirties were erotic in a different way – the odd flash of Marlene Dietrich's stockinged knees, the well-filled sweaters of Paulette Goddard, the cunning under-lighting that imparted a special sumptuousness to white flesh. Now there was too much candid anatomy, too much of the piston-action of the male and the insincere ecstasy of the female. Frankness was becoming a substitute for narrative movement. The thrust of the story, unimportant to the great post-war names like Fellini, Visconti and Antonioni, had once been the chief virtue of film – fifty pages of novel condensed to ten seconds of urgent montage. There was a new dullness around under the guise of the shocking. An Italian company was advertising *La Banana Meccanica*. I nodded grimly at it and went to be assaulted by *Tommy*. For this the volume had been switched to the maximum. *Génial*, pronounced the French critics.

LIANA AND I were briefly in Bracciano when I was adventitiously pushed back to the practice of my métier, or what I considered to be my métier. A young American photographer had found my address and arrived with a number of pictures he had taken of Rome under the rain. To wish to photograph Rome under a dull sky was original enough: sun and Italy were supposed to go together. In effect, the young man, who gave his name as David Robinson, had photo-graphed a double Rome – one sitting on its rain-puddled reflection. He wanted to make a book of these pictures and he required a text. The notion of a brief novel stirred in me. One of the characters should be a Roman photographer, and her photographs and the text should complement each other. I naturally thought of a woman photographer, black-haired, short-skirted, seductive. I was going to put a version of my wife into the novel. The title was already available – *Rome in the Rain* – and this title was to be preserved in all the foreign-language editions of the book. In America it had to be the sexier *Beard's Roman Women*, and this became the British title too. I told Robinson to find himself a New York agent and have the agent write to me.

I wrote the novel fairly rapidly in the summer of 1975, mostly in the Bedford Dormobile. I began it in Montalbuccio and finished it in Monte Carlo. We were looking for somewhere to live in Monte Carlo, or what we called Monte Carlo. We really meant the Principality of Monaco, which has three main regions – Monacoville, site of the princely palace on a hill, a valley called the Condamine, another hill with a casino, Mount Charles or Monte Carlo. But if you refer to Monaco in Italy, it is always assumed that you mean München or Munich. I have sometimes had to jump out of the wrong train at Rome's Termini station. American immigration officers rarely know of Monaco, despite America's having given a princess to the place, but they all know of Monte Carlo. 'A kinda French Las Vegas, right?' Not quite right.

We left Andrea in Montalbuccio, though not alone. Our former secretary-companion Francesca, the black beauty, had long gone from our life. She had been guilty of certain irregularities, some of them to do with money; she had been trying to make us the hospitable centre of a number of fellow-Ethiopians, some of them cousins; she had been trying to screw the author of *Arancia a Orologeria*, said now to be very rich. Her place had been taken by a Welsh beauty named Susan Roberts, a prospective interpretress for the European Parliament whose French was good but whose Italian needed practice. She could type and drive a car; she was, being Welsh, tidy. Her voice struck me to the liver, the voice of cultivated South Wales. It was very nearly the voice of my dead wife, and it was a voice that was to disturb the hero of *Beard's Roman Women*. Susan and Andrea saw us off from Montalbuccio in high summer. 'You will not see us again,' we boasted, 'until we have bought a dwelling on the Côte d'Azur.' Liana drove away and then had to stop to let a cat out.

Liana needed town life, but the flat in Rome was being taken away from us by its landlord, who needed to give it to his shortly-to-be-married son. In any case, there was far too much criminality in Rome. Liana was sick of being robbed of her passport and then blamed by the Questura. The tenants of a lower floor had been not

merely burgled but shot. We too had been burgled, though not shot
since we were in Bracciano at the time. The burglers had taken a
three-thousand-dollar Stellavox tape-recorder and a quantity of
maternal jewellery. Graham Greene had seemed once to posit the
doctrine that Catholics were closer to the moral realities than
Protestants. This may be true, but there is nothing like a Catholic
city, unless it is a Muslim one, for bare-faced robbery. Go up to
Scandinavia, where the pastors lament that God has died, for
decency of behaviour and respect for property. The Catholic Mafia
and Camorra set the world's standards for villainy. Christ has taken
on the burden of our future sins as well as our past ones. St Paul raged
in vain against that heresy. Moving to Monaco, if we could, we
would be in a Catholic principality, but there the police, so we heard,
were not in collusion with the criminals. There were a lot of police:
Milanese millionaires had to be protected.

It was time, too, for me to regularise my exile. I had been living in
Italy without the state's permission; I was a displaced person. I needed a
carte de séjour to show that I was an acceptable guest of a foreign country.
Before I could be accepted in Monaco I had first to be accepted in France
and answer questions at the French Embassy in Rome. Why do you
wish to live in France? *Parce que je suis écrivain et j'ai besoin d'une culture
vive que je ne pourrais pas trouver sauf en France.* Anything like a failure of
British patriotism goes straight to the French heart. As for the
relationship between France and Monaco, France did not really like to
see that independent enclave stuck on its Côte d'Azur. Monaco should
be French as Gibraltar should be Spanish. General de Gaulle had been
angry to see so much French business taking advantage of Monaco's
tax-free status and he had threatened to cut off Monaco's water,
electricity, gas, postal services and railway transport. There was a clause
in a Franco-Monegascan treaty which provided for the French
absorption of the principality if Prince Rainier III did not beget an heir.
He married Grace Kelly and secured the Grimaldi line.

Before 1975 was over, there was a very urgent reason for getting
out of Italy. Andrea was at last acquiring an English education. He
was a pupil of St George's School outside Rome, where Italian was
studied as a foreign language and he was taught not only to play the
clarinet but to read music. He was happy there, with his school cap
and his blazer. He would get up in winter Bracciano darkness, eager
to hitch-hike to school and be the first in. He fell in love with a
fellow-pupil, all too blondely Anglo-Saxon, named Elizabeth. He
woke me at five with the demand for a song for her, words and
music. Blearily I wrote and set

Elizabeth, Elizabeth,
Here is my heart.
Elizabeth, Elizabeth,
Don't let us part.
You can be my life,
You can be my death,
Winter's frosty knife,
Summer's balmy breath –
You, you, Elizabeth,
Elizabeth, Elizabeth.

This pleased him well enough and he ran off through the dark. But, in dark or light, he was being watched. He was a foreigner, the son of a German who had made money out of violence.

One of the Tagliaferro family came to call – a member of the Sicilian branch, not the Maltese. He was a retired mafioso, and he claimed to have worked with Lucky Luciano. He had come to settle down in Anguillara on the coast of Lake Bracciano (a town noted for its eel dishes, with eels on its coat of arms, and indeed, an eel in its name) and he wanted me to ghost his autobiography. I did not at once dare to reject the assignment. Let me, I said, finish the book I am at present writing and then we will meet again for a detailed discussion. He talked of the *vicissitudìni* of a varied life, of the odd *necessità* of dressing the wicked in *capotti di cemento*. He was a man of impressive presence and old-world courtesy. We smoked his Monte Cristo cigars and he drank my airport malt whisky. He came back later to warn me that my son Andrea was on the kidnap list. It was not to be a Mafia kidnapping, he assured me, and he would have nothing to do with it anyway, being retired from the trades of extortion and revenge. It was a group whose location and member-ship he knew but would not divulge; he could vouch for both its greed and efficiency. We had better get out of Bracciano. We were, I said, leaving anyway.

But this was not yet. In the summer of 1975 we were looking for somewhere to leave for. We could see that the Principality of Monaco was above our social rank. The bohemian daughter of a contessa and a scruffy writer were ejected from at least one restaurant (La Rascasse) for being ill-dressed. Our motor caravan was not welcome. Among the sybarites, in blazing heat, while Liana searched for an apartment, I wrote *Beard's Roman Women*. This was partly in the bedroom of a small hotel run by Swiss homosexuals. I nourished myself on bottled beer and madeleines. The German

version of the book – *Rom im Regen* – has only just been published,
and I was in winter Zürich between the last paragraph and this to read
aloud from it. Hence I have had occasion to return to the very nearly
true story it tells. This story is about the refusal of the dead to die. '*Im
regnerischen März 196–, etwa eine Stunde bevor er sich zum Flughafen
fahren liess, hatte er die überzähligen Liremünzen in den Trevibrunnen
geworfen.*' In fact, it was in the rainy March of 1959 that I threw my
coins in the Trevi fountain, daring Rome to call me back. Rome is
sullied for the protagonist, Ronald Beard, by his wife Leonora's first
portal haemorrhage, which floods a hotel bedroom.

Beard's wife dies of cirrhosis, like mine, and an American film
producer calls him to Los Angeles to console him. At a party Beard
meets a young and beautiful Italian photographer, Paola Lucrezia
Belli, falls heavily for her and goes back with her to Rome – to my
own apartment on Piazza Santa Cecilia, Number 16A. The Trevi
magic always seems to work. It is in Rome that he hears from an old
Far Eastern friend that Leonora, whom Beard saw die in an Ealing
hospital, is not after all dead: she has been seen drinking in London.
This seems to be confirmed when he receives telephone calls from
her. The calls turn out to be malignant impersonations: Leonora is
certainly dead, and the Far Eastern friend admits mistaken identity.
What I was doing was externalising into fiction the nightmares I was
having and still occasionally have. A wife returning from the dead
may be a phantom, but there is nothing fantastic about the moral
issue that is raised. Is a vow of eternal love cancelled by death? Is a
new love an infidelity? What would any widower do if, confirmed in
a fresh and happy relationship, his supposedly dead wife walked in,
smiling and healthy, saying: 'Here I am. Sorry I was away so long.
Now let's get down to living and loving again'? Then she and the
new love confront each other. It was wise of St Paul to preach that
there would be no giving in marriage beyond the grave and that a
sacrament already sealed would be unsealed.

Ronald Beard in the book feels like a murderer, as all widowers do.
He expiates his guilt by leaving his Italian mistress, who goes back to
her husband anyway. He marries a younger cousin of his first wife, a
virtual simulacrum of her, with the same blond looks, Welsh accent,
culinary skills. But the fates are not satisfied. They strike him down
with a fatal and faintly comic disease, and Beard has to wonder
whether he is being punished for being a widower or for failing in the
courage to reject his native culture (he has scuttled back to it) and
embrace an exotic one. He proposes to die on the stairway of the
apartment block in Piazza Santa Cecilia. The climb is toilsome

enough to give him a heart attack. In their flat Paola Lucrezia and her husband are listening on their hi-fi to a setting of Dryden's 'Song for Saint Cecilia's Day', not Handel's. He essays the climb three times but does not die. He goes off, more or less satisfied, with his Far Eastern friend to get drunk. The rain is heavy over Rome but, miracle, they manage to find a taxi.

I would perhaps understand the book better if Vincenzo Labella had fulfilled his promise to make a film out of it. It would not have cost much, even with – as was proposed – Sean Connery in the lead. I was even persuaded to write the music, including the piquant modernish setting of the Dryden poem. That music joined the pile of· manuscript scores which weigh down the lid of my piano. The Dryden, and its anonymous setting, are clearly in the book because the bones of St Cecilia lie under the altar of the basilica which names the piazza. She stands for death and resurrection translated to an oneiric or musical zone and thus rendered harmless. Paola Lucrezia Belli is related to St Cecilia's antipode, whose statue stands not many yards away – Giuseppe Gioacchino Belli, before whom Beard falls in a puddle, protesting that he is not drunk but dying. Belli stands for the earthy, coarse, unregenerable. I was doing some work on Belli.

Liana found an apartment on the rue Grimaldi in the Condamine. It was on the top floor and there was no elevator. It was large, being two flats knocked into one, and, as this was Monaco, it was expensive. Jesus of Nazareth, or the television script about him, would hardly help to pay for it. The prospect of a late middle age of hard work, with no let-up in deference to fatigue and waning powers, made me somewhat sour, especially in a locale dedicated to moneyed leisure. I wanted to taste some of this *douceur de vivre* I had heard so much about.

The French would take a long time to decide on my suitability for residence on the Côte d'Azur, and then the Monegascan police would deliberate on my suitability for residence on their own minute part of it. The right to live in a tax-free area of the world is naturally a precious gift, not that authors can ever live tax free, since they pay tax wherever they publish. Authors, lacking the concession given to commercial enterprises in Monaco, are, with what looks like gross injustice, more closely watched by *la police des étrangers* than any other Monaco residents. There is always the danger that they will write scandal about *la famille princière*, which was and is and always will be the cynosure of sensational journalists. No week goes by, as I can testify from my knowledge of European bookstalls, without a picture of Princess Caroline or Princess Stéphanie on some cover or other. In the 1970s the love-life of Prince Rainier III and Princess Grace was grossly probed and groundless libels of an impending separation were bleated and blared. The police kept track of this kind of treason among its writer residents and had an extensive stock of tapes of scandalous utterances made on radio or television abroad. One journalist I knew came back from a trip to New York, where he had made a mild allusion to the premarital *amours* of Princess Grace on television, to be greeted with an invitation to hear his own voice on record and an order to leave the Côte d'Azur within twenty-four hours. I had no fear of such expulsion: I was not that kind of writer. And, before putting myself in danger of it, I had first to be allowed in.

So it was from Rome that Liana and I flew to New York, she to stay there for a while while I went straight to Iowa City. I was not only to hear my symphony performed; I was to teach the modern novel for half a semester. My two hundred students did not hear the symphony; the students of music did not know that I was a novelist: the division between the sister arts is hardly to be healed by eccentrics like myself. I picked up Liana in Winnipeg, where Len Carriou's company performed, not well, my translation of *Cyrano de Bergerac*. There she fell in love with the local goldeneye fish and crammed our luggage with broiled fragments of it. We were lodged in an old house on the corner of the Iowa campus and she saw, sooner than I did, the virtues of an agrarian state. For here the wealth was basic and genuine: it sprang from the soil and not from the manipulations of commerce. The scents on the air were of wheatfields, and the sophistication of the culture the university promoted was balanced by the primitivism of the farming Mennonites, who allowed no engines on their acres. An open-air pig-roast was seasoned with a performance of *The Importance of Being Earnest*. The faculty refurbished its culture in Europe and was contemptuous of New York, though it conceded intellectual merit to Chicago in the east and theatrical value to Minneapolis in the north. When Burt Lancaster, accompanied by Gianfranco de Bosio, arrived via Cedar Rapids, the university population was not over-impressed. It had other things on: a marathon reading of *Ulysses* and an endless collective epic poem festooning, in a toilet-paper copy, the streets of Iowa City.

Lancaster and Gianfranco had come to persuade me to write a film script on the life of Schroeder, the schizophrene who had interested Freud. Lew Grade, who seemed to be on the way to ruin through projects unrealisable and hence wasteful of front-money, was prepared to finance a script. I told them to put off discussion of the project until my music had been performed. Like any composer whose imaginings have not been tested through the realities of the concert hall, I was tremulous with fear. Jim Dixon, the conductor, a big humorous steak-eating man, consoled me: in the preliminary rehearsals the music had sounded well enough. I had made a misjudgement about *Flutterzunge* on the flutes, and the one harpist (I should have written for two), a neurotic girl who had invited the Head of the Music Department to sleep with her, was screaming about the impossibility of certain pedal-changes and my failure to specify all the notes of her *glissandi*. The harp, the most dispensable of all the instruments, even in Debussy, gives the most trouble. As for the tenor soloist, who had just taken his doctorate, I had put too many notes in his weak region: he could sing high C and it would be as well to alter the score to accommodate this gift. There was trouble with the timpanist, who was black. Like many blacks, he insisted that he had a natural sense of rhythm, but this Jim Dixon had denied. 'You ain't got no rhythm, baby,' he had said. Jim Dixon had none of the fashionable squeamishness about race. He told the story of the pianist Rubinstein, who had been in Tel Aviv and was asked what he thought of it. A fine city, he had said, but too many Jews.

The night of the concert came. I gave a cocktail party before it and had lost some of my fear. Burt Lancaster and Gianfranco de Bosio were in the audience, and the Head of the Music Department had said to Burt: 'I hope to Christ we haven't bought a turkey.' The concert began with Brahms's 'Tragic' Overture and then came forty minutes of my music. They had not bought a turkey. There were, for me, visual thrills I had dreamt of for over forty years – the bells of the three trumpets raised, the extravagant wiping of the cymbals, the fists of the xylophonist racing up and down his bars of wood. The harpist spitefully neglected to play one of her *glissandi*. The tenor was weak on most notes except his prized high C. The baritone was first-rate. It was he who had to bring the work to an end with spoken lines of Shakespeare: 'The words of Mercury are harsh after the songs of Apollo. You that way. We this way.' And then a fortissimo C major triad. This earned a laugh. It is rarely that one laughs in a symphony.

I wished my father had been present. It would have been a filial fulfilment of his own youthful dreams. My father was in my mind when the university organised a weekend film festival with the director Sidney Pollock as guest. One of the films presented was Fritz Lang's *Metropolis* in its uncut version, and I volunteered to accompany it on the piano. My father had done this, twice nightly, thrice on Saturdays, but he had had only the much edited reduction, which granted his hands a rest after ninety minutes. I played for nearly four hours. I was given little wisps of marihuana in thanks. I was back into music, but I had neglected such performing skill as I had. I would never now, as old age approached, be a pianist. But America accepted me as a composer.

Burt Lancaster and Gianfranco de Bosio flew east from Cedar Rapids with my promise of a script on Schroeder. Meanwhile I had three other projects to fulfil in the sphere of show business. One was a series on the life of Freud for Canadian television, one an off-Broadway musical about Trotsky's visit to New York in 1917, the score to be composed by Stanley Silverman. The third undertaking was the toughest. The disaster movie had proved a profitable genre, and Brown and Zanuck at Universal wanted to make a film of the ultimate disaster – the end of the world. What they had in mind was a futuristic version of *When Worlds Collide*, which had scared people in the 1950s. People were always happy to be scared, and now film technology had advanced to a pitch which could make them sup full of horrors. *The Towering Inferno* had shown only a skyscraper on fire, and *Jaws* had only been about a man-eating shark. Now the shark would be a heavenly body rushing into the earth's orbit and eating the Rockies after the *hors d'oeuvre* of Manhattan. Zanuck and Brown naturally thought in terms of the end of America and an American spaceship saving the élite of America, who would build a new America somewhere in the outer blackness. They called upon a British writer to show all this.

At a cocktail party in Iowa I met Professor Van Allen, the discoverer of the Van Allen belt (two regions, so I learned, of charged particles above the earth, the charges coming from cosmic rays trapped by the earth's magnetic field). I discussed the end of the world with him, and he thought there was nothing improbable in the notion of a collision of the earth with an intrusive heavenly body. Indeed, this was more likely than a nuclear destruction engineered by the superpowers: blind nature remained our best destroyer. Encouraged, I set about creating a rogue planet called Puma from a distant solar system, blundering into ours to make a single circuit in the wrong direction, eating the moon first and then opening its jaws for earth, meaning America.

I wrote not a film treatment but a brief novel. I wrote the Freud script and the Trotsky libretto at the same time. All three sat in the same folder in instalments of varying length, and when all three were finished I saw that they were aspects of the same story. They were the story of the twentieth century, in which the major discoveries have been of the human unconscious, the possibility of extra-terrestrial colonisation, and of the salvation of human society through world socialism. Writing respectively a television series, the libretto of a musical, and a science fiction novella, I had really written a tripartite novel in a form appropriate to the television age. The television zapper has trained us to take in quasi-simultaneously a number of diverse programmes: why not apply this zapping technique to prose fiction? I called the novel *The End of the World News*. The Zanuck–Brown film was never made, for the film financiers saw no future in an ultimate disaster; the Canadians grew scared of a Freud series; Stanley Silverman developed a composer's block. I wrote the music myself for the Trotsky project and put it in a drawer, though I performed one of the songs on BBC radio. For the rest, I was able to salvage for a kind of sub-literature what the livelier media rejected. I hate waste.

This work was done in Bracciano. We were a long time hearing from the French and the Monegascans about permission to move to the Côte d'Azur. As is often the way, I now regretted leaving Italy, or at least Lazio. I had become strongly attached to the Roman dialect, which Andrea spoke, and, above all, to its poet Giuseppe Gioacchino Belli. When I was not writing about Freud, Trotsky and the end of the world, I was translating Belli's sonnets, using the Petrarchan form so easy for the Italians, so hard for us. There were a lot of these sonnets – 2,279 – in three fat volumes, and I sometimes thought of dedicating my life to their translation. It would have been a useless venture, for who in the Anglophone world would care about an obscure dialect poet? There were some, not all Romans, who believed Belli to be the greatest poet of the nineteenth century, but his greatness rested in his use of a dialect difficult to translate. Robert Penn Warren, on one of his regular visits to Rome, gave it as his opinion that the nineteenth-century greatness had to be shared between Belli and John Keats. Belli lived in Rome, working as a Vatican censor, while Keats merely died there. Did they, I wondered, ever meet?

The psychic faculty that had made me foresee the assassination of Kennedy had been a long time sleeping, but it awoke when I was asked to read some of Keats's poems at the house on the Spanish Steps where he died. Reciting the odes, I became aware of a kind of astral wind, a malevolent chill, of a soul chained to the place where the body died, of a silent malignant laughter that mocked not my reading but the poems themselves. Later, making a television film on Rome for Canada, I recited the last sonnet – 'When I have fears that I may cease to be' – on the steps outside the Keats house. It was high summer, and the sky was cloudless, but within the space of fourteen lines of iambic pentameters a storm arose, the rain teemed, I and the television team were drenched, and the final couplet was drowned by thunder. The camera caught all this. I am not imputing a demonic vindictiveness to the soul of John Keats. It seemed to me rather that a fierce creative energy, forbidden its total fulfilment by a premature physical death, frustrated into destructiveness, was hovering around the house where he died. Fanciful, true. Let it go, forget it. But if Keats had lived to, say, Belli's age – Belli died in 1861 at seventy-two – would he not have outgrown his consumptive romanticism and, with that Shakespearean wit and intelligence manifested in his letters, moved on to a fuller poetry, doing Browning's work better than Browning? Could he have learned from Belli how to employ the colloquial, the obscene, the blasphemous?

I translated seventy-odd sonnets of Belli, restricting myself to those that dealt with religious themes and gave full scope to the employment of the blasphemy of the Roman gutters. It seemed to me that a reasonable farewell to Rome and environs would be a recitation of my translations in the one place where an audience could be raised – the American Academy. I had an actor friend who was willing to recite the originals. This was Mario Maranzana, a Triestine who could manage most of the Italian dialects. He had dubbed the speech of the prison officer in *Arancia Meccanica*. For him I had contrived a Falstaff play out of the better Italian versions of Shakespeare. He was himself a Falstaffian figure, gross, full of gross language. *Cazzo* was never out of his mouth. He had a refined schoolteacher wife named Maria Luisa. Looking for her he would shout: '*Dov'è mia puttana di moglie?*' He called himself a communist and Solzhenitsyn a traitor. Obscene and blasphemous Belli was up his street. We gave our joint recital at the Academy, with Mario Praz and Paolo Milano in the audience: they, if anyone could, could judge of the accuracy of the translations.

Here is the sonnet that dealt with the Annunciation:

> You know the day, the month, even the year.
> While Mary ate her noonday plate of soup,
> The Angel Gabriel, like a heaven-hurled hoop,
> Was bowling towards her through the atmosphere.
> She watched him crash the window without fear

And enter through the hole in one swift swoop.
A lily in his fist, his wings adroop,
'Ave,' he said, and after that, 'Maria.

Rejoice, because the Lord's eternal love
Has made you pregnant – not by orthodox
Methods, of course. The Pentecostal Dove
Came when you slept and nested in your box.'
'A hen?' she blushed, 'for I know nothing of – '
The Angel nodded, knowing she meant cocks.

The last two lines could not be a literal rendering. The Italians call a
penis a *cazzo* but also *un uccello*, a bird. I was lucky to have at least an
avian colloquialism in English. There were other names for the
organ, too, and Belli listed only a few of them in a sonnet with a
coda. The English falters badly:

Here are some names, my son, we call the prick:
The chair, the yard, the nail, the kit, the cock,
The holofernes, rod, the sugar rock,
The hickory dickory dock, the liquorice stick,
The lusty Richard or the listless Dick,
The old blind man, the jump on twelve o'clock,
Mercurial finger, or the lead-filled sock,
The monkey, or the mule with latent kick.

The squib, the rocket, or the roman candle,
The dumpendebat or the shagging shad,
The love-lump or the hump or the pump-handle,
The tap of venery, the leering lad,
The handy-dandy, stiff-proud or a-dandle,
But most of all our Sad Glad Bad Mad Dad.
And I might add
That learned pedants burning midnight tapers
Find Phallus, apt for their scholastic papers,
And one old man I know calls it Priapus.
His wife has no word for it but a sigh –
A sign that life has somehow passed her by.

That was unsuitable for the biblical sequence. I imagined Keats
translating it or, not having enough Roman, drawing on the stocks
of Georgian euphemisms. Keats was watching all the time. I would

quieten his unquiet spirit by putting him in a little novel and having him meet Belli. Then I would have an addendum of the unholy sonnets. I would call the book *ABBA ABBA*, signifying less a despairing call on the father who betrays us all than the octave structure of the sonnet-form, the only language Keats and Belli could have in common. But the time for writing this was not yet.

MANY PAGES back, I mentioned what seemed to me at the time a trivial action: I broke an egg on the head of my son Andrea because he was being fractious about his food. He had to wait long for his revenge, which he exacted while we were preparing to emigrate to Monaco. While I was heavily asleep on the bad Bracciano wine, he cut my hair with very sharp scissors, so that I emerged cropped like an old-time criminal. I had to be photographed for the benefit of the Monegascan police, and a scowling unreformed thug invited their confidence. They must have looked deeper than the horrid, or far from horrent, surface, for they let me in. Or perhaps, in those, these, days, long hair was, is, the true criminal badge. So the cropped author and his family set themselves up on the top floor of Number 44, rue Grimaldi, in the Condamine, or port area, of the Principality of Monaco.

That is still my address, or my chief one. I cannot invite the reader to visit me there if he or she spends a holiday on the Côte d'Azur, or comes to report journalistically on the Grand Prix or the annual Television Congress. Too many have appeared uninvited, and this interferes with my work. American students have climbed to the third floor with their rucksacks, assured that they would receive a welcome, be fed freely, permitted to doss down on the parquet, and then to slink off in the foredawn with the odd first edition or trinket of the Pasi family. Mere holidaymakers have tried to make me part of their holiday. The apartment is all too easy to find. It is a ten-minute walk from the railway station, on the one-way artery that leads to Nice. It is a two-minute stroll from the sea front, though it looks out, from the back windows, on the verandahs of the Bristol Hotel, and, from the front, on to a rather charming vista of *belle époque* houses, all of which will, in due time, be demolished to make room for skyscrapers. For Monaco is no longer a delectable oasis of *art nouveau*, restful except in the Casino gambling salons, where the players sweat over their plaques and the running of the ball. It is a miniature Manhattan.

Like the real Manhattan, it has to expand upwards. It cannot push out into the Mediterranean or back into France, where the Alpes Maritimes stand guard. There is an illusion of lateral continuity, since there are no frontiers to mark the beginning of French territory. If you cross the Boulevard des Moulins you are into France, and there was once a time when the Monaco police would carry gambling suicides over that street on to the soil of Beausoleil, so that scandal could be accorded a country well able to accommodate it. During the Second World War the Nazis did not respect Monaco's neutrality and they set up SS headquarters in the Hôtel de Paris, just opposite the Casino. They had to accept the rulings of the Société des Bains de Mer, however, when buying gambling chips with their worthless occupation marks, and were ejected from the salons if they wore uniform. They did not despoil the Casino roof of its lead, since the SBM insisted that it was a historical monument. Monaco maintained its dignity and still does.

Aristotle Onassis once gained a sort of control over the principality, owning the majority of the shares of the SBM, and he had some notion of Prince Rainier III's marrying Marilyn Monroe to attract the tourist trade. He was a vulgar man, and Prince Rainier, with the astuteness that the Grimaldi family has always shown – it is, after all, the oldest monarchical line in Europe – outwitted the tycoon with a cunning manipulation of the SBM's charter and drove him out. When the Hitchcock film *To Catch a Thief* was made on the Côte d'Azur, the prince met its star, Grace Kelly and, in a genuine love match, married her. She played the role of princess superbly, seduced the French into keeping their paws off the territory, secured the Grimaldi succession, and presided over Monaco with a glamour that was no mere factitious emanation of her cinematic *métier*. The beauty could be observed at close hand, the dignity was genuine, the kindness was no act.

Liana and I first met her and Prince Rainier when Yehudi Menuhin and his wife Diana came to the principality for a concert. I had met Yehudi on a BBC television programme, had reviewed his autobiography, and maintained a correspondence with him. He invited us to a lunch in a Monte Carlo restaurant, his portion of the meal being wholly vegetarian, and the princely pair were the other meat-eaters. From then on Liana and I were regular guests at the palace parties. Grace was perhaps the last of the great hostesses. She could charm the French and control Frank Sinatra. Sinatra never quite understood the nature of her status, regarding the term princess as a kind of metaphor, rather in the manner of New York Jews. Or else he would assume in her a depotic power from which she was constitutionally debarred. He would be embroiled in a brawl in a Monte Carlo bar, find himself in the courteous hands of the police, and then telephone the palace with 'Grace, you gotta get me outa this'. One of his show-business friends, Sammy Davies Jr, regarded the princely family as an appurtenance of his own greatness: arriving at Nice airport to find no Grimaldi greeting, he noisily caught the next plane out. But Sinatra could, when he wished, assume the standards of culture and courtesy which a palace party demanded. He discussed with me very learnedly the orchestration of Stravinsky's *L'Oiseau de Feu* and speculated as to how some of its devices could be applied to what his trade calls a backing.

Princess Grace's lady in waiting was Madame Gallico, the widow of the author Paul Gallico, a cultivated English lady who knew all about literature. So my situation, so far as the princely family was concerned, was that of acceptance as a genuine author. This meant a measure of cultural duty to the principality, such as the judging of the annual flower show, attendance at amateur drama festivals, the occasional lecture in the Théâtre Princesse Grace, even the proposal to set up a kind of open university. Grace, after all, had practised an art and I was practising one. There was a *rapport*, there was an occasional palace lunch, followed by a walk through Monacoville, during which the cloaked bare-headed Grace would greet and kiss the older inhabitants. Her charm was a constant property. Her death was a great loss.

All this lay in the future when, in 1976, Liana, Andrea and I walked the bare boards of the third-floor apartment. Furnishing it would be a piecemeal process: no furniture van was allowed to clutter rue Grimaldi. The denuding of the Trastevere flat meant the transfer of everything in it to a small house in Callian, a village in the Var, which Liana almost distractedly bought when passing through Provence on the way to Monaco. In rue Grimaldi there was a table with a typewriter on it; there were mattresses but no bed. Indeed, it was not for another five years that a French bed, far narrower than the old *letto matrimoniale*, was to climb the stairs. It was books that filled the apartment – review copies and most of the library of the *Ile de France*, bought, along with all the galley ladles and a dozen sailor suits suitable only for ship's monkeys, by Liana at a Monaco auction.

Perhaps Princess Grace and I were alone in regarding literature as a commodity not to be disdained in a territory dedicated to pleasure. True, there was a fine miniature opera house, a ballet company, a resident orchestra, a music academy, and a theatre or so, but this was not really a reading country. When rich British expatriates wanted a book, they would telephone the little English bookstore and ask to be sent round whatever headed the week's bestseller list. When video-cassette players became popular, a club was formed with a thousand-pound-a-year subscription which would deliver by air recordings of British sit-com series. Bestsellers were then no longer needed. There seemed to be no writers in Monaco except myself and a reclusive German who produced bestselling pornography. There was, true, Basil Lord, who had become very rich from writing second-language textbooks for commis waiters, and soon there was to be Shirley Conran. There was also the Joyce scholar George Sandolescu, who had been smitten by Joyce when hearing me lecture on him at London University. There were perhaps obscure poets of the Monegascan dialect. There was certainly nobody committed to producing the kind of unsaleable fiction to which I was dedicating my middle age. But surely, approaching sixty, I was past middle age? The climb to the third-floor apartment with shopping-bags, the more arduous climb up the hill-road to Monte Carlo – these were, and still are, useful gauges of senescence.

Reviewing some years ago a book called *Joseph Conrad: Times Remembered* by Conrad's son John, I wrote as follows:

> I shopped in the supermarket, dragged three bags up three flights, peeled potatoes, cleaned Brussels sprouts, put the joint in the oven, washed yesterday's dishes, made the beds, swept the floors, then sat down to Mr Conrad's reminiscences of life at the house called Oswalds.
>
> 'The indoor staff, the crew as JC called them, consisted of Arthur Foote, valet/butler, Edith and Florrie Vinten, house-maids, sisters of the chauffeur, and Mrs Sophie Piper who did the cooking under my mother's guidance, and if there were more than three guests for a meal extra help was enlisted from the village.'
>
> Jessie Conrad suffered from her leg, so the nurse Audrey Seal joined the crew. There were two fulltime gardeners and the aforesaid chauffeur. Conrad, note, was not a rich author even though he was a great one. This was the way a man of letters in the twenties was supposed to live. One cannot help a breath of envy of the kind that escaped from Auden when he versified about Mozart not having to make his own bed.

I am not grumbling – God forbid that I should grant that opening to

critics ready to pounce on a lower-middle-class whine – but I am
certainly regretting the waste of time on unpaid chores that could
have been better spent on earning a living. In a pleasure resort
crammed with hotels, domestic service would have been impossible
to find even if we could have afforded it. True, we were amassing
property which Liana shrewdly declined to sell, but cash was the
problem, and cash had to be earned. Earning it meant that I did little
about producing what I called literature.

In the spring of 1976 I spent six weeks in the University of New
York at Buffalo as a writer (or non-writer) in residence. Professor
Leslie Fiedler, who held the Samuel Clemens chair, invited me. I
approved in many ways of Leslie, whose view of literature was
highly unacademic. He did not see why the techniques of aesthetic
appraisal should be reserved to Henry James and George Eliot. He
was very American in his belief that American literature had
travelled a path quite different from that of Europe – more romantic
and 'Gothic' than realistic – and that the properties of high American
literature could be pursued in lowlier genres – the detective story, the
romantic bestseller, even the comic strip. It was a holistic approach
to fiction of which any fiction-writer had to approve, since his aim is
to extend his audience beyond the mandarin without, if he can
manage it, compromising intellectual and artistic values. Leslie had
been, like myself, caught in the Tom Collins net which promised
huge advances on minimal synopses, and he was at work on a book
about freaks which sounded like a genuine Tom Collins project,
though Leslie broke the toils and published the work without that
dangerous aegis. I was put up in a decrepit motel near the campus.
There was no bath, and I subsisted on room-brewed tea and junk-
food from a supermarket. The squalor helped me to think I was
saving what I earned.

While Leslie Fiedler was extending the bounds of the readable, the
students I had to visit were doing their best to limit them. They
produced poems and short stories which, like *Finnegans Wake*, had
neither beginning nor end, since, unlike *Finnegans Wake*, they were
written on paper glued into rounds, like Christmas cracker caps. The
blacks said it was impossible for a white guy to write fiction with
genuine blacks in it. How about Faulkner? How about *Pudd'nhead
Wilson*? That had to be shit, man, you couldn't burrow into the black
soul with pinko fingers. The girl students denied that any male
novelist could create a female character. How about Madame
Bovary? How about Anna Karenina? How about, for God's sake,
Cleopatra? Transvestite males, the lot of them; it was an *a priori*

business: if you were a man you weren't genetically endowed to know what it was like to be a woman. On the other hand, a woman could produce a man: weren't women doing it every day? The blacks had no doubt that they enclosed the whites. I was made to feel very old-fashioned, like Shakespeare. Othello, of course, was at best an Uncle Tom, at worst a clown in burnt cork.

I was made to feel even more old-fashioned when I took a tape of my Iowa symphony to the music department. The head of the composition section was a Bronx man who spoke of dis and dat and de woiks of Beethoven (the mention of the name provoked a delicate sneer among the students, one of whom was a transvestite). My first movement would be okay for a battle scene in a B movie: as serious music it did not begin to exist. What then was serious music? There was no clear answer, but to compose an oboe concerto which produced the same sounds with different fingerings was a serious exploration of sonority: this was what the head of composition was doing. What you had to do (and this sounded much like what was being taught in Paris by Boulez) was to find out what the frontier was between noise and those sonic organisations called musical notes. I fled, deeply discouraged, and read Jeremy Taylor in my motel hovel.

At fifty-nine I was past any woman's being attracted to me, except for the one who had learned to be attracted into marriage when I was fifty-one. But there was a woman instructor at Buffalo who had had a bad marriage. She had come down to breakfast every morning to find on her cereal plate diagrams of the sexual position to be enjoined that night. Out of that marriage had been born a son, now teenaged, bearded, stoned, and violent, who threatened his mother with an axe. His mother, who had gained her doctorate with a dissertation on Lydgate, needed comfort and thought she might find it in me. She drove me to see Niagara Falls ('*Endlich fortissimo,*' Mahler had pronounced on it), but I had the usual difficulty in crossing the border into Canada. We had lobster and steak on the same plate at the Surf and Turf. She took me to a high school where, known only as the author of an article on the Marquis de Sade, I lectured on the Marquis de Sade. She was a woman of great attraction and her mind was well-stocked with mediaeval literature. I sighed, shutting my cabin door on her, watching her, through the smeared window, work her lovely legs into her car. In future, I vowed, I would not visit the United States unaccompanied by my wife.

Marriage is a discipline, and so is love. America had become a great place for the satisfaction of transient itches, and the gods who presided over genital herpes and AIDS would make it suffer. No sex without love, I vowed, and all love to be monogamous. Besides, I was growing old. A Creative Writing student had brought me a story in which one of the characters died at sixty. What did he die of? Of old age, I was told. The lad looked at me sternly, as if he knew of my anachronistic urges. The lovely expert on Lydgate kissed me with passion at Buffalo airport. It was a sort of farewell kiss, and not only to Buffalo. Faithful and continent I flew to Washington.

1976 was the bicentennial of the American revolution. Revolution had put into the minds of America's Shakespeare scholars that Shakespeare had been dead just 360 years. So there was a kind of mystical celebration of Shakespeare in the nation's capital. Three men were to give the keynote addresses – Alistair Cooke, a Mancunian like myself but now, like TWA, a bridge over the Atlantic river; Jorge Luis Borges, whom I had met sporadically in a number of American colleges; the man whom the great Argentinian had humorously called the Borges of England, now to be amended to *el Borges mancuniano*, or possibly *mancuniense*. It was on this occasion that I met my old tutor from the University of Manchester, Dr L. C. Knights, reflecting that wheels were coming full circle, that I would probably remeet all of my past before being snuffed out in my brief future. It was on this occasion too that Borges and I spoke Anglo-Saxon together. It was at a party in his honour at the Argentine Embassy, and there were too many spies around listening for incriminatory words from the distinguished sceptic. The conversation was really an antiphonal recital of Caedmon's hymn about Frumsceaft or Creation, and it went like this:

Burgess: Nu we sculan herian heofenrices weard
Borges: Metodes mihte and his modgethonc
Burgess: Weorc wuldorfaeder swa he wundras gehwaes
Borges: Ece dryhten ord anstealde.

I may have got the dialect wrong, but the point was that it got the spies worried. This could be accounted a triumph for scholarship.

I delivered my speech, from which great scholars like L. C. Knights, G. Wilson Knight and Dame Helen Gardner stayed away; it partly took the form of a short story on Shakespeare's possible contribution to the King James Bible. Nobody has yet solved the mystery of why Psalm 46 has the word 'shake' 46 words from the beginning and 'speare' 46 words from the end (if you ignore the cry 'Selah'), the year of the proof-correcting being 1610 (4+6) and Shakespeare 46 years old. It is not a matter of interest to scholars.

There is a short story by Kipling called 'Proofs of Holy Writ' which shows Shakespeare arguing with Ben Jonson about biblical *mots justes*, and from it I took the idea – not confirmed by any known documentation – that the Jacobean poets had been brought in to polish the proofs of the poetic books of the Bible. In my story Shakespeare, weak in Latin and Greek and totally without Hebrew, is left out of the great work and, sensitive about his provincialism and lack of higher education, broods. He ends by inserting his name in Psalm 46, hoping for a rebuke that will at least show that the higher scholars have heard of him, but the 'shake' and the 'speare' are merely blandly accepted as adequate amendments of 'tremble' and 'sword'. I still ask the question: who found out about what is either a sly self-glorification or a strange but suggestive accident? That I was excited about this proved that I was not a scholar. I collected my silver medal and my fee, tucking it away with my Buffalo cheque, and took a plane from Dulles airport. I had made a little money, but I was supposed to be earning my living from writing.

I DID write, but my writing was for the void. I earned much of my living by writing scripts for films and television series that were, as I knew while writing them, destined not to be made. There was, to start, the ultimate disaster movie, which I called *Puma*. I was summoned by Zanuck and Brown to Culver City to meet their elected director, John Frankenheimer, but he was busy at Paramount editing a film about Palestine Liberationists dropping bombs from the Goodyear blimp on to the spectators of the Golden Bowl game in Florida. A gesture in the direction of making *Puma* was a storyboard created by Universal artists – four walls of a room covered with a strip cartoon of the narrative. But I could hear the heart going out of the project – something to do with the shaking of the heads of the banks. I was stuck in a suite in the Beverly Wilshire Hotel, reading *Humboldt's Gift* and wondering why Bellow had not been filmed. I was robbed of a thousand dollars by a room-cleaner or one of her confederates, but I dared not complain. That would have been a sure way of getting a Mexican knife in my back. This was not a good hotel. A few weeks previously a visiting British agent had collapsed of a heart attack there and been bundled into the hands of the police as an unseemly drunk: he had died in the wagon. The food was bad. I was not mollified by the free basket of fruit and the welcome to Amigo Burgess. I would not be seen again in Los Angeles.

Back in Monaco I was persuaded to write a script on Mary
Stewart's novel *The Crystal Cave*, which was about Merlin. The
young producer, Tom Auslander, was very excited about gaining
the rights to a work by so distinguished a novelist, and he expected to
be congratulated on having persuaded her to let me transfer (so long
as I carried it with care, spilling not a drop of its exquisite essence) her
masterpiece to the screen. After all, she disapproved of my *A
Clockwork Orange*. I got mad: Christ, I was no Henry James, but nor
was she any George Eliot. Lynne, my first wife, had been wise in
warning me against self-disparagement: people would always be too
ready to accept one's undervaluation of oneself. The English, if not
the Irish or Welsh, posture of modesty in respect of ability or
achievement was certainly out of place in the tough world of show
business. So I said to Tom Auslander that I was doing him and the
bestselling lady a bloody favour, and I produced a script that was, I
knew, a good deal more compelling than the book. Auslander then
requested that I forgo the second half of my fee so that he could pay a
genuine script-writer to convert my effort into something mediocre.
That was the term he used. Mediocrity was safe and within the
comprehension of the financiers.

Things had changed little in the film world since the days of the
illiterate trekkers west from the New York clothing industry
(Auslander had been brought up in that). There was a relic of those
days still in the script shorthand MOV, meaning mivout sound.
Peter Ustinov had been willing, with myself as scenarist, to star in a
film about Edward Lear, but the response among producers had been
of the order of 'Lear? Wasn't he a king or sumpn?' and, when told
about 'The Owl and the Pussycat', 'Streisand just made a movie with
that title. A real stinkeroo. Way down south at the BO.' My novel
The Wanting Seed came up again as a possible vehicle for Sophia
Loren, with her husband Carlo Ponti producing, but financiers were
scared of cannibalism as the solution to the world's feeding problem.
Cannibalism was not mediocre.

I wrote two television series – one on 'Vinegar Joe' Stilwell, the
American general who cursed Louis Mountbatten as a Limey
playboy, the other on the life of Aristotle Onassis. I even, at the
request of the production company, went to New York to argue the
major television networks into accepting the latter. But they were
interested only in Onassis's marriage to John F. Kennedy's widow.
Stilwell seemed to have been forgotten. But, whether these projects
might have been acceptable or not, there was something increasingly
frightening about the thesis-sized contracts that went with them.

The author was to give up all rights in his work, submit to all changes, and even transfer the very name of author to the producer. The pay was on subtle sliding scales that, to the deliriously uncomprehending head of the untrained contract-reader, seemed to portend the paying back with interest of the advance if the project were to be abandoned. Samuel Goldfish, who turned himself to Goldwyn, had merely called writers shmucks with Remingtons. They had now become the ultimately screwable.

What seemed promising, chiefly because there was a cisatlantic honesty and even generosity in the three-page contract, was a feature film on the life of the Persian hero Cyrus. The project was Iranian. The Iran of the Shah wished to enter the world of international cinema, and what better subject for its initial multi-million-dollar venture than the Persian superman celebrated by Xenophon and Herodotus? The emphasis was to be on Iran's Aryan past, but there would be in the film a sequence of great interest to the Jews, since Cyrus entered Babylon by way of its sewers, slew Belshazzar, and put an end to the Babylonian captivity. One of the Shah's cousins was placed in charge of the enterprise. He was a charming man, with a charming wife educated at Roedean, and he fed me in Paris exquisitely on *sabzi khordan, panir, nane lavash, mast va vakhiar, chelou, khoreshe fesenjan, halvaye shir* and the finest Iranian caviar. He fed Vincenzo Labella exquisitely too. Vincenzo was never far away when there was a film project that had a chance of realisation. He had been absent and silent when the American projects had come up. There seemed every possibility that *Cyrus* would be made: there was plenty of Iranian money available. I read my Xenophon and Herodotus and histories of Persia and produced a good loud script. But then Ayatollah Khomeini stepped in, slaughtered Iran's pre-Islamic past and, while he was about slaughtering, slaughtered the producer of *Cyrus* and his Roedean wife.

I actually succeeded in making a film called *Gli Occhi di New York* – The Eyes of New York – for the firm of Mondadori in Milan. This was, and is, a great publishing organisation whose output in print is enormous. How enormous I saw when visiting the Mondadori printing works outside Milan. Huge engines worked twenty-four hours a day on the production of both quality literature and rank rubbish. These opposed commodities shared the same bed, a new edition of Vergil and a Mickey Mouse cartoon book joined like Siamese twins in the printing, to be surgically parted after. Producing print was not enough for Mondadori. They wished to enter the field of the commercial cassette – audio and video. Liana and I put together an anthology of British Victorian humour for the first category, but nobody at Mondadori found it funny. Then Mondadori came into the possession of a vast amount of American film stock and commissioned Mike Billingsly and myself to sift through it in search of something that would make a saleable sixty-minute videocassette. What emerged from the sifting was material about Ellis Island, vignettes on New York primitive painters, and some shots of Manhattan graffiti. I wrote a script which gave a factitious unity to all these elements, recorded it, and wrote an hour-long score for flute, clarinet, violin, violoncello and piano. The film was assembled, very stylishly, and all the work was paid for, except for the music. The Italian procedure as regards film music was for royalties to be paid, for composer and performers alike, out of lease or sale of the film itself. As the cassette was never put on to the market, the musicians got nothing. Mondadori had second thoughts about invading the world of non-print media.

The only film in which I was involved which actually reached the screen and, indeed, made money was one produced by the American Michael Gruskoff and directed by Jean-Jacques Annaud. This was *Quest for Fire*, based on the novel *La Guerre de Feu* which was published as long ago as 1911 by the Belgian J. H. Rosny. The book is not known in Anglophonia, though many European children have read it. It is a fanciful romance about primitive man, presenting a Rousseauesque noble savage not really acceptable to Darwinians. It is a dream more than a scientific reconstruction of the Stone Age, but it is a dream that has sold more than twenty million copies. Jean-Jacques was known for his film *Black and White in Colour*, a study of French attitudes to their former colonial subjects. The French did not want to see it but it was successful outside France and, indeed, received an Oscar as the best foreign film of 1978. His next film, *Coup de Tête*, was acceptable to France and made enough money to enable him to spend two years looking for finance for *Quest for Fire*.

Lest it should appear that I am concerned only with recording the trials of a writer, I will recount the difficulties that Jean-Jacques had in making *Quest for Fire*. He got a script from Gérard Brach (Roman Polanski's collaborator) and a number of unknown young actors who had to learn the gestures and language of anthropoids. A little money came in, and a low-budget production was set up with a small British technical crew. The locations were to be in Iceland and Kenya. Then Gruskoff, in Paris making *Nosferatu* with Werner Herzog, met Jean-Jacques and became interested in his project.

Columbia too grew interested, but underwent one of those

bewildering changes of management of the kind that had ditched the Warner Brothers Shakespeare film. Having said yes, Columbia now said no. Gruskoff then went to Twentieth Century-Fox. The former tough-guy actor Alan Ladd was head of the company and Gruskoff taught him enthusiasm for *Quest for Fire*. Then Ladd resigned, but not before passing that enthusiasm on to his successor, Sandy Lieberson. Money now entered the project, and by the time shooting in Iceland was ready to begin, two and a half million dollars had already been spent on it. But problems arose in the shape of Iceland's quarantine laws, the strictest in the world, which forbade the importation of Stone Age animals. These were elephants and lions, made suitably shaggy for the film, which were being brought from Africa. By the special building of a quarantine ship, the promise of total segregation on the sets, and the construction of a special airstrip, the Icelanders were persuaded of the non-violation of their laws. The team worked on the central tableland of Iceland, far from any human habitation except the tiny village of Hella. The team needed this village so badly for accommodation that they persuaded the villagers to go on a pre-paid Mediterranean cruise for the whole period of the filming.

But now the Screen Actors' Guild called all its members out on strike, and every American-backed film project automatically closed down. Gruskoff was on the telephone for eighteen hours a day, seeking finance from very unlikely sources. At last the Hungarian-born John Kemeny, who ran the International Cinema Corporation in Montreal, agreed to look for ten million dollars, starting with the two and a half million that Twentieth Century-Fox wanted to be urgently repaid. The negotiations took time. The beasts went back to their zoos, the villagers to their village, the airstrip froze over. But the film was made, seen, and remains popular.

My part in the enterprise was the creation of a plausible language for the men and women of the Stone Age. This would be the first sound film ever to employ an artificial language that would resist dubbing. There would be no subtitles either. Everything said would have to be made clear by the context of action. Both Jean-Jacques Annaud and Michael Gruskoff had some vague notion that the Stone Age people of Europe spoke the old Aryan tongue we call Indo-European, but they were several scores of thousands of years out. What they would certainly not be speaking was a tonal language of monosyllabic roots like Chinese; nor would they be grunting and hallooing in Tarzan fashion. Their language – or languages, since several tribes were breaking their long isolation in search of fire –

would have a faint resemblance to what we know of Indo-European, with an accidence of some complexity, meaning terminal gradations in nouns and verbs. The uninstructed like to believe that primitive languages were simple. Not so: they became simple, or simpler, as men learned how to generalise. Modern English is far simpler than Anglo-Saxon. Stone Age man might have distinct words for sun or moon, according to its position in the sky. But to speak of words in the earliest stage of language is probably false – whole statements rather, as yet unanalysable into parts of speech.

I did not dare to be too pedantic, since our actors would not be professional philologists. They had to be equipped with a very small vocabulary of lexemes, and, at the same time, with the anthropologist Desmond Morris in charge, a fairly exact inventory of gesture. Without gesture a lot of the speech would make little sense to the audience. And, of course, the linguistically ignorant find the Max Müller theory of language being specialised gesture rather comforting. It was hard to get either Morris or the actors to accept that words are arbitrary. I had to fasten my invented vocabulary to some dictionary or other. Thus, a tree could be thought of as *dondr*, a fanciful ancestor of the root of *rhododendron*, and a forest could, in the Oriental manner, be expressed by reduplication: *dondr-dondr*. An animal could be *tir*, forerunner of German *Tier*, and a stag, carrying a forest on its brow, could be *tir dondr-dondr*. The prepositions could be simple phonemes, in the Russian mode, so that 'The stag in the forest' would be *tir dondr-dondr v dondr-dondr*. As for the key-word of the film, it would very likely be expressed in some form which avoided naming the thing directly: *atr*, related to Latin *atrium*, meaning a place blackened by fire, would do. Vocabulary is less important in language-invention than structure: it was structure that the audience would have to hear. One British film critic was very foolish in thinking that all he heard was apeman inarticulacies. It was the young for the most part who heard very differently. It was feared that the film would raise unwanted laughs, but it did not. It was worth making. And though the payment for the linguistic contribution was a handful of hundred-franc notes from Jean-Jacques Annaud's pocket, I did not, as I did for a fully paid-up script unused, feel cheated.

Another way of getting money was to travel in person to collect book royalties unpaid. Since I had no agent, and some publishers will not shell out unless importuned, this knocking at foreign doors was enforced on me. There was no point in going to Tel Aviv or Warsaw – too far, too difficult, not much to buy with unexportable stage money – but Spain was next door to France, and in Barcelona not only Spanish but Argentinian earnings awaited collection. Paco Porrua, a Buenos Aires man who, like so many from the Argentine, had emigrated to the mother country in search of political freedom, was holding thousands of pesetas in Sitges. Liana, Andrea and I loaded ourselves into the Bedford Dormobile in high summer and made for the Pyrenees. The Monaco police were glad to see the back of us. They did not like our vehicle, and they granted no place in which to park it. It was too plebeian, too *Wandervogel*, too much associable with fat brown German legs and picnics of beer and sausage. What they wanted from us was something High German,. like a Mercedes. They would have to wait a long time for that.

After several breakdowns we arrived at Sitges, parked under a grilling sun, and moved into a single cheap *habitaciòn*. We found Paco Porrua, and he loaded us with pesetas. As G. K. Chesterton said, the only real money is specie. I bulged with the stuff. When Andrea wanted something useless, such as a collection of Toledo knives, a sombrero, an ill-woven poncho, or a succession of highly coloured *helados*, I was quick with 'Certainly, my boy'. I fed us all, including Paco Porrua, on Argentinian steaks and rough red wine. Andrea got gently drunk for the first time in his life. It had to happen sometime. He plunged into the sea to clear the fumes and then flopped down as if dead in the *habitaciòn*. The time has come to say something about Andrea.

As i approached sixty and Andrea passed thirteen, I accumulated a fair load of parental guilt. If I had been a schoolmaster in Banbury or a bank clerk in Ealing, Andrea would have had an adequate suburban education and been sensibly monoglot. But, living in Europe as he did, and moving from one part of Europe to another, being, moreover, the product of an Anglo-Italian connection, he never quite knew what his native language was. He had spoken Moghrabi Arabic in Malta, switched to Roman and then to Tuscan, and now had been thrust into a French-speaking environment. He settled into trilinguality but was not happy about it. He had been taught in Italian state schools, moved briefly to a private one where English was the teaching medium, and now found himself in Monacoville under French nuns. In an end-of-term concert he was dressed up as a courtier of Louis XIV and made to play Lully on his recorder. Music, the transcendent language, kept him sane. But then he moved to a technical college on the border of the principality, where there were French students as well as Monégasque. Here there was a good deal of defiant French chauvinism, and Andrea, doubly the foreigner, was chosen for execration. The history lessons were chauvinistic, with the British winning the battle of Waterloo only by ungentlemanly cheating. Andrea the *italien* was of a race too lowly for the French to take seriously – spaghetti-munchers who sang oilily on construction-sites – but Andrea the *anglais* was assaulted in the school urinals. He fought back, but he grew weary of fighting. He denied, anyway, that he was English. There was Scottish blood in the family, thanks to my mother, and Andrew filled up his arteries with it, denying the Irish inheritance. He chose a nation to which he could be devoted. He wore the tartan of the Wilson sept of the Gunn clan, learned Gaelic, read Burns and Hugh MacDiarmid. He was to be called Andrew Burgess Wilson.

When the school vacation came round, he would, armed with a student ticket, take a train to London and then another train to Inverness. With his rucksack and his west Scottish accent he would roam the Highlands. His Scottish patriotism became profound and his attitude to Anglo-Scottish history contentious. There is no reason in the world why we should not make our patriotism a matter of free will. Andrew chose Scotland, and he could not have chosen a better nation. Back in Monaco, in kilt, sporran, and Scottish jacket, he walked out with me in the evenings, me carrying my swordstick. This was to attack coarse French youths who cried '*Pédé!*' As Andrew advanced into his late teens, he became an *aficionado* of Scottish malts. He drank like a Scot. He was in danger of becoming an alcoholic. That was safer than being a drug addict.

At the technical college he was trained in what is called *le technologie de la cuisine*. He became a *cuisinier* or cook, but left the college uncertified because of some vague scandal about a bottle of industrial Grand Marnier. He worked as a *chef* in the snack bar opposite our apartment and fell in love with the mistress of Gérard, who owned the place. He worked as a *sous-chef* in one of the two restaurants in Callian in the Var, where the wife of the proprietor fell in love with him. He worked in the galleys of luxury yachts hired by wealthy Milanese or Americans. He worked in the kitchens of Le Fouquet in Paris and then as sole *cuisinier* in a *bistrot* on the boulevard Saint-Michel. In Paris he lived high and alone in a garret near Les Halles, descending to street level to be mugged. In London, with the help of Lord Forte, he secured a post in the kitchens of the Grosvenor House hotel, grew disgusted with union restrictivism, came back to

Monaco. He did odd jobs and, in the evenings, studied the oboe at the Monaco Academy of Music. As I write, he is playing the oboe and the cor anglais in London. He has, if belatedly, fulfilled my own ambition to become a professional musician.

My guilt is in order. Artists (and I have to call myself an artist, not out of the pretension that critics scoff at but because I try to practise an art) do not, with the best will in the world, make good fathers. The fathering of works of art distracts them. They are too nomadic. In *Pudd'nhead Wilson* Mark Twain says of the houses in Dawson's Landing: 'When there was room on the ledge outside of the pots and boxes for a cat, the cat was there – in sunny weather – stretched at full length, asleep and blissful, with her furry belly to the sun and a paw curved over her nose. Then that house was complete, and its contentment and peace were made manifest to the world by this symbol, whose testimony is infallible. A home without a cat – and a well-fed, well-petted, and properly revered cat – may be a perfect home, perhaps, but how can it prove title?' Since 1968 I have never had a house with a cat or any other pet, and to be brought up without pets is not good for a child. True, in Bracciano we had briefly a jackdaw named Ara, a target for the *cacciatori* with their bloody guns, and in Monaco an unspayed tabby called Bruce, who leaped from the third-floor window to seek a mate. But that symbol of permanence – the cat or dog growing old, its conservatism honoured, the only external changes it knows those of the seasons in the back garden – left my life when I went into exile. For exile is a negative condition: one is not living in a place so much as not living in a place. Andrea-Andrew needed a dog and a garden. And he needed a country he could call his.

When one is prone to guilt, guilt will attach itself to bad weather and delayed trains. Andrew was clearly depressed by the affluent narrowness of Monaco and its over-efficient police force, as well as its prick-teasing French girls with names like Zizi and Dodo, and when he attempted suicide it was clearly my fault for bringing him to the principality. He was involved in a very nasty car accident on the road to Nice, and his left leg and thigh were converted to a bag of Scrabble pieces. This was my fault again. If I was guilty about Andrew, I was guilty also about his mother. The cat Bruce attempted to assert ownership of a typescript of mine and Liana got to him just as the musk-spraying began. She fell over one of Sir Terence Conran's artefacts – a giant mock matchstick with a lighter stuck in the end – and cracked her leg on it in two places. That was my fault for wanting a cat; my fault for writing a book. Liana was expensively operated on in the Hôpital Princesse Grace and then submitted to expensive home therapy. Guilty about writing, I had to write harder than before to pay bills.

Determined to write my novel about the death of Keats, I suggested that we move to tranquil Callian, where there was no Grand Prix and no touristic noise. The Bedford Dormobile was under repair at the time, so Liana, Andrew and I drove in a hired Renault. A French truck nudged us on to a soft shoulder on a secondary road, and the Renault, a very lightweight vehicle, went over and over and ended upside-down in a ditch. We managed to unfasten seat-belts before the car caught fire, though we would have been out of it more quickly had we not been wearing seat-belts. I, like the fool I was, am, went on puffing at a Schimmelpenninck. Andrew, cool and brave, got the luggage out. Then the car destroyed itself. How far this could be blamed on John Keats I do not know. On our way to Rome in the newly serviced Bedford Dormobile, Liana realised that the brakes had been drained of fluid and not recharged with it. She had to drive smack or smash into the scaffolding of a construction site. We were going to Rome to film Keats's grave in the Protestant Cemetery and Keats's lodgings on the Spanish Steps.

KEATS SUBMITTED to being put in the novella *ABBA ABBA* without any further protest, but the novella itself could not possibly repay the time and ingenuity spent on it. The seventy-odd Belli sonnets which I had translated for the second half of the book (and which cunning critics saw were the justification for the first half) had taken more man-hours than I cared to count. Such Irish readers as I met liked the work, and one even said it was a whore of a book, but the British were cold. I received a letter from a reader, a man well-read and highly articulate, who said that *ABBA ABBA* was unreadable. He went further and said that all my fiction was unreadable but conceded that I was a tolerable journalist. This was a not uncommon view. In the spring of 1979 I was summoned to a luncheon at the Savoy Hotel in London to receive a plastic plaque and a cheque for two hundred pounds as Critic of the Year. This was on the strength chiefly of the book reviews I had published in the *Observer*. Mrs Margaret Thatcher had just come to power and she, aware of the importance of the Fourth Estate, did me the honour of quoting the citation that honoured me in her after-luncheon speech. Then she gave me the plaque and the cheque. We were photographed smirking. This was not quite the honour I wanted.

I had the reputation of being a reliable critic. I sent unhealthily clean copy with great speed. On receiving a book, any book, for review, I at once went to bed with it. Then, lest I forget what the book was about, I got up to clatter off my thousand words or so. I was not really being conscientious. If I delayed reading the book I would infallibly lose it. If I delayed writing I would have to read the book again, being always forgetful of most new things I read. Another reputation I had was of being an expert on evil. This was presumably because of *A Clockwork Orange*. When some public enactment of evil – such as the attempt to murder the Pope – needed explication in two thousand words or so, I was sometimes called on by the *Daily Mail* to write an exercise in popular theology, usually in not much more than an hour. The technique of writing for a popular paper was gnomic – each sentence brief but each sentence a paragraph, sometimes made to stick out in heavy type like a wall motto. I began to pride myself on a kind of professionalism. When the features editor of the *Daily Mail* told me I was a good journalist, I began to wish to forfeit the desire to be a good writer.

For the *New York Times*, and especially its Sunday magazine, I turned myself into an expert on France and the French. The fee for a lengthy article on the Pompidou Centre or on Yves Saint Laurent was, by European standards, derisory, but one was permitted lavish expenses. To attend an Yves Saint Laurent *défilé* and then to interview the homosexual master (photographs of little Berber boys all over his bedroom) was not the kind of subliterary work I had ever envisaged for myself. I was a bull in the china shop of his *atelier* and, to shocked *oo la las*, breathed Schimmelpenninck fumes all over rolls of silk which I then knocked over. That assignment was as absurd as having to cover the World Football Cup in West Berlin for *Time*. The real absurdity was having to explain Italy to the Italians. This task was given to me by the great Indro Montanelli, who ran the Milan newspaper called *Il Giornale Nuovo*.

Montanelli was a veteran anti-fascist and a cunning editor who saw the advantage of paying a million lire to a foreigner who, not having been brought up on the Ciceronian style which characterised so much Italian journalism, could speak bluntly and sharply to the Italians and, when the blunt sharpness went too far for most readers, be excused as a mere ignorant Britisher. The features editor would telephone through to demand a thousand words or so on a given subject, often bizarre, and I would dictate these to Liana, who would

at once type them in Italian and then read them to a copy-taker. Some
of the subjects specified had to do with the Joannine-Pauline papacy
(I and II) and the hidden truths behind their more enigmatic
pronouncements. What had Sir Walter Scott (whom John Paul I
admired) to do with Catholic dogma? When John Paul II insisted that
(a) hell existed and (b) the resurrection of the body was no metaphor,
what precisely did he mean? Define hell for the benefit of our
atheistic readers. What is the difference between the angelic and the
saintly? I got into severe trouble with the Italian clergy when I
suggested, in an article on the Turin shroud, that Christ probably did
not die on the cross and that his supposed resurrection was a mere
resuscitation. It was demanded by high Vatican officials that I be
expelled from Italy, although I was actually living on the French side
of the frontier. Montanelli was able to soothe orthodoxy by pointing
out that I was British and that the British were naturally heretics: the
publication of my blasphemous article had been a deliberate irritant;
the provocation of clerical anger and a powerful reassertion of the
doctrine of resurrection had been, after all, all for the good of the
Italian soul.

The *Corriere della Sera* offered me two million lire for the
occasional article on the *terza pagina*. Montanelli was angry when I
left him, speaking loudly of treachery, but he was being insincere:
loyalty means little in journalism and least of all in any Italian
activity. The *Corriere* had a larger circulation than the *Giornale*, and
its third page articles were closely read. One thing that had to be
attacked there was the villainy of Italian bureaucracy and, even more,
the brutality of its border officials. Liana and I had once travelled by
train from Milan to Chiasso across the Swiss frontier, there to
deposit some money in a bank I will not name. On the return trip she
had been dragged from the train, so that she fell heavily, and her
handbag had been ransacked roughly for evidence of illegal exportation of money. I had had to stand fuming and impotent. Later, our
son Andrew had been removed from the train at Chiasso because he
rightly protested at having had his British passport insolently
thrown to the compartment floor. Then he had been beaten on the
testicles with a rubber truncheon and refused permission to reboard
the France-bound train, last of the day. He found a *carabiniere* to
whom to protest, and this *carabiniere* had turned his back while the
action with the *manganello di gomma* had been resumed. This clearly
had to get into an article, though obliquely, as an almost casual
illustration of frontier police behaviour. Had I been living in Italy, I
would certainly have been visited and roughed up. I was politely

invited to go to Como and discuss the alleged brutality amicably with the authorities, but I knew better than to fall into that trap.

It was assumed, by readers who did not see the small print at the end of my published articles, that I wrote them straight into Italian. I learned to do this, though not for the *Corriere*, but had to ask Liana to check my spelling and my subjunctives. To be published in Italian – not just articles but books – always led to eventual personal appearances in the larger cultural centres of the peninsula. The Italians have the charming custom of 'presenting' a new book, which means inviting the public to free drinks at one of the larger bookstores – which are owned by publishers – and a couple of learned dissertations by professors, followed by the author's eloquent promotion of his own work. Italian, in its Tuscan form, calls for phonetic rehabilitation on the part of an English speaker – the use of new muscles and a *bel canto* placing of the voice. I suppose I must now regard Italian as my second language. Having to speak it at a scholarly level has made me readier to rebuke Italians for speaking English badly. I had a bizarre success with an article for the *Corriere* on the absent *acca* of Italian. I was angered by a television presentation of the film *Pygmalion*, in which Professor Henry Higgins, having taught Eliza to say, 'In Herefordshire, Huntingdon and Hertfordshire hurricanes hardly ever happen', was announced at the embassy ball as "Enry 'Iggins'. The article had some effect on television announcers, who tried to stop deaspirating proper names like Hemingway. The pedagogic instinct dies hard, but Italians are not easy to teach. They refuse to understand what a *schwa* is, except in Naples, where *spaghetti* rhymes with 'better'.

The Italians and I have never been able to meet on an issue far more important than phonology. I mean the reputation of the late Pope John XXIII. When, in the 1970s, the issue of his canonisation came up, the *advocatus diaboli* file seemed to have only one entry, but that was enough to prevent his being whizzed straight into sainthood. The objection to his elevation was my own, and it continues. It was while living in Rome that I asked the Church, in the press, on radio, on television, to consider Christ's statement, 'By their fruits shall ye know them.' If Pope John XXIII had been so saintly, why was Catholicism falling to pieces? He may not have been responsible for all the innovations of the Second Vatican Council, but he had let them go through. The vernacular Mass was a disgrace. I had met priests in America who no longer knew what they believed in. It was considered virtuous for a cardinal to have forgotten his penny catechism and say that love and love alone counted. The cult of a fat personality had driven out the old intellectual rigour of the faith. When I first attacked Joanninism to an Italian journalist I was given the headline *Burgess è fascista*.

I had in mind the composition of a novel of some length in which a profoundly innocent pope became an agent of evil. I had written in Bracciano in 1972 sixty or so pages of it. There was even a title ready. We had been driving in the Alps in the Bedford Dormobile and seen and heard yelping lean-headed eagles. Or rather Liana and I had seen them; Andrew slept. When told what he missed he said indignantly: 'I have seen eagles in my life.' *Eagles in my Life* seemed a reasonable title: Andrew even designed a cover – all multicoloured peaks and crags but no eagles – for a novel of that name. But I grew scared of the length and proleptically weary of the work involved. The books I wrote in the middle and late seventies were meant to be urgencies that justified putting off the great task, though not one of them was urgent. When a writer writes about other writers it is a sign of a loss of creative vitality or else an evasion of the generation of it. I wrote about Keats and Belli, which was perhaps an inventive venture enough. I wrote about Ernest Hemingway. I wrote about George Orwell. I wrote, for the Milan publishing house of Tramontana, a two-volume history of English literature – twelve hundred pages in all. It was called *Scrissero in Inglese* – They Wrote in English. The sheer bulk seemed to excuse my not producing a bulky novel.

When my little Hemingway book came out, I was asked to write and appear in a sixty-minute film for television called *Grace Under Pressure*. This was to deal with Hemingway's life, work and death and to attempt an assessment of his achievement. It was also to try to explain why he killed himself. The London Weekend Television team, with Tony Cash as director and myself as performer, flew to Chicago, picked up two station wagons, loaded them with uncountable metal boxes, unloaded them at a Holiday Inn, and then were told there were no vacancies. It was that kind of trip: meticulous booking at the London end met no counterpart at the Mid-West end. Hotels had ceased to take letters seriously. Delayed by a storm when flying from Salt Lake City to Kansas City, we arrived at the booked hotel after six in the evening to be told that our rooms had been cancelled. We were reluctantly and belatedly accommodated for an extra charge, and I was given a room with television but no bed. I did not complain until we checked out: then I granted myself the luxury of a tirade. It was more self-pity than genuine anger. There had been a time when America knew me as a writer; it did not take long to be forgotten. And here I was bowing down to Hemingway, the author of two good novels but a bad man. I could not forgive him for his treatment of Ford Madox Ford, the greatest British novelist of the century. In the humid house in Key West where Hemingway had lived, I was asked by a curator to marvel at the miracle of superlative fiction being produced by two typing fingers: there, see, was the Hemingway machine. In Salt Lake City I telephoned Professor Geoffrey Aggeler, a Catholic in a Mormon university. He, who had published a book on me, might restore my faith in myself. But he thought the telephone call was a hoax: what would I be doing in Salt Lake City?

Between that paragraph and this I saw the Hemingway film again. It is good television and good biography. It discloses little of the extreme depression I was suffering. There was a moment of pathological self-abasement which the camera did not record. Outside the Kansas City hospital where Hemingway first became fascinated by castration (it comes in the early story 'God Rest Ye Merry Gentlemen' and is given fuller treatment in *The Sun Also Rises*) there is a citation from Shakespeare: 'The quality of mercy is not strained.' I kept referring to Hemingway as Shakespeare until, in Take Ten, I got things right. That elevation of a good novelist into the world's greatest poet signified how low on the literary scale I considered myself to be. Shivering at the graveside in Idaho, I tried to explain why Hemingway shot himself in that house over there (from whose windows Mary Hemingway was watching us). He had reached a plateau of achievement and could not move. He was paralysed and might as well be dead. I was sixty-one, Hemingway's own age when he put the gun in his mouth, and I knew what it was like not to be able to write. But one advantage of not being Hemingway was that I was not big enough to be a public character who, to impose a melodramatic end on a failed life, had to be his own big game. There was humble work to do – making a film on Hemingway, for instance – and a living could be earned. But I wanted to write a masterpiece and did not have the courage to do it.

Liana had quietly written to Little, Brown in Boston to ask them to commission a book from me – anything to make me feel that I was still wanted. Little, Brown asked for a book on Orwell's *Nineteen Eighty-Four*. The apocalyptic year was still some time off, but one could already see that the Orwellian nightmare was not going to be waking reality. What was 1984 really going to be like? I could try to answer that question by writing my own sub-Orwellian fantasy, daring the rebukes of critics for having the temerity, with so little talent, to try to put Orwell right. First, though, *Nineteen Eighty-Four*

had to be explained to American readers who had thought that
Orwell was an arch-conservative warning against Soviet communism, and the vapid use of the term 'Orwellian' for any vision of
the future, very common among American journalists, had to be
rectified. Dallas airport, which looked like the H. G. Wells film
Things to Come, had been called Orwellian. Nobody seemed to
realise that Orwell's imagined future was actually the past –
specifically the year of 1948 – and that he had played the game of
handing the government of a war-weary Britain over to disgruntled
intellectuals.

Orwell's game, I believed, was more a metaphysical one than a
political. Turn Oxford philosophical idealism into collective
solipsism and you got Ingsoc. No existing political system, I argued
in my book, could end up as a metaphysical oligarchy: there was no
prophecy at all in Orwell. The future I envisaged for Great Britain in
1984, or, to avoid plagiarism, 1985, would be the consequence of
syndicalism being given a tougher philosophical base than it already
had. The Trade Union Congress, or TUC, would identify itself with
the state, and Britain would become Tucland with a new national
anthem:

> Muscles as tough as leather,
> Hearts proofed against the weather,
> Marching in friendly tether,
> Cradle to grave.
> Scorn we a heaven hereafter –
> Built it with love and laughter
> Here, firm from floor to rafter –
> Tucland the brave.

The strike weapon would operate not sectionally but collectively. As
my union official Devlin puts it, 'The time's coming, and it won't be
long, it may well be before nineteen ninety, when every strike will be
a general strike. When a toothbrush maker can withdraw his labour
in a just demand for a living wage and do so in the confidence that the
lights will go off and people shiver and the trains won't be running
and the schools will close. That's what we're moving to, brother.
Holistic syndicalism, as Pettigrew calls it with his love of big words.'
Pettigrew is the ideologist of the TUC. He posits the thesis that there
are two human worlds, an inner and an outer, and one must not
encroach on the other. The inner world is for dreams and visions,
including the vision of God, but 'history is full of the wretchedness,

the tyranny, oppression, pain occasioned by the imposition of an inner vision on the generality. It began, perhaps, with Moses, who had a vision of God in a burning bush and, through it, initiated the long trial of the Israelites. Saint Paul sought to impose his idiosyncratic vision of the resurrected Christ on an entire world. So with Calvin, Luther, Savonarola – need I go on?' The world of work, which is controlled by syndicalism, must not be touched by values applicable only to the inner world. The hero of the story, Bev Jones, has seen his wife burnt to death in a hospital enfired by the IRA; the fire brigades, being on strike, have not moved a muscle to extinguish the fire. Bev, a former history teacher and now a confectionary worker, resigns from his union and speaks out for humanity. But the concept of humanity is not acceptable in Tucland – only the material bettering of the worker's condition. Human emotions like rage belong to the inner world.

Bev Jones is so called because three great dead liberals had the syllable Bev in their names – Bevin, Bevan and Beveridge. Aneurin Bevan spoke wisely when he said that syndicalism and socialism are two different things. For the worker has to accept the dynamic of a dichotomy: if the state becomes his employer, then he has to fight the state. Pettigrew envisages 'a withering away of the unwritten political constitution which was always held to be one of Britain's instinctual masterpieces. A parliament has become a time-wasting formality, as you know. We need only an executive and a civil service. A political college is already in process of formation, wherein the executive of the future will be trained. This executive will require, for the mystical purposes of continuity, a permanent head . . . The devotion of the British Worker to the British Royal Family is of long standing, and it expresses an instinctual sense of the value of a nominal executive that is outside the sweaty world of the political professionals.'

The monarch of my imagined future Britain is Charles III. His mother has abdicated. He has a dark-haired queen and begets a son called William. I wrote the book before the Prince of Wales married a blonde beauty, but I got the name of his son right. For the rest, the novella called *1985* is as false a prophecy as *Nineteen Eighty-Four*. I wrote it when the trade unions of Great Britain were behaving irresponsibly. The Europe in which I was living was particularly shocked by the year-long disappearance of *The Times*, because the print unions refused to use the new technology. If I did not approve of the strike weapon, it was because it had been considered immoral in the teaching profession when I had been a grammar school master, because it was not of any utility to a freelance writer, and because it had been used treacherously during the war when I, a soldier, had not been permitted to strike. A year after the publication of my book, in Britain and America, a new and powerful Toryism came into being, with a fierce lady at its head. By 1985 the strength of the unions had declined.

British critics were quick to notice that I was out of touch with British life. My fictional workers were old-fashioned stereotypes puffing Woodbines and eating plum duff and custard. The reality was more sophisticated, with holidays on the Costa del Sol, lasagne and Hamlet panatellas. Although I had covered the World Cup for *Time*, I knew nothing of the new football strategy. To match Orwell's appendix on Newspeak, I provided an account of what I called Worker's English, 'in which grammar should be simplified to the maximum and vocabulary should achieve the limitations appropriate to a nonhumanistic highly industrialised society'. But I was hopelessly out of date in thinking that Britain was still highly industrialised, and the simplification of English was being left to the teenagers and the tabloids. Some of my wider prophecies merely extended into the future what was already there in 1978 – the Language of Professional Evasion, for instance, like this specimen of presidential press-conferencese: 'There are various parameters of feasibility, all of which merit serious examination in the context of the implications of your question, Joe. The overall pattern of strike capability on both sides of the hypothetical global dichotomy is in process of detailed scrutiny, and the temporal element involved cannot yet, of course, be quantified with any certainty. Does that answer your question, Joe? Thank you, Mr President.' I prophesied three-screen television in every home but missed totally the growing vogue of the pornographic videotape.

More than anything I failed to notice that sexual permissiveness could not last. 'The permissive age will persist through 2000, and films and magazines will work hard at devising new variations on the basic copulatory theme . . . Abortion will be cheap and easy. A gloriously apt correlation between the disposability of the foetus and the availability of sex, since both proclaim the cheapness of human flesh.' I did not foresee AIDS, but nobody did. Any attempt at fictional prophecy is bound to fail: no creative imagination can match what seems to spring so casually out of the historical process. But what we mean by futfic or future-fiction is the creation of alternative worlds which do not have to relate to the possible or plausible. Remake the past, as Keith Roberts does in *Pavane* and Kingsley Amis in *The Alteration*, and you are safe. Both imagine what the present might have been like if there had been no Protestant Reformation. This is legitimate, entertaining, even mind-expanding. But move into the future and you are in danger of seeming to ask to be taken seriously as a prophet. The trouble with me was that I had written, in *A Clockwork Orange*, a forecast of juvenile violence that had come all too true. Some people, especially in the United States, wanted to believe that that was all I had written. In late 1978 I had to get down to showing what I really could do. Ford Madox Ford had had that intention when embarking on *The Good Soldier*.

THAT WAS not Ford's preferred title, but *The Saddest Story*, which was, was considered too depressing for wartime publication. The book I began to write was eventually brought out under the title *Earthly Powers*. This was insisted on by Michael Korda of Simon and Schuster in New York. As he shortly afterwards published a novel of his own called *Worldly Goods*, he may, with Hungarian cunning, have been planting the rhythm of that title in advance. My working title was *The Instruments of Darkness*, straight from *Macbeth*, but I discovered that this had already been used for a book on the history of radar. I then took from Hobbes's *Leviathan* a title that Korda said was too long and unmemorable – *The Prince of the Powers of the Air*. The working title got into Italy as *Gli Stromenti delle Tenebre* and the Germans used the prince in *Der Fürst der Phantome*. The French called the novel *Les Puissances des Ténèbres*, a compromise between the first and the last titles. The question is always arising – how important is the title of a novel? Not very, I think; I would be satisfied with something like *Novel Number Twenty*, on the analogy of symphonies. There is no copyright on titles, and there is always the danger of accidental duplication, even triplication: there are three books called *No Laughing Matter*. I have already mentioned my novel *One Hand Clapping* and its eclipse by a biography of John Middleton Murry under the same name. Titles are a great nuisance. I think of *Earthly Powers* as *The Prince of the Powers of the Air*. Korda's title does not mean anything, though critics bravely tried to show how apt it was.

In the great days of the novel, meaning of serialisation, length, sometimes inordinate, was imposed by publishing procedure. Dickens's novels show a technique of accumulation, essentially picaresque: structure is not important. Write a long novel today –

one, say, of 650 printed pages – and you have to erect a scaffolding in advance of setting down the first word. The structure can be arithmological in the mediaeval manner, meaning that the number of its parts has a symbolic significance. The number of chapters I proposed matched the number of years of the man telling the story. He celebrates his eighty-first birthday in the first chapter: let then the total of chapters be eighty-one. 81 is 3 × 3 × 3 × 3. I spelt this out at the beginning. 'I looked at the gilt Maltese clock on the wall of the stairwell. It said nearly three . . . We were three steps from the bottom . . . I minced the three treads down to the hall . . . Three steps away . . . lay a fresh batch of felicitations brought by Cable and Wireless motor cyclists.' It was only when proofs came from the printer that I saw that I had miscounted; there are eighty-two chapters. It did not, does not, matter greatly. Joyce said of *Ulysses* that, when his eighteen episodes had marched across their Homeric bridges, those structures could be blown to the moon. And, when you come to think about it, a man who has celebrated his eighty-first birthday has to be in his eighty-second year.

This extensive structure had at its core a mere anecdote. A pope is to be canonised. The Vatican needs evidence of saintliness – a miracle, for instance. When he was a mere priest, the pope cured a child of terminal meningitis through the power of prayer. This child grows up to be a sort of James Jones, the leader of a religious sect who orders his followers to commit suicide. God, permitting the miracle, clearly intended its beneficiary to perform an act of great evil. Free will does not come into it, since a disease has free will and its lethal progress has been reversed. If the child had died he would not have caused the deaths of others. What curious game is God playing? If God is also the devil, the prince of the powers of the air, then it is as likely that evil will come out of good as the other way round. Perhaps more so. If our century is to be explained at all, it is in terms of God's becoming his opposite.

It seemed to me, writing the book, that the reader had a right to reject this terrible thesis. As the whole story of the consequence of the miracle is told by an ageing man whose memory is unreliable, especially as, being a novelist, he confuses true enactments with ones of his own invention, then rejection of his narration, in part or in whole, is justified. That he is unreliable, like the narrator of *The Good Soldier*, is evidenced by a number of small errors of memory. He insists that he met James Joyce in Paris when, according to Ellmann's biography, Joyce was taking a holiday at an English seaside resort. He claims to have been seduced by George Russell, when, according to *Ulysses*, Russell was burbling about formless essences in the National Library. Russell was, moreover, thoroughly, if unaggressively, heterosexual. The narrator claims to know German well, but he makes *Schloss* masculine instead of neuter. There is no excuse for this, as he is referring to a novel by Kafka. There is a multitude of small errors, all of which were duly noted by the critic Francis King CBE and presented as evidence of the unreliability of this real author, not that invented one. George Steiner was very upset by *der Schloss*: he seemed to think that neither the author nor his editors had a German dictionary handy. In other words, there were critics who failed totally to understand the technique of the book. The way of voluntary rejection is signalled on practically every page. The book is a contrived text, not a record of facts, real and invented, that call for belief or a suspension of disbelief. Most novels assume a covenant with the reader, saying in effect: this is all fabrication, but pretend that it is not; expect consistency of motive and action, as in real life; forget that it is no more than trickery. There is as much Borges as Burgess in *Earthly Powers*, which is what Burgess acquiesces grudgingly in its being called. In other words, no covenant.

The book was big and looked like an American bestseller, but it was more a parody of the genre than the real thing. Indeed, it had very little hope of selling well in America. There was too much ambiguity in it, there was an open attack on reformed Christianity, and evil was not presented as a glamorous property in the manner of *Rosemary's Baby* or *The Exorcist*. The narrator was homosexual, which made its appeal sectional, and there was not a great deal of action. Nevertheless, I hoped for a sizeable advance in America. The book, unfinished, was first sold unseen to Rizzoli in Milan: Mario Spagnol, who then moved to take charge of Longanesi, had the right editorial antennae. We clinched the deal over luncheon in Paris, and at this luncheon Gabriele Pantucci appeared. Gabriele was Rizzoli's agent in London. A tough polyglot Milanese, with American connections and a new American wife – the tall and lovely Leslie Gardner, who had worked for the BBC in London and was now setting up her own literary agency – he sought to take the book, when it was finished, to New York, set himself up in the Plaza, and from there auction the property. This was the new way of publishing a book. The days of reciprocal loyalty were over. You sold to the highest bidder, signed a one-book contract, and prepared to see the book sell what it could and then disappear. And – the Rizzoli sale was exceptional – you sold the book first in America.

In January 1980 *The Prince of the Powers of the Air* was a hundred pages or so off its conclusion. Then Liana broke her left leg in two places and had to be operated upon in the Hôpital Princesse Grace. The smashed bones were joined with patches of metal: hospital rest and medication were imposed and I climbed daily at sundown up to the Jardins Tropiques to see my recovering wife. In sympathy my own left leg began once more to show that its arteries were seizing up and I limped, groaning. Gabriele came to say that he proposed taking my typescript to New York in February in order to ensure pre-Christmas publication, and I had to rush the book to its end. Liana came home and was put to bed in the salon: the bedroom still had only a mattress. I cooked. A physician came at eight in the morning and a physiotherapist at eleven. I claudicated, moaned, wrote. I identified myself with the ancient Somerset Maughamesque narrator of the novel, was prepared to accept death when I had typed the final page but feared bad dreams. Apart from the novel, I had a busy year ahead of me.

I went to Antibes to interview Graham Greene for the *Observer*. I limped up the hill to Monte Carlo station, caught the stopping train – Cap d'Ail, Eze, Beaulieu-sur-Mer, Nice, St Laurent-du-var, Cros-de-Cagnes, Cagnes-sur-Mer, Villeneuve-Loubet, Biot. Greene's apartment was only a hundred yards up the hill from Antibes station, but I had to take a taxi. Greene, in his middle seventies, living with a *chic* French *bourgeoise* whose leg was not broken, was fitter than I at sixty-three. We talked and I bought him lunch. He seemed pleased at what he termed my suffering venerability and, when I sent him the typescript of our colloquy, accepted that this was a true account. I did not, of course, use a tape recorder. Later he contributed to 'Sayings of the Week' in the *Observer* the following remark: 'Burgess put words in my mouth which I had to look up in the dictionary.' This turned me against him. He had long, it seemed, had something against me: back in 1966 I wrote an article on him in which I suggested that he had been touched by the Jansenist heresy. In 1980 he had abandoned hell and sin and was on the way to dispensing with God, but the imputation of Jansenism still rankled. He was like a murderer annoyed at being called a shoplifter. There was in him, I thought, a little of the smugness of the achieved writer, though, to give him his due, there was not more of it than when I had met him first in 1957. I do not think he liked my novels. I was pretty sure he would not care for *Earthly Powers*. I had elected the Joycean way in the sense of deliberate hard words (to check the easy passage of the reader, in the manner of potholes on a road) and occasional ambiguity, Greene had made the popular novel of adventure his model. But I feel that the real barrier between us was that between the cradle Catholic and the convert. Greene has said that cradle Catholics are weak on theology (does he include St Thomas Aquinas?). One who has become a Catholic by choice is bound to feel himself superior to one who, crying at the douche and then licking the salt, is merely unwittingly baptised into it. Evelyn Waugh, despite the legend, had more charity. He was certainly the better Catholic.

In the spring I had a large undertaking – the delivery of the T. S. Eliot Memorial Lectures at the University of Kent. The preparation of four scholarly talks is the equivalent of writing a book, and, indeed, Faber & Faber expected a book: it was a recognised part of the undertaking. But by now I had learned what Simon and Schuster in New York and Hutchinson in London were offering for the new novel, and I was loath to part for a Faber pittance with the hard-milled flour of cerebration, which is tougher work than writing fiction. I called my lecture series 'Blest Pair of Sirens'. It was an attempt to show the relationship between music and literature, and, paying the traditional homage to the nominal sponsor, I began with a discourse on the musical element in *The Waste Land* and *Sweeney Agonistes*. This meant playing the piano and even singing, claudicating from lectern to instrument in a tangle of microphone leads, for I was recording both for the university and the BBC. I praised Eliot for recognising the importance of jazz and popular songs and, indeed, of popular art in general. He was always promising to attempt a critical evaluation of the detective story but, I said, 'He probably failed, as he did in his essay on Kipling, to find the right tools for dissecting what, being merely good, was the enemy of the best. He admired Conan Doyle's Sherlock Holmes stories but did not see how they could be literature. And yet, at the most solemn moment of the first scene of *Murder in the Cathedral*, he lifts, verbatim, some lines from "The Musgrave Ritual".'

Mrs Valerie Eliot rebuked me, at a dinner based on the French cuisine which was curiously and Kentishly heavy, for accusing Tom (who had read the Holmes stories to her while she was mending his socks) of plagiarism: he had assumed that everybody would recognise the citations. I was not convinced; I had always had grave doubts about Eliot's taste and, indeed, intelligence. He was supposed to have preferred *My Fair Lady* to *Pygmalion*, which meant that he admired stupidities like

Arabians learn Arabian with the speed of summer lightning
And Hebrews learn it backwards, which is really rather frightening

and solecisms (which Shaw would not have permitted) like

> I'd be equally as willing
> For a dentist to be drilling
> Than to ever let a woman in my life.

Mrs Eliot was not impressed by me. I had set some of Enderby's poems for a soprano accompanied by flute, oboe, violoncello and keyboard, at the request of the 'cellist Michael Rudiakoff at Sarah Lawrence College, and I followed this with a version of *The Waste Land* for the same combination with a narrator. Mrs Eliot permitted only two performances, but she was prepared to see *Cats* run for ever. God preserve us from literary widows.

I called my first lecture 'Under the Bam', which referred not only to a song in *Sweeney Agonistes* but to the original Persian of the *Rubaiyat* of Omar Khayyam. The Cyrus of the day, in the first quatrain, takes the dome of a mosque and inverts it to make a cup, so that it may be filled with the dry white wine of the dawn. The Persian word for dome is *bam* and for cup *jam*. I was suggesting that the study of English verse be housed in the halls of a wider study of rhythm and stress – be, in fact, under the *bam* of music. This led me on, in the succeeding lectures, to a consideration of Hopkins's sprung rhythm from the musical angle and to symphonic form in *Ulysses* and counterpoint in *Finnegans Wake*. I ended the series with an enquiry as to the meaning of music and, to establish belated credentials, blasted the lecture hall with a movement from my ballet suite *Mr W.S.* This was meant to accompany a dance sequence in which the Globe playhouse is opened with *Totus Mundus Agit Histrionem* fluttering on the flag and the 'All the world's a stage' speech mimed. Then I limped into Canterbury to view the cathedral. I had never seen it before.

I was confused. This was the shrine of Chaucer's pilgrims, good or bad but certainly believing Catholics all, but now it seemed more to be the property of the Blessed Thomas Stearns Eliot. Was English Catholicism possible? Had it ever been? The great continuity to the English was the English Church, whether Catholic or reformed. In the delicious Kent spring I recognised myself to be a foreigner, meaning probably an Irishman. I saw myself scowling at the bland self-satisfied Canterbury streets in the enwindowed mirror of a furniture shop, and I recognised the Irishness very clearly, simian upper lip and all. Georges Belmont, paying a visit to Moscow on behalf of contemporary French literature, had kindly urged the state publishers, going beyond his brief, to consider my work, ending jocularly: 'If you do not publish him he'll plant IRA bombs in the Kremlin.' I felt like planting bombs in the dainty tea-shops of Canterbury, and yet on behalf of whom or what? Chaucer's pilgrims? I was confused. I am still confused. I do not know what I am.

But this year was dedicated to looking for roots. BBC television was to transmit a series called *Writers and Places*, taking British writers back to the sources of their discovery of vocation, and I flew with David Wallace, the BBC director, back to Malaya, or Malaysia as it was now called, to revisit the place where I began to write publishable work. We went to Ipoh in Perak, driving there from Kuala Lumpur, to fix up a hotel for the technical team that would follow, proposing to do most of the filming in Kuala Kangsar. This was not quite the place where I began to write my first published novel, *Time for a Tiger* – that had been in Kota Bharu on the north-east coast – but Kuala Kangsar, the royal town, and the Malay College just outside it were, in thin disguise, the locales of the novel. Kuala Lumpur, the Muddy Estuary, was not what it had been in my day. It had outgrown its origins as a provincial town of colonial departments and Chinese hotels and now had metropolitan pretensions. We put up in an American-style hotel with Chinese and Malay girls kinkily dressed as cowboys in a restaurant called the Ranch House; we found that the sophistication of air conditioning and elevators to the twentieth floor was not supported by the public supply of electricity. Lifts suddenly stopped between floors and ageing American tourists suffocated. We got lost on the road to Ipoh – my fault entirely: I am stupid with signposts and have no sense of direction – and found ourselves ready to plunge into a toffee-brown stream at which angry monkeys drank. But Ipoh, when we found it, retained its old shabbiness, and our hotel was full of hoicking and the loud quack of Hokkien. The team arrived, in it Maureen Hammond, the production assistant, a girl too beautiful for a Malaysia which had forgotten European glamour in the flesh: she was soon set upon by lubricious Tamils and Bengalis.

I spoke Malay again, or *Behasa Negara*, and there was a whole generation which, not having heard a white man speak it, gaped and could not believe its ears. I could still write the language in Arabic script, but, following the example of Indonesia, Malaysia had adopted the Roman alphabet entirely and made the kind of spelling reforms against which I had warned sternly back in 1957. The phoneme *ch* was represented by *c*, even before back vowels, so that Coca-Cola ought to have been, though it was not, pronounced very eccentrically. For that matter, *o* was supposed to have disappeared and the high back vowels spelt indifferently as *u* – *kampong* was now *kampung*. Malay was still having trouble finding a word for 'you'. An advertisement announced that Guinness was good for everybody – *Guinness baik untuh anta*, but *anta* for 'you' was Indonesian and not in use in Malaysia. The beverage itself was downed, and so were gin, whisky and brandy: I had an evening in one of the Sultan's town residences where, surrounded by acrylic nudes, Malays got disgustingly drunk. Strict Islam was slow, following the example of Iran, to impose itself on the middle class and the aristocracy, but there were plenty of the reactionary young around, including girls in solemn black, to urge teetotalism and the hand-chopping of thieves.

Malay College was no longer an English public school for Malays: the medium of instruction was *Bahasa Negara*, the Islamic slant in the teaching was powerful. A photograph of Jimmy Howell, my former headmaster, looked down sourly on the young Malay principal, leading prayers in the dining hall. Certain of my old students were around, chiefly in Ipoh, prosperous businessmen growing to fat, brown fingers quick to activate pocket computers, Longines watches on their plump wrists. I had, they admitted, taught them well: what they particularly remembered was my refusal to give them Chaucer in the Nevil Coghill translation: they had got to the heart of English through its mediaeval form, when the phonemes were close to their own. They were international men, and it had been my intention to make them so: they were always flying to Hongkong or Tokyo, armed with English. And yet the intention of the government, Malays dictating to Indians and Chinese, was to impose the Malay tongue on everyone and punish those who did not speak it. The Malays were on top, *bumiputra*, sons of the soil, but the real work of the country was, as it had always been, in the hands of the immigrant races. There were Malay administrators and army colonels, but no Malay airline pilots or cybernetic engineers.

I had lived in this exasperating, damnably seductive country when a bitter war had been waged in the jungle against the communist terrorists. There had been Malay soldiers then, as well as decent young British national servicemen who were shot and garotted on behalf of an emerging nation quick to forget those heroes, who were as much white leeches as the drunken rubber planters. Now the army was entirely Malay and, the *dzarurat* or emergency being long over, it saw no need for discipline. Filming on the road between Ipoh and Sungei Siput (where the emergency had begun), we became uneasy at the sight of a laughing Malay platoon stumbling through a ditch. Laughing, they raised their rifles at us, unrebuked by the platoon commander, and fired over our heads. They were such bad shots that a bullet pinged our hired car. There is a tendency to hysteria in that race, expressing itself in the diseases of *amok* and *latah*, and their awareness of political supremacy encourages it. Even lowly Malays demanded that Indians and Chinese call them *tuan* – a title formerly reserved to *hajis* and white men. I had foreseen the unhappiness of Chinese tycoons and Indian lawyers back in 1957: I had even written about it in *Beds in the East*.

For all the changes that had emerged since the departure of the British, the country remained enchanting, the girls devastatingly seductive, the food succulent. I, and the whole team, experienced that flood of wellbeing that marks one's first days in the tropics but soon gives way to lassitude, melancholia, and anorexia. But my own recovered appetite for Chinese and Indian *makan* and gin *pahits*, and an erotic flicker that I forced myself to douse, were not reflected in the gloomy solos recorded by the sweating technicians. I called the programme 'A Kind of Failure'. I had tried to bring Western culture to Malaysia, but technology, which is not culture, had laid the way open only to the grossest consumerism. If there was Western culture at all, it was *Dallas* on television and, in the bazaars, the romances of Barbara Cartland, one of the most dangerous women in the world. No literature or music was coming out of Malaysia. The Sultan of Perak, Yang Maha Mulia Idris Shah, had swallowed the West, meaning a fleet of Mercedes, a saxophone on which he played 'Spanish Eyes', muzak very loud in the Istana, his acrylic monstrosities, drawing from Islam not a religious discipline but the posthumous delights of the Koran realised in life – a regular change of wives, houris, *arak* or three-star Martell.

Why should an Oriental state have a national theatre or a symphony orchestra or a library above the level of the Ipoh Club's cupboard of tattered bestsellers? After all, there was a native culture – the *wayang kulit* or shadow play, kampong oboes and fiddles, the recitation of improvised *pantuns*. Yes, but the native culture was disappearing; the Malays were living in the towns and the young were riding Hondas. The leap into modernity had been immense – straight from the jungle to IBMs and discothèques and electronic games. I do not know whether there is an obligation to absorb Beethoven and Shakespeare along with the technology that serves them: that technology is, after all, neutral and international, and quadrophonic apparatus and the visual display unit have no sense of values. But I wondered how long a country like Malaysia could survive without being able, as it were, to tap the oceanic. It is only Islam these days that is filling the spiritual vacuum, and it is filling it with the wrong substance.

Walking the dark streets of Ipoh at night I was accosted by a Chinese girl of exceptional beauty. She offered me not herself but a kind of born-again Christianity. 'Repent,' she pleaded. 'Do repent. Follow the way.' Not the *tao* but the literal word of the Bible. She was near-hysterical in her evangelistic fury. She frightened me. Ipoh, made rich on tin and rubber, had yawned its huge vacuum at her, and she was filling it with the only thing she could find. All I could do was accept one of her ill-printed hand-outs, with a crude drawing of a Chinese Jesus dripping black blood, and promise to repent.

After Malaysia, Scotland. Not only the Edinburgh Festival, where I spoke and debated, but the hinterland I did not know. My mother's roots were up there somewhere, and our son Andrew seemed to have found them. He spent much of his time in a kilt in the Inverness area, but he had come down to the George Hotel to be our guide. There had been a total remission of the arterial pain in my left leg while I was in Malaysia, but it came back with force on Princes Street. My face, I knew, was grey and twisted: I could scarcely hobble fifty yards. Liana hobbled more healthily on her metal crutch, but we both, to an ancient but thriving Victor Pritchett, looked like casualties in the cause of literature. In Inverness I drank deeply. I drank very deeply. I had not been so drunk since a long wait at Salt Lake City airport, which, being international, had to dishonour the Mormon principles of the town and sell me a bottle of gin so that, the Book of Mormon open before me, I could beguile a prolonged take-off delay (the God of Joseph Smith had unleashed a storm over the mountains). The deep drinking brought on a fresh remission. I was grateful to Scotland. I wrote an overture for the Scottish National Orchestra in gratitude, and this was performed. I never heard it: the Musicians' Union forbade an unpaid recording. But I keep meeting musicians who played it.

In the autumn I had to deliver the four John Crowe Ransom Memorial Lectures at Kenyon College in Ohio. It was tempting to consider repeating the 'Blest Pair of Sirens' series, but I hate serving food reheated. I found new things to say about the relationship between literature and music and I spoke of those elements in what I call Class 2 fiction which draw it close to music. 'Class 1 fiction, in which language is transparent, fulfils its end when transposed to the cinema screen. Class 1 novels are better as films than as verbal constructs. In Class 2 fiction, on the other hand, the opacity of language is exploited, and structure may have a significance apart from mere plot. When literature yearns towards the self-referential, it is trying to become music.' The claudication had returned, and the kindly people of Ohio were worried. They did not like to see me smoking so much: smoke was silting up the arteries. Indeed, the no-smoking era was beginning in the United States – bitter rebukes for my gross little cigars and hands wildly waving away the effluvium. On television I saw a discussion group of women, frenzied Maenads deploring some new wrath of God, I could not tell what. It turned out to be herpes of the genitals; AIDS was still to come. This blessed country was never free of curses. I flew, forbidden to smoke cigars, to London and the Savoy Hotel. Liana was there waiting.

I was in London to publicise what was now definitively *Earthly Powers*, a big book of 649 pages with, on the back of the jacket, a photograph of myself in a cheap checked shirt, squinting at the world and seeming to be spitting out a grape pip. There was a cocktail party to launch the book, and at it I met Larry Adler, the famous American harmonica player. I had written harmonica pieces for the late John Sebastian. On my sixtieth birthday I had appeared on BBC television and accompanied on the piano another harmonica player, Tommy Reilly, who played a piece I had specially written for him. Now it only remained for me to compose for Larry the eagle and one of the minor patterns of my life would be fulfilled. I wrote him a dissonant baroque suite but, so far as I know, he has never played it. No matter: God has put me on earth to, among other things, write for the harmonica. The connection between that instrument and the kind of books I wrote was in doubt, but the three supreme players were somehow drawn to me as I to them. Something to do, perhaps, with my essentially vulgar psyche aspiring to high art, the sad suck-and-blow of the Somme elevated likewise.

I had heard vaguely of the Booker Prize, awarded each autumn for the best fiction of the year, and I now discovered that *Earthly Powers* had been put in for it. I came back one late afternoon from a radio interview to find a television team installed in my Savoy suite. It appeared that I and William Golding, who had just published *Rites of Passage*, were close contenders for the award, and I was to tell such televiewers as were interested how I felt about it. I felt nothing. Gifts of money are always acceptable, but I would rather, which I have never thought possible, receive them from unknown admirers, not from contentious committees. The mould was broken with Harriet

Shaw Weaver: the conviction of Joyce's genius that she had could never be transferred to a pack of jurors. Being up for the Booker Prize entailed going to a grand dinner at which the name of the winner would be announced. I would not go. I was near-dead with jet-lag; I had not brought my dinner jacket. In the little world of British literary journalism my absence was, and still is, interpreted as sulking, which it was not. It could not be unless I had prior and illegitimate knowledge of the winner. It was evident to me, anyway, that my novel was not Booker material. It was hard reading for the jurors, and it smelt of the wrong properties, one of which was Catholic Europe.

On this trip to Great Britain I agreed to make a short television programme for Granada, the exotically named commercial chain which entertains Lancashire. The year which had taken me back to Kuala Kangsar now took me all the way back – to Manchester, the Xaverian College, Moss Side. Moss Side was a green ruin: the shops over which I had lived as a boy were no more; the off-licence on Moss Lane East had become a West Indian shebeen, was later boarded up, was finally demolished. There was something unnerving about this destruction of the past. The great city itself, the old Cottonopolis with its chophouses and cultivated German Jews, had sunk into a post-imperial refuge for brown and black people who had, as I had, as most of Malaysia had, a nostalgia for colonialism. But the present and the future lay with unhappy independence.

The year ended with a trip back to the United States, this time with Liana, to publicise, far more rigorously than in amateurish Britain, the novel which America had insisted on calling *Earthly Powers*. It was a primary selection of the Book of the Month Club, a rare distinction for a British work. There was a celebratory dinner at the Four Seasons in Manhattan: the rack of lamb was too tough to eat; one longed for hungry dogs emerging from under the table cloth. I travelled to Chicago, Boston and Washington and spoke on radio shows which started at midnight and ended at dawn. I was ill. I was delirious. I said something about the desirability of America's return to the British colonial system. Liana went to bed, ill, in the Plaza. We took the Concorde back to London. It was three hours late in taking off, which nullified its one advantage over the old-fashioned jet. My delirium had not abated. Our fellow-passengers were old and ugly, as they had to be, since, to afford the fare at all, they had to be rich or distinguished or both. Delirious, I insisted that we all be issued with delicately hammered gold masks in the likeness of Apollo or

Aphrodite. It was unfair that so much hideousness should mock the sleek beauty of this supersonic eagle.

I HAVE recounted the activities of 1980 not because I consider them to be interesting in themselves but because they indicate how easily the writer's life can cease to be one of writing. In 1981 I was determined to hide myself from a world that wanted me merely as media fodder. I would write, it did not much matter what so long as I wrote. I made a television version of *The Waste Land* and then lost it. I started a novel tentatively called *All the Men and Women*, which was to be about the history of the English stage. It began with the pageants of Corpus Christi in the late Middle Ages and this section was mostly written in Middle English. *Earthly Powers* might conceivably make me rich, but this would not. Shirley Conran, who had settled briefly in Monaco for strict commercial ends, found what she could understand of it somewhat dirty. There was lambation of somebody's coynte.

Shirley Conran was a highly successful journalist who had become famous with a book called *Superwoman*. Women should be strong and independent and not waste their time stuffing raw spaghetti. Shirley did not in herself embody her concept of hard femininity. She was attractive, willowy, vulnerable. She came regularly in the evenings to No. 44 rue Grimaldi and I would cook her a curry. She brought with her pages of a novel in progress. She had not previously written any fiction, but she had made up her mind to produce something highly commercial. Her aim was not literary; she had perhaps in mind something of the Class 1 variety which could only be fulfilled on a screen, small or large. In my innocence I could not take seriously the instalments she brought me to read and, of my goodness, correct, improve, respell, reparagraph. The title *Lace* I approved, though I thought it ought to be given an extra dimension by becoming the acronym of something – Lambdacismal Aggregation of Christographic Eohippism, perhaps. She listened kindly. Her lovely eyes betrayed none of the pity she must be feeling. She knew what she was doing. She finished the book and, having used Monaco, left it. Michael Korda of Simon and Schuster paid her a million dollars, an astronomic advance compared with what he had paid me. Good luck to her and him. Who wants literature anyway?

To be fair, however, *Earthly Powers* did not do badly, except in America where it was heavily remaindered. In France, as *La Puissance des Ténèbres*, it headed the bestseller list for months; Georges Belmont and Hortense Chabrier, its superb translators, won the Charles Baudelaire prize and the book itself was *le meilleur livre étranger de l'année*. It was helped, as so many French publications are, by a weekly literary programme on the *deuxième chaîne* of French television called *Apostrophe*, whose anchorman was Bernard Pivot. Most literary people in France, above all publishers, watch the programme and then stay tuned for *Ciné-Club*. Pivot had decided, some years before the publication of *La Puissance des Ténèbres*, that the three most important, or at least significant, novelists of Europe were Alberto Moravia, myself, and Günter Grass (the order is the descending one of age – ten years between us). This would seem a bizarre selection to the British literary establishment. We were given a programme to ourselves, in which Moravia's French was superb, mine adequate, Grass's, despite his years as an art student in Paris, non-existent. For me, *Apostrophe* has always been compelling to watch when foreigners, especially the British and Americans, get on to it. How much French will Norman Mailer, Gore Vidal, Sir Angus Wilson, Julian Barnes, Nadine Gordimer prove themselves able to speak? Gore Vidal, who claims to have met André Gide, should have been as fluent as Oscar Wilde, but he spoke little, and what little he spoke was very close to Italian. Henry Kissinger spoke no French at all. Sir Angus lisped charmingly: '*La Reine me lit, j'en suis sûr.*' Barnes, who won a prize for *Le Perroquet de Flaubert*, was shy. Jane Fonda, publicising one of her aerobic manuals, was superb. George Steiner speaks all the languages.

George and I were on the same programme. He had just published the French version of his little romance about an ancient self-justifying Hitler being recovered from the Brazilian jungle. He claims that this exposure sold a hundred thousand copies of his book. I fancy that, as I was higher than he on the bestseller list in *L'Express*, I must have sold more of mine. My novel was clearly seen as being, like his, a European book. It led me deeper into Europe than anything I had previously published. It meant trips to Oslo and the start of an almost familial relationship with Stockholm, where I learned how the Nobel Prize was awarded and divined that it would never be awarded to me. It meant a long *Winterreise* through Germany, with a call at Vienna, on those excellent German trains. But it meant not writing. I had sadly to accept that an author must sell his books and if, preferring to write, he refuses to sell them then he must accept the blame if they do not sell.

Liana and I escaped from the Grand Prix in Monaco to the village of Callian in the Var, where our little house lay on the rue des Muets in the core of a little labyrinth of streets. I put together my thoughts on music and literature in a brief book, then fixed myself up at an outdoor café table with ballpoints and scoring paper and set Hopkins's 'The Wreck of the Deutschland' for baritone soloist, chorus, and large orchestra. It could not, of course, be done, but I had to prove this to myself. I could not compose my own rhythms; I had to follow Hopkins's, and his sprungness got lost in the choral counterpoint. This work was interrupted by a call to go to Cesena in Italy. Having married into the country, I had to obey such calls. This one came specifically from the Marchese Curzio-Maria, one of Liana's aristocratic relatives, who was president of the local branch of the Rotary Club. He wanted me to speak at one of his dinners, and the subject was to be Malaysia.

Italy had a very fantastic relationship with the country, a sub-literary one. A man whose name was Emilio Salgari, unknown in Britain and totally ignorant of its colonial system, had written, in extreme poverty, adventure stories set in the Malay archipelago. One of these was about an heroic Malay pirate named Sandokan who fought bitterly against the benign rule of the white raja Brooke. It was false history but popular with children. It had now been made into a television series, so that all of Italy might know how brutal the colonial British were and how highly *simpatico* was a thug who made his white victims walk the plank. In contradiction of this travesty my own Malayan trilogy – called bluntly *Malesia!* – had just appeared as a single book in Italy. Liana had translated it and worked hard on the translation. She had appended notes and a glossary devised to teach such Italians as read the book various truths that Salgari had not wished to know. Here was an occasion for me to tell the Rotarians of Romagna something about the unglamorous East and to illustrate it with the videocassette of the programme that had been filmed in Ipoh and Kuala Kangsar. As in a film, a telegram arrived during the dinner to announce that I had won with *Malesia!* the Premio Scanno.

Italy is generous with literary prizes. It did not read my books with any avidity but it showered awards upon me – the Premio Malaparte in Capri, the Premio Fernet Branca in Milan, both for general literary achievement, the Premio Bancarella for something or other, the Premio Comisso in Treviso for my book on D. H. Lawrence, others. I list them in no spirit of boastfulness: Italy thinks she has a duty to literature, and this duty is expressed in regional awards rather than in big national bestowals that hit headlines. One does not shout about them. One takes the money (unexportable from Italy) and the plaque or figurine, bows, leaves, forgets, unless one is concerned with hinting at the comparative pusillanimity of a country that has produced the greatest literature in the world. I went from Cesena to Scanno to do something rather more important than receiving a prize. I went to embrace and kiss the cinema actress Monica Vitti, whom I adore and who also was being honoured for her services to art. She was very thin. Most film goddesses are – Sophia Loren, for instance, and Jeanne Moreau. Incidentally, *Gli Stromenti delle Tenebre* received no prize. Italy could see clearly what it was about, and it did not like my traduction of a popular pope. When I got back to Cesena I was glad it had not yet been published.

This was because there was a Rotarian (he wore the badge which, to me, has always been sinister since Sinclair Lewis's *It Can't Happen Here*) whose name was Don Guiliano Botticelli. He was a round cigarette-smoking priest who approved of me. He had read me and considered me the better type of British Catholic, not like Graham Greene. He followed me closely on the *terza pagina* of the *Corriere della Sera*. I did not dare disclose to him what my Catholicism had become – a nostalgic culture with very little faith in it, a stick for trouncing Anglicans, a stand to be taken somewhat hypocritically in articles on evil for the *Daily Mail*. He had a delightful decaying little mediaeval church on the main street of Cesena and, with the Curzio-Maria family, though not Liana, I attended a Sunday mass there. It was, of course, in the vernacular, but the old displaced Latin shone through its vulgar deformation. God tried to drag me back. He filled me with tears and elation; he promoted large appetite for lunch and love. Little Wilson, disguised as Antonio Borghese, was being invited to come to terms with *il gran Dio*. A man I once met who had served a twelve-month prison sentence told me he had taken to reading John Stuart Mill in his cell. If ever he went back to jail, he swore, he would read John Stuart Mill again. If ever I return to Cesena I shall attend a Sunday mass.

To END this chronicle, this time-bound account of a life which has not been spent wholly in time, I have to return to a Catholic town closer to my family than Cesena and celebrate an author other than myself. In 1982 Dublin remembered that James Joyce had been born there a hundred years before. There was to be junketing on Bloomsday, 16 June, and Radio Telefis Eireann was to join the BBC on 2 February, Joyce's birthday, in presenting my own tribute to a

writer I have known longer than most of the Joyce professors – a
musical version of *Ulysses*. I called the work *The Blooms of Dublin*,
thinking of *Abie's Irish Rose* and *The Cohens and the Kellys*. The BBC
announcer, inspired, cut out the definite article, thus emphasising
what had once flowered in the city and not an implausible half-Jew
whom no Dubliner could believe might ever have lived there. Of
course, Leopold Bloom was really Ettore Schmitz or Italo Svevo. I
had written a libretto and a short score some time previously; now
the hard labour of orchestrating filled the autumn and early winter of
1981. It was done in the dreamlike state appropriate to a task that
borders on the mechanical: Liana and Andrew watched television;
Shirley Conran discussed *Lace*. What was not mechanical was the
overture. If the work as a whole stayed close to the tonalities of the
music hall, there had to be at least one number which reflected
Joyce's crabbed ingenuity. My overture was a double fugue in five-
eight time, but it collapsed, Joyceanly enough, into a cracked church
bell and the voices of old crones in shawls reciting the Hail Mary.
The rest of the score is, I think, the kind of thing Joyce might have
envisaged, or eneared, for his characters. He was the great master of
the ordinary, and my music is ordinary enough. I had felt for some
time that he might have had demotic musicalisation in mind, as he
was not averse to cinematisation: after all; Molly Bloom is a
professional soprano, Stephen a tenor who is rebuked for not
developing his voice, and Bloom has to be a baritone. In the Ithaca
episode of *Ulysses* a song about little Harry Hughes (Hugh of Lincoln
in disguise) is not merely sung but notated. The former mayor of
Cork, a Jew, could not forgive Joyce for this rare intrusion of
apparent antisemitism: if Stephen, as we are told, is singing this song
and Stephen is the young Joyce, then the author himself stands
accused. But I was able to soothe this fine Corkman by pointing out
that the song is notated in the bass clef, which no tenor music ever is,
and that it goes down to a low A which no tenor could ever reach.
Bloom and Stephen are becoming identified in this chapter, and it is
really, if it is anyone's song at all, Bloom's. The song is for a baritone;
ergo, Bloom is a baritone.

John Tydeman and Michael Heffernan were in charge of the very
fine radio production of my centennial tribute. Actors and singers
were engaged in Dublin and London, and the whole work was
recorded in the studios of Radio Telefis Eireann in the January of
1982. Feverish but immensely efficient post-production work in the
BBC studios in London brought the recording to completion with
dubbed-in Dublin sounds – the very church clock of Sandymount,

the very ravens of Glasnevin cemetery – and *Blooms of Dublin* was put out simultaneously from Dublin and London on the evening of Joyce's hundredth birthday.

There was little doubt as to how British listeners would respond – with guarded pleasure, with contempt, with indifference. It was feared that Irish listeners would react more positively, with a stock response of anger and resentment. Their ears would not be innocent: the very name of James Joyce, even and especially to those Irish who had not read him, is the trigger to a kind of mythical explosion of vituperation among men and shudders among women ('Have you read the bloody thing at all? It's bloody unreadable, for a bloody start. And it's a bloody tangle of dirt, filth and uncleanliness'). The Irish trouble began even before the work was recorded. Tydeman, Liana and myself arrived in Dublin on the feast of Epiphany to find all Ireland shrouded in snow. This was nature's response to Joyce's story 'The Dead', in which snow is general all over Ireland – a meteorological phenomenon unheard of in that mild wet land washed by the Gulf Stream. There was no transport available from Bloom's Hotel to the RTE studios in Donnybrook, and there seemed no hope that the singers, actors and orchestral players would turn up.

By a Joycean miracle, everybody turned up – some sliding down snowy hill-slopes; others hiking through snow-broth – in order to decide not to perform. The actors, led by a union official who was to play the part of the Citizen's dog Garryowen, went on strike for obscure Irish reasons which had nothing to do with morality; the musicians, and especially the female members of the chorus, refused to be involved in filth. The musicians' union informed the orchestral players that they could not refuse to perform on moral grounds, so the recording went ahead under heavy protest. A second violinist declared: 'I'll play, but I won't play well.' This threat was fulfilled.

But, in general, professional integrity prevailed over moral doubts. When a dirty word appeared in the sung text, it was, naturally, only to be sung by the males, and the ladies were sent out of the studio. The terrible outburst of obscenity from Privates Compton and Carr in the Nighttown scene was given to English actors, so Dublin morality was not seriously sinned against. There is very little allegedly obscene language in *Ulysses*, and such as we find is always in the service of a legitimate aesthetic shock. When Bloom describes the Middle East as the 'grey shrunken cunt of the earth' he is using an exactly appropriate term. Change it to 'womb' and the biting force of the consonants vanishes. Make Private Carr change 'fucking' to 'bloody' and the climax is muffled. Dublin, a hundred years after the birth of one of its greatest sons, was still not ready for modernistic honesty.

The true shocks were reserved to the intellectual critics, especially the musical ones. These expected opera, not a Broadway musical. Matyas Seiber had composed a cantata called *Ulysses*, which, in spite of the titular claim, is only a setting of the words 'The heaventree of stars hung with humid nightblue fruit'. There was shock at my using those same words for a tiny duet between Stephen and Bloom, to be sung with the tired simplicity proper to the end of a long day. The general critical view was that I had fulfilled about ten per cent of the musical potential of *Ulysses*. But how inappropriate, even stupid, a Schoenbergian enlargement would have been. The late Hans Keller, who seethed and raged in the *Listener*, revealed in an exemplary manner the limitations of musical criticism. He splashed metaphor about – paralytic, consumptive – and deplored my sickly amateurism. I did not defend myself. As for now – *de mortuis*.

In June a number of writers assembled in Dublin to honour Joyce – William Empson, Angela Carter, Luciano Erba, Pierre Sabatier, Dennis Potter, Chinua Achebe, myself, others. On Stephen's Green a bust of Joyce was unveiled (a gift to Dublin from American Express). Before the unveiling I stood alone and looked up towards the shrouded image. It was a totally windless day; in the leaves of the trees no motion. And yet I could swear that I saw the agitation of the veil in a burst of silent laughter. Joyce had won, he had slaughtered the philistines. But I was not happy about Joyce.

I had done my best for him, as so many had. I had produced three books, innumerable articles, a musical work, all in his honour. I did not expect, despite the Joyce magic, the grateful touch of a hand that is still. The gratitude should be all mine: Joyce, more than any man, had taught me the value of literature and tried to instil in me a sacerdotal devotion to art. But he had not lived the Johnsonian life, he had never known the proud debasement of Grub Street. He had practised high art under the umbrella of the last Maecenas, rejecting literature and its grubby journalistic offshoots as a way of making a living. His son George had ended as a pathetic unemployed alcoholic, his daughter Lucia in a madhouse. He had squandered everything except his talent. It was not good enough, and Dublin knew this. In the afternoon of 16 June the whole city became a stage for street theatre – the Wandering Rocks episode of *Ulysses* was brought to life, its characters trod the pavements – and honest unliterary citizens muttered: 'What dhe hell does dat fella dhere tink he's doing dressed like me bloody grandfadher? Dhere ought to be a bloody law.' A city is not something enclosed in a book: it is living people trying to earn for their wives and sons and daughters, and among these were little Wilsons transubstantiating words into bread.

Still, this was Joyce's year, and it was a long one. With the Swedish director Eric Nielson I made a film about Joyce but also about Stravinsky, who shared the centenary and, for the Joyce-mad prepared to extend Bloomsday not only forward to the crack of Bloom but back to Eve and Adam's, was born the day after the sacred feast. In the film I tried to destroy Joyce's Dublin with the music of *Le Sacre du Printemps*, but Joyce was there ready to build it up again. The film was shot mostly in Bracciano. I switched on the television in my house there and saw, horrified, the body of Princess Grace, struck dead by an infarctus while driving a car. We had been together, earlier in the summer, to celebrate Joyce in Monaco. There had been an Irish dinner afterwards (bacon and cabbage transformed into something ethereal by the genius of the French cuisine) and I had played Irish songs on the piano. Grace had become a European, meaning an Irishwoman. Now she was gone. Soon I would be involved in the creation of her best memorial – the Princess Grace Irish Library. This became eventually a centre of Joyce studies. You could not get away from Joyce, even if you were a Monegascan princess from Philadelphia. At the end of the year I dedicated a plaque to Joyce in Fouquet's restaurant in Paris. Stephen Joyce was there, the boy born out of the dark past while a grandfather died, one who had been another victim of genius. Genius, like patriotism, was never enough.

EPILOGUE

YOU AND I have both had enough of the time I have had, whose back I loaded with words for sale. Enough of the *Nacheinander*; let us dwell briefly in the *Nebeneinander*.

The terms are appropriate, since I write this envoi in Switzerland. Admittedly in Italian-speaking Switzerland, but German is spoken here also, and there is a kind of self-abasement in *Svizzera esterna* when it contemplates the power and achievements of *Svizzera interna*, meaning Zurigo or Zürich. I am in Ticino, south of the Alps, a few kilometres away from Lugano. My address is *Casella Postale* or *Postfach* 77, CH 6942, Crocifisso di Savosa. Liana and I have not settled here. We are still residents of Monaco, and I am a *résident privilégié* who will not have to apply for a new *carte de séjour* for another ten years, if I live that long. There is a tiny quota of *Nebeneinander* in Ticino for foreigners who do not seek permanent residence in the Confederatio Helvetica: they are allowed to buy chalets without paying the full complement of taxes, although the imposts we pay are heavy enough. The chalet was purchased by Liana, on mortgage, and I tried to efface myself totally and present her to the Swiss as a *sole feme* not well-off whom a man occasionally visits. But the Swiss are not easy to fool, and, though the chalet and the bank account that disburses the mortgage instalments are in her name, they have pinned me down as an earner and a heavier one than I really am.

Why, when there is an adequate apartment on rue Grimaldi, Condamine, Principauté de Monaco, do we spend some months every year in Ticino? Chiefly because we are crowded out by books, the Monaco summer, heralded by the Grand Prix, is oppressive, and we have a fancy for air well above sea level, mountain crests with occasional snow on them, the sense of space. Moreover, there is in Gravesano a doctor named Werner Nussbaumer who looks after my mitral valve.

Let me indulge a spatial lust and describe where we are. We come up the Via Cantonale from Crocifisso di Savosa or down it from Porza to turn into a parking space common to a cluster of like chalets. We come up or down in, of course, a Mercedes of the diesel-consuming variety. We garage this or leave it in the open and climb stone steps past the chalet of our neighbour, who is a Sicilian owner of two ice cream parlours in Lugano, and enter a sizeable dwelling. The foyer is cluttered with half-unpacked suitcases and plastic bags from the *supermercato* called Innovazione which may have small change nestling in their lower folds, and it clanks with empty bottles. The daughter of an Italian aristocrat and the son of a Moss Side tobacconist have not learned the bourgeois virtue of tidiness: we leave that to the Sicilian next door. To the left is a washroom-toilet, useful for an old man whose bladder broods during car-journeys and then makes urgent signals when it hears the brakes applied. We then enter the dining area of a long *salone* of split levels down whose two steps I frequently trip. The area has two dining tables. The first bought is so strewn with old letters that some day may be answered that it must not be disturbed; the second bought is for eating on, but that too has accumulated a burden of paper, though I jealously guard a minimal space just large enough for a plate, knife and fork, tumbler, and bottle of Argentinian or Bulgarian or Turkish Burgundy. Liana will not eat at a table. She prefers to recline on a couch in the Roman manner and, in the manner of a woman, eat what to a man must look like snacks, always at odd hours. The kitchen, which is to the left of the dining area as one enters the house, was already equipped when we took possession with Swiss or German refrigerator, oven, electric cooking plates, dish-washer. There is a table intended for the preparation of food and even the eating of it, but this is covered with jars of harissa, tiny red peppers in vinegar, Cumberland sauce, the dried residue of mint jelly, hard crusts for processing into breadcrumbs or for feeding the hens of the proprietress of a little restaurant called La Ticinella, knobs of cheese, wizened limes, shop cake, a tin or two of, to me, uneatable Italian biscuits, a near-empty carton of *Milch-lait-latte*, a swift water-boiler for the making of tea, an electrical crumb-sucker made by Black and Decker, a tea-soaked packet of Rothman blue. This clutter is all my fault.

In the *salone* proper there is a three-piece suite, a concession to bourgeois taste; there is also a television set and a video recorder. There are book-shelves, but the spines of the books are hidden by ranks of video-cassettes, some of which have spilled on to the floor.

Very few of these are commercial (*Citizen Kane, Meet Me in St Louis, Top Hat, Room Service, The Life of Brian*); the great majority represent Liana's tapping the current of time in the form of television news, interviews with Italian or Central European notables, urgent programmes on AIDS, as well as old films with Totó or Alberto Sordi. We see a great deal of television, in Italian, French and German and even the strange Swiss dialects associated with the blowing of the *Alpenhorn* or young people dancing in village squares to the accompaniment of accordions while the eternal Alps look down. By my chair there is an old Schimmelpenninck tin used as an ashtray, a copy of the second volume of Tovey's edition of Bach's forty-eight preludes and fugues, and a wad of music manuscript paper bought in Cologne on which, over my morning mug of tea (six tea-bags), I try to emulate Bach and compose at least a fugal exposition.

Outside is a garden somewhat overgrown, with a Byzantine *pozzo* or well or baptismal font bought in Mezzovico. There are plastic bags of fertiliser in it. Near by, under the eaves, is a pile of firewood not to be used, since the fireplace is full of old copies of *The Times* and also the ceramic coat of arms of the Pasi family, cracked and not yet submitted to menders. Also the heat of the house comes from below. To the left of the stairs going up, with their clanging iron banisters, are stairs going down to the *cantina* or cellar. This houses a washing machine, an oil-burning heating apparatus of very solid German manufacture inscribed with German warnings complete with exclamation points, and that obligatory feature of new-built Swiss houses – a nuclear shelter. The massive metal door is too heavy for even two persons to open or shut and it opens on to a grim cell rather than use which one would prefer to be nuclear-blasted. It is filling up gradually with such copies of the *Corriere della Sera* as do not lie on various floors of the habitable part of the house. One comes up to ground level and, mounting from it, observes a stairwell covered with paintings which are the work of Liana's mother, the now dead contessa. She left these to Liana along with bibelots of the twenties and a few million lire. Everybody in Italy, incidentally, is a millionaire.

The pictures show an eccentric talent, eclectic too. There are montages of torn envelopes and female faces with cat's eyes, explosions with HELP! and WOW! and BANG!, all meant to disturb. There are also more sedative still-life paintings in the style of Cézanne. Time has turned all these art-works into pictograms unread: the climber or descender has become blind to them. The climber comes to a landing with another stairway leading to the final floor and a kind of roof-garden. The landing opens into three rooms – a study, a study which is also a bedroom, the master or mistress bedroom itself. In here there is a large *letto matrimoniale* in which Liana and I sleep in each other's arms or, if too warm, back to back and even some distance one from the other. A door in this room leads to Liana's bathroom, which has a bath. My own bathroom, which is across the landing from the bedroom, has no bath and hence is ill-named, but it has a shower, a container of liquid soap in the shape of a pineapple, a wash-stand and mirror and a battery-run clock of large size. There is also one of these clocks on the wall of the bedroom. Under the clock is Liana's bedside table, which is part of the bed, and on it is a telephone. There is also a telephone next to the television set downstairs, but she prefers to use the bedroom telephone even when not in bed, for her number-book is on the table as also documents sometimes to be referred to when she is called or is calling. I never call.

On the floor beside her bed there are, at the moment, the following objects: a copy of the *Observer*, copies of *L'Espresso* and *Panorama*, a life of Sidney Smith, *Senilità* by Italo Svevo, her own translation of *The Crying of Lot 49* by Thomas Pynchon, an English anthology compiled by myself and published by Tramontana of Milan with the title of *Letteratura Inglese: I Campioni*, a musical setting of mine of Gabriele D'Annunzio's *La Pioggia nel Pineto*, an open packet of Rothman blue, two discarded pairs of *collants*, a French book on Goya, Samuel Butler's *The Way of All Flesh*, the inevitable *Corriere della Sera* open at an article by myself on *Il Linguaggio del Femminismo*, a British Airways eyeshade, a clean *reggipetto*, a book called *A Million Menus*, a local telephone directory and a letter to myself from an American Bible publisher begging me, for a thousand dollars, to write six thousand words on the Epistle of St Jude. *The Way of All Flesh* informs her that this kind of commentary has already been done, and at great length, by Dr Skinner, headmaster of Roughborough School.

On the floor beside my side of the bed are copies of the *Times Literary Supplement* containing nothing by myself, Charles Dickens's *Our Mutual Friend*, Denis Wheatley's *Strange Conflict*, a near-empty packet of Ormond Junior cigarillos, a cigarette lighter inscribed Kindstrom's, Konfektyr o Tobak, Linnég 9-11, Tel: 60 69 56, 114 47 Stockholm, a cube of camphor, and a pair of rumpled blue socks. On my own table are a lamp with a parchment shade depicting Etruscan leisure activities, a miniature copy of the Segerstad Sword in Stockholm's Statens Historiska Museum, a dirty coloured handkerchief and a cube of camphor. Against the wall nearest my side of the bed is a kind of wardrobe made of heavy cloth attached to a metal frame: it is in the shape of a British telephone booth and is inscribed TELEPHONE. It is matched by, against the wall by the door of Liana's bathroom, a kind of wardrobe of similar size and shape that is meant to look like the front of a London bus. On the wall between the windows that give on to a balcony is a chart of Swedish money-pieces of varying degrees of antiquity, its title *Svenska Mynt*. Next to the telephone booth wardrobe is a huge map, bought in East Berlin with gratefully accepted West German marks, of the Roman province called GALLIA.

Let us now leave the bedroom, naked if you wish, for we have no pyjamas, and enter the room where I work, which Liana calls my *studio* and I my study. It has an architect's table with two pot-plants on it, the inevitable clutter of letters unanswered, a pencil-sharpener in the shape of a piano, a device for punching holes in papers to be filed, three paper-stapling machines, one of which works, a tin that held a cake made by King's Master Bakers of YORK and now an ashtray, a yellow tin of Ormond Junior cigarillos, several dried-up ballpoint pens, packets of Tipp-Ex, a pair of blunt scissors, Johnston's Pocket Atlas of the World, a London street index, the pages I have just typed, the typewriter I have typed them with (Olivetti Studio 45, serviced by Sergio Lavagetti, Bellinzona 092/25 53 69), and a plastic-covered road map of Francophone Switzerland which serves as a base for the Olivetti. On the wall before me is a *carte du monde*. Behind me are shelves with books and, above them, the athletic silver cups which Liana's poor dead sister Grazia won. There is another table with an electric typewriter whose buzzing I resent. There is a photocopier, also a humidifier, a pair of ankle boots that no longer fit me, a miniature televisor that no longer works, and various typewriter cases that do not contain typewriters. Get up creaking from the slat-seated chair that striates the fundament if not mollified with a little cushion ornamented with my zodiacal sign of Pisces, and leave the room, turning immediately right and entering Liana's study and my computer room. There is a bed there on which sleep unsolicited typescripts from literary aspirants. There is Liana's table, chair, Olivetti. There is an IBM personal computer which I do not like but cost much and has to be used, though not for the writing of books. I typed the first line of *The Waste Land* on it and it would not accept the second because of the alleged bad syntax of the first. To type an acute accent or an umlaut is a major operation. Whole pages of hard work unaccountably disappear. The printing machine insists on justifying the lines and produces gate-toothed copy of little elegance. Let us go upstairs.

Upstairs there is a toilet, the fourth and last, and a shower. There is also the music room, with an upright piano, a Jacobi-Bürger. There are the complete piano works of Chopin, a volume of Beethoven's sonatas, the *Sarnia* of John Ireland, *Le Tombeau de Couperin* and *Ma Mère L'Oye* of Ravel resting on the lid. There are records, few of them bought, most of them reviewed during a brief stint as record-reviewer for the *Spectator*. There is an apparatus that plays records and cassettes and records cassettes. There is a compact disc player with a limited repertoire – the *King Arthur* and *Fairy Queen* of the astonishing Henry Purcell, the *London Symphony* of Vaughan Williams and the Violin Concerto of Elgar. Because of some fault in manufacture or my carelessness in handling it, the latter prolongs the first movement indefinitely, repeating much of the exposition *de capo* and not amenable to the gentle shove of a finger. I accept the electronic age, which I sometimes call the homoelectric age, but very uneasily. Let us go downstairs again, there to be insulted, in note, telegram or the spoken dialect of Palermo, by the Sicilian ice cream man who objects to our mode of parking the Mercedes, belatedness in sweeping away snow or autumn leaves, loudness of our *televisore* after ten at night when his son Fabio is sleeping, the tearing open of our plastic *poubelle* bags by the male cats which howl after his unspayed female. He is soon to be a local councillor, right wing of course.

In her novel about Venice, *Serenissima*, Erica Jong has some well-heeled characters going off to stay with Liana and Anthony Burgess in their house in Lugano. She probably has a vision of something like Baron Thyssen's Villa Favorita or the Milanese mansion that glowers on the hill above us. We rest in the comparative humility proper to a writer and his wife, and nobody comes to stay with us. Perhaps astonishingly, we find that we have no friends. We do not, of course, need them. That high unconsortable one,/ His love is his companion. But there seems to be some money in the bank – how much or little I do not know. I shrink from bank statements as from statements of royalties. I do not even carry specie in my pocket, leaving all disbursements to Liana. She files away French and Swiss francs, German marks, Dutch florins, Scandinavian crowns, dollars, sterling, all with great efficiency, and calls upon them at need.

The fact that I have prospered moderately seems confirmed by the declining need to accept any and every proposition offered by publishers, editors and the ringmasters of the cultural sideshows of large commercial firms or cartels. I will not, of course, write at sub-Skinnerian length on the Epistle of St Jude; nor will I fly to Brunei to interview my old pupil the Sultan, reputed to be the richest man in the world; nor will I go, at the request of the magazine called *Rolling Stone*, to the Soviet province of Georgia to discuss Georgian *glasnost*. The requests from commerce are best rejected by asking for an exorbitant fee, travel by Concorde, and a hotel suite. But to the great firms and combines money is better paid to me than to the taxman, and I find myself hoist. Yet demands for maximal comfort cannot always be met by the promoters: one can find oneself in the absent hands of strikers or frustrated by one's own stupidity as a traveller. I will give one example of this dual derangement.

I was called on, in Monaco, to fly to San Juan in Puerto Rico to talk about communications to a conference of American magazine proprietors. At the airport of the Côte d'Azur, whence I had first to fly to Paris en route for New York, I was asked to check my suitcase. But I said I preferred to do that at Charles de Gaulle airport, after having stuffed with duty-free liquor and panatellas the ample space that travelling light provides. But it turned out that this was the last chance to stow luggage for New York. At Charles de Gaulle airport there were buses to take one to the various terminals for overseas flights, and I lugged my bag aboard a bus that took me to the wrong one. That it was the wrong one I only discovered when stuffing time had arrived. I had to replace my goods back on their shelves, under the supervision of a bossy thin blonde suitable for the post of monitrix at the Cannes Film Festival, and take another bus. This time I arrived at the Concorde terminal, where I stuffed without opposition. The bar for Concorde travellers opened, but ice was slow to arrive. An attack of malaria came over me. When ice arrived I drank deep. I hefted my bag aboard and was schoolmistressly rebuked for not checking it. Then the Concorde staff decided on a three-hour strike. The bar was closed. Three and a half hours late we took off and were served an endless dinner of nameless fish compounds and strange meats. We arrived at Kennedy airport. I had missed my flight to San Juan. The next one would be at midnight. The terminal was crammed with Puerto Ricans and there was no room to sit down. I tried to sleep off my malarial attack on the floor, head on goods-crammed bag. I was kicked awake by a cop. That cop threatened me with arrest for an unspecified irregularity. Then, while his hand was in, he took away a Puerto Rican youth for leisurely threatening. I grabbed the youth's seat. I was sitting next to a Puerto Rican girl reading Ernest Hemingway. She kept saying:

'What that word mean? And what that?' We boarded. We landed at San Juan airport in the very small hours. There were no taxis. There was no means of reaching the remote fortress-like hotel where I and the magazine proprietors' conference had been booked. At four in the morning a gipsy motorman offered to take me whither I wished to go for fifty dollars. He scoured the island but could not find the hotel. At five-thirty-five he found it. It was in sumptuous grounds guarded by men in green uniforms with rifles. At six I was in bed. At six-thirty I was awakened with, 'Hi. You wanna go jogging?' Never again. I will not leave Europe. Not often, anyway.

I AM very much in Europe here in Lugano. This is the remotest point of the triangle formed with Monaco and Milan. It is a triangle within whose body shady deals are done, governments cheated, money stacked, high denomination plaques thrown on to green baize. Switzerland itself is not quite Europe: it remained aloof from Europe's last agony, as did Ireland, though it bought Nazi coal and was cautious about letting in refugees. It touches true Europe at four points, and it knows that its three linguistic cultures are mere tributaries of the main rivers. What true Europe is, however, nobody quite knows. Milan Kundera defines a European as one who is nostalgic for Europe, and he is probably right. Evelyn Waugh's words about the dismemberment of Christendom refer, proleptic-ally, to that nostalgia. If, living out of Great Britain for more than twenty years, I have become a paying guest of Europe rather than a European, it is the better to indulge the soft-centred dream of belonging to a culture that I do not wish to believe is dead, though I know, when I shake myself fully awake, that it is, and that Europe is only a land-mass shockingly divided.

The European parliament is always, in a kind of desperate search for a neo-European philosophy, arranging congresses at which great unanswerable questions are posed: What is Europe? What is European culture? How is the European language problem to be solved? In 1984, having appeared on a German television pro-gramme in Hamburg – the theme was, of course, the Orwellian prophecy – I flew via Munich to Venice to provide my own answer to that last question. The French, of course, had no doubt as to what the obvious answer was. They had no doubt, either, as to what Europe should be – a political unity accepting French leadership, rejecting American influence, closer to the Third World than to either of the superpowers. I spoke, to their incredulity and that of others, of the necessity of reviving Latin as the chief second language of Europe. It could be called Eurolatin and stripped of a good deal of its grammar; it had always been amenable to calques and loanwords and neologisms. The alternative, and a rather compelling one in view of the international technical vocabulary, especially in medicine, was Greek, but this was felt to be going too far. Anyway, if I wanted Latin, there was always French available, said the French, and French was the linguistic ideal to which Latin had always been moving. The French were glad that I did not endorse English as the second language of Europe. They were even gladder to hear that I did not consider English to be, any longer, a European language.

And, of course, it is not. The nature of modern English is decreed in America, and British English is a disregardable dialect of ECA or East Coast American. The modern novel in English is Bellow, Roth, Updike. The problem of the contemporary British novelist – my problem – is knowing who to write for. To write for the British is not enough: it means choosing for subject-matter the trials of emancipated women living in Hampstead or holidaying in small hotels by Swiss lakes or, worse, chronicling Thatcherite England in the various idioms of Thatcherite England. To write for America, where the large advances are, is a temptation, but American publishing houses want the British less and less, unless they can turn themselves into Americans, as the cunning Shirley Conran has done, or, like John le Carré, show the instability of the British intelligence system. The alternative is to write for Europe, and this means living in Europe: being removed from Britain, there is no danger of being bemused by what the British daily press considers important or assuming that ephemeral modes of speech are fixed or normative. It means not writing about contemporary Britain at all. This, naturally, is a disadvantage.

My rejection of English as a European language among the cold stones of February Venice was taken as hearteningly and unexpectedly unchauvinistic, but my advocacy of Latin was taken for what it was – homesickness for the Christendom of the thirteenth century. The surprising world success of Umberto Eco's *Il Nome della Rosa* may have had something to do with such homesickness – even in America. It was comforting for nostalgics to find that Sherlock Holmes, disguised as William of Baskerville, was only a traditional Aristotelian logician and that semiotics and intertextuality – books talking to books – were discovered in the Middle Ages. My homesickness for Catholic Europe could partially be comforted by living in a highly sceptical Europe that still carried the visible marks of its old religious unity, but perhaps my true motive was more self-serving – being close to European literary markets. This was, is, in the spirit of the EC but not of the less materialistic Europe dreamed of by European ideologists.

A writer deals with language and, if he is lucky, that language is what he begins to learn in his cradle. I have learned some of the languages of Europe and delivered public speeches in them, but I could never, as Samuel Beckett did of choice and the clever Hungarian refugees of London did of necessity, abandon my native tongue for one unwarmed, or uncooled, by my native climate. I am still a child of cold England, but only in the sense that I love its language and its literature. I cannot go back there to live, and, on brief visits, I see myself as an outsider. The rift of religion, region and class should have been healed a long time ago, but it is not. Like a colonial, I have a sense of exclusion, a chip on the shoulder. Sometimes, with a kind of peasant scorn, I provoke my class superiors to declaring this as a truth I have not the wit to know. This happened some years ago in Bristol.

I was in Bristol to attend a literary dinner. I had been escorted there by the public relations officer of a publisher. He was a failed actor, usually drunk, and, in the hotel where the dinner was held, he tottered down the stairs frankly pissing. My suit was commended in the bar, or perhaps derogated, as being Felliniesque. It was not an evening suit. Most of the paying guests wore dinner jackets. At the top table were an actress who had just published her first book, one for children, and a television personality who had made a picture album out of a television series. I had just published a book myself, I forget what. When my turn came to speak I decided to denounce the assembly as the descendants of merchants made rich on tobacco, sherry and slavery who did not care a damn about literature and, if Thomas Chatterton had been born into their century, would have been as indifferent as their forebears to his suicide. This was not expected to go down well, and it did not. But a Bristolian patrician in evening dress interpreted my denunciation rightly. I had a chip on my shoulder, he said, because I came from Manchester. He should have said more, but it was enough to have come from beyond the great divide. The north will never come to terms with the south, or west. The children of industrialism and the scions of land, or of Bristol commerce, have little to say to each other. Literature is honoured by putting on evening dress and attending a literary dinner. Writers may be accepted as Celtic drunks or Cockney upstarts, that is as amusing clowns, but they are not, unless they live in old Bloomsbury, ladies and gentlemen. Writers are essentially Mancunians.

In European countries, the regional divisions of language and culture have no class associations. In Italy, especially, there is no sense of the dialect of Friuli or Romagna occupying a status inferior to that of Milan or Rome. Goldoni wrote in Venetian and is honoured for it; Porta wrote Milanese and Belli Roman. It is the damnable class structure of Britain, and the centralising influence of London, Oxford and Cambridge, that impose a single literary language, as well as a set of social standards, that, to Europeans, make our contemporary writing look chillingly homogeneous, over-genteel, and, paradoxically enough, provincial. D. H. Lawrence raged against British bloodlessness, married a foreign aristocrat, and went to write abroad. Britain still will not forgive him for being the son of a Nottinghamshire miner who spoke German and Italian without a public school accent. The British literary ideals are E. M. Forster and Virginia Woolf, who kept sex out of the novel, reserving perversions of it to private life, and confirmed the prejudices of the British ruling class. Virginia Woolf called *Ulysses* 'the book of a self-taught working man . . . of a queasy undergraduate scratching his pimples'. Naturally, not an Oxford or Cambridge undergraduate – some working man's son at Owen's College. It would have done her good to be seduced in a Manchester back-alley.

Our lives are built on prejudices, and I will not attempt to hide mine. Living in Europe, rarely hearing English spoken, rarely enough speaking it myself, my British class prejudices are soothed out of existence. The chip on the shoulder is hardly visible. Whether I am a gentleman or not is unimportant. My patriotism is reserved, as Lin Yu Tang said it should be, to the food I ate in childhood, also to certain ungentlemanly British authors, chief of them that great provincial William Shakespeare. Europe accepts me – as the winner of the *Prix Europa*, as a *Commandeur des Arts et des Lettres*, as a spokesman for European letters at the parliament of Strasbourg. In England it is only the language that matters.

AM I happy? Probably not. Having passed the prescribed biblical age limit, I have to think of death, and I do not like the thought. There is a vestigial fear of hell, and even of purgatory, and no amount of re-

reading rationalist authors can expunge it. If there is only darkness after death, then that darkness is the ultimate reality and that love of life which I intermittently possess is no preparation for it. In face of the approaching blackness, which Winston Churchill facetiously termed black velvet, concerning oneself with a world that is soon to fade out like a television image in a power cut seems mere frivolity. But rage against the dying of the light is only human, especially when there are things still to be done, and my rage sometimes sounds to myself like madness. It is not only a question of works never to be written, it is a matter of things unlearned. I have started to learn Japanese, but it is too late; I have started to read Hebrew, but my eyes will not take in the jots and tittles. How can one fade out in peace, carrying vast ignorance into a state of total ignorance?

The rage I wake to and take to bed is a turbulence not always related to an object. It seems like a pure emotion looking for an object. It cathartises itself into salty howling, then exhaustion, then it starts again. I remember in South Lancashire in my youth meeting an old woman who had just lost her husband. She said, 'I've been crying all morning, and as soon as I've finished this treacle pudding I'll get back to it.' There is always the danger of enjoying the tears or the rage, making a kind of prolonged orgasm out of frustration. Sometimes I fasten hopeless tears on to three images. One is of a small knock-kneed schoolboy, stockings falling down, satchel unhandily strapped to back, late for school, running to school and whimpering because he knows he will be punished. Who is the boy? It may be myself. One is of something I merely heard about. An owl screamed in misery because its eggs had shattered: some rodenticide or other had rendered the shells thin as paper. The third I saw in Kota Bharu: a large beetle lay dead; on its back there seemed to be a painted mask intended to frighten its enemies. There is a poem by Coventry Patmore in which a widowed father strikes his son and sends him to bed; then in remorse he visits the sleeping child, his cheeks still wet from sobbing, and weeps himself because the boy has placed his toys on his bedside table in an effort – 'ranged there with careful art to comfort his sad heart' – to make order out of a life temporarily ruined. I cry at that poem. I cry at any attempt to sustain life through the feeble accumulation of things. *Sunt lachrymae rerum, et mentem mortalia tangunt.* Newman spoke of Vergil 'as of a prophet or a magician; his single words and phrases, his pathetic half lines, giving utterance as the voice of Nature herself, to that pain and weariness, yet hope of better things, which is the experience of her children in every time.' I do not doubt that Robert Burns wept over the mouse

and its wee bit housie in ruins. One's frustration at impotence to put
the world right, expressed in rage, one's shame at the hopeless tears
one starts to enjoy – these make the prospect of death a little easier.

Meanwhile *il faut tenter de vivre*. The young Jane Eyre, sternly
asked what she, foul sinner, must do to avoid hell, answers that she
must keep herself healthy to put it off as long as possible. I cannot
keep myself healthy – too many bad habits deeply ingrained, cardiac
bronchitis like the orchestra of death tuning up under water – but I
submit to the promptings of an energy that might be diagnosed as
health perverted, for true health enjoys itself and does not wish to
act. The energy, which I call creative, is given to the thousand words
a day I vowed to produce after the failure of the neurologists'
prognosis freed me from writing more. But the rumour has been
going around that I will soon be done with writing.

The *Corriere della Sera* has announced that I am giving up the novel
for music. This was in connection with the performance of a work of
mine in Geneva, a twenty-five-minute composition for two flutes,
two oboes, two clarinets, two bassoons, one horn, one trumpet,
timpani, piano, vibraphone, xylophone and glockenspiel. The
Corriere sent its chief music critic to appraise the work. He did not, as
a British critic might feel himself obliged to, recommend that I go
back to the gallipots of fiction, but he complained that (a) it needed to
fulfil its meaning by being attached to a film and (b) it was very
English. I do not know whether he meant Purcellian or Brittenesque,
Britten and Purcell being the only English composers known in
Europe: my work was intended to be international. It is called *Mr
Burgess's Almanack*, a British enough title, and he seemed to think
that I was impressionistically painting the running of the English
year. But the title is a trick. The calendar and the chromatic scale have
in common a division into twelve. As the year moves from January
to December, so in my work the musical intervals I exploit
harmonically run from the minor second to the octave. There are
two intervals (called perfect) which demanded a kind of bumpkinish
clodhopping in the Holst or Vaughan Williams manner; these are the
fourth and the fifth. It was the fancied Englishness of these tonalities
that the *Corriere* critic must have pounced upon. The work was finely
played mostly by Americans, who lead the sections of the Orchestre
Suisse Romande, and all they found in the music was notes, some of
them difficult.

Still, this imputation of Englishry was interesting. Music, which
we think to be an international language, is profoundly national,
even profoundly regional: you can even pin Schoenberg and his

pupils down to a capital city. I sometimes feel that the growth of my musical sensibility came to a full stop in 1934, when Elgar, Holst and Delius died. These three composers move me inexpressibly because they are English. What the English quality is I do not know; it is over-fanciful to suppose that they are presenting Turner landscapes in sound or conveying the taste of ale in a country inn. The mystery of music cannot be probed. If a love of England, whatever England is, can be aroused in me, Elgar above all will do the arousing. I could quite happily sit down and write Elgar's third symphony for him, knowing his idiom inside out, having pored over his scores, able, in fact, to reproduce page after page of his Symphony No. 2 in E flat from memory. Europe knew him once, but now knows him no longer. The trio of the 'Pomp and Circumstance' march in D major is played in Italian television commercials under images of ladies and gentlemen taking Twining's tea, but only the most eccentric, or Anglophile, musicologists are interested in *Falstaff* or *The Dream of Gerontius*. I have to play Elgar records with a shut door and force my own musical projects to exploit a harsher idiom. I have to beware of nostalgia.

The setting of Gabriele D'Annunzio's *La Pioggia nel Pineto*, a copy of which is on the floor by Liana's bed, has been sung in Amsterdam. My *Singspiel* version of *Uhrwerk Orange* has been performed in Bonn: this was an insolent affront to Beethoven's birthplace, since most of the songs and choruses are perversions of Beethoven. I have now to dig myself deeper into Europe with an opera based on the life of Sigmund Freud, having painfully started to prepare a libretto in Viennese German. I do not know whether this can be done. It will be hard to find a baritone willing to stop singing halfway through because Freud's voice has been stilled by cancer of the jaw. Anna Freud, soprano, takes over from him, and, in a final fantasy before death, he recovers the tones of a denouncing prophet to smash the tables of the law upon cowering Jung, Adler, Rank and Ferenczi. It seems to me that here we have a golden opportunity to use atonality and profound dissonance to represent the workings of the unconscious, while conscious action can be conveyed through the tonalism of Mahlerian music, café waltzes, bands in the park. Perhaps it will never be done, though two thousand sheets of scoring paper await under a map of *Die Biblischen Länder* (another purchase in atheistical East Berlin, West German marks gladly accepted). Meanwhile there are a few books to be written.

There are also books already written. They were written not merely to earn bread and gin but out of a conviction that the manipulation of language to the end of pleasing and enlightening is not to be despised, despite what the postman greeting an unshaven yawner may think. I have done my best, and no one can do more. I may yet have my time.

Index